AN
HISTORICAL INTRODUCTION
TO
PHILOSOPHICAL THINKING

Studies in Philosophy

Consulting Editor:

V. C. CHAPPELL
The University of Chicago

AN
HISTORICAL
INTRODUCTION
TO
PHILOSOPHICAL
THINKING

---

by *CH. PERELMAN*

UNIVERSITY OF BRUSSELS

Translated by
KENNETH A. BROWN

Random House • *New York*

CONTENTS

AN
HISTORICAL INTRODUCTION
TO
PHILOSOPHICAL THINKING

INTRODUCTION

What is philosophy?

This question deserves careful examination. It might be helpful before replying to ask what the question presupposes. Are we seeking a definition of the word *philosophy?* If so, what do we expect of a definition? Should it describe the thing denoted by the word, or should it attempt to specify some usage of language at a particular time and place? Sometimes, indeed, an entirely different role is ascribed to definition—that of declaring how the author intends to use the word. This he may do arbitrarily, or he may give his reasons.

In this introduction we shall try to answer the question: How has the word *philosophy* actually been used since it was first introduced into the Greek language? It is obvious that the use of the word has evolved over the centuries and that every creative philosopher has supplied a definition adapted to his own major interests.[1]

The word *philosophy* seems to have been used for the first time by Pythagoras (sixth century B.C.). He argued

[1] *Cf.*, for example, "Philosophy and Philosophical Studies," *Encycl. Brit.*, 1964, XVII, 56–61.

that since true wisdom was possessed by God alone, man could at best be a lover of wisdom.[2] The idea of philosophy is thus born out of an extension of the idea of wisdom. The "wise men" of Greece were believed to be virtuous because of their knowledge. In their opinion, action was determined by knowledge. This idea that knowledge leads to virtue is a constant feature of Greek thought and has important extensions in Western thought generally.

Philosophy has been from the first opposed to religion and history. It is opposed to religion because, instead of holding to a traditional and local doctrine, it seeks to establish on its own account a system of propositions which can claim universal acceptance. It is opposed to history—at least to history conceived as a chronicle of events—because from its beginnings philosophy has been concerned with explanations and reasons in an attempt to acquire understanding.

It should be noted that not until the end of the eighteenth century was a distinction made between philosophy and natural science.

It was only in the fifth century B.C. that the first sciences —the mathematical sciences—became organized into an autonomous system of knowledge. This is the reason the Greek word *mathemata* stands both for science in general and for the mathematical sciences in particular.

To geometry and arithmetic, the first sciences to be developed, were soon added astronomy and harmony, which attempted through the study of mathematical relations to explain the motion of the stars and the ratios of musical tones. Contrasted with these sciences there developed under the influence of the fifth century Sophists the literary disciplines—grammar, rhetoric, and logic; these dealt respectively with correct literary usage, the technique of persuasion, and the principles of demonstration.

These seven disciplines were regarded in antiquity as preparatory to philosophy; in the Middle Ages they determined the organization of the first universities. Along with the faculties of theology, law, and medicine, the faculty of

---

[2] Diog. Laert., I, xii.

philosophy (or the faculty of arts) included two curricula preparatory to the teaching of philosophy—the *trivium* and the *quadrivium*. The trivium was made up of the literary disciplines (grammar, rhetoric, and logic) and the quadrivium of the mathematical disciplines (arithmetic, geometry, astronomy, and music). Under the name *natural philosophy*, the natural sciences formed part of philosophy. This is the reason that even in the seventeenth century Newton's basic work, in which he proved the law of universal gravitation, was entitled *Mathematical Principles of Natural Philosophy*.

Beginning in the seventeenth century, the natural sciences one by one became established as autonomous disciplines—physics with Galileo, chemistry with Lavoisier, botany with Linnaeus, biology with Darwin and Claude Bernard, and experimental psychology with Wundt. The study of social phenomena, which Comte sought to establish as an independent science under the name of *sociology*, attempted progressively to become detached from philosophy through the use of statistical methods. Mathematicians such as Boole, de Morgan, Schröder, Frege, Peano, Whitehead, and Russell contributed to the transformation of logic into a branch of mathematics.

This progressive separation of the individual sciences from their common source suggested about 1830 to the French philosopher Auguste Comte the "positivist" theory of the development of human knowledge. According to Comte, human thought develops by passing successively through three stages—the theological, the metaphysical, and the positive. In the theological stage men seek to explain all phenomena through the intervention of various divinities; in the metaphysical stage their explanations call upon all sorts of occult forces; in the positive stage—that of science—men are content to assert the facts and the relations which exist among them. Philosophy appears in this perspective a stage of human thought to be outgrown, just as the theological stage has been.

It cannot be denied that Comte's analysis is correct regarding certain areas of knowledge where scientific answers have completely replaced theological or philosophical concepts. But that is quite another thing from saying that *all* human problems can be solved by calling on the experimental or deductive methods of science alone. The study not of what is but of what ought to be, what has the greater value, what is preferable, and what should determine our choices and our conduct can be abandoned to scientific methods only when we are dealing with purely technical problems. But that is far from being the case. Not only does the solution of our fundamental problems elude science and technology; the very hypothesis that philosophy can be dispensed with is itself a philosophical hypothesis, resting on presuppositions which we shall examine later.

The pages that follow are intended as an historical introduction to the problems of philosophy, not as a complete and detailed history of philosophy. They are designed to help the reader gain an insight into the most significant philosophical problems and to acquaint him with the nature of philosophical reasoning.

C.P.

I

GREEK PHILOSOPHY

BEFORE PLATO

The School of Miletus

Courses in the history of European philosophy usually begin with a discussion of the thinkers who made up the school of Miletus—Thales, Anaximander, and Anaximenes (*c.* 640–525 B.C.). This tradition appears to be a result of the historical accident that Thales was the first philosopher dealt with by Aristotle in his *Metaphysics*.

But it is obvious that philosophical thought could have had no absolute beginning; every idea is an extension of some other idea, and we know today how much the thinkers of the Milesian school were influenced by the Egyptians and the Babylonians.[1] If it were our intention to study these thinkers in detail, we would have to begin with the tradition on which they built. But our purpose in discussing them is to gain a better understanding of the great systems of Plato and Aristotle. Thus we shall present only the essentials of their thinking, the way in which they made their appearance as initiators of the great philosophical tradition of Greece.

---

[1] Cf. R. Berthelot, *La pensée de l'Asie et l'Astrobiologie*, Paris, Payot, 1938.

Their basic problem was to determine what was the basic stuff of which the universe is made.

The very diversity of things gives no suggestion of what the basic stuff or material might be, but the idea of change does lead to the idea of permanence. Underlying the development of any particular thing (child—adult—old man) is a presupposition of its oneness. In spite of change, something remains constant. Belief in change is possible only if a certain permanence be granted. Without this permanence there would be substitution rather than change; one thing would replace another.

This idea was clearly put by Diogenes of Apollonia, a disciple of Anaximenes:

> My view is, to sum it all up, that all things are differentiations of the same thing. And this is obvious; for, if the things which are now in this world—earth and water, and air and fire, and the other things which we see existing in this world—if any one of these things, I say, were different from any other, different, that is, by having a substance peculiar to itself; and if it were not the same thing that is often changed and differentiated, then things could not in any way mix with one another, nor could they do one another good or harm. Neither could a plant grow out of the earth, nor any animal nor anything else come into being unless things were composed in such a way as to be the same. But all these things arise from the same thing; they are differentiated and take different forms at different times, and return again to the same thing.[2]

For Thales this basic stuff is *water;* for Anaximenes it is *air;* and for Anaximander it is what he calls the *unlimited* (*to apeiron*).

It must be emphasized that these concepts of *water* and *air* had then a very different meaning from that they have today. When Thales spoke of water he was not thinking

---

[2] J. Burnet, *Early Greek Philosophy* (4th ed.), pp. 353–54.

of the chemical compound H_2O, but of liquids generally and anything that could become liquid, like fusible metal. This means that the real stuff of the universe is represented by things in their liquid state. In this connection we should not forget that the ancients considered the physical appearance of bodies essential, not their chemical properties.

By *air* Anaximenes understands not merely the gaseous state, but breath, wind, mind, and soul. Bodies are derived from air by condensation and become air again by rarefaction. But air is not merely physical stuff; it is also the driving force in the transformations of a body from one state to another. It seems possible that this concept was borrowed from Anaximander.

The *apeiron,* or "unlimited," of Anaximander is the first purely rational concept which can be found in Greek philosophical thought. The nature of the *apeiron* is described in a rational rather than an empirical or experimental manner. Since it is the fundamental stuff which abides throughout all transformations, the *apeiron* cannot be described in terms of sensible qualities. It is the basis of everything—indestructible, immortal, uncreated; as the source of all things it has motion and perpetual life.

The concept of the *apeiron* may be interpreted in two ways:

1. The *apeiron* is the primitive chaos in which the various qualities perceived by the senses stand in opposition to each other and are indistinguishable from each other. Individual bodies come into being through the separation of particular qualities from this chaos.

2. The *apeiron,* according to Plato and Aristotle, is not a mixture of all qualities; it has none of them, but receives them all.

In this contrast between primordial stuff on the one hand and the changing appearances perceived by the senses on the other, it should be observed that primacy is given to the universal rather than to the particular; the particular always in the end gives way to some other particular. The Greek mind seeks what is permanent, unchanging, and universal, even when the universal cannot be described with precision. This explains why pure mathematics was a product of the Greek mind.

With the school of Miletus can be compared Heraclitus of Ephesus (second half of the sixth century B.C.). He too raises the problem of permanence in the universe; he reaches the conclusion that nothing abides. Everything is in perpetual flux—"All things flow." He compares the universe to a river: if the river be regarded as a collection of droplets of water, all its elements are in constant change. "This world," he says, "which is the same for all, no one of gods or men has made; but it was ever, is now, and ever shall be an ever-living Fire, with measures of its kindling and measures of its going out."[3]

The Pythagoreans and the Eleatics

The importance of the structure of things was emphasized by Pythagoras of Samos (sixth century B.C.), whose name is known to every student of geometry. At Crotona in Magna Graecia, Pythagoras organized a society which was both mathematical and mystical in character, and which came to regard itself as an elite alone worthy of ruling.

The universe, according to the Pythagoreans, is made up of numbers; but by numbers they understood certain numerical relationships which are to be found in the universe—the ratios of musical intervals, for example. At the same time their conception of number was geometrical: numbers were points arranged in geometrical patterns, for example:

3 ⠒   4 ⠿   9 ⫶⫶⫶   6 ⫶⫶   etc.

As a result, they regarded the universe as made up of figures, relationships, and forms. Form, not matter, is the important thing.

---

[3] *Ibid.*, p. 134.

It might be wondered what mathematics has in common with a mystical mind. This association is understandable if one accepts the premise that mathematics can explain everything. There will then be a tendency to explain everything by symbols, and it is easy to move from that point into mysticism.

Pythagorean thought was transformed by Parmenides of Elea (fifth century B.C.), who can be considered the first rationalistic metaphysician among the Greeks. He offers a logical principle which provides the basis for his discussion of the external world. This point of departure is the first formulation of the *Law of Identity,* which appears to be completely self-evident: *Being alone is; not-Being is not.* On his interpretation of this principle rests his whole conception of the universe.

Since he was a Pythagorean, Parmenides pictured the universe with the help of numbers—points—comparing these to the stars in the firmament. *Being* for him is represented by the points which constitute the universe. The space which separates the points is *not-Being.* If this is the case, only the points exist; the intermediate space does not exist. Once the existence of space is denied, it is impossible to distinguish between different things. All the points tend to conglomerate, and thus the universe consists of an immense compact sphere; motion is inconceivable. This point of view was criticized by Melissus of Samos, a disciple of Parmenides. *Being,* according to Melissus, is infinite both in space and time, for if it had a spherical shape, it would have to be surrounded by *not-Being,* which is impossible.

Qualitative changes, considered merely as processes of condensation and rarefaction, are therefore impossible, since they presuppose the existence of the void. There is no possibility of generation and corruption. Consequently *Being* cannot change; it alone exists, and exists eternally.

From the application of his logical principle to the universe Parmenides draws paradoxical consequences: the universe of our senses is nothing but appearance; it is a universe of mere opinion. He simply denies any meaning to appearances; they have no value whatever. He does not even attempt to explain the sensible universe, for he rejects the data of the senses.

This view could not be consistently maintained. Some account had to be given of the existence of the world of the senses, and some explanation had to be offered for our being able to distinguish it from the "real" world, which was so very different. That is why Parmenides' successors tried to account for appearances in a rational view of the universe.

Nonetheless the Greeks held onto one principle in the thought of Parmenides: *Reality is uncreated and imperishable;* otherwise all generation would be a creation of being from non-being, and all destruction a passing from being to non-being. The concept of creation *ex nihilo* is from then on wholly foreign to Greek thought.

This principle of the conservation of reality later leads to the principle of the conservation of matter.

The Atomists

The search for an explanation which would mediate between appearance and reality gave rise to two forms of *atomism:*

1. *Qualitative atomism,* introduced by Anaxagoras of Clazomenae (c. 499–428 B.C.).

Anaxagoras was the first Ionian philosopher to come to Athens and introduce philosophical questions there. He is said to have been a friend of Pericles. The fundamental principle of his physics is that *the Whole can neither be diminished nor augmented, for it is impossible that there be anything in addition to the Whole; the Whole is always equal to itself.* Change is to be explained by the mixture and separation of the things that are.

To this Parmenidean principle he thus adds the concept of modification. His idea is that there exists an infinite number of independent qualities which enter into everything in varying proportions. Our senses perceive only the qualities which are most strongly represented; the others are imperceptible. That is why sense perception fails to give a complete picture of the universe.

All qualities pre-exist eternally in bodies in such a way that modifications are only apparent. A quality appears only when it is separated from its contrary.

Anaxagoras introduces the idea that there is a difference between force and matter. It is Mind (*nous*) which endows the universe with perfect motion—i.e., circular motion. This motion in the universe is what provides for the appearance and disappearance of the qualities.

Thus in Anaxagoras we have the first example of a dualistic conception of the universe based on the distinction between mind and matter.

2. *Quantitative atomism,* introduced by Leucippus of Miletus (a contemporary of Anaxagoras) and Democritus of Abdera (second half of the fifth century B.C.).

The atomism of this school is based upon the hypothesis that reality is made up of corpuscles which differ from each other only in their spatial qualities—in size, shape, and arrangement.

The universe, then, is made up of an infinity of tiny invisible bodies, indivisible (*atomos* means indivisible), compact, and eternal, which may be compared to so many tiny universes, or Parmenidean Ones. These atoms are in perpetual motion, therefore there must be a void. Thus not-Being is.

Atoms and their combinations alone are real. All sense impressions are the result of atoms and their combinations. Color, temperature, odor, taste, and sound give us no idea of reality, but are merely what we perceive of that reality. All our perceptions are derived from collisions between the atoms which make up the perceived object and the atoms making up the subject who perceives.

The atomists seek to explain the sourness or sweetness of a liquid by its atomic make-up—sourness from "hooked" atoms, sweetness from round and smooth atoms. This picture of the universe is thus derived partly from logical principles and partly from theories created to explain the world of appearances. This points up a weakness in the argument of the supporters of the real world, since the "reality" of these atomists is based on appearance, and on closer examination appearance is more certain than "reality."

This multiplicity of opposing theories about the universe gave rise to a certain skepticism, which the supporters of opinion and common sense made use of against the physical theorists. Philosophers began to turn toward man.

The Sophists

Among these philosophers were the Sophists of the Age of Pericles. They are known to us principally through the dialogues of Plato. The most important of them were Protagoras of Abdera, Hippias of Elis, Gorgias of Leontium, and Prodicus of Ceos. They were the first professional philosophers, for up to this time philosophers had been priests, politicians, businessmen, physicians. The Sophists traveled about the Greek world seeking students and living from their fees. They taught their students the art of persuasion, the art of winning in contests of oratory. They were the first also to devise courses of instruction for the elite. Now, by extending the practice of reasoning and questioning, they fatally extended the spirit of criticism, and in the battle between Plato and the Sophists we may see one aspect of the battle between the aristocrats and the democrats of Athens in the fifth and fourth centuries.

The ideas of the Sophists are largely known to us through the writings of their opponents. Nevertheless there is no doubt that in their own time they were influential and admired men.

Protagoras of Abdera (485–411 B.C.) was the greatest of the Sophists. He enjoyed enormous prestige and was treated with respect even in the pages of Plato, who makes him one of the interlocutors in his dialogue the *Protagoras*.

Protagoras' pronouncement "*Man is the measure of all*

*things, of the things that are that they are, and of the
things that are not that they are not"* is capable of two
differing interpretations:

1. *Man* means man generically, humankind, what is
common to all men.

2. *Man* means each man considered as an individual.

When *man* is interpreted in this latter sense, we arrive
at a subjectivism which provides no way to discover rules
applying to all men.

These two interpretations, the universal and the indi-
vidualistic, are both naturalistic, since they imply a theory
of knowledge deriving from some view of human nature.

The Sophists took their stand on the side of common
sense against the science of the physicists; they are important also for the position that most of them took in the
debate over "nature" and "law." The physicists sought to
derive the rules of conduct from nature. They advocated
the idea of "natural law"—rules of conduct which could be
derived from some particular nature, divine or human.
This idea, which accepts the predominance of nature over
law, is based on a confused understanding of what law is.

Law may be understood in two senses:

1. A constant relationship controlling phenomena or
one in accordance with which phenomena occur. Thus law
describes what is. In the sciences law is descriptive; it is
never to be regarded as prescriptive or normative.

2. A principle in accordance with which one *ought* to
act. Here law is normative rather than descriptive.

In the idea of natural law these two concepts are confused; an attempt is made to deduce normative law from
descriptive law. This is a common confusion, since there
is often a transition from the normal to the normative. For
example, the actual behavior of a group establishes a law
of conduct.

The Sophists, for the most part, refused to grant to
"nature" superiority over law. And although Protagoras
always supported law based on social conventions against
law derived from "nature," both of the current interpretations of his aphorism can be regarded as asserting that

human knowledge is based on human nature. That is why in his book on the Sophists the Belgian philosopher Eugène Dupréel[4] interprets Protagoras' "man" as a social being molded by his society.

On social questions Protagoras was a conservative. Since reason was imperfect he criticized the notion of basing social reform on reason. Similarly he criticized those who rejected sense experience, since it was from sense experience that they derived their rational concepts. In this sense he was a skeptic.

There are two kinds of skepticism:

1. *Methodological skepticism* begins with doubt, but regards this doubt as a point of departure for attaining certainty (e.g., Descartes).

2. *Systematic skepticism* is doubt which disparages one method of knowing while advocating some other method (Pascal casts doubt on reason in order that faith may prevail).

Protagoras' skepticism is systematic, since he wishes the knowledge which is derived from common sense to prevail over theories the foundation of which is purely rational.

Gorgias of Leontium (483–376 B.C.) is known as one of the founders of rhetoric, the technique of persuasion. To give his subject a respectable standing as the center of humanistic culture in Greece he attempted a thoroughgoing criticism of the theory of truth held by Parmenides. He was in a good position to do so, since he had been a pupil of Zeno of Elea, who was in turn a pupil of Parmenides.

While Parmenides had sought to build a positive theory of the universe, Zeno supported him negatively by criticizing the theories of his master's opponents. This he did in his famous paradoxes, such as that of Achilles and the tortoise.

Gorgias attempted to show that there is no truth at all. He criticized the Eleatic theory by offering three theses:

1. Being does not exist.

---

[4] *Les Sophistes,* Neuchâtel, Editions du Griffon, 1948.

2. If it did, it would be unknowable.

3. If it were knowable, it could not be communicated.
He argued as follows:

1. If Being did exist, it would have to be (a) eternal or (b) created at a given time; and it would have to be (c) one or (d) many. But it is neither eternal, created, single, nor many.

a. If it were eternal, or unlimited in time, it would also be unlimited in space, as Melissus of Samos had shown. But Zeno of Elea had proved that everything that is is in a place which determines its limits. The doctrines of Melissus and Zeno, who develop the theory of Parmenides, end in a contradiction; for an infinite Being limited by something else cannot be conceived. Therefore we cannot accept the eternal and infinite Being of Parmenides.

b. If it were created, it would have to be derived from not-Being, which contradicts the fundamental principle of Parmenides.

c. If it were one, it would have a certain magnitude. But, since all magnitude is divisible, it would have to be conceived as made up of several parts.

d. If it were many, each part would have to be a one, but this one in turn would have a certain magnitude (and would consequently be divisible into parts), for it is impossible to have a whole made up of parts which have no size. There are difficulties in this reasoning which remain to be cleared up—particularly with regard to the infinite (cf. Kant).

2. Our knowledge consists of ideas; so it is impossible to know anything that is not an idea. If reality were different from our ideas, it would be unknowable. But if reality consisted of our ideas, how could we make a distinction between what is real and what is imaginary? Yet without such a distinction the possibility of error is incomprehensible. This presents us with the problem of the relation between thought and reality.

3. If being were knowable, this knowledge would still be incommunicable, for all knowledge is connected with

a knowing subject, and two subjects cannot know the working of each other's minds. The only communicable thing is the words or the signs by which we express ourselves.

This raises the problem of the relation between thought and language. Can it be determined just what within our consciousness we are able to communicate? When a word is spoken, an idea is expressed; that seems to be something objective. But to that word are attached connotations which are not communicated and which are therefore subjective. The word *man,* for example, can call up widely varying connotations.

These are crucial problems, dealt with in different ways in psychology and the theory of knowledge.

The speculations of the Sophists proved to be disturbing. At least some of the problems they raised appeared insoluble.

Socrates and His Disciples

Socrates of Athens (469–399 B.C.). While we do possess a few fragments of the Presocratics, we have nothing at all written by Socrates. So far as we know, he in fact wrote nothing. For an account of his teaching we are entirely dependent on the testimony of his contemporaries, and that testimony is contradictory. Thus the reconstruction of his thought presents grave difficulties.

Socrates is known to us through the dialogues of Plato, the *Memorabilia* of Xenophon, and Aristophanes' comedy *The Clouds,* in which he is ridiculed.

It is difficult to say just what was the actual thought of Socrates. Plato attributes to him ideas which are clearly Plato's own. And even though tradition represents Socrates as having turned away from the study of nature to devote himself to the study of man, Aristophanes presents him as principally concerned with natural phenomena.

Moreover, it may be wondered how faithfully the traditional Socrates who is given to us by Plato represents the historic Socrates.[5] Rather than attempt to settle this discussion here, we shall be content to study the ideas usually attributed to Socrates.

Although Socrates set himself in opposition to the Sophists, he was, like them, uninterested in the natural sciences; and, like them, he devoted himself to the study of man and the human mind. The Delphic maxim "Know thyself" was his guiding principle.

If there was any one characteristic in which Socrates differed from the Sophists—a characteristic insisted on by Plato—it was in his belief that discussion and argument should be directed not toward defeating an opponent but toward discovering the truth. While the Sophists' technique was primarily one of rhetoric, Socrates advocated what Plato called dialectic, a technique for discovering truth through discussion.

Socratic dialectic has two characteristics:

1. When, for example, Socrates carries on a discussion with Callicles in Plato's *Gorgias,* he clearly attempts to gain his interlocutor's acceptance of each link in the chain of his argument. (Proceeding by questions and answers, he addresses himself to a single person rather than to a large audience, as did the Sophists.) He uses this dialectic as a technique for attaining the truth. There is a dangerous leap here from the agreement of an interlocutor to the truth of the proposition he grants.

It is thus in the name of dialectic as opposed to rhetoric that Plato, following Socrates' lead, undertakes to speak for truth against mere opinion.

2. Dialectic deals with the meanings of words: the conclusions clarify these meanings. Socrates was much less concerned with experience than with the *true* meanings of words. Thus it was that Plato—it is difficult to distinguish Plato's ideas from those of Socrates—sought to define abstract concepts like justice, while Aristotle studied the actual constitutions of states. Socrates and Plato put their

---

[5] See A. E. Taylor, *Socrates.*

emphasis on the problems of language, the search for valid definitions of universal ideas. The importance of the universal as opposed to the particular was to be finally justified in the long run, but Socrates was already insisting that "Science deals only with universals."

The idea of the universal was to be considered again by Plato himself. (In a somewhat arbitrary manner Plato's early dialogues, written under the influence of Socrates, are usually believed to express Socratic ideas, while the later dialogues contain ideas worked out by Plato himself.)

Socrates is also well known for having proposed the moral doctrine that *no man does wrong voluntarily.* He bases his contention on the ground that everyone seeks happiness, seeks what he believes to be his own good. But in a curious fashion he confuses the good sought by the individual with the universal idea of the good. Since every man seeks happiness by achieving the good, it follows that wrongdoing can come only through ignorance. This is the morality of the wise man, who acts morally because he has a knowledge of the good. This presupposes implicitly that knowledge of the good brings about achievement of it. We have here a rationalistic conception of the relation between knowledge and action.

If it be granted that there is only one standard of comparison for acts which are very different, and if, also, there be granted a unity of values, then, and only then, are all acts comparable. The notion of guiding our conduct by a science requires that the comparison of different values be possible and that there be a kind of calculus of values. The Greeks were highly receptive to this sort of rationalism.

However, this morality of the wise man is not the only moral theory known to man. The morality of a saint is based not upon a calculus of the values of acts but upon love and the spirit of sacrifice. In addition to the spirit of sacrifice, the hero has courage, and nothing requires him to be a calculating wise man. In the same way the prophet is not a wise man; he is inspired.

Socrates did not merely preach the morality of the wise man; he lived as one all his life. Condemned to drink the hemlock (for reasons which seem to have been partly political), he preferred to submit to the laws rather than to flee, for he proclaimed that disobedience of the laws would bring greater evil than his death.

Socrates was very influential through both his doctrines and the example of his life. He had many disciples, who formed widely differing schools. Their concerns were essentially moral theory (the problem of happiness) and logic. With natural science they were hardly concerned at all.

Among these disciples was *Aristippus of Cyrene* (435?– 356 B.C.), who founded the Cyrenaic or *hedonistic* school. Once it is granted that everyone seeks happiness, it becomes necessary to define happiness. Aristippus defines it as pleasure (*hedonê*); his whole theory of morals may be summed up in the question: How must one act to experience the greatest pleasure? But the idea of pleasure needs to be clarified: Is it the most intense pleasure that is to be sought, or the most lasting? Is it an intense pleasure followed by pain, weariness, and grief, or a pleasure which results in a sense of well-being?

With pleasure as a common denominator of all acts, we thus arrive at the possibility of an arithmetic of pleasure, an idea to be developed later by Epicurus and again in the eighteenth century by Jeremy Bentham.

According to Aristippus we are conscious only of our sensations, never of their causes. The reality which causes our perceptions is unknowable. On this point Aristippus is in agreement with Gorgias. We cannot know whether what we assert about some object is better grounded than any other assertion. Truth can result only from a *comparison* of different perceptions which derive from the same object. It thus becomes necessary to establish an internal criterion of coherence among different perceptions. For example, a stick dipped in water appears broken, but touching it shows us our mistake.

Aristippus holds truth to be merely relative; he insists on the progressive character of knowledge, which is ever seeking to integrate an always-increasing number of particulars.

Antisthenes the Cynic and his follower *Diogenes of Sinope* were little concerned with theoretical knowledge; they considered it both impossible of attainment and unimportant. The only good worth seeking is virtue, and virtue consists in following nature. All the rest—the various laws and rules of society—are mere conventions, and the wise man need not bother about them.

Euclid of Megara (*c*. 450–368 B.C.), another pupil of Socrates and of the Eleatics, founded the *eristic* school. Instead of devoting himself to the problems which had occupied his master, however, he was concerned with methods of discussion. He attached great importance to logical problems. Through the use of paradoxes, the eristic school attacked the hypotheses current at the time.

Consider this hypothesis, which was widely held during the period: Every word has a clear and precise meaning, so that it is possible to divide things into two classes: (1) those to which the word applies and (2) those to which it does not apply. The weakness of this hypothesis is brought out by paradoxes:

Example 1.　Socrates is a man.

But Socrates is not a man.

Therefore Socrates is not Socrates.

This argument employs two different meanings of the word *is*. In "Socrates is a man" the word *is* indicates membership in the class of men. In "Socrates is not a man" *is* is taken in the same sense as in the sentence "Socrates is the teacher of Plato"; that is, as a sign of identity. The paradox is thus based on the ambiguity of the verb *to be*.

Example 2.　A person concealed by a veil.

If I see someone concealed by a veil, I do not know him. But suppose this person is my father. I know my father, but I do not know the person concealed by the veil. Therefore I know someone and at the same time do not know him.

The verb *to know* cannot be taken in an absolute sense, and therefore knowledge is relative.

Example 3. Much and little; large and small.

These words are relative. For example, a large fly is smaller than a small elephant. How large, then must something be to be called large?

The ideas of large and small vary according to the standard of comparison, and the standard depends on what kind of things are being compared. The meaning of many ideas depends on the conditions under which they are applied, and it is impossible without absurdity to determine this once and for all. How large must a large number be?

Example 4. The bald man; the heap.

How few hairs must a man have to be bald? If $n =$ bald, does $n + 1 =$ not bald? Or, again, beginning at what number do several grains of wheat constitute a heap?

Examples 3 and 4 raise the problem of how concepts are used. Are the limits of our concepts well defined? Can we determine their degree of approximation?

It was a problem of this sort that was studied in the nineteenth century by two physiological psychologists Fechner and Weber. They introduced the concept of the *differential threshold* (limen), a psychological minimum below which no difference can be perceived.

Consider, for example, two straight lines which do not have exactly the same length. When do we perceive a difference between them? If the difference is minimal, we do not perceive it.

Take two wooden spheres, one hollow, the other solid. Suppose we fill the hollow sphere with sand until the two seem to have the same weight. Let us then add or take away one grain. Naturally no one can detect any difference.

There are, then, differences we do not perceive, yet the sum of these imperceptible differences can result in a difference we *do* perceive.

Thus it may be perceived that A = B, B = C, C = D,

and yet the fact that A ≠ D may very well be perceived also. The differences between A and B, B and C, and C and D lie below the threshold of differentiation, while the difference between A and D lies above it.

This problem has also given rise to a development within the field of logic. According to classic theory, a concept divides entities into two classes: those to which it applies and those to which it does not. But there is another way of representing the ideas we conceive—that of ordering the objects of discourse rather than classifying them. Instead of being simply classified as large, for example, or heavy, objects are arranged in some kind of order—greater than, heavier than . . . etc.

For example, suppose that A be put to the right of B if B is heavier than A. In this way A and B may be compared, and such an ordering could be established by a set of scales. For this to be possible, however, the relation "heavier than" must be:

1. *Asymmetrical:* If B is heavier than A, A cannot be heavier than B.

2. *Transitive:* If B is heavier than A and C is heavier than B, C must be heavier than A.

Thus all the objects may be arranged in a series in some determined order, a series whose basis is a relation. If we introduce some object to represent zero on the scale—air, for example—every object which is heavier than air is "heavy," and every object which is lighter than air is "light." Thus the ancients used to speak of bodies which were heavier than air as heavy bodies.

By introducing the idea of measurement, science seeks to go further than merely ordering things. To pass from the concept of ordering to that of measuring, a unit of measure must be established. The various units of measurement must be subjected to the laws of arithmetic ($2u + 2u = 4u$), and they must be homogeneous.

Some scientists have even tried to introduce metrical concepts into areas where they are not applicable. Bergson criticizes the psychologists who invented psychometry on the ground that the differences they study are not quantitative (numerical) but qualitative. The logical problems connected with these ideas have been studied by Hempel and Oppenheim.[6]

---

[6] C. Hempel and P. Oppenheim, *Der Typusbegriff im Lichte der Neuen Logik,* Leiden, Sijthoff, 1936.

PLATO
(427–347 B.C.)

Unlike the philosophers who came before him, Plato has left us many writings—some thirty dialogues and ten letters. But the difficulties of interpretation are no less numerous or serious; Plato frequently makes Socrates the central character in his dialogues, and thus arises the question of distinguishing Plato's theories from those of Socrates.

This problem is made still more difficult by the fact that we sometimes find in Plato contradictory views. Since his work extended over a period of many years, it is conceivable that the author's mind underwent an evolution which could account for the inconsistencies. We may expect, then, to find in him Socratic teachings, the views of the younger Plato, and those of his ripe maturity.

For a long time, however, the ideas of the younger Plato were indistinguishable from those of his maturity, since the order of the dialogues was not known. They were classified on the basis of personal preference, and there was no hesitation on the part of scholars to regard some of them as apocryphal.

This difficulty was increased by the way in which Plato presented his ideas. One of his favorite devices was to convey them in the form of myths. Sometimes it is difficult to determine what should be interpreted literally; just where myth begins is often uncertain.

In his *Légende Socratique et les Sources de Platon*[1] Eugène Dupréel has advanced the hypothesis that Plato merely occupied himself with themes supplied him by the Sophists. This critic thus builds up the Sophists at the expense of Plato, whom he does not consider a philosopher of any originality. Whether one agrees or not, there is still a difficult problem here.

Since the beginning of the twentieth century Platonic studies have been greatly aided by the work of a Polish scholar, W. Lutoslawski. Through his development of an idea suggested by L. Campbell in 1867, Lutoslawski worked out a method for determining the order in which Plato's dialogues had been written, and thus disposed of many earlier controversies. His technique is known as the *stylometric* method.

THE STYLOMETRIC METHOD

When we speak and write we use two kinds of words:

1. Some words depend on the subject at hand. Thus in dealing with literature we use such words as *poetry, books, author,* rather than *city, river, country.*

2. There are other words, however, whose use depends particularly on the person who is doing the talking and writing. They are marks of a mental tendency which determines the author's style, and every author has a preference for some of these words, like *however, for, actually.*

Moreover, when a man's work spreads out over several years, his style becomes modified; but this more or less conscious evolution occurs in a continuous way.

By means of an exact calculation of a writer's use of such connective particles, Lutoslawski showed how the evolution of a style could be followed. To verify his method he applied it to the writings of Goethe, the chronology of which is known with exactitude. His results were conclusive.

When this method is applied to the works of Plato it

---

[1] Brussels, Sand and London, Oxford University Press, 1922.

becomes possible to establish the order of the dialogues. Since we know that the *Laws,* which was left incomplete, was his final work, we can arrive at a chronological order. Thereby we come to know the evolution of Plato's thought. Doubt, however, still remains concerning how much of Plato is really Socrates.

Yet it is not necessary to say that what we here label as Plato's thought is the precise historical truth. We will limit ourselves to presenting and discussing this Socratic–Platonic philosophy as it has influenced the history of Western thought.

PLATONIC THOUGHT

To gain a better understanding of the ways in which Plato's theories are related to those of Socrates, we may restate the Socratic doctrine that science deals only with what is universal. Science does not seek truths which are transient. It makes use of concepts and structures which go beyond experience.

To the degree that a science, such as zoology, deals with an animal, let us say a cat, it is not concerned with some particular cat, but seeks to express principles applicable to all cats. In this way general ideas are indispensable for all scientific constructions.

Plato shares the view that everything that is perceived by the senses (i.e., everything material) is constantly changing. But he does not completely share the view of Heraclitus that since everything in nature changes, no science is possible at all. There must be certain permanent structures which are not subject to the changing flux. It is by reason of this permanence that science is possible.

Plato's philosophy, in fact, attempts to provide a view of reality which will explain how that reality can become an object of science. In this sense Plato is a rationalist, for he believes he has found in reality certain characteristics which make possible a rational study of it. Above the world of sensation and change, he believes, there is a world which is unchanging, the world of *ideas* or *forms,* and the world of perception is merely a reflection of it.

THE THEORY OF IDEAS

The usual common-sense view is that our ideas are derived from experience. We select certain common qualities which can be applied to collections of things. But this account of the process runs up against a preliminary difficulty: To discover, for example, what all cats have in common requires knowing which animals are cats; and we can know this only if we know what characteristics they have in common with other cats.

Thus it is apparent that in the problem of knowledge there is a kind of vicious circle. To separate out the universal ideas from the individuals belonging to a certain class, we must already know that they belong to that class.

For Plato the problem is very simple: Individual things belong to the same class to the degree that they participate in the same *idea* or *form.* Ideas, in this sense, are not thoughts or creations of the mind, for in that case they would depend on the mind that conceived them and would be different for each mind. Ideas for Plato are objective and permanent.

Plato worked out his theory of ideas by reflecting on the nature of mathematical objects, which are the same for all those who deal with them. That is why the inscription over the entrance to his school (known as the Academy, since it was located in the Grove of Academe) read: *"Let no one ignorant of geometry enter here."* He intended thereby to emphasize that before undertaking the study of philosophy a student must acquire the techniques of abstract mathematics. Thus Plato's thought belongs to the tradition of Pythagoras and Parmenides.

Lying at the basis of Plato's philosophy is the belief that amid the changing world of experience there exist permanent structures which derive from the participation of concrete things in the lasting realities which constitute the *world of ideas.* These realities are eternal, unchanging, and invisible, apprehended not by the senses but by thought alone.

Plato immersed his students in an atmosphere not only of rational mathematical thought but also of mysticism. The theory of ideas is presented in a highly poetic manner in the well-known passage from the *Republic,* the Myth of the Cave:

And now, I said, let me show in a figure how far our nature is enlightened or unenlightened:—Behold! human beings living in an underground den, which has a mouth open towards the light and reaching all along the den; here they have been from their childhood, and have their legs and necks chained so that they cannot move, and can only see before them, being prevented by the chains from turning round their heads. Above and behind them a fire is blazing at a distance, and between the fire and the prisoners there is a raised way; and you will see, if you look, a low wall built along the way, like the screen which marionette players have in front of them, over which they show the puppets.

I see.

And do you see, I said, men passing along the wall carrying all sorts of vessels, and statues and figures of animals made of wood and stone and various materials, which appear over the wall? Some of them are talking, others silent.

You have shown me a strange image, and they are strange prisoners.

Like ourselves, I replied; and they see only their own shadows, or the shadows of one another, which the fire throws on the opposite wall of the cave?

True, he said; how could they see anything but the shadows if they were never allowed to move their heads?

And of the objects which are being carried in like manner they would only see the shadows?

Yes, he said.

And if they were able to converse with one another, would they not suppose that they were naming what was actually before them?

Very true.

And suppose further that the prison had an echo which came from the other side, would they not be sure to fancy when one of the passers-by spoke that the voice which they heard came from the passing shadow?

No question, he replied.

To them, I said, the truth would be literally nothing but the shadows of the images.

That is certain.

And now look again, and see what will naturally follow if the prisoners are released and disabused of their error. At first, when any of them is liberated and compelled suddenly to stand up and turn his neck round and look towards the light, he will suffer sharp pains; the glare will distress him, and he will be unable to see the realities of which in his former state he had seen the shadows; and then conceive someone saying to him, that what he saw before was an illusion, but that now, when he is approaching nearer to being and his eye is turned towards more real existence, he has a clearer vision,—what will be his reply? And you may further imagine that his instructor is pointing to the objects as they pass and requiring him to name them,—will he not be perplexed? Will he not fancy that the shadows which he formerly saw are truer than the objects which are now shown to him?

Far truer.

And if he is compelled to look straight at the light, will he not have a pain in his eyes which will make him turn away to take refuge in the objects of vision which he can see, and which he will conceive to be in reality clearer than the things which are now being shown to him?

True, he said.

And suppose once more, that he is reluctantly

dragged up a steep and rugged ascent, and held fast until he is forced into the presence of the sun himself, is he not likely to be pained and irritated? When he approaches the light his eyes will be dazzled, and he will not be able to see anything at all of what are now called realities.

Not all in a moment, he said.

He will require to grow accustomed to the sight of the upper world. And first he will see the shadows best, next the reflections of men and other objects in the water, and then the objects themselves; then he will gaze upon the light of the moon and the stars and the spangled heaven; and he will see the sky and the stars by night better than the sun or the light of the sun by day?

Certainly.

Last of all he will be able to see the sun, and not mere reflections of him in the water, but he will see him in his own proper place, and not in another; and he will contemplate him as he is.

Certainly.

He will then proceed to argue that this is he who gives the season and the years, and is the guardian of all that is in the visible world, and in a certain way the cause of all things which he and his fellows have been accustomed to behold?

Clearly, he said, he would first see the sun and then reason about him.

And when he remembered his old habitation, and the wisdom of the den and his fellow-prisoners, do you not suppose that he would felicitate himself on the change, and pity them?

Certainly, he would.

And if they were in the habit of conferring honours among themselves on those who were quickest to observe the passing shadows and to remark which of them went before, and which followed after, and which were together; and who were therefore best able to draw conclusions as to the future, do you think that he would care for such honours and glories, or envy the possessors of them? Would he not say with Homer,

"Better to be the poor servant of a poor master,"

and to endure anything, rather than think as they do and live after their manner?

Yes, he said, I think that he would rather suffer anything than entertain these false notions and live in this miserable manner.

Imagine once more, I said, such an one coming suddenly out of the sun to be replaced in his old situation; would he not be certain to have his eyes full of darkness?

To be sure, he said.

And if there were a contest, and he had to compete in measuring the shadows with the prisoners who had never moved out of the den, while his sight was still weak, and before his eyes had become steady (and the time which would be needed to acquire this new habit of sight might be very considerable), would he not be ridiculous? Men would say of him that up he went and down he came without his eyes; and that it was better not even to think of ascending; and if any one tried to loose another and lead him up to the light, let them only catch the offender, and they would put him to death.

No question, he said.

This entire allegory, I said, you may now append, dear Glaucon, to the previous argument; the prison-house is the world of sight, the light of the fire is the sun, and you will not misapprehend me if you interpret the journey upwards to be the ascent of the soul into the intellectual world according to my poor belief, which, at your desire, I have expressed—whether rightly or wrongly God knows. But, whether true or false, my opinion is that in the world of knowledge the idea of good appears last of all, and is seen only with an effort; and, when seen, is also inferred to be the universal author of all things beauti-

ful and right, parent of light and of the lord of light
in this visible world, and the immediate source of
reason and truth in the intellectual; and that this is
the power upon which he who would act rationally
either in public or private life must have his eye fixed.

I agree, he said, as far as I am able to understand
you.

Moreover, I said, you must not wonder that those
who attain to this beatific vision are unwilling to
descend to human affairs; for their souls are ever
hastening into the upper world where they desire to
dwell; which desire of theirs is very natural, if our
allegory may be trusted.

Yes, very natural.

And is there anything surprising in one who passes
from divine contemplations to the evil state of man,
misbehaving himself in a ridiculous manner; if, while
his eyes are blinking and before he has become accustomed to the surrounding darkness, he is compelled to fight in courts of law, or in other places,
about the images or the shadows of images of justice,
and is endeavouring to meet the conceptions of those
who have never yet seen absolute justice?

Anything but surprising, he replied.

Any one who has common sense will remember
that the bewilderments of the eyes are of two kinds,
and arise from two causes, either from coming out
of the light or from going into the light, which is true
of the mind's eye, quite as much as of the bodily eye;
and he who remembers this when he sees anyone
whose vision is perplexed and weak, will not be too
ready to laugh; he will first ask whether that soul of
man has come out of the brighter life, and is unable
to see because unaccustomed to the dark, or having
turned from darkness to the day is dazzled by excess
of light. And he will count the one happy in his condition and state of being, and he will pity the other;
or, if he have a mind to laugh at the soul which
comes from below into the light, there will be more

reason in this than in the laugh which greets him who
returns from above out of the light into the den.

That, he said, is a very just distinction.[2]

In this myth Plato works out a new view of the world.
The prisoners are men whose souls are still chained to the
earth by their bodies; the soul which is freed from the
body turns toward the intelligible world to lead a higher
existence.

It should be noted that this concept of the superiority
of the soul to the body is not at all typical of the Greek
tradition. When Homer says that Achilles would prefer a
life of travail to existence as a shade, he understands by
the life of a shade the life resulting from a separation of
the soul from the body. For Plato, on the contrary, it is
the life of man on earth that is a life of darkness and
shadows.

We begin with a kind of common-sense hierarchy which
holds that the real thing is better than the shadow. In
Homer the real life is life on earth, and the afterlife is
only a half-life. This is the primitive idea of the impalpable
shade, the double, which is of less value than the body.
But, due to the influence of doctrines derived from Asia
(Persia) and of the Orphicism which the Pythagoreans
introduced, there arose the doctrine that life on earth is
a life of shadows, while in life after death the soul is freed
to rise to the real world, the intelligible world.

The cave analogy clarifies this philosophical concept of
the superiority of the world of ideas to the world of sense.
In the Myth of the Cave a special role is given to the sun,
interpreted as the idea of the Good. The supreme position
given to the idea of the Good (also interpreted as the idea
of the Beautiful) shows us that Plato's thought is fundamentally teleological. To understand things we must know
what purpose they serve. All explanation in Plato is *final*
rather than causal.

This brings us back to the problem of man. When Soc-

---

[2] *Republic* vii, 514a–518b. (Jowett tr.).

rates considers the movements of a man who is getting up, the important thing, he says, is not to study the action of his muscles, but to learn for what purpose the movements are being made. Instead of placing man in nature, the philosophy of Plato tries to explain the whole of nature as dependent on human concerns.

This way of looking at things, of explaining things through purposes or ends, requires a being who proposes those ends—a divine being. To realize how Platonism anticipates Christianity in this respect, one need only think of the idea of the Good as another name for God. Indeed the mystical aspect of Plato's thought anticipated a number of developments in Christian thought.

Although Plato's point of departure was, to a large extent, his mathematical conception of ideas, the mystical element in Platonism was closely bound to an ethics which looked down on earthly and corporeal life. For beauty of bodily forms it substituted the ideal of spiritual beauty.

This aspect of Platonism was to develop under the influence of ideas derived from Asia—particularly those of Christianity—and emerge as Neoplatonism, whose most important representative was Plotinus. Because of his influence on St. Augustine, Plotinus was to have a great effect on medieval Christianity. It was only in the Renaissance that Plato himself—whose thought contained more than mysticism—was rediscovered.

The world of sense (the world of appearance and opinion) and the world of ideas (the real and intelligible world) are not completely divorced from each other in Plato's thinking. The world of sense is simply a reflection of the world of ideas. But how can man, who lives in the cave of the world of sense, succeed in finding a more lasting world?

In one of the dialogues, the *Symposium,* it is love (*eros*) which Plato regards as the driving force behind man's search for something more satisfying than the sensible world. Love is the expression of the soul's restlessness in its search for a better understanding of ideas.

This quest is a progressive one. We begin with love for

a beautiful body. From that we are led, according to Plato, to enlarge our center of interest and become attached to beautiful bodies; thence we proceed to beautiful actions, and from these are led to intellectual beauty—to the beauty of reason. Finally we attain to the idea of universal beauty, to beauty itself, the idea of the Beautiful, which is one with the idea of the Good. We are led by the inadequacy of an imperfect love to aspire after a reality which can satisfy us. Thus we see how through love we are raised above what is material to higher values. Our experience with what is sensible is merely the starting point for our ascent.

The mystical character of this whole concept should be noted. The mere substitution of God for the idea of the Good transforms it into an assertion that the love of God is the goal of our existence.

Plato thus creates a religious mysticism which is accompanied by a rather curious phenomenon: a justification of the love of man for man. This kind of forbidden love has always been characteristic of military civilizations, of which Sparta was an example in Plato's day. Now at that time there were two political factions, the democratic and the aristocratic. The latter made Sparta their model, even in its less admirable aspects.

Plato distinguishes two kinds of human love: the love of a man for a woman, and the love of a man for a man. His preference is for the second kind, since it allows us more easily to free ourselves from our material body. He regards the love of man for woman as binding us to the earth and preventing our ascent toward the world of ideas.

What is the role of experience in knowledge?

The fact that in geometry we reason about imperfect figures as if they were perfect requires us to accept the view that there is a kind of knowledge which is prior to experience. Experience is nothing but the occasion which recalls to us things already known. It is the stimulus for recollection (*anamnesis*).

But if experience serves as the stimulus for recalling an

idea the soul knew beforehand, then the soul must have existed before the body. Thus it is that along with his theory of ideas Plato adopts a doctrine of *metempsychosis:* the soul undergoes a whole series of wanderings and transformations. It passes from one body to another, and between any two terrestrial lives it leads an independent existence; during this time it may catch a glimpse of the world of ideas. Each existence, then, is a reincarnation, and thus the soul can be reminded on each occasion of experience of things it had glimpsed while it was separated from its bodily wrappings.

Plato's linking of his theory of knowledge to his theory of the soul is brought out in the dialogue *Phaedrus:*

> Of the nature of the soul, though her true form be ever a theme of large and more than mortal discourse, let me speak briefly, and in a figure. And let the figure be composite—a pair of winged horses and a charioteer. Now the winged horses and the charioteers of the gods are all of them noble and of noble descent, but those of other races are mixed; the human charioteer drives his in a pair; and one of them is noble and of noble breed, and the other is ignoble and of ignoble breed; and the driving of them of necessity gives a great deal of trouble to him. . . .
>
> Zeus, the mighty lord, holding the reins of a winged chariot, leads the way in heaven, ordering all and taking care of all; and there follows him the array of gods and demi-gods, marshalled in eleven bands; Hestia alone abides at home in the house of heaven; of the rest they who are reckoned among the princely twelve march in their appointed order. They see many blessed sights in the inner heaven, and there are many ways to and fro, along which the blessed gods are passing, every one doing his own work; he may follow who will and can, for jealousy has no place in the celestial choir. But when they go to banquet and festival, then they move up the steep to the top of the vault of heaven. The chariots of the gods in even poise, obey-

ing the rein, glide rapidly; but the others labour, for the vicious steed goes heavily, weighing down the charioteer to the earth when his steed has not been thoroughly trained:—and this is the hour of agony and extremest conflict for the soul. For the immortals, when they are at the end of their course, go forth and stand upon the outside of heaven, and the revolution of the spheres carries them round, and they behold the things beyond. But of the heaven which is above the heavens, what earthly poet ever did or ever will sing worthily? It is such as I will describe; for I must dare to speak the truth, when truth is my theme. There abides the very being with which true knowledge is concerned; the colourless, formless, intangible essence, visible only to mind, the pilot of the soul. The divine intelligence, being nurtured upon mind and pure knowledge, and the intelligence of every soul which is capable of receiving the food proper to it, rejoices at beholding reality, and once more gazing upon truth, is replenished and made glad, until the revolution of the worlds brings her round again to the same place. In the revolution she beholds justice, and temperance, and knowledge absolute, not in the form of generation or of relation, which men call existence, but knowledge absolute in existence absolute; and beholding the other true existences in like manner, and feasting upon them, she passes down into the interior of the heavens and returns home; and there the charioteer putting up his horses at the stall, gives them ambrosia to eat and nectar to drink.

Such is the life of the gods; but of other souls, that which follows God best and is likest to him lifts the head of the charioteer into the outer world, and is carried round in the revolution, troubled indeed by the steeds, and with difficulty beholding true being; while another only rises and falls, and sees, and again fails to see by reason of the unruliness of the steeds. The rest of the souls are also longing after the upper world and they all follow, but not being strong enough they are carried round below the surface, plunging, treading on one another, each striving to be first; and there is confusion and perspiration and the extremity of effort; and many of them are lamed or have their wings broken through the ill-driving of the charioteers; and all of them after a fruitless toil, not having attained to the mysteries of true being, go away, and feed upon opinion.[3]

Plato adopts a tripartite division of the soul on the analogy of a concept fairly common among the Greeks, the division of human faculties into:
1. *Reason,* located in the brain.
2. *Noble instincts,* located in the heart.
3. *Base instincts,* located in the abdomen.

This concept was to be taken up again by Aristotle, who distinguished the vegetative soul, the sensitive soul, and the rational soul.

With this threefold division in mind, Plato assigns the traditional four cardinal virtues:
1. *Wisdom,* the virtue of reason.
2. *Courage,* the virtue of the noble instincts.
3. *Temperance,* the virtue of moderating the base instincts.
4. *Justice,* the virtue of a kind of harmony among the three faculties.

In the *Republic* Plato carries this figure over into his discussion of politics. He recognizes three classes in society, each corresponding to one of the three faculties of the soul.
1. The class of workers, regarded as the lowest class. (Admiration for work is a modern idea.)
2. The class of warriors, which corresponds to the noble instincts.
3. The class of lawmakers, those who guide the state. They correspond in the city to the faculty of reason.

Justice is the result of a certain harmony among the

---

[3] *Phaedrus,* 246a–248b. (Jowett tr.).

three social classes; it is established through the philosopher-king. This is an entirely aristocratic ideal, based on the concept of fitness and competence.

In the *Phaedrus* myth, quoted above, Plato illustrates the classic duality of Greek thought, the opposition of truth to opinion, of science to common sense.

Plato uses one remarkable argument to prove the superiority of truth to opinion. He sets up a hierarchy of gods and men. The intellectual nourishment of the gods, he argues, can only be superior to that of men. Divine knowledge (eternal truth) can only be superior to the changing opinion of men.

Is this argument worthless? There is a real problem here. Plato, who represents himself as a rationalistic thinker, is one of those whose technique is farthest from the classic manner. Here we find neither a syllogism nor an inductive argument. It is an instance of reasoning which depends upon a technique of persuasion of which modern man since the time of Descartes has lost the theory without losing the practice.

Another example is to be found in the connection Plato establishes between the high and the good and the low and the evil. A kind of spatial arrangement is made of human faculties:

Low: in the direction of the earth and the sensible world, with what that world provides of physical stimuli.

High: in the direction of the heavens, the world of ideas, the Good.

There is a correlation between what is low and the result of low instincts and, by implication, an evaluation of the lower and the higher. We have here a concept which is obviously capable of religious development.

It should also be noted that this establishment of a connection between the heavens and morality is mirrored in our own language—a further example of the way in which language influences thought. To the degree, indeed, in which we learn a language we enter into a philosophical, moral, and religious tradition. This explains why, in order to present some philosophy which is foreign to current ways of thought, a new vocabulary has to be created to avoid old associations which are contrary to the new thought.

Plato believed that his theory of ideas, which alone made science possible, had to be granted by everyone, since it alone made possible a knowledge of the future. Indeed, if sensation were our only source of knowledge, we could never know the future, since it cannot be perceived.

Knowledge of the future must stem from a certain relation among the past, the present, and the future, a relation which is external to all sensation and lies in the realm of ideas. If we derived this relation from sensation, there would be no certainty that a connection which existed in the past would be valid in the future.

This problem of knowing the future was taken up again in the eighteenth century by the English philosopher David Hume. It is the problem of induction, which makes possible the derivation of general principles from particulars.

Plato explained the mutual relations between different realities by his *theory of participation*.

THE THEORY OF PARTICIPATION

According to Plato, a judgment asserts a predicate of a subject, an analysis later formalized by Aristotle. A judgment is the assertion of a relation between a subject and a predicate, and this judgment is true if there exists a participation between the subject and the predicate.

For example, consider the judgment "A is B." This judgment is true if the idea of A participates in the idea of B. *There are different kinds of participation.*

A thing can participate in ideas. Each of the properties of the thing participates in the idea of each of its properties. In this way the subject participates in the composite idea. When I say "Socrates is a man," Socrates participates in the idea of man; and when I say "All men are mortal," I affirm the participation of the idea of *man* in the idea of *mortal*.

Thus the relation of participation may hold not merely

between things and ideas but within the realm of ideas itself.

Participation plays an important role within this realm of ideas, since every idea participates in a more general idea. A kind of hierarchy is thus established: the concrete thing participates in certain ideas, and these in turn participate in ideas of a more general character.

In thus asserting a plurality of ideas Plato disagrees with the Eleatic view that reality is one and invariable (Parmenides and Zeno).

In two dialogues which are regarded as the most abstruse and difficult of all of Plato's works, he himself offers a criticism of the theory of ideas and confronts it with a revised theory. These dialogues are the *Parmenides* and the *Sophist*.

The *Parmenides* is a dialogue between Parmenides, Zeno of Elea, and Socrates; it turns into a discussion between Parmenides and Socrates. Here, however, in a departure from Plato's usual practice, Socrates is given only a secondary role. He is the one who is being interrogated; Parmenides is the interrogator. Plato uses this means to devote himself to a criticism of the theory of ideas.

In the *Sophist* Plato sets forth the theory of ideas as modified by the criticisms presented in the *Parmenides*.

THE *Parmenides*

Parmenides' reasoning begins with certain obvious principles. If "reality" is found to be in contradiction to the conclusion of a train of thought which has a solid basis, "reality" must be deceptive. In order to determine what is true reality, Parmenides falls into an extreme rationalism.

This is the method which in Plato's dialogue Parmenides applies to the theory of ideas. The answer to his criticism is to be found by making more flexible the basic logical principles which seemed evident to Parmenides, but which may appear strange to us, who have profited by Plato's criticism.

Socrates and Parmenides are not in agreement on the

matter of participation. For Socrates there is a relation between the thing and the idea which is like the relation
between subject and predicate. The Eleatic view is different.

According to the theory of participation, several things
may participate in the same idea. For example, all men
participate in the idea of *man:*

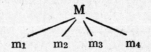

Let us consider the converse relation, that between the
idea and the several things which participate in it. There
is an Eleatic principle which affirms that everything that
exists exists in a determinate place. On this point Socrates
is asked: If several different men participate in the idea of
man, do they participate in the whole of the idea or in a
part of it? The two cases may be considered:

1. The whole of M is present in each man.
2. Only a part of M is present in each man.

1. If each of the individuals participates in the whole
of an idea (if the universal idea of *man* is to be found in
each particular man), it must be admitted that one and
the same idea is in different places at once (since it is
intimately related to each man). Thus we arrive at a
ubiquity of ideas, which, according to Parmenides, is impossible.

To understand this point of view it must be realized that
ideas are considered here as incapable of being in several
places at once. As a consequence Plato disaffirms the local-
ization of ideas.

If we grant, to resume the argument, that the idea of
man is wholly present in every man, we must grant that
there are as many Ms as there are men. Since every man
is doubled by an M, the sensible world is doubled by a
superfluous world; for when we create an idea in addition
to every particular thing which participates in it, we are
not justified in saying that all these ideas are identical to
each other.

If, indeed, this reasoning is pursued—if every M participates in an M′—we fall again into precisely the same difficulties.

Plato then suggests that ideas have nothing to do with space. But this raises a very serious problem: How are we to conceive the relation between objects which have nothing to do with space and objects which are in space? There would have to be something to unify the spatial and the extraspatial, and that something would have to be in space.

A similar problem arises in connection with the soul and its relation to the body.

2. In dealing with the hypothesis that each particular thing participates in only part of the idea and not in the whole of it, Parmenides imagines a number of men covered by a sail. They are all covered by the same sail, but each of them is covered by only a part of the sail.

This suggestion gives rise to another objection of the Eleatics, who are inspired by an absolutist logic (Being alone is; not-Being is not). If A is great, it participates in the idea of "greatness in itself." Similarly, if B is small, it participates in the idea of "smallness in itself." But if B, B′, and B″ all participate in the idea of smallness and at the same time participate in only part of that idea, they participate in an idea which is smaller than "smallness in itself"; this is obviously impossible.

COMMENT: Of any concept it is important to distinguish characteristics that determine its meaning from its properties as an idea. The cases where these properties fit the characteristics are rare, although they do exist. Thus it is the case in the concept of *concept*. The characteristics of a concept consist of the conditions which everything to which the concept is applied must realize (e.g., the concept *black*; every object to which this concept is applied must be black). This is not so with the properties of the concept itself. The concept *black* is not itself black; the concept *long* is not a long concept. This distinction had not been made at the time of Parmenides. For him, as for Plato, the idea of smallness is a small idea.

The reply, then, to this argument of Parmenides has two

aspects: (1) to divest ideas of any spatial quality and (2) to deny the identity between the characteristics of a concept and its properties as a concept.

FURTHER OBJECTIONS BY PARMENIDES:

1. Whenever we apply the same concept to several things, we explain this as a participation by these things in the same idea. For example, many different men participate in the same idea of *man*. But are we not then forced to say that these individual men and the idea of *man* together participate in still another idea of *man* which accounts for what they have in common? The situation is something like this:

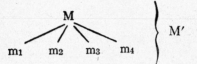

For Parmenides this other idea is the "third man." But if we accept this principle, it would be similarly necessary that this third man, together with all the others, participate in still another idea, a fourth man. This reasoning could be continued infinitely, and we would have an endless chain on our hands. This is the well-known "third-man argument."

2. Consider two objects, a man and a horse (m and h); m is different from h, and this difference is explained by their natures. Their natures are explained by the participation of m in an idea, M, and of h in H.

But if their difference is explained only by their participation in different ideas, was there a difference between them before this participation?

How could two identical things come to participate in different ideas? There must have been some sort of difference which predisposed one of them to participate in the idea M and the other to participate in H.

But this predisposition must in each case participate in the idea of that predisposition, M' and H', and so on. It is impossible for us to solve the problem on these terms— i.e., to explain the origin of the differentiation.

Parmenides thus accentuates a great weakness of the theory of ideas. In whatever direction he turns he is unable to explain the existence of things which are different (reality for him is a perfect, undifferentiated sphere, and his arguments about ideas only confirm this view). Since he can give no rational explanation of differentiation, the problem is raised without being solved.

At the beginning of the twentieth century the French scientist and philosopher Meyerson wrote a book, *Identity and Reality*, in which he defended the thesis that all explanation is a reduction to identity. Since all explanation consists in a reduction to identity, the whole universe, if it is rational, reduces to an immense identity.

3. Whenever we affirm that a proposition is true, we mean that the subject participates in the predicate. But here arises a paradox: the subject participates in contradictory ideas.

Suppose, for example, that we examine a chair; this chair is a single thing. I say *the* chair; there is only one of it. Yet it is made up of parts, and is therefore a plurality. So the chair participates in both the ideas of unity and plurality.

Similarly, if I say "The chair is brown," the subject *chair* participates both in *brown* and *being.* On the other hand, if I say that it is not black, then *chair* participates in the ideas both of Being and not-Being.

Furthermore, since it is identical with itself but different from other chairs, it participates in both the ideas of identity and difference.

This line of reasoning reduces to absurdity the doctrine that every object participates in only one idea.

THE *Sophist*

In this dialogue Plato seeks an answer to these objections and grapples with a real difficulty in Parmenides' concept of being.

He raises the question: What is a Sophist?

"A Sophist," he replies, "is a hunter whose quarry is

young men, and whose purpose is to extract money from them in exchange for teaching them."

And what does he teach them? Appearance.

But what is appearance? It is the false face of reality, which seems to be real without actually being so. In the guise of Being it is really not-Being.

Yet, since the Sophists make appearance the subject matter of their teaching, and since it is possible to talk about it, appearance must possess a kind of being. It is no longer correct to say: Being is; not-Being is not. Thus we are in definite opposition to Parmenides, who denies the existence of not-Being. If Being is, not-Being, in some sense, also is. These concepts are not absolute. This is a revision of Plato's original theory of ideas. Not-Being is not absolute nonexistence.

Plato thus takes into account the criticism he had put into the mouth of Parmenides. He finds his solution in the relatedness of ideas. The being which ideas have is not an absolute being.

He reaches the conclusion that things in the world of sense participate in ideas and that those ideas in turn participate in more general ideas, until finally we reach eight basic ideas:

$$
\begin{cases} 1.\ \text{identity} \\ 2.\ \text{difference} \end{cases} \qquad \begin{cases} 5.\ \text{unity} \\ 6.\ \text{plurality} \end{cases}
$$

$$
\begin{cases} 3.\ \text{rest} \\ 4.\ \text{motion} \end{cases} \qquad \begin{cases} 7.\ \text{being} \\ 8.\ \text{not-being} \end{cases}
$$

These ideas participate in each other; they form a system of categories which are not conceived as absolute. What Plato counters against the absolutism of Parmenides is the relatedness of ideas.

PLATO'S PHYSICS

Plato's main task after he had perfected his theory of ideas was to give an explanation of physical matter and distinguish between the universe of sense and the immaterial world of ideas. To this problem he turns in the *Timaeus.* Here he sets forth his theory of matter and places his physics on a mathematical basis.

We shall see in what a tentative and almost embarrassed manner he deals with the subject. Almost throughout he expresses himself through the use of analogy.

The following passage comes at a point in the dialogue where he has just explained that when the same name is given to several objects it is because they participate in the same idea:

And the same argument applies to the universal nature which receives all bodies—that must be always called the same; for, while receiving all things, she never departs at all from her own nature, and never in any way, or at any time, assumes a form like that of any of the things which enter into her; she is the natural recipient of all impressions, and is stirred and informed by them, and appears different from time to time by reason of them. But the forms which enter into and go out of her are the likenesses of real existences modelled after their patterns in a wonderful and inexplicable manner, which we will hereafter investigate. For the present we have only to conceive of three natures: first, that which is in process of generation; secondly, that in which the generation takes place; and thirdly, that of which the thing generated is a resemblance. And we may liken the receiving principle to a mother, and the source or spring to a father, and the intermediate nature to a child; and may remark further, that if the model is to take every variety of form, then the matter in which the model is fashioned will not be duly prepared, unless it is formless, and free from the impress of any of those shapes which it is hereafter to receive from without. For if the matter were like any of the supervening forms, then whenever any opposite or entirely different nature was stamped upon its surface, it would take the impression badly, because it would intrude its own shape.

Wherefore, that which is to receive all forms should have no form; as in making perfumes they first contrive that the liquid substance which is to receive the scent shall be as inodorous as possible; or as those who wish to impress figures on soft substances do not allow any previous impression to remain, but begin by making the surface as even and smooth as possible. In the same way that which is to receive perpetually and through its whole extent the resemblances of all eternal beings ought to be devoid of any particular form. Wherefore, the mother and receptacle of all created and visible and in any way sensible things, is not to be termed earth, or air, or fire, or water, or any of their compounds or any of the elements from which these are derived, but is an invisible and formless being which receives all things and in some mysterious way partakes of the intelligible, and is most incomprehensible. In saying this we shall not be far wrong; as far, however, as we can attain to a knowledge of her from the previous considerations, we may truly say that fire is that part of her nature which from time to time is inflamed, and water that which is moistened, and that the mother substance becomes earth and air, in so far as she receives the impressions of them.[4]

The analogy in which Plato compares matter to the mother, form to the father, and the created object to the child was to be adopted by certain Church fathers, who said that in human generation the father supplies the soul and the mother the body of the child. Nothing could better indicate the low estate in which woman was regarded in antiquity. A very curious tendency is to be noted in ancient thought whereby anything compared to woman acquires by analogy an inferior status.

The concept of matter which we find in the *Timaeus* is opposed to that of the early natural philosophers, who

---

[4] *Timaeus,* 50b–51b. (Jowett tr.).

believed that fundamental matter was an element such as air or fire.

For Plato such natural elements had already received the imprint of the world of ideas. He can define matter only abstractly and in a negative way—matter is defined as what receives the imprint of the world of ideas and consequently can have no quality of its own.

This is a concrete example of one of the recurrent problems of philosophy: when a thinker frames a dualistic theory in which he posits two fundamental elements, his major problem then is to see how these two elements can be related in such a way as to account for the reality we perceive. Thus any philosophy which wishes to avoid foundering in obscurity always tends toward some kind of monism.

The problem posed here is that of the opposition between the sensible world and the "real" world. Whenever we have to deal with basic elements whose characteristics are entirely different, the problem of uniting them presents grave difficulties. The status of matter rests in suspense in Plato; this is why his philosophy in the long run has had influence only on thinkers who attach little importance to the sensible world.

The subsequent development of Platonism was a working out of its two major aspects:

The religious and mystical aspect. This gave birth to Neoplatonism, which, through St. Augustine, influenced the development of Christian thought up to the end of the twelfth century.

The formal and rationalistic aspect. This exercised its influence from the time of the Renaissance in such rationalistic developments as we find in Descartes.

Plato's thought does not sufficiently explain the character of the sensible world. Consequently those who attach a greater importance to experience are attracted by the mind of another thinker who was deeply concerned with what is material and what is mutable and human. That thinker was Aristotle.

III

ARISTOTLE
(384–322 B.C.)

Student, follower, and opponent of Plato, Aristotle, who had entered the Academy at the age of eighteen, remained there for nineteen years until Plato's death in 348. Yet, despite the teaching of his master, the philosophical system he developed was radically different from that of Plato, for he was deeply interested in biological problems and in the phenonema of nature.

This may be explained perhaps by the environment in which he grew up. Born in Stagira, a city of Macedonia, he belonged to a family of physicians. His father, Nicomachus, was physician to Amyntus, the king of Macedonia and father of Philip of Macedon. Aristotle was a childhood friend of Philip, and to him was later entrusted the education of the future king, Alexander the Great.

(This last point has been doubted. How, it is asked, could the student of such a great master as Aristotle have lived in a manner which so little conformed to the teaching he had been given? Aristotle had preached moderation— the Golden Mean—a virtue which did not characterize Alexander the Great. If the pupil did not seem to have retained much of his master's teaching, it is even more surprising to note that Aristotle learned little from the achievements of Alexander. He did not seem to realize that the era of little Greek city-states was over and that the day of great empires was dawning. When he described the ideal city, he spoke of a city whose limits could be seen from some lofty spot and whose inhabitants would number no more than one hundred thousand. Although he had studied the constitutions of the Greek states, Aristotle was still living in the past. The argument against Aristotle's having been the teacher of Alexander does not seem worth taking seriously.)

Aristotle is primarily concerned with the problem of change. He distinguishes four kinds of change:

1. *Change of place:* motion.
2. *Change of quantity:* variation in the size of a thing, without change of quality.
3. *Change of quality:* such as growing old.
4. *Change in substance:* birth, generation, destruction, corruption.

A characteristic trait of Aristotle's thought is worth noting in this connection. *The idea of change is the more general idea;* the idea of motion is merely grafted onto it— motion is a special case of change. Among Aristotle's opponents, the Atomists, and, later on, among the mathematical philosophers like Descartes, change is regarded as a special case of motion. They looked upon motion as the more general idea.

The idea of change leads directly to the idea of matter, for matter underlies change and explains the possibility of change. Only in matter is change discernible.

What is matter?

Here we are face-to-face with the problem already raised by Plato. However, in a manner quite different from that of Plato, who expresses himself figuratively and seeks to bring about understanding through analogies, Aristotle relies on using ordinary language: What do we actually mean by matter?

When we see an object—a gold ring, for example—what does its matter consist of? It is the gold. And so we distinguish in the ring:

the *matter,* which is gold;

the *form,* which is circular.

Similarly, if we consider an ivory die, we can distinguish

the *matter,* ivory, and the *form,* the cubical shape. The die consists, then, of matter and form. This is true of every material object—it is made up of matter and form.

But when we think of matter in the plural—gold, ivory, iron, wood—what do they have in common? Why do we call them all *matter?* It cannot be their distinctive qualities which cause them to be matter, for they differ from each other; gold is not iron.

Our reply nowadays is that matter has mass; but for Aristotle the problem arose out of an extension of Platonic thinking: *matter can have no qualities at all.*

But can it then be said that matter exists? Can a thing which has no qualities exist?

If matter does not exist, it is simply not-being. But then how can any form enter into not-being to result in a material body? The idea of creation *ex nihilo* disappeared from Greek thought after the time of Parmenides.

At this point Aristotle makes a distinction which, as a result, is familiar to us, the distinction between actuality and potentiality:

actual reality (in act): what has well-defined properties; an actual being which is now in the fulness of being.

potential reality (in potentiality): what exists in potentiality and may become actual reality. (A chair is brown, but in potentiality it is white, for I can paint it; it is wooden, but in potentiality it is ashes, for I can burn it.)

On the basis of this distinction Aristotle defines matter as potential reality which may become actual. This way of looking at it makes it possible to define motion as the *actualizing of what is potential.*

Insofar as an object is actual, it has definite properties; but, due to the fact that it is material, it is subject to change.

All the properties that we can study in things derive from their form.

This whole concept may be compared with the Platonic theory, with which it appears to have a certain kinship. Like his master, Aristotle holds that everything perceived by the senses is material and changing, and that science is concerned with form—the various qualities which, for Plato, were derived from the world of ideas. But there is also a great difference between the two thinkers. For Plato the world of ideas is the real world, and the world of sense is a mere reflection of it. For Aristotle, on the other hand, *the world of sense is the real world;* the forms or ideas he regards as abstractions from sensible objects. There is no world of forms or ideas independent of matter. Forms are in the objects themselves.

Aristotle's view here is thus much closer to that of common sense, which emphasizes the importance of experience. Matter and form, for him, are principles abstracted from concrete objects.

As for the concrete object, we see that it changes, develops. The seed becomes the plant; the child becomes the man. What is it that determines the character of the change? Does it have any direction?

Aristotle distinguished four different causes at work in the development of every particular thing:

1. *Material cause:* its matter.
2. *Formal cause:* its form.
3. *Efficient cause:* what we usually mean by *cause* today.
4. *Final cause:* the end to be attained.

These four causes are easily distinguished in objects made by man—a statue, for example:

1. *Material cause:* the marble.
2. *Formal cause:* the idea in the mind of the sculptor.
3. *Efficient cause:* the sculptor himself.
4. *Final cause:* the end or purpose in view (making money, for example).

For natural objects, on the other hand, the formal cause takes the place of both the efficient cause and the final cause. How, then, does change come about in natural objects? The answer to this is based on the principle accepted by Aristotle and his contemporaries that anything in motion derives its motion from some other thing.

This idea differs notably from what we hold today. We conceive of things as always in motion—uniform motion in a straight line—in accordance with the principle of inertia. But Aristotle's view is that the normal state of a body is at rest. He therefore has to account for motion.

If a body, A, is in motion, this motion comes from some other thing, B, concerning which there are two possibilities:

B is at rest.

B is in motion.

In the latter case, the motion of B must be explained by some other thing, C; and so on.

But can we make an infinite regress into the past, explaining cause by cause? Can we grant an infinite chain of causes stretching back from a motion which is undoubtedly actual?

Aristotle does not believe in actual infinity. For him the infinite is the possibility of always finding a being, object, or number greater than the being, object, or number under consideration. For example, to say that a series of numbers is infinite means that it is always possible to find a number larger than any given number; but this larger number is itself finite.

He does not accept either an actual infinity or the possibility of imagining an infinite series of causes, for the infinite cannot be exhausted—the actual effect would never be reached.

We cannot make an infinite regress; we must stop somewhere. We must grant that there is a first cause, a starting point in the series of causes:

$$A_1 \rightarrow \quad A_2 \rightarrow \quad A_3 \rightarrow \quad A_4 \quad \quad \ldots \quad \quad A_p$$

This first cause Aristotle calls the *prime mover*.

But if there is a prime mover, it cannot be in motion, for it would have to derive its motion from some other thing. It is therefore unmoved, and thus has in itself no principle of change, no potentiality: it is entirely in act. It is what Aristotle calls *pure act*, containing within itself no material cause. It is immaterial.

How are we to understand this? Can there be a purely immaterial reality?

At this point Aristotle remembers that there had been introduced into the Greek philosophical tradition a concept which was similar to this—the *nous* of Anaxagoras (cf. p. 13). Aristotle conceives *pure act* to be of the nature of thought—a special and peculiar kind of thought, since it is unmoved.

What can be the object of a thought which does not change? Can this unmoved thought think about a universe made up of things which are changing? This would mean keeping track of changing things, which would seem to be impossible for something that was unchanging. A motionless thought could think about nothing but the prime mover; in other words, it could think about nothing but itself, for it is the only unchanging thing in the universe. It is in this way that Aristotle presents his idea of God: prime mover, pure act, first cause.

How then does God act on the universe? Like a man who makes something? No, for the man changes. On the other hand, how can God act, since he is a motionless cause?

This unmoved cause, says Aristotle, acts not as an efficient cause, but as a final cause, an end, an ideal, which other beings seek to approach. God is not a creator; he is what makes possible the harmony of the universe. Through their tending toward God, things realize the universal order, the *cosmos*. This is what proves God's immobility, for a changing ideal would indeed be unattainable.

What does this action consist in?

1. It is the defining principle of universal order.
2. It is the directive principle of the motion of things.

God differs from everything else in being pure act; and, insofar as everything is moved by God, it moves toward the realization of its own essence; its development consists in realizing its form.

This whole idea is obviously linked to the concept of biological growth. It is characteristic not only of Aristotle's philosophy of nature, but of his moral philosophy as well. The essence of a thing defines its structure and the goal of its development. To know how human life should be conducted requires that we know what is the proper essence of man.

The ideal nature of things, however, may not be fully realized. In this connection it should be noted that the term *essence* is equivocal. It may mean (a) the actual structure of a thing, or (b) the structure which it ought to achieve. Its meaning is thus a combination of the static (the structure) and the dynamic (the goal to be achieved). In this double sense it provides a basis for ethics. Man ought to act in conformity to his essence.

The line of reasoning by which motion is traced to a prime mover is followed by Aristotle in a number of other areas. Bearing the label "Aristotle's principle," it can be stated: *Infinite regression is impossible; there is always a first cause.*

This same principle operates in all causal explanation. In the case of material cause, for example, there must be a prime matter which is potentially real.

Again, when it comes to making definitions, to understand the meaning of a word we must ultimately have recourse to intuitive concepts, grasped because they are self-evident.

Or, to take another example, in proving a proposition we must use other propositions; but these must ultimately rest on certain basic axioms which serve as a point of departure. These are the so-called *laws of thought:*
1. *The law of identity:* A is A.
2. *The law of noncontradiction:* A cannot be both B and not-B.
3. *The law of the excluded middle:* Either A is B or A is not-B.

What we have called Aristotle's principle can be applied also in understanding that there is an ultimate end of our action. Just as the impossibility of an infinite regression from cause to cause requires a prime mover, there must also be a final end.

Aristotle's principle can be applied, then, in the most widely diverse areas of philosophy, but Aristotle still has to defend his doctrines against criticism. What can be done if a skeptic refuses to accept the laws of thought, which admittedly cannot be proved?

Then, says Aristotle, consider the skeptic's position. Either he is silent, and there is no discussion at all, or he tries to justify his position. In the latter case the argument of *retorsion* may be used against him.

Aristotle's point here is that reasoning cannot be carried on at all without using the three laws of thought. If the skeptic denies this, Aristotle points out that he uses the principles even in denying them. In fact only through the use of the law of noncontradiction can the skeptic deny these laws. Thus he is in contradiction with himself, since he is assuming the validity of the very principle he attacks.

Aristotle holds that a proposition is true when it corresponds with what is real. He was the originator of the concept known as the *mirror theory of truth*, a theory which has been developed through the modern distinction between language and *metalanguage*.

When I speak I use words, but what I am talking about is not the words (which are, after all, only tools) but the things the words stand for. When I speak about Plato I am speaking about the philosopher. But when I say PLATO in five letters, the object of my discourse is the word itself.

The expression *this proposition*, refers to the expression itself. In order, then, to speak about a word I must use the name of the word. An expression which refers to certain objects must not be confused with an expression which refers to itself. That is why we speak of PLATO the word in contrast to Plato the philosopher.

If we pass from words and the things the words represent to propositions and the facts they deal with, these same considerations are valid. Thus I can say that the proposition "It is raining" is made up of three words; but the fact that it is raining is not made up of three words: rain is not made up of words.

The mirror theory of truth therefore amounts to saying

that the proposition "It is raining" is true if, in fact, it *is* raining.

THEORY OF KNOWLEDGE

In contrast to Plato, Aristotle assigns a great importance to knowledge derived from the senses; for him this is the starting point of all knowledge.

Sense knowledge consists in the actualizing of two factors, one subjective and the other objective, which exist only in potentiality:

1. The quality which is to be manifest in the experience.
2. The capacity of the sense organs to perceive.

Aristotle recognizes that the various sense organs are specialized. But then a problem arises: How are we to integrate the data of the different senses which collaborate in the perception of the object? Aristotle regards as undebatable that ideas such as that of motion or unity are obtained through the collaboration of several senses. This is to be explained, according to him, by the existence of a *common sense,* which relates the data of the various senses to each other. The organ of this common sense is the heart.

When we experience an object, we always lay hold upon its form, never upon its matter. That is why the soul is called the locus of the forms.

THE LAWS OF ASSOCIATION

Aristotle was the first to set forth the laws of the association of ideas. Ideas, or perceptions, he said, become associated in three different ways:

1. *Association by similarity:* as we look at an object we think of one which is similar.
2. *Association by contrast:* the passage from one concept to another which is opposed to it (cold–hot).
3. *Association by succession in time:* the passage from one idea to that which follows it in the usual order (Tuesday–Wednesday).

Through association of ideas by similarity we are able

to work out concepts which deal only with the *essential qualities* of things.

A distinction must be made here:

1. *Essential qualities:* the qualities by virtue of which an object is the kind of thing it is, and which are present in every object to which the concept applies. They constitute the essence of the object.

2. *Accidental qualities:* qualities which need not be present in every object to which the concept applies.

This distinction provides a connection between Aristotle's theory of a concept and his theory of definition.

DEFINITION

By definition we sometimes mean simply the process of abbreviation whereby through linguistic convention we replace a complex symbol by one which is more readily handled: for example $4 + 1 = 5$. Here we are dealing with a *nominal definition.*

Aristotle is primarily concerned with what are called *real definitions.* For him it is the business of natural science to find real definitions, to discover the essential characteristics of what is defined. It is more than a matter of linguistic convention; it is the discovery in definition of the essence of the thing. This kind of definition constitutes the real goal of knowledge. It is important to remember in this connection that Aristotle believes the essence of a thing to lie within the thing itself.

Today we make the distinction between accidental and essential qualities; but the distinction is relative, depending on the point of view. For Aristotle the distinction lies in the very nature of things; it is an absolute distinction. Whoever studies nature must make his thinking conform to the hierarchy revealed by his study.

The very structures, or forms, which Plato believed to have an objective and independent existence Aristotle introduces into the things themselves.

What does a good definition consist in? It must indicate the essential nature of the object. A distinction needs to be made at this point between two aspects in which a concept may be viewed: *extension* and *intension*.

1. The *extension* of a concept is the class of all objects to which the concept properly applies. The extension of the concept *man*, for example, is the class of beings of whom it may be said that they are men. Put another way, the extension of a concept is the class of all possible subjects of which the concept may be truly predicated. For example: John is a man; Peter is a man; Paul is a man. The extension of the concept man is made up of John, Peter, Paul, and so on.

2. The *intension*, or connotation, of a concept consists of the properties, or qualities, which all objects to which the term applies must possess. If the concept, taken in its whole extension, is the subject of a proposition, the totality of qualities truly predicated of the subject constitutes its intension. For example: All men are mortal; all men are rational; all men are . . . and so on.

Aristotle sets forth the principle that intension and extension vary inversely with each other. If only part of the extension of a term is considered, the intention is correspondingly increased. For example, if in place of all men I consider only white men, I lessen the extension but increase the intension.

But this principle is not true in the case where certain properties imply certain other properties. For example, if a property A implies another property B, all objects which have A will also have B; thus to consider A alone does not increase the extension.

This principle makes it possible to classify things, so that the concept with the lesser extension will be contained within the concept with the greater extension. For example, men are animals. Certain properties belonging to man must be omitted from the intension of the concept *animal*. This type of classification makes it possible to distinguish genera from the species they include.

In this hierarchy of concepts beginning with the individual, represented by a proper name, and proceeding to the most general, there must be concepts which from the absolute point of view are the most general.

Each species is subsumed under the genus, which, in turn, is a species within a more inclusive genus. Genus and species are relative ideas. But ultimately there is a genus in itself, which is a predicate by nature.

From the Aristotelian point of view, *a good definition places the* DEFINIENDUM (the term, concept, or species to be defined) *in its proximate genus and then gives the* DIFFERENTIA (difference) *which distinguishes it from other species in that genus.*

Man	is	a	rational	animal.
↑			↑	↑
definiendum			*differentia*	proximate genus

definiens

In the language of the later Scholastics, a definition proceeds *per genus et differentiam.*

The proximate genus is the genus which ranks next above the concept to be defined. A concept which is too inclusive, too far removed from the *definiendum*, should not be taken as the proximate genus. For example, there is no sense in trying to define man by putting him in the genus of Being in general.

Aristotle believes that there is an objective hierarchy of concepts, not one which depends upon a subjective point of view. That is why we must seek a proximate genus, place the definiendum in that genus, and then indicate the specific *differentia* which distinguishes the concept from other species in that genus.

There is no way, however, of defining those most general concepts which Aristotle calls the *categories.*

To determine what these categories are (and here his procedure is quite different from that of Plato) Aristotle starts from the empirical basis of language; examines substantives, verbs, and adjectives to determine what are the most general categories to which these (Greek) words belong. His list of categories numbers ten:

1. *Substance:* man, horse.
2. *Relation:* double, to the left of.
3. *Quantity:* five, few.
4. *Quality:* white, ill.
5. *Time:* yesterday, soon.
6. *Place:* at Athens, over there.
7. *Action:* expressed by the active voice of verbs.
8. *Passivity:* expressed by the passive voice of verbs.
9. *Posture:* expressed by verbs of state: I am seated.
10. *Possession:* expressed by forms of the verb *to have.*

These categories cannot be defined; they can be known only intuitively. They are the most abstract genera of thought, and there is no way to explain them. The search for these most general concepts which can be directly known constitutes a new application of what we have called Aristotle's principle.

ARISTOTLE'S LOGIC

Aristotle analyzes all judgments as being of the form *A is B.* These judgments are what he calls *predicative,* for they consist of a subject, a copula, and a predicate. Whatever may be the structure of a given judgment—whether it consist merely of a subject and a verb (Paul eats) or a subject, a verb, and an object (Paul eats an apple)—Aristotle modifies it by altering the verb to a copula and a present participle (Paul is eating; Paul is eating an apple). Everything following the copula is considered to be part of the predicate. This analysis, of course, is different from that of modern logic, in which propositions, rather than terms, are regarded as the starting point.

From the standpoint of *quality*, Aristotle regards judgments as either affirmative or negative: A is B; A is not B. From the standpoint of *quantity* they are universal (All A is B; No A is B) or particular (Some A is B; Some A is not B), depending on whether the subject is taken in its full extension or not. It is apparent that on the basis of this twofold classification there are four different kinds of judgment. In medieval times the first vowels of the two Latin verbs *affirmo* and *nego,* provided a convenient way of designating these propositions: A—universal affirmative; E—universal negative; I—particular affirmative; and O—particular negative.

Reasoning

Aristotle makes a distinction between two kinds of inference: (1) *immediate inference,* in which the conclusion is drawn from a single premise; and (2) *mediate inference,* in which the conclusion is based on two or more premises.

The principal forms of *immediate* inference are based on (a) *opposition,* (b) *obversion,* and (c) *conversion.*

a. *Opposition* is derived from a consideration of the question: Given the truth or falsity of one of the four kinds of judgment, what may be concluded concerning the truth or falsity of the other three when they have the same subject and predicate? The relations between the four judgments can be brought out through the aid of a square in which the top corners represent the two universals and the left-hand corners represent the two affirmatives:

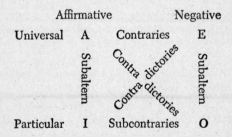

	Affirmative		Negative
Universal	A	Contraries	E
Particular	I	Subcontraries	O

Contradictories (A and O, E and I) are so related that the truth of one implies the falsity of the other, and the falsity of one implies the truth of the other.

Contraries (A and E) are so related that if one of them

is true the other must be false, but they may both be false; the falsity of one does not imply the truth of the other.

Subcontraries (I and O) are so related that they cannot both be false, but they can both be true; the falsity of one implies the truth of the other.

Subalterns are not symmetrically related; the two particulars are each subaltern to the universals having the same quality, I to A and O to E. In each case if the universal is true, the particular is also true; and if the particular is false, the universal is false.

b. The second kind of immediate inference is *obversion*. Given a judgment which asserts some predicate of a subject, it is possible to establish the relation between the subject and the negative of that predicate. If A is B, what is the relation between A and not-B? Clearly the quality of the judgment must be changed: From All A is B it must be concluded that No A is not-B. Some A is B implies that Some A is not not-B. No A is B implies that All A is not-B. And Some A is not B implies that Some A is not-B.

c. *Conversion* is a process whereby, from a judgment which asserts a predicate of a subject, we pass to a conclusion in which the predicate of the premise becomes the subject of the conclusion and the subject of the premise becomes the predicate of the conclusion. If A is B, what is the relation between B and A?

With the universal negative (E) and the particular affirmative (I) conversion is simple:

No A is B → No B is A and Some A is B → Some B is A

Conversion of the universal affirmative judgment can be made only by limitation:

All A is B → Some B is A

As for the particular negative judgment, no conversion is possible, since the judgment Some A is not B tells us nothing about the relation between B and A.

The classic form of *mediate* inference analyzed by Aristotle is the *syllogism;* and the classic model of the syllogism is shown by the formula:

If all A is B

and if all B is C,

then all A is C

The form of this argument can be indicated in a diagram:

All A is B

All B is C

Therefore all A is C

Every syllogism contains three propositions (two premises and a conclusion) and three different terms (P, S, and M), each used twice. One of these terms (M), which appears in each of the premises, is known as the *middle term.* The other two terms each appear once in the premises and once in the conclusion. They are known as the *major term* (P), which is the predicate of the conclusion, and the *minor term* (S), which is the subject of the conclusion. The premise containing the major term is known as the *major premise,* and the premise containing the minor term is known as the *minor premise.* By convention the major premise is usually stated first.

Four so-called *figures* of the syllogism are usually distinguished, depending on the position of the middle term:

I		II		III		IV	
M	P	P	M	M	P	P	M
S	M	S	M	M	S	M	S
S	P	S	P	S	P	S	P

It might appear that each premise of the syllogism, as well as the conclusion, could be one of the four possible forms, A. E, I, or O. This would mean that for each figure there would be $4 \times 4 \times 4 = 64$ possible combinations. These possible combinations of premises are called moods. And since there are four figures of the syllogism, there could be 256 possible moods. Actually only 24 of these turn out to be valid, for only from them can a true conclusion be inferred if the premises are true. (If one of the premises is false, nothing may be concluded as to the truth or falsity of the conclusion.)

A mood of the syllogism is valid only if it conforms to a set of eight rules governing the validity of syllogisms. Understanding of these rules requires the introduction of a further concept, that of *distribution*. A term is distributed when an assertion is made about the whole of its extension. Thus in the universal judgments, A and E, the subject is distributed; in the negative judgments, E and O, the predicate is distributed (since all or part of the extension of the subject is excluded from the *entire* extension of the predicate). Put another way, A distributes its subject, O distributes its predicate, E distributes both subject and predicate, and I distributes neither.

The rules governing the validity of the syllogism may be stated as follows:

1. The syllogism contains three, and only three, terms.

2. The middle term does not appear in the conclusion.

3. No term may be distributed in the conclusion which is not distributed in the premises.

4. The middle term must be distributed at least once in the premises.

5. If the premises are affirmative, the conclusion must be affirmative.

6. From two negative premises no conclusion may be drawn.

7. From two particular premises no conclusion may be drawn.

8. The conclusion always follows the weaker premise. (A negative premise is considered weaker than an affirmative, and a particular weaker than a universal.)

Modern logic has shown that the syllogism is only one among many forms of mediate inference. Syllogistic reasoning is based essentially on classification. Modern logic is based on the analysis of mathematical reasoning. It is an operational logic, since it analyzes the structure of mathematical operations and calculations.

IV

THE PHILOSOPHY

OF THE

HELLENISTIC PERIOD

The changes which occurred in the Western world after the death of Alexander the Great in 323 B.C. cannot be too greatly emphasized. We enter, indeed, a new era of civilization—the Hellenistic—in which the whole atmosphere of the ancient world becomes different.

Up to now we have studied the history of Greek thought as worked out by the Greeks themselves in the homeland and in the colonies. But the conquests of Alexander resulted in an expansion of Greek culture throughout the Near East, northern Africa, and the periphery of the Mediterranean world. From the cultural point of view Rome was little more than an outgrowth of Greece. Only in the areas of administration, law, architecture, and engineering were the Romans genuinely creative.

One sign of the dominance of Greek culture throughout the Western world was the fact that all people of any distinction—all those who prided themselves on their cultivation—spoke Greek, the language common to the civilized West. Greek continued to be spoken in the eastern Mediterranean until the fall of Constantinople in 1453.

The campaigns of Alexander, military expeditions, brought about the spread of Greek culture. It required the prestige of arms to demonstrate that cultural superiority which, often enough, is not recognized when military superiority is lacking. This relation between armed might and culture is a curious and unfortunate phenomenon of civilization.

Even though Alexander's empire was divided among his generals after his death, Asia Minor, Africa, and even Rome remained strongly influenced by Greek culture from the third century B.C. until A.D. 1453—more than seventeen centuries.

But this culture was not something purely Greek. To it were added mystical and religious elements which were very un-Greek, and which gave birth to all kinds of syncretistic concepts deriving from quite various sources.

The center of this Hellenistic civilization was neither Athens nor Rome; it was Alexandria. And at Alexandria, up until the great fire in 640—a period of some ten centuries—the most divergent civilizations were to come in contact with one another. Here, under the protection of the Ptolemaic dynasty, institutions for organized scientific study came into being. It was at Alexandria over many years that astronomy (the Ptolemaic system, which placed the earth in the center of the universe), geography, grammar, and geometry (Euclid) were developed.

After the destruction of the library in Alexandria, Byzantium remained the center of ancient culture until the Renaissance.

Only recently has the importance of these Hellenistic civilizations at Alexandria and Byzantium been adequately recognized. History often resembles those false genealogies drawn up to establish the importance of the present by reference to some glorious past. By virtue of the fact that we have lived under the influence of a Roman and Latin Church the influence of Alexandria and Byzantium has been neglected.

CHARACTERISTICS OF THE HELLENISTIC PERIOD

During this period Greece is no longer the mistress of her destiny. The time is one of frequent civil war. The problem of politics no longer occupies the forefront of philosophical concern; the philosophers who are heads of the various schools at Athens, and who are "barbarians" in their origin, are primarily concerned with individual happiness. They deal with the question: In what way must we live in order to be happy?

Thinkers of this period compared philosophy to a fruit tree. Its roots are logic, the trunk and branches are physics, and the fruit is ethics. The whole of philosophy is dominated by ethics, the search for a rule of life.

All these moral theories, whatever they may be, reach the same conclusion: Happiness consists in *ataraxia*—the state of being undisturbed, of preserving peace of mind.

The Stoics

The Stoic school, the first to be established, was founded about 300 B.C. by Zeno of Citium (a city in Cyprus), who came to Athens to study with Greek masters, and who was in time made an honorary citizen.

In the long history of the Stoic school, extending over several centuries, three periods have been distinguished.

Early Stoicism is represented by Zeno (336–264 B.C.), Cleanthes (c. 331–232 B.C.) and Chrysippus (d. 204 B.C.), who became the great man of the school.

Middle Stoicism is represented by Panaetius of Rhodes (d. before 111 B.C.) and Posidonius (c. 135–51 B.C.), who gave instruction to Cicero and was a friend of Pompey. Rhodes was the center of Stoicism during the second and first centuries B.C.

Later Stoicism made many converts at Rome during the first and second centuries A.D. The most important of these were Seneca (c. 4 B.C.–A.D. 65); Epictetus (first century

A.D.), a freed slave; and the emperor Marcus Aurelius
(121–180).

Despite the great number of the works of Chrysippus
(he is said to have written more than four hundred books)
we have only fragments of his writings. For an account of
his system we are forced to go to two sources:

1. Diogenes Laertius, who in the third century A.D.
wrote *Lives and Opinions of Eminent Philosophers.* Although this work is useful, it has a somewhat journalistic
character.

2. Marcus Tullius Cicero, the most valuable source.
In a number of his works in dialogue form he presents
discussions among representatives of the various philosophical schools—Epicureans, Stoics, and Academics (Pla-
tonists of the Academy). Thus, thanks to the prestige of
Cicero's style and the fact that he wrote in Latin, the
ideas of the earlier Stoics have been preserved. In Plutarch
and Sextus Empiricus are also found expositions of Stoic
ideas. These fragments of ancient stoicism have been
gathered together by the philologer von Arnim.

The Stoic philosophers of the later school laid the greatest stress on ethical theory and seem to have been influenced by the ideas of nascent Christianity.

It is interesting to note that Seneca was a nobleman,
Epictetus a freed slave, and Marcus Aurelius an emperor.
Stoicism is a philosophy in which no stress is placed on
social classes. Furthermore, it represents no national point
of view; it is cosmopolitan, and for this reason it helped
bring about the unification of the Roman empire. The
jus gentium—the law of nations—was in large measure
influenced by the Stoic philosophy.

Although Epictetus and Marcus Aurelius lived in Rome,
it is noteworthy that they both wrote in Greek. So strong
was this tradition that when Cicero wrote his philosophical
works in Latin, he thought it useful to apologize to his
readers for not writing in Greek—yet he was living in the
"golden age" of Latin civilization.

In a similar way during the seventeenth century, the
"golden age" of French civilization, Descartes wrote his

Discourse on Method in French and apologized for not writing it in Latin.

These changes are characteristic, for they show what the language is that dominates any particular epoch:

1. Greek up to the barbarian invasions.
2. Latin until the Renaissance.
3. Italian in the fifteenth and sixteenth centuries.
4. French in the seventeenth and eighteenth centuries. We might note as a typical example a work written in French by an Englishman and dedicated to the King of Prussia.
5. German for science and philosophy in the nineteenth century.
6. English in the twentieth century.

Interestingly enough, this succession of languages is related to political domination, which becomes extended through a cultural hegemony.

In their theory of knowledge the Stoics are sensationalists: all knowledge for them is based on sensation, on data derived from the senses; in this they are opposed to the earlier schools, which gave a preponderant place to reason.

Through our senses we perceive images to which we must give assent. These perceived images bring about a certain inertia in our minds and force our acceptance; they impose themselves on us. Likewise concepts are formed spontaneously through the combining of images, but we are able to control them by comparison. Science is regarded as a systematic elaboration based upon concepts and common notions.

The Stoics developed in antiquity a logic of propositions intimately related to their general philosophical outlook.

For Aristotle, as we have seen, the basis of knowledge is to be found in the abstract which explains the concrete— the basic element of knowledge is the concept, the term, whose combinations result in propositions. Thus with Aristotle, if a meaningful proposition is to be made out of *All A is B*, the variable letters must be replaced by concepts. For example, if A = *man* and B = *mortal*, we can derive the proposition *All men are mortal*.

For the Stoics, the letters stand not for terms but for propositions. The Stoics recognized five logical schemata:

1. If p then q
   But p
   Therefore q

   The *principle of deduction*. If one proposition is the condition for another and that condition is fulfilled, so also is the consequent.

   For example: If *n* is divisible by 4, *n* is divisible by 2.
   But *n* is divisible by 4.
   Therefore *n* is divisible by 2.

2. If p then q
   But not-q
   Therefore not-p

   The *principle of transposition*

   For example: If *n* is divisible by 4, *n* is divisible by 2.
   But *n* is not divisible by 2.
   Therefore *n* is not divisible by 4.

3. It is false that p and q
   But p
   Therefore not-q

   If two propositions cannot both be true, the truth of one establishes the falsity of the other.

4. Either p or q
   But not-p
   Therefore q

5. Either p or q
   But p
   Therefore not-q

But an equivocation lurks in the meaning of "either . . . or": It may mean one or the other of two things:

1. At least one of the alternatives is true; the other may be true.

2. If one of the alternatives is true, the other must be false.

The fifth *schema* is valid only if p and q cannot both be true.

For centuries these five Stoic schemata were misunderstood by logicians, who knew only the logic of Aristotle. They replaced the variable letters by terms instead of propositions and understood the verb *is:* e.g., "If p then q" became "if p is then q is."

It was not until the twentieth century that the Polish logician Lukasiewicz showed that the Stoics were really dealing with a calculus of propositions.

This provides an interesting example of a common historical process. Ancient doctrines are interpreted in terms of current knowledge, and the progress of contemporary science can thus make possible a better understanding of the history of the past.

The Epicureans

Epicurus (341–270 B.C.) was the founder of the Epicurean school. There were two dominant influences on him:

1. The Atomists, particularly Democritus (see p. 13).

2. The Cyrenaic school, whose head was Aristippus of Cyrene (see p. 21).

The first influenced his physics, the second his ethics.

Although Epicurus is reported to have been a voluminous writer, we have very little from his own hand. There are three principle sources of information about his doctrine:

1. Diogenes Laertius, who devotes the whole of his tenth book to the study of Epicurean theories and preserves three important letters.

2. Cicero, Sextus Empiricus, and Plutarch, whose works contain expositions of Epicurean doctrines.

3. The *De Rerum Natura* of Lucretius, a philosophical poem of the first century B.C. in which the Epicurean

theories are developed, the most important and complete source remaining to us.

Epicurean physics resembles that of Democritus except that for Epicurus the atoms "swerve" and have a power to deviate from their trajectory; this provides a systematic basis for human freedom.

THEORY OF KNOWLEDGE

In his theory of knowledge Epicurus holds that knowledge depends on:

1. Sensation.
2. Conceptual elaboration.
3. Feeling (a great novelty).

Epicurus is a sensationalist; he believes that knowledge is based on sensation and that sensation cannot deceive us.

But if sensation cannot deceive us, how can error be explained?

Error occurs only in our conceptual assertions, not in our sense perceptions, for two reasons:

1. We use concepts which have been badly framed.
2. Every proposition, in some sense or other, goes beyond the data of experience; to the degree that it does so, error is possible.

For example, I look at a tower in the distance, and from my place of observation it appears round; on drawing nearer, I see that it is square. Therefore the proposition "The tower is round" is false.

How does the error arise? If I draw away, the tower again appears round.

My mistake consists in saying "The tower is round." This statement goes beyond the data of experience.

Let us note that even if I say "The tower appears to be round," I seem to imply that it would be round for others in other circumstances and at other times, whereas it appears round only to me. Already I have made a generalization from the conditions of experience. This is why science must describe with rigor and precision the *condi-*

tions of experience. The sciences have progressed to the degree that they have made these conditions precise.

The theory of induction worked out by the Epicureans is known to us through a treatise by Philodemus of Gadara, who was head of a philosophical school at Naples in the first century B.C. This treatise was among the eighteen hundred papyrus scrolls discovered at Herculaneum and published during the nineteenth century.

Induction proceeds from what appears (which is known through observation or testimony) to what does not appear. By reason it draws conclusions from like to like, unless contrary experience prevents the acceptance of those conclusions. This kind of reasoning had already been developed in the *corpus* of Hippocratic medicine in the fifth and fourth centuries B.C.

It is through *feeling*, according to Epicurus, that we experience pleasure and pain. And it is on the feelings of pleasure and pain that all ethics, conceived as a collection of rules for moral conduct, is based.

If we were creatures who had no feeling, we would be unable to judge good and evil. These words would have no meaning for us. Therefore it is because we have feelings that ethics in general can be constructed.

EPICUREAN ETHICS

Morality consists in the pursuit of happiness; happiness consists in a life in which the maximum of pleasure is enjoyed.

But in contrast to the school of Cyrene, which made no distinction among pleasures, Epicurus regards pleasures as qualitatively different. He distinguishes three varieties:

1. Necessary pleasures.
2. Useful pleasures.
3. Superfluous pleasures.

Necessary pleasures involve the satisfaction of our natural and indispensable needs, such as eating and drinking. This satisfaction may be attained in the simplest way by eating bread and drinking water. Drinking wine is not a necessary pleasure, and getting drunk is superfluous.

Epicurus insists on the fact that the necessary pleasures are always satisfied in a natural way, while it is more difficult to satisfy the useful pleasures and even more difficult to satisfy the superfluous pleasures. This proves, believes Epicurus, that nature is well ordered.

Epicurus makes a further distinction between the pleasures of motion and the pleasures of rest.

The pleasures of motion are brought about by a change of state. They satisfy a need by making that need disappear. Thus, if I am thirsty, I experience pleasure by quenching my thirst. This pleasure has brought about a certain change of state.

On the other hand, not to experience the need of drinking is also a pleasure: it is a *pleasure of rest*.

The first pleasure is active; the other is passive.

From the Greek point of view, to feel a need is a proof of imperfection, for it means a tendency toward change. The gods, who are perfect beings, enjoy pleasure in rest.

This distinction between the pleasures of motion and the pleasures of rest brings to mind two ways of viewing progress. In antiquity from the time of Parmenides on (with the exception of Heraclitus) progress was regarded as a tending toward perfection, toward stability. Ordered stability, harmony requiring no change, is better than motion. This concept is tied up with the valuing of what is ancient and traditional.

Certain streams of modern thought, particularly romanticism, have habituated us to seek what is new, original, and to be valued for that very reason. But one must not lose sight of the fact that for centuries what was new had to be justified as a continuation of what was old. There is a relation here to the two ideas of pleasure that we find in Epicurus. The *pleasure of rest* is the form of pleasure preferred by the ancients. This ordering of pleasures would not be acceptable today.

In a paradoxical way this ethics based on pleasure has

the same goal as that of other contemporary ethical systems —*ataraxia,* the state of being undisturbed.

The system of Epicurus is in the mainstream of Greek thought, since it is based on a kind of calculus of pleasures.

This whole theory was greatly extended in the eighteenth century in the *utilitarianism* of the English thinker Jeremy Bentham (1748–1832). He held that good is not simply the pleasure of the individual, but the greatest interest of the greatest number, worked out by a calculus of pleasures. In this arithmetic of pleasures Bentham introduced various criteria for determining the value of pleasures: pleasures which are certain, pleasures which are lasting or transient, intense or moderate pleasures, pleasures followed by good or ill consequences, and so on.

But this moral arithmetic presupposes the possibility of comparing pleasures, of being able to quantify them through some coefficient of their importance. All acts must be comparable on the same basis; that is the condition underlying the application of reason to human conduct. Rational conduct is conduct which is in agreement with this moral arithmetic, and this, in turn, requires that moral values be reduced to the same denominator.

This leads us to the objection raised by Henri Bergson in his *The Immediate Data of Consciousness.* He criticizes the introduction of any calculus in the area of consciousness; for, in order to set up such a calculus, measurement must be introduced, and only what is spatial can be measured. Thus to measure time we measure spatial movement, like that of the hands of a watch.

It is possible to compare spatially either the causes or the effects of sensation, but we can never measure directly the phenomena of consciousness. They are heterogeneous, which means they are qualitatively different, and there is no way of reducing them to a mere quantitative difference. This criticism applies to any arithmetic of pleasures, for pleasures are phenomena of consciousness.

It should be noted further that the ancient philosophers associated morality with reason (considered as a certain knowledge of natural phenomena):

For Plato morality consists in conformity to the natural order.

For Aristotle morality consists in realizing human nature.

For the Stoics it consists in following nature.

For the Epicureans it consists in a calculus of pleasures.

There are some difficulties in the way of connecting ethics with science. Can the transition be made from science, which tells us what is, to ethics, which deals with normative laws? Can one pass from what is to what ought to be?

The answer can be affirmative on only one condition: the end morality strives to attain must be known precisely.

If actions be regarded as means for arriving at the end proposed by ethics, science can provide the technique for arriving at that end. If the end is known, the whole of ethics is reduced to the study of the best means of realizing it, and a moral technique based on science would be conceivable. Morality would be a kind of applied science if there were no doubt about the end in view.

That is what the ancients meant when they said that everyone seeks happiness.

But there is a quality which distinguishes science from ethics: When we have to act we must make a choice as to how to act; our response cannot be put off indefinitely; and once the choice is made we are committed. In science, on the contrary, it is permissible to suspend judgment until the right answer is found. The reply "I do not know" can always be made.

In matters of morals the element of time plays a large role which it does not play in the sciences. A knowledge better than that of today may be possible tomorrow; but if one is required to act today, can one reply that he will wait until next year?

On the other hand, one must conform to the currently accepted moral standards. Though ethics may have a progressive character, one cannot arrange the board ahead of time. The laws on which we act must be applicable to the twentieth century, not to the twenty-fourth.

It is possible to speak of relative—not absolute—moral

progress when moral rules are better adapted to the present day needs than the usages and customs of earlier decades.

So far, however, as ethics is tied to science, there is one drawback which affects the rules of ethics. These rules would be valid only so long as science could explain them; if a rule appeared incomprehensible, one would have the right to reject it.

Furthermore, science is dominated by the notion of truth as something which is grasped only approximately; one seeks to come closer and closer to it. Science is progressive; it is forever modifying its provisionally accepted principles. Therefore in tying morality to science one seems to give to morality the character of possible rectification which is typical of science. Ethics then takes from science its unstable character. This would be a revolutionary concept in ethics.

On the other hand, if moral rules were fixed, if morality became rigid, this condition might lead to a congealing of the sciences; it might give them a dogmatic character which would transform them into something approaching religion. A great number of religious beliefs are congealed scientific ideas of an earlier era.

The Skeptics

All Greek philosophy can be regarded as a battle between dogmatism and skepticism. Just as there are several varieties of dogmatism, so also there are several varieties of skepticism, for the ends and means of skepticism are not always the same.

The whole Greek sophistical movement, which regarded itself as the defender of common sense (*doxa*) against science (*epistēmē*), was itself a form of skepticism. But why one doubts and what one doubts have to be known. These two problems are bound together.

The thinkers of antiquity who are usually called skeptics formed a movement the importance of which has been underestimated by dogmatic philosophy; to the degree that one espouses an idea one tends to neglect its adversaries—a phenomenon characteristic of a successful ideology. It tends always to disregard not only the contemporary ideas opposed to it, but those of the past as well. A whole period of our Western civilization was so dominated by religious dogmatism that very little has been preserved for us of the writings of the skeptics. They are known to us through Cicero, Diogenes Laertius, and Sextus Empiricus (*Outlines of Pyrrhonism* and *Adversus Mathematicos*).

Three periods of post-Aristotelian skepticism may be distinguished:

1. The first period is represented by Pyrrho of Elis (*c.* 365–275 B.C.) and his pupil Timon. The skepticism of this period is known as Pyrrhonism. Pyrrho, who was the high priest of the city of Elis, opposed the deduction of rules of action and conduct from science; in so doing he opposed the morality of the wise man.

The basic reason for his opposition, as he saw it, was that in order to deduce rules of action from some concept of reality one must know the reality. But we never know a reality absolutely and we can never again gain absolute certainty. We can only compare perceptions with other perceptions. That is why we must construct no philosophical system; we must be silent.

Pyrrho therefore left no writings, and we know of him only what Timon wrote in his satirical verses, the *Silloi* (lampoons).

The ideal he pursues is *ataraxia*. Since nothing is certain, nothing need trouble us or force us to act. But in practical life we cannot be content with negation, and since we must sometimes act, the best course of conduct, according to Pyrrho, is to conform to laws and customs.

He became high priest of his city because there was no certainty as to the existence or nonexistence of the gods and because religion was a custom to be observed.

As a form of skepticism Pyrrhonism is an expression of social conservatism; the only rule of conduct is a kind of inertia. There is no reason for change, and Pyrrho's purpose is to criticize reason as an instrument of social reform and revolution. Pyrrhonism is an absolute and conservative skepticism.

2. The second period of skepticism covers the third and second centuries B.C. It is represented by the Middle and the New Academy, which grew out of the Platonism of the Old Academy.

The best-known representative of the Middle Academy was Arcesilaus of Pitane (315–240 B.C.), and the outstanding thinker of the New Academy was Carneades of Cyrene (219–129 B.C.).

How could these thinkers represent themselves as carrying on the Platonic tradition? How could their thought be derived from the dogmatism of the Old Academy?

At that time two dogmatic schools occupied the forefront—the Stoics and the Epicureans, both of whom were sensationalists. When it came to sense experience Plato had been a skeptic. He showed the variability and the obscurity of sense knowledge, and his writings provide many arguments against it.

It is precisely because the Academy opposed the sensationalist dogmatism of the Stoics and Epicureans that there developed an arsenal of arguments to prove the imperfection of sense knowledge; a great number of these arguments were taken from Plato himself.

Water, for example, held at a constant temperature will seem cold or hot depending on whether our hands are hot or cold. Our perceptions are different under different circumstances.

These thinkers are likewise opposed to the dogmatism which results in social conformity. The *criterion* they suggest is what is reasonable; that is, what is the most probable.

Thus Carneades shows that a single sensation is more likely to lead us into error than several sensations which agree with each other. He proposes a theory of coherence as a basis for making a decision.

In the long run we must decide for ourselves in favor of what appears most probable and reasonable to us. We can never make a choice based on dogma.

It is apparent that in this theory the freedom of the

individual to make a choice plays an important role. It is not surprising that it was Carneades who invented the theory of free will.

THE THEORY OF FREE WILL

Here we must see in what way the theory of human freedom was presented during this time.

The two schools contemporary with the Academy, the Stoic and the Epicurean, advanced theories about freedom which were completely opposed to each other.

The Stoics believed that all the parts of the universe (macrocosm) were interdependent. This idea was reinforced by Oriental influences, Babylonian particularly, which introduced *astrology* into Stoicism. Astrology established a relation between celestial phenomena and human life in such a way that through understanding the meaning of the positions of the stars and planets, the "language of the stars," predictions could be made about the unfolding of human life.

Human freedom therefore had no role to play. The life of man was fettered; the course of life was established by destiny. For some twenty centuries astrology was considered the science *par excellence,* and until the Renaissance it was believed to be the most important natural science.

When what was predicted failed to come to pass, it could always be argued that the conjunction of the heavenly bodies had not been accurately observed at the moment of the individual's birth, or that errors of calculation had been made. Thus astrology helped to bring about the development of an exact science—astronomy. In the same way the attempts of the alchemists to transmute the baser metals into gold gave birth to chemistry.

These studies, chimerical as they were, therefore contributed to the progress of practical and useful sciences.

What has been called a battle between science on the one hand and philosophy and religion on the other during this long period was really a battle between astrology and philosophy and religion.

For the Stoics the free man is he who adapts himself to his destiny—to natural laws. "The fates lead the man who is willing," wrote Seneca; "the unwilling they drag." The freedom of the sage is the freedom of the man who submits to destiny. But there is no free will.

The Epicurean theory, on the contrary, introduces universal indeterminism; since atoms have the ability to deviate from their path, it is no longer possible to establish laws of nature.

The Epicureans believe that man enjoys an absolute freedom. Curiously enough, however, they believe that the same freedom exists for things as well as men. *They enlarge the scope of freedom too much.* No distinction is made between the freedom of conscious and of unconscious beings.

By virtue of its position between these two extremes, the thinking of Carneades is in opposition to the dogmatism of both the Epicureans and the Stoics. To the degree that there is an element of probability in our knowledge, the concept of human freedom is introduced as a basic factor in moral and theoretical judgment.

3. During the third period, the first two centuries A.D., skepticism is bound up with problems of the applied sciences, the result of a debate between two rival schools of medicine: the *empiric* and the *dogmatic* schools.

The dogmatists were astrologers. They explained the condition of man as a function of his natural environment. Since a knowledge of nature was required, they applied themselves to it and were therefore physicists.

The members of the empirical school denied the possibility of any absolute knowledge. Their trust was in immediate experience with no search for explanations in physics. For them it is appearance which is certain and "reality" which is debatable.

Their ideas are known through the writings of Sextus Empiricus, who tells us of two of his predecessors, Aenesidemus and Agrippa.

These three thinkers are known to us only through Sextus Empiricus, but it seems likely that they were part of a long tradition of skepticism. When Sextus Empiricus offers proofs that knowledge is impossible, he attributes no authorship to these arguments. The idea of literary property is in fact a modern one; until the time of the Romantics the truth of an idea was more important than its originality. Novelty was a sign of error, and therefore no one was afraid of plagiarism. On the contrary, it was better to present a new idea as a form of a very old one.

Aenesidemus offered ten *tropes,* or modes, of error—ten arguments against the possibility of objective knowledge:

1. *The first trope.* This mode is based on the differences of the means of perception in general. If we have sense organs, animals have them too, and they are differently constituted from ours. It is obvious that sensations depend upon the sense organs. Consequently men and animals perceive things in different ways. What proof is there that human perceptions reveal the true picture of reality? It is quite arbitrary on our part to say that we truly perceive reality.

2. *The second trope.* Even supposing that human knowledge is the only exact knowledge, it must still be admitted that there is no unanimity in the tastes and opinions of men; some like what others dislike. These feelings must depend on men's way of perceiving. If some like what others dislike, it must necessarily be because their perceptions are different. What, then, is true human perception? (Men can disagree with each other, of course, because they have the *same* tastes.)

3. *The third trope.* There are differences among the different senses. What is pleasing to one sense may be displeasing to another. What is pleasing to the eye may be displeasing to the taste. Our senses may give the impression of a red apple, smooth and delicious, but may there not be different qualities existing in the apple itself? Perhaps there is only a single quality perceived in different ways by the senses; perhaps if we had more senses we would perceive more qualities. On the other hand, it is quite evident that the universe of a blind man is quite different from that of a man who can see. The properties

we attribute to objects are closely tied up with the number and the keenness of our senses. We cannot deduce from our perceptions the existence of an absolute reality.

4. *The fourth trope.* There are differences in the perceptions of a single person which depend on the circumstances of perception; that is, on the state and condition of the person perceiving. Certainly there are perceptions which differ according to whether the person is wide awake, half-awake, or completely asleep; whether he is fasting or surfeited, happy or sad, young or old, calm or excited. Since these perceptions vary according to the state of the perceiver, how could a normal state be identified which would provide "true" perception?

5. *The fifth trope.* There are differences in perception which result from the position, distance, and location of the object. A body appears heavier in air than in water; an odor more striking in a warm room than in a cold one; a boat larger near at hand than in the distance. But what is the true size? A stick dipped in water appears broken; when removed it is intact. Thus we perceive things not as they are, but as they appear to us under various conditions, and we cannot separate them from these conditions.

6. *The sixth trope.* This mode of error has to do with the purity of our perceptions. Perceptions are never isolated, but are always mixed with other perceptions. The color of a face varies as the person is in a warm or a cold place. What is true? To find out, qualities would have to be isolated, and this is impossible.

7. *The seventh trope.* Objects, moreover, produce different effects in accordance with their quantity. The same substance can be either a medicine or a poison, depending on quantity. Wine weakens us if we drink a large amount, but in small quantities it is a stimulant.

8. *The eighth trope.* There are perceptions which are by nature relative. When we describe their properties, we must do so by comparison. For example, an object has no absolute size; it is not large or small unless it is compared with something else.

9. *The ninth trope.* The frequency or rarity of things

affects our perception of them. The first aerial bomb has a different effect from that of the twentieth. The price of a thing depends not on itself but on its rarity. Water is expensive in the desert, but costs hardly anything in the home.

10. *The tenth trope.* There are certain differences in judgment which are the response to the different manners, customs, and laws observed among different peoples.

GENERAL COMMENTS

1. *The conditions of perception.* Aenesidemus was correct in saying that we cannot, on the basis of certain observations, attain absolute truth. We cannot reach a result independent of the conditions of observation. This principle is well understood in science, where the conditions of observation are integrated into the description of the results of experiments.

What Aenesidemus criticizes is an exaggerated extrapolation which does not take into account the variability of the conditions of observation.

2. A number of these tropes are derived from the fact that the predicates *good* and *bad* are often applied to the same thing. We note that Aenesidemus puts all properties on the same level—for example, color, taste, usefulness, and harmfulness. He would have gained in clarity had he distinguished facts from values and the objective study of nature from the study of value judgments about nature. Failing to make that distinction, Aenesidemus gave the same untrustworthiness to both.

He ought to have distinguished between law (fact) and norm (value). By neglecting this distinction he extended his skepticism from the area of practice to the area of theory. But do all judgments have the same status?

From the end of the eighteenth century the idea has spread that there must be a distinction between judgments of fact and judgments of value. The former describe reality; the latter our attitude toward that reality.

But how are judgments of fact to be related to judgments

of value? What are the limits of each? This is an important problem for modern logic.

In contradistinction to Aenesidemus, who criticized sense knowledge, Agrippa formulated five tropes in criticism of rational knowledge.

1. *The first trope.* If rational knowledge is based on sensible knowledge and the latter is relative, the derived knowledge can be no more certain than that on which it is based.

2. *The second trope.* If we try to use as our base the fact that men agree, we must admit that such agreement is exceedingly rare. The result is that we must find some other way to prove the propositions we affirm. Accordingly, the three tropes which follow deal with propositions.

3. *The third trope.* If a proposition is to be proved, its proof requires that other propositions be granted on which it can be based. But these in turn must be proved through other propositions, which must then be proved. The result is that if proof of everything is required, we are forced into an infinite regress—which is impossible.

4. *The fourth trope.* What happens if we stop at some point and accept a proposition arbitrarily? Why must we accept the propositions which constitute the point of departure for a demonstration?

Here we find implicitly the criterion of evidence.

5. *The fifth trope.* If two propositions are based on each other we have a reciprocal inference; that is to say, a vicious circle. For example, two strangers, A and B, come to my door. A tells me "B is thoroughly honest," and B says "A always tells the truth." What value can be given to these assertions, since B is the guarantor of the truthfulness of A, and A provides the warranty for B?

In logic, propositions which are deduced from other propositions have only the validity of the propositions on which they are based. In a purely formal deduction the degree of trustworthiness cannot be increased beyond that accorded to the premises.

Sextus Empiricus lived at Alexandria and was a self-styled skeptic. He opposed in his outlook both the dogmatic philosophers who believed in absolute truth and the Academics who denied its possibility.

The skeptics in fact avoided committing themselves.

Both the dogmatists and the academicians granted certain appearances, but gave them different interpretations. The point at issue was the status of these appearances: how to get from them to absolute truth.

For Sextus Empiricus a choice must be made among the appearances. It is first of all a choice of human appearances rather than those of animals. But then are we to base our choice on the criterion of unanimity?

Suppose we then affirm the truth of propositions on which men are in unanimous agreement. But if we seek the agreement of all men, does such an agreement exist? When can we say that there is agreement among all men? We would have to question them all, and this would be not only an enormous but an impossible task, for all men include not only those who have died but those who are yet to be born. Such a total unanimity in space and time is completely illusory, therefore this quantitative criterion cannot be adopted.

Perhaps, then, we can use a *qualitative* criterion.

Let us accept as true what is affirmed by competent men, by authorities.

But are there authorities? And who is competent to say that someone else is an authority? Perhaps there is disagreement among the men who are regarded as authorities; who is competent to say which of them is the best authority? And how do we know that some even better authority may not appear tomorrow?

Since this external criterion is unsatisfactory, what is to be done? We must try to find an internal criterion.

If propositions which have been proved are granted to be true, what is the criterion of a good proof? If we affirmed that we had found such a criterion, it would be necessary to prove it.

But then, are not the academicians right in saying that

it is impossible to know reality absolutely? If they believe it has been proved that truth is unknowable, that very proposition must somehow be demonstrable, and with the help of the same criterion we could prove other propositions.

Therefore, says Sextus Empiricus, the position of the academicians is paradoxical.

Consequently all that can be done is to reject an inadequate proof without saying that an adequate one is impossible.

A criterion is never absolute. It can appear adequate to some group of men at some time without having to be adequate forever. Even the idea of proof and demonstration can be understood with different degrees of rigor and precision.

Skepticism reduces intellectual knowledge to a decision which the investigator has to make. Later on a more convincing proof may be established, forcing him to abandon a demonstration considered adequate up to that time.

Rules are established as a function of present knowledge.

The rules of logic were worked out by analyzing what appeared to be the most valid rules of formal proof. It may be wondered whether the same rigorous requirements are applicable in other areas of thought.

Neoplatonism

The influence of the skeptical thinkers might have brought on a crisis in dogmatism, but, though their thinking had some triumphs, its main effect was to weaken the internal structure of Greek thought and to provide conditions favorable to the introduction of mystical tendencies, Oriental in origin.

It was primarily at Alexandria that the skeptical movement developed. Here were mingled a variety of peoples—Jews, Egyptians, Phoenicians, Assyrians, and the like—most of them Oriental. At Alexandria the great trade routes which united the European and Asiatic worlds converged, and here in this great city philosophies and religions of the most varied character came into contact and influenced one another. Thus was born a period of *syncretism* in which philosophical thinking appropriated the most widely diverse ideas—ideas not only from Greek thought but also from Oriental religions, in particular from Babylonian and Hindu religions.

Philo Judaeus (*c.* 30 B.C.–*c.* A.D. 40) was the founder of a movement which sought to understand religious thinking rationally. He interpreted the Bible as a collection of allegories and argued that Moses had anticipated the thought of Plato.

This was also the era in which various Gnostic movements developed. These were variants of primitive Christianity—or (perhaps it might rightly be said) modes of thought of which Christianity was merely a variant.

At Alexandria also are found the first writings of the Greek Church Fathers—Clement of Alexandria (*b.* 150) and Origen (*c.* 185–*c.* 254), both of whom sought to introduce Christian thought into the Hellenistic Greek tradition.

The last and most notable of the Greek philosophers was Plotinus of Alexandria (205–270). He was the founder of Neoplatonism, perhaps the most important doctrine at the end of the third century, a doctrine which had an extraordinary influence on Western philosophical thought up to the twelfth and thirteenth centuries.

We know the ideas of Plotinus only through his pupil Porphyry, who gathered together the thought of his master in a volume of fifty-four writings consisting of six books of nine writings each, a work known as the *Enneads*.

These writings did not provide a completely articulated system; rather they suggested one in a style that was informal and lively.

Plotinus' thought leads to mysticism, but not to a vague and irrational mysticism. Plotinus is a philosophical mystic who gives philosophical reasons for his mysticism.

His thought, in some ways very close to Hindu thinking, takes much of its inspiration from the Plato of the *Symposium* as well as from Aristotle.

The chief characteristic of Plotinus' thought is the introduction into Greek philosophy of a new way of knowing, something quite apart from sensationalism or rationalism or skepticism. This way of knowing, which proceeds through neither reason nor the senses but transcends these conventional sources, is *mystical ecstasy*.

This mystical knowledge is incommunicable, for to explain it conceptually would be to deform it. No merely discursive thought can attain to the supreme knowledge which is revealed in mystical ecstasy—knowledge of the One.

How did Plotinus reach this conception of the One?

He reached this conception of a highest principle by insisting on the superiority of cause over effect—the earlier over the later—an idea very close to that of Aristotle's prime mover. But he generalizes the principle, affirming that what is antecedent is always superior to what is consequent, that the cause is always superior to the effect. In so doing he sets up a hierarchy of being.

For us today the idea of superiority is relative. In different relations a thing might be both superior and inferior to something else. But for Plotinus there is only one criterion of superiority. The problem is to know how that superiority manifests itself.

The criterion is *unity*. This makes possible the establishment of a hierarchy of being. The superiority of one thing over another is shown by the degree of unity it has. Unity is therefore bound up in the very nature of things. The more a thing is one, the more real and perfect it is.

Plotinus sets up a hierarchy among these unities. For example, if one speaks of a herd or an army, one is dealing with units made up of separate components, each of which is a unity itself. If one speaks of a house, one is dealing with a greater unity since, though the house is built of separate materials of varied origin, the house itself is very much a unity.

Among living beings there are some which are more virtuous, beautiful, or just than others. Their superiority consists in a certain unity of values which are not in opposition within them but constitute a kind of internal harmony.

An immoral person is one who has failed to introduce into his soul this harmony among different values, and who has thus failed to attain a higher unity.

Intellectual beings who are not capable of division in space and time have a higher unity, although thought and the object of thought are still dissociated. There remains a kind of duality.

Plotinus therefore cannot accept the God of Aristotle as the perfection of unity. As Aristotle's God thinks about himself, is he perfect because he thinks or because it is about himself that he thinks?

Perfect unity transcends the distinction between subject and object. This unity requires that there be no distinction between the knower and what is known.

Knowledge of the One cannot be rational knowledge; it cannot depend on words, because a word is the extension of a thought, and thought is the extension of an object.

In reaching the state of ecstasy individuality itself must disappear. In this state one feels himself no different from the One; he has lost consciousness of his personality. This whole idea is analogous to the *nirvana* of Buddhist philosophy.

Such an ecstatic experience is neither lasting nor frequent. Plotinus himself is said to have experienced it only four times in his life. But our whole life must be lived in preparation for this ecstasy.

All that can be said about the One is borrowed from an inferior world; it cannot define the One positively. Any attempt to do so would detract from its unity. The One can only be defined negatively—by describing what it is not, in comparison with which it is superior. God is superior to anything that can be said about him. This is a theology of negation.

It is only by analogy that the nature of the One can be suggested. Plotinus describes it as a kind of immaterial source of light and heat; and the farther removed things are from this source, the less light and heat they possess.

The universe is like a series of concentric spheres which

diminish in reality and perfection in proportion to their distance from the central source of being—the One. They diminish in this order:

1. The One.
2. The sphere of ideas (*nous*).
3. The sphere of the soul.
4. The sphere of matter.

Plotinus similarly develops a moral hierarchy, proceeding from the lower to the higher:

—an ethics of pleasure (Epicurus) on the level of matter.

—Stoic ethics on the level of the soul.

—Aristotelean ethics on the level of reason and contemplation.

—mystical ethics associated with the One.

Such is the philosophy with which Christianity as it developed in the fourth century would have to do battle.

V

THE BEGINNINGS OF CHRISTIAN PHILOSOPHY

Neoplatonism is the last great philosophical system to offer us a vision of the universe which, influenced as it was by Oriental elements, still preserves the purity characteristic of Greek thought.

This purity cannot be better characterized than by saying that for the Greeks, as well as for Plotinus, the personality of the individual plays an unimportant role in the philosophical system. When the Greeks speak of man, they look upon him as representing the human species with no emphasis on his own personality.

What the Greeks propose is a humanistic ideal in which all individual characteristics are removed. Consequently the classical tradition speaks only about the universal character of humanity. Thus in the mystic ecstasy described by Plotinus the individual loses his personality.

With Judaism and Christianity a new way of thinking is introduced into the Western world, and it is interesting to trace the contribution of the religious ideas derived from the Old and New Testaments. In opposition to classical Greek thought, which is dominated by the ideas of order, of universality, and of what was called the *cosmos,* in which man plays but a lowly part, the ideas which are about to be introduced put the central emphasis on the relation between God and man.

The God of Judaism and Christianity is very different from the divinities of earlier philosophers. He is a personal God, not an abstract principle far removed from man. He is a perfect will, just and charitable. To ascribe human attributes to the deity in this way—even though these attributes are extended to the extreme—emphasizes the importance these human attributes are to have in the new philosophy. The central position is to be given to personality.

On the other hand, by sharing, even in a lesser degree, some of these attributes of God, man shares also a certain divinity and thereby is distinguished from the other animals.

This God is also a *creator*, an idea contrary to Greek thought, in which God was regarded as an architect, as one who gave order to otherwise unformed matter. The new idea of creation *ex nihilo* was completely foreign to Greek thinking, which since Parmenides had rejected the notion that being could come from non-being.

The fact that God is a creator transforms the very idea of creation. Since God can create *ex nihilo*, and since man himself is a creator on the model of God, there exists philosophical ground for human freedom.

Although the God of Aristotle or of Plotinus (being an ideal) can be ignorant of all that happens in the universe, this unconcern cannot characterize a creator God, for he must know what he creates.

And since God has created every human soul, man acquires an individuality and must be accountable to God. Animals, on the other hand, are simply grouped into genera and species by specific attributes.

This human soul, which God observes and knows, is tributary to him. The idea of accountability to God is to dominate religious thinking. The fundamental problem is that of knowing how to live in order to win eternal salvation.

Knowledge—insofar as it is of interest to religion—is only one means of gaining salvation; it is concerned with the set of rules that we must know and follow in order to gain that end.

Can man attain salvation by his own efforts? No, for morality separated from all religion is insufficient. Then how can the rules which must be followed to attain salvation be known? Faith is needed. But man is incapable of gaining faith without the divine intervention. Here Christian thought is influenced by St. Paul and later by St. Augustine, both of them converts.

Since faith, as well as baptism, is necessary for salvation, the intervention of *divine grace* is needed in order to follow the prescribed rules.

Christian thought thus introduces a novel element: the role played by certain suprarational factors which alone make it possible for man to attain faith. *Divine grace,* through which man attains faith, can thus be considered as a divine form of love.

In this fashion a novel concept was introduced into Greek philosophy: *the role of love and charity in a divine being.* Up to this point love had been regarded as a transient madness, a kind of ecstasy.

The form of divine love which is grace makes love stable and durable, since it extends to all men through eternity.

It is to be noted that these various factors—creation, the importance of the individual, the idea of grace, and the idea of love—can be considered irrational factors insofar as they concern the individual.

Another innovation was that of the sense, of the meaning of life, the meaning of history, problems which had never been considered by the Greeks.

If creation by Providence be granted, then it may be wondered what is the purpose of that creation. It may be ascribed to the plans of an omniscient and perfect being. Thus the first philosophy of history is given us by St. Augustine in *The City of God.*

These ideas can be explained only by their first appearance as religious concepts. And this group of new concepts influenced all the thinkers we are to study up to the time of the Renaissance.

CHRISTIAN PHILOSOPHY

Here another problem arises: Can we really speak of a Christian philosophy? And can there not be more than one? Indeed, in the Middle Ages a number of religious philosophies were intermixed.

If a man is completely wrapped up in the search for truth, how does the fact that he is a Christian influence his thinking? Is there any sense in speaking of a Christian mathematics or a Christian physics? Or, more generally, what does the idea of Christian truth mean?

Does the possession of religious faith influence the thinking of a philosopher? This problem has given rise to some of the greatest controversies among historians of medieval philosophy. Is it possible at all, in fact, to speak of a Christian philosophy?

If the final truth of a philosophical system is to be determined by religion, how can it be called a philosophy? If the final truth can be known only through the study and interpretation of sacred writings, that study belongs to theology, not to philosophy.

We now confront a dilemma: If it is philosophy, how can it be Christian? If it is Christian, how can it be philosophy?

Some thinkers have affirmed that there are universal truths which are given only by religion, by Christians who have been illuminated by God.

Anyone who addresses hearers who share his faith presupposes the acceptance of certain texts and dogmas on which his argument is based. Thus a theologian assumes that certain dogmas are already granted, and he does not discuss their basis. His only task is to explain and interpret them. Religion demands the acceptance of certain articles of faith.

On the other hand, whoever develops a philosophical system undertakes to address everyone and to convince everyone. Between philosophical thought and religious thought there is a difference in audience.

The theologian assumes the acceptance of certain texts from which he develops his thought, while the philosopher can assume only what everyone is willing to admit—truths that are valid for everyone.

In what he believes will be acceptable to everyone the philosopher may, of course, be wrong. He can assume, for example, that those who question the truth of what he is saying are simply deficient in good sense. But he must always find a justification for his theories.

This is how it came about that when believers argued with nonbelievers and consequently could not base their reasoning on dogmas which their interlocutors were unwilling to accept, they were forced to philosophize.

It is the audience that determines the nature of the premises used by the philosopher. These premises are quite different from those of the theologian, who falls back on evidence derived from sacred writings.

We are in a position now to understand why a Christian philosopher, starting from premises which everyone grants and which are therefore stripped of all religious or dogmatic character, seeks to reach conclusions which are in agreement with his religious tenets. The starting point of his reasoning, therefore, has a philosophical character.

Christian philosophers have understood, however, that they could not give a philosophical demonstration of all the articles of faith. They have had to distinguish between (1) the *credibilia*—things which must be believed—and (2) the *demonstrabilia*—things which are capable of proof.

A number of Christian dogmas have had to be reduced to simple articles of faith; further, the grouping into *credibilia* and *demonstrabilia* has varied from system to system.

PHILOSOPHICAL PROOF

Can proof in philosophic questions be regarded as having the same character as proof in the deductive sciences of mathematics or geometry?

If it could, then it would be possible, as in geometry, to transpose the order of axioms and theorems.

But this transposition is impossible in philosophy. Though the basic principles might be granted by everyone, the conclusions are accepted by only a certain number of men. The conclusions are quite different from the original premises, and the process of arriving at them can only be explained by a difference in the nature of the proof.

Philosophy therefore cannot be thought of as a deductive science. In the deductive sciences proof can be worked out by the mechanical application of procedures in which every step is warranted; it would be possible to create a machine to demonstrate certain propositions.

But this is by no means the case with philosophical demonstration. The method here is *dialectic* or *rhetoric*. The arguments which are used in passing from one proposition to another more closely resemble those of law than those of mathematics. They are not mechanical arguments at all.

The goal of philosophy is to influence the mind and win its agreement, rather than to perform purely formal transformations of propositions.

If philosophy is looked upon merely as a deductive science, the concept of a religious philosophy makes no sense at all. As it happens, religious beliefs do influence the working out of a philosophical system. And it is these most deep-seated beliefs which stand in judgment of the doctrines which the philosopher believes with less intensity.

The nature of philosophic proof can be worked out only within philosophy itself.

How can the validity of certain proofs be determined?

If a philosophical system is intended to establish a certain coherence in thought, it must rest upon the most valid ideas of that system of thought. There are several ways of establishing coherence. If one is faced with two incompatible propositions, A and B, it is possible either to:

1. Deny A.
2. Deny B.
3. Find factors of compatibility between them.

This choice can be made only on the basis of the best-established convictions. It is therefore very important to know what are the best-established elements of any system of thought.

In Christian thought these are the dogmas of religion.

St. Augustine (354–430)

St. Augustine was born at Tagaste, in what is now Algeria. He was the son of a pagan father and a Christian mother.

His father wanted him to become a teacher of rhetoric, a representative of pagan culture, while his mother (St. Monica), who had had him baptized at his birth, hoped he would become devoted to his own salvation. As a consequence his life was a poignant internal conflict until his thirtieth year, when he became completely converted to Christianity.

Later he became bishop of Hippo in north Africa and was perhaps the greatest theoretical writer of the Church. Of all the Latin Fathers Augustine was the most influential in establishing the dogmas of the Roman Church.

His works, amounting to several thousand pages, have been collected in the *Patrologia Latina* and edited by Migne. (There is a similar collection of the Greek Fathers.) His best-known writings are the *Confessions* and *The City of God,* the first philosophy of history worked out on a Christian basis. He also wrote several commentaries in which he took a position on such critical problems as grace, free will, and original sin.

Augustine above all others contributed to the formulation of Christian doctrine. His historical importance is very great, since it was his writings which were best known to Christian philosophers in the centuries that followed.

Augustine was thirty when he actually became a Christian. Earlier he had come into contact with Greek thought, pagan thought, in particular Neoplatonism. But the two most important opposing positions with which he did battle were skepticism and, in the realm of morality, Manichaeism.

What was his position with regard to skepticism?

Whoever constructs a system of thought based on religious and dogmatic principles must face the question: Have we the right to believe in absolute truths? Is it possible to know truths which are basic and absolute?

Augustine admits that such truths cannot be known through sense experience.

On what basis, then, can such truths be established?

Augustine reaches the conclusion that the only thing about which he has no doubt is the fact that he doubts. Now if he doubts he thinks; and if he thinks, he is acting, and therefore must exist. We find here a line of thought later taken up by Descartes in his *"cogito ergo sum."*

This truth, which seems indubitable, has been reached through an inner intuition completely independent of sense experience. It is an eternal and immutable truth.

But if your mind can think an eternal truth, it cannot be the author of it, for the effect cannot be more perfect than the cause.

If this truth is eternal and immutable, the mind that created it cannot be less eternal and immutable. A transient cause cannot give rise to an eternal effect. The cause of this truth must be just as eternal as the truth itself.

It is in this way that St. Augustine finds his *proof of the existence of God:* eternal truth must be thought by an eternal mind.

For Plotinus, as we have seen, the One is the center of all reality, transcending every quality and every property that could be attributed to him. But the Christian God is an eternal and intelligent being; because of this He can be the author of eternal truth.

To the degree that our ideas are eternal they are but the tracing of divine thought.

Reality exists only through its conformity to the ideas of God.

This idea of reality is to persist through all philosophy influenced by Christian thought.

God, who has given us revelation, has also given us the power of reason through which we understand His ideas.

This is Augustine's solution to the problem of the relation between philosophy and religion. It is inconceivable that the two ways of knowing that God has given us could be in opposition. Reason better enables us to understand dogma. Thus Augustine sought to explain the dogma of the Trinity by analogy with our own being.

But the way in which Augustine deals with the problem of evil and of freedom is more interesting to us today.

He emphatically opposes the Manichaean doctrine (influenced by Persian thought) that universal history is the result of a conflict between two principles: *good* and *evil.* If these principles are embodied as God and Satan, the divine power is limited by an opposing principle and the existence of evil in the universe can be explained.

Although this Manichaean theory runs counter to orthodoxy, there are traces of it to be found in the Christian religion. Without it, difficulties arise in understanding the doctrine of redemption. With whom did God have to deal in redeeming mankind? The fact that God had to redeem man through the sacrifice of His Son, instead of merely bestowing forgiveness, implies a contract between two beings who deal with each other on the basis of power.

In rejecting Manichaeism St. Augustine had to face a problem: If God is all-powerful and completely good, how can the existence of evil be explained? How could sin and evil have come about in a world created by God? Even if evil sprang up in the mind of a fallen angel, how could a mind which entertained such evil have been created? How does it come to pass that God's work is not perfect?

All these questions are raised in Book VII of the *Confessions:*

"Who made me? Did not my God, who is not only good, but goodness itself? Whence then came I to will evil and nill good, so that I am thus justly punished? Who set this in me, and ingrafted into me this plant of bitterness, seeing that I was wholly formed by my most sweet God? If the devil were the author, whence is that same devil? And if he also by his own perverse will, of a good angel became a devil, whence, again, came in him that evil will, whereby he became a devil, seeing the whole nature of angels was made by that most good Creator?"[1]

"Behold God, and behold what God hath created; and God is good, yea, most mightily and incomparably better than all these; but yet He, the Good, created them good; and we see how he environeth and fulfills them. Where is evil then, and whence, and how crept it in hither? What is its root, and what its seed? Or hath it no being? Why then fear we and avoid what is not? Or if we fear it idly, then is that very fear evil, whereby the soul is thus idly goaded and racked? Yea, and so much greater evil, as we have nothing to fear, and yet do fear. Therefore either is that evil which we fear, or else evil is, that we fear. Whence is it then? seeing God, the Good, hath created all these things good."[2]

And there is Augustine's reply, a reply which corresponds completely with that of Plotinus:

"And it was manifested unto me, that those things be good, which yet are corrupted; which neither were they sovereignly good, nor unless they were good, could be corrupted: for if sovereignly good, they were incorruptible, if not good at all, there was nothing in them to be corrupted. For corruption injures, but unless it diminished goodness, it could not injure. Either then corruption injures not, which cannot be; or, which is most certain, all which is corrupted is deprived of good. But if they be deprived of all good, they shall cease to be. For if they shall be, and can now no longer be corrupted, they shall be better than before, because they shall abide incorruptibly. And what more monstrous, than to affirm things to become better by losing all their good? Therefore, if they shall be deprived of all good, they shall no longer be. So long therefore as they are, they are good: therefore whatsoever is, is good. The evil then which I sought, whence it is, is not any substance: for were it a substance,

---

[1] Augustine, *Confessions* (tr. E. B. Pusey), VII, iii.
[2] *Ibid.*, VII, v.

it should be good. For either it should be an incorruptible substance, and so a chief good: or a corruptible substance; which unless it were good, could not be corrupted. I perceived therefore, and it was manifested to me, that Thou madest all things good, nor is there any substance at all, which Thou madest not; and for that Thou madest not all things equal, therefore are all things; because each is good, and altogether very good, because our God *made all things very good.*"[3]

"And to Thee nothing whatsoever is evil: yea, not only to Thee, but also to Thy creation as a whole, because there is nothing without, which may break in, and corrupt that order which thou hast appointed it. But in the parts thereof some things, because unharmonizing with other some, are accounted evil: whereas those very things harmonize with others, and are good; and in themselves are good."[4]

What was Augustine's conception of evil?

Evil is only relative: it is the privation of that higher good which would allow the attainment of incorruptibility —of perfection.

The criterion of absolute good and perfection must be the degree of reality a thing has. The more reality it has, the more qualities it possesses, the more perfect it is.

When it comes to God's creatures, they are good to the extent that they are considered in themselves. They are bad only in comparison with others who have more qualities than they. They are not fundamentally bad, but only possess a certain degree of corruptibility.

But how can sin be explained? Why should men be eternally damned for more or less illusory errors? The problem is all the more serious since God is omniscient and knows the future from all eternity.

We are then, in a degree, predestined to good or to evil.

How then are we to understand the damnation of a predestined being, especially since this damnation is not only

---

[3] *Ibid.*, VII, xii.
[4] *Ibid.*, VII, xiii.

just, but since only those who have faith and have been baptised will be saved? Simply to live a moral life is not enough. Salvation is denied to men who are completely just but unbelieving—like Socrates—and is even denied to infants who have died before baptism.

Must they be regarded as eternally damned?

Let us consider the tragic instance of infants who die before baptism. In the time of St. Augustine it was believed that such infants would go to hell.

St. Augustine also asserts that even if one has heard the divine word, one may not be immediately convinced.

He then develops the theory of grace, which can be found in the epistles of St. Paul. God grants grace to whom he wishes. But since grace is not accorded to all, how can eternal punishment be justified?

Being infinitely good and just, God can punish only after the sin. But why does He punish infants who have died before baptism?

It is at this point that Augustine introduces a concept which is in great part derived from his logical thinking: the *doctrine of original sin.*

There must be sin of which all humanity is guilty. This is the sin of Adam's disobedience to God. Since that sin man has lost his eternal life. The Hebrew interpretation is that mortality results from original sin. But Augustine gives a different interpretation to the Biblical assertion that man has lost eternal life. Eternal life for him is life in the heavenly paradise.

Only those to whom God has accorded grace will enjoy eternal life; the others are damned.

It is understandable how this whole tragic concept—particularly as it applied to infants who had died before baptism—was modified later by the concept of *limbo,* a place between heaven and hell which received such infants.

A new element has thus entered, which serves to differentiate Christian ethics from pagan ethics—the notion of divine grace.

Pagan morality depends on the idea of merit. Christian

morality is characterized by the notion of grace, which is one of the essential differences between it and Greek thought.

It should be noted, however, that in the course of later centuries, up to the time of Erasmus, Christian thought progressively attempted to bridge the gap which separated these two ancient ideas. Protestantism under Luther and Calvin represented a reaction, a return to St. Augustine, from whom, with Thomas Aquinas and Scholasticism, Christian thought had drawn away.

VI

CHRISTIAN

PHILOSOPHY IN

THE MIDDLE AGES

The break between antiquity and the Middle Ages is marked by a twofold invasion of the world of ancient civilization—the barbarians in the north and the Arabs in the south.

During the fifth and sixth centuries and part of the seventh, the barbarians progressively invaded the whole of civilized Europe. Centers of culture still remained in the eastern Mediterranean, notably at Alexandria and Constantinople, but in the seventh century, following the Arab invasions, the Western world was cut off from Greek civilization except by sea. The famous library at Alexandria was burned in 640, and this fire was only one of the events signalizing the fall of the ancient world. Not until after the battle of Poitiers in 732, when Charles Martel stopped the advance of the Arabs, did the Western world become stabilized and its institutions and culture begin their slow development.

The outstanding feature of the philosophy of the Middle Ages is its domination by religion. Its practitioners are almost all clerics belonging to one or the other of the great monotheisms—Judaism, Christianity, or Mohammedanism. In the chapters which follow we shall be concerned primarily with Christian thinkers because of their importance in later European philosophy. What we say about Mohammedan and Jewish thinkers will be limited to their influence on Christian philosophy.

Until the founding of the first universities, the intellectual centers of the Middle Ages were exclusively religious. They were monasteries and abbeys which were provided with libraries, and the clerks alone were able to make use of them. Monte Cassino, founded by St. Benedict in 529, and the abbey at Jarrow in the south of England were two well-known examples.

One of the last pagan thinkers, Boethius, author in 524 of *The Consolation of Philosophy,* was even looked upon as a Christian martyr, pagan though he was, so difficult it was to believe that anyone concerned with philosophy could be anything but a Christian and a cleric.

For Christians the problem of knowledge did not arise in the same way as it had in antiquity. Knowledge for them was not an end in itself, but a means of attaining salvation.

From now on the first problem is to know what must be believed in order to attain salvation, a religious preoccupation that has the result of progressively limiting individual reason and requiring more and more dependence on authority.

In the sixth century the use of individual reason became limited by the establishment of an authority to decide what must be believed. Reason's function was thus limited to determining in what works true doctrine might be found.

But the Church intervened not only to determine what texts were to be regarded as sacred but also to point out who were the Fathers in whom one might have confidence that they had interpreted the texts in conformity to doctrine. To avoid heresy was important.

Up to this point reason had been limited only in religious matters. But from the seventh century on, the use of reason was restricted in all matters, even those not concerned with salvation.

In 599 Pope Gregory the Great forbade the reading of pagan books which might produce ideas of pride and enjoyment contrary to the Christian spirit. In the seventh century Bishop Isidore of Seville forbade such reading to monks. Such works were regarded as useless and dangerous.

Thus we witness a kind of decline of the prerogatives of reason until the middle of the eighth century, after the battle of Poitiers. This era constitutes the lowest point in Western culture. It was soon followed by a reaction. This reaction, known sometimes as "The First Renaissance," was brought about under Charlemagne.

But the word *renaissance* should not give rise to too many illusions. This renaissance consisted in the formation of a small group of persons trained to perform certain functions (priests, functionaries). They were taught to read and write, which was a rare accomplishment in that illiterate time when men who had withdrawn into monasteries constituted the only islands of culture. The monasteries of Ireland and the south of England, notably the famous abbey of Jarrow, were to make possible the restoration of culture in the West.

It might be recalled in passing that at this time Byzantine culture, traditionally regarded as negligible, continued its steady development.

When Charlemagne decided to establish institutions of learning in France he was obliged to call on the clerics of England and Ireland. One of these was Alcuin of York (*c.* 735–804), educated at the abbey of Jarrow.

Characteristically Alcuin was required to explain his purposes: the propagation of knowledge would be a useless and harmful thing if it did not contribute, at least indirectly, to human salvation. Capable priests must be trained (a constant policy of the Church) and missionaries must be sent through the pagan world.

Alcuin insisted that it was not his intention to invent or find new truth. The function of instruction would be to transmit to future generations what the generations of the past, aided by revelation, had been able to learn and make known to the world. To the degree that some knowledge lies outside the sacred texts, it makes possible the understanding of things as they have been created by God.

Medieval thought is forced to justify incurring the possible dangers of knowledge by saying that such knowledge does not tend toward anything new which might depart from tradition: newness is the enemy. For several centuries, until Renaissance times, a new idea was looked upon as something pernicious, execrable, heretical. In the later Romantic period originality and novelty were valued. But in medieval times those who had novel ideas sought to show that they were nothing but old ideas in a new form. Thus at the time of the Reformation Calvin himself attempted to show that he was only returning to the ancient doctrines from which the Church had drawn away.

In the ninth century appeared the first truly original thinker of the Christian Middle Ages: John Scotus Erigena.

At that time there had been some spread of learning, but it was a Latin learning, for Latin was the language of the Church. In the middle of the eighth century Pope Paul I had sent to Pepin the Short a Greek manuscript believed to have been written by Dionysius the Areopagite, a disciple of St. Paul. Both a philosophical and theological work which dealt with "divine names," it belonged more or less to the tradition of Neoplatonism. It was later shown that the author was actually a monk who lived two centuries after Plotinus and who wrote in a Neoplatonic spirit.

But the work was in Greek, and for a century it remained unusable. In the middle of the ninth century Charles the Bald called on one of the few men in Western Europe who knew Greek. This was John Scotus Erigena, who lived in Ireland (whence the name *Scotus*—the Irishman). He translated the work into Latin. Afterward he wrote a treatise, *De Divisione Naturae,* which was inspired both by the Pseudo-Dionysius and by St. Augustine.

The first period of medieval philosophical thought is thus influenced entirely by Christian thinkers whose inspiration was Platonic or Neoplatonic.

The number of ancient writings known to the Middle Ages was strictly limited, and they were discovered little by little. During the first thousand years Christian thought was based on the Gospels, on the Epistles, on the writings of certain Church Fathers (especially St. Augustine), on a number of works of Plato (particularly the *Timaeus*), on Boethius, on Scotus and the Pseudo-Dionysius—all of them Platonic or Neoplatonic.

Other writings appeared gradually; it was not until the tenth and eleventh centuries that the first works of Aristotle—those dealing with logic—began to appear. In the twelfth and thirteenth centuries other Aristotelian writings, which were to have a profound effect on medieval thinkers, became known.

It was due to Mohammedan thinkers, who translated and commented on the works in Arabic, that these writings came into the Western tradition. Among the most important of these scholars were Avicenna (980–1037), a Platonist, and Averroes (1126–1198), an Aristotelian.

But this acquaintance with ancient works through the Arabs could occur only by stages as the situation became stabilized, as fear of Mohammedan invasions ceased, and as commercial relations were established.

These Greek works were translated first into Arabic; then they were translated into Hebrew by Jews who lived in Arab areas; then by other Jews they were translated into Latin. Thus they passed through several translations before reaching the Western world.

Works which were too difficult, received directly in Greek, would not have been understood. Medieval thought continued to make new spurts of development as new works from antiquity became available. Its growth has been likened to that of a fire which is built up by continuously adding fuel.

Medieval thought at first sought its inspiration from the Scriptures, then from Christian writings which were Neoplatonic in nature, then from Platonism itself, and finally from Aristotelian writings, which were the farthest removed from the original inspiration.

John Scotus Erigena was a religious thinker who belonged in the Augustinian tradition. He held that reasoning must be based on faith: "If you do not believe you will not understand." Reason can prepare the ground for faith and illuminate it. This idea, however, already grants to reason a degree of autonomy: interpretation can be more or less independent.

Actually, the more texts there are, the more the interpretations differ, and even the Fathers themselves differ profoundly in their interpretations of the sacred texts. How then can a coherent doctrine be created except through choosing among the varying interpretations? And this choice can be made only through the exercise of reason.

On the other hand, to conceal the novelty of an idea, that idea had to be offered under the patronage of some ancient text. Everything new had to be presented as a commentary on something old.

In this ingenious way dogmas evolved without running head-on into the rigors of orthodoxy. How could some dogma be bent if the texts were inflexible? The only way was to show that the new interpretation was better than those which had been made before.

So in the ninth and tenth centuries virtually all philosophical writings appear as commentaries on ancient texts, and they are the more likely to appear in this guise if the thought contained in them is new and original.

Pagan works came more and more to be read and interpreted on the ground that truth is divine and that if the pagans discovered a number of truths, those truths must be recaptured from them as illegitimate possessions of theirs.

Beginning with the tenth century, contacts with the Mohammedan world increased with commerce and the Crusades. Several Mohammedan writings came to be known. There followed, therefore, a period of religious controversy in which each side undertook to prove that it was in possession of the true religion.

From the very fact of trying to persuade non-Christians of the truth of the Christian religion the arguments had to become more philosophical and less theological. Arguments other than those based on sacred texts were needed, for they had to be based on grounds the opponent would admit.

Logic, therefore, founded on the *Organon* of Aristotle, was developed. In the Middle Ages it was called *dialectic*. Its purpose was to force the acceptance of the truths of religion and refute the tenets of religion's opponents.

St. Anselm of Canterbury (1033–1109)

The most important thinker of the eleventh century, perhaps the most important of the High Middle Ages, was St. Anselm of Canterbury. Like most of the scholars of his time, he led a wandering life. Born at Aosta in northern Italy, he carried on his studies in France, particularly in Normandy, and was then summoned by William the Conquerer to become Archbishop of Canterbury. At that time distinctions of nationality were of little importance. Even in the thirteenth century, when the University of Paris had become the most important center of Western thought, the four greatest masters at that university were non-Frenchmen.

The ties of religion, and in particular the monastic ties, were so strong that distinctions of nationality played no role at all in the development of medieval thought.

St. Anselm belongs in the tradition of St. Augustine and John Scotus. Like them, he viewed reason as dependent on faith. The only function of Christian philosophy was the better understanding of religious dogmas. This is expressed in two characteristic formulas which explain the relation between religion and reason:

Philosophy is faith seeking to make itself intelligible (*Fides quaerens intellectum*).

I believe in order to understand (*Credo ut intellegam*).

In this approach there is no place for thinking which is independent of religious dogmas.

In this spirit must be understood the argument, later called by Kant the *ontological* argument, for the existence of God.

THE ONTOLOGICAL ARGUMENT FOR THE EXISTENCE OF GOD

This argument was misunderstood not only by St. Anselm's successors but also by his contemporaries, who tried to find in it a proof of the existence of God.

St. Anselm did not address himself to the problem of the existence of God, which for him was evident. This was the problem he was concerned with:

I believe in God.

How am I to conceive of the God in whom I believe?

If I believe that God is the supremely perfect being and that there can be no other more perfect, then from the fact that I so conceive Him, He must have an objective existence independent of my thought; if He did not, He would not be supremely perfect.

Even the contemporaries of St. Anselm misinterpreted this argument as a proof of the existence of God, an argument purporting to prove the existence of God from the very idea of God—hence its name the *ontological argument*. Such an argument would be a passage from the order of thought to the order of being, of ontology.

Even in Anselm's day one of his contemporaries, the monk Gaunilon, who belonged to the Aristotelian tradition, provided an objection to the whole idea. We cannot conceive of an essence unless beforehand there is some existent thing of which we can affirm that it possesses that essence. This indeed is Aristotle's view of the matter: we cannot have ideas to which no real things correspond.

For example, the concept *man* can be employed only if men exist and depends upon the knowledge we have of them. Consequently it is possible to formulate the concept of God only if there is a God. The concept of God cannot be used to prove the existence of God, since that concept is possible only if God exists.

THE DEBATE OVER UNIVERSALS

St. Anselm took a stand in one of the great logical-metaphysical disputes which stirred up the thinkers of the tenth and eleventh centuries. This was the dispute over universals (*universalia*).

The controversy dealt not with the existence of particular things but with the status to be assigned to such general ideas as *humanity* and *justice*. If these ideas have an existence, what kind of existence is it?

This question had already given rise to a disagreement between Plato and Aristotle. Fundamentally it is the problem of the existence of Platonic ideas.

Do such ideas actually determine the structure of things, or are they purely intellectual concepts formed by our mind and based on particular things?

Plato came out for "*universalia ante rem*," and Aristotle for "*universalia in re.*"

The discussion hinges on determining whether:

Universals are prior to the thing they designate: *universalia ante rem.*

Universals are in things: *universalia in re.*

Universals are posterior to things: *universalia post rem.*

The historical origin of this dispute is rather interesting. Porphyry, the pupil of Plotinus, had written an elementary treatise on logic which Boethius had translated from Greek to Latin. Although it was a work for beginners, Boethius commented that Porphyry had raised the following question:

"As for *genera* and *species,* do they have a real existence or do they rather exist only in our thoughts? If they exist, are they corporeal, and if they are incorporeal are they in our thoughts alone or are they also in the things we sense?"

Boethius finally decided that these questions were too difficult for beginners.

At least three different positions came to be taken with respect to the problem:

Nominalism. Universals are merely words (*nomina*) which have no existence outside our thoughts.

Realism. Universals have an objective existence.

Conceptualism. Universals determine the structure of things, and our mind abstracts them from things. This is an intermediate position.

The principal representatives of these views were:

Nominalism: Roscelin of Compiègne (1050–1120).

Realism: Anselm, William of Champeaux (1070–1121).

Conceptualism: Abélard (1079–1142).

When purely logical problems like these are applied to the field of theology they bring difficulties in their wake. Roscelin insisted that only individuals (i.e., things which would be destroyed if they were divided) have real existence. Thus he would attribute real existence not to an army but to each particular soldier. Basically this notion agrees well enough with common sense.

But difficulties arise if this principle is applied to some of the Christian dogmas, in particular to the concept of the Trinity. Which is real—God, or each of the persons of the Trinity? If God alone is real, one falls into the heresy of Unitarianism. If each of the persons of the Trinity is real, one falls into the heresy of tritheism. This illustrates the difficulties which can result from applying the principles of logic to religious doctrine.

Fundamentally this is the difficulty faced by any religious philosophy. If it insists that all religious problems transcend the possibility of human understanding, the outcome is a kind of mysticism which leaves no place for philosophy. On the other hand, if our minds are believed capable of understanding all the problems of religion, revelation is superfluous, and every unbeliever ought to be led to faith through reason. Faith could then be supported entirely by reason.

Thus every thinker who attempts to be at once a believer and a philosopher must maintain an equilibrium between the two extreme positions of rationalism and mysticism. Every religious philosophy must therefore seek a compromise between these extremes. Yet there is no hard-and-fast rule for determining the exact frontier between these two positions. There have always been conflicts in establishing the boundary between the mystical and the rational.

This discussion brings to mind the distinction between the *credibilia* and the *demonstrabilia*. It is the chief problem of thinkers whose orientation is religious.

From the eighth century to the time of Descartes in the seventeenth century there was a progressive development of confidence in the power of human reason.

At first there was little wish to know anything but the sacred Scriptures and the writings of the Fathers. Then, little by little, profane works came to be known. Finally there was a strong desire to be limited no longer to commentaries and the interpretation of ancient texts.

On the contrary, William of Conches in the twelfth century took a stand in favor of affirming propositions which were not derived from sacred writings. The charge of heresy should not be brought against what is not found in the Scriptures but against what is opposed to the Scriptures.

Abélard worked out the *sic et non* method. This consisted in neutralizing the assertion of some religious authority by quoting the assertion of some other religious authority. Often enough among the Fathers contradictory opinions were found on the same subject. Abélard set up a table of pronouncements, the affirmative on one side and the negative on the other. Thus we are left perfectly free to make our own decisions, since in either case we have the support of competent religious experts. Reason is thus freed from dependence on authority.

Under the influence of Aristotelian thought, which penetrated more and more deeply into Western Christianity, a new attitude of mind began to develop among the philosophers. It came to be admitted that there were a host of problems which had no connection with religious faith.

Until the end of the twelfth century reason occupied an intermediate position between a primitive and an enlightened faith. But in the thirteenth century the idea developed that there are areas in which reason is absolutely sovereign.

This high point in medieval Christian rationalism is represented by Albert the Great (1206–1280) and by his pupil St. Thomas Aquinas (1225–1274), who is regarded as the greatest Christian thinker. Both men became professors at the University of Paris, the former coming from Cologne and the latter from Aquino in Italy.

St. Thomas Aquinas (1225–1274)

St. Thomas' principal work was the monumental *Summa Theologica*. He was author also of the *Summa contra Gentiles,* a more strictly philosophical work, and numerous commentaries on Aristotle, the Pseudo-Dionysius, and others.

One of St. Thomas' principal concerns was to delimit the boundary between philosophy and theology. He wished to free philosophical thought from theology and grant it a certain independence.

In this connection it might be noted that in the eighteenth century the German philosopher Immanuel Kant similarly undertook to separate the areas of religion and science; Kant's purpose, however, was to protect religion.

St. Thomas grants that, in addition to the theological problems concerning the relation between God and man, there is a whole series of problems which concern the structure of nature—purely philosophical problems. (Remember that at this time the disciplines of natural science had not yet become separated from philosophy.)

It is not always easy to keep the philosophical and theological domains separate, however, for even in dealing with natural phenomena Christian philosophy must take dogma into account. This may be illustrated by an example which will enable us at the same time to appreciate the originality of St. Thomas, who follows Aristotle whenever he can.

When St. Thomas deals with the problem of the relation between the soul and the body, he has to diverge from the classic conceptions of Plato and Aristotle; he must account for the dogmas of the immortality of the soul and the resurrection of the body. Whereas for Aristotle the soul is simply the form of the body and perishes with it, for Plato the soul, to the degree that it is immortal, is completely independent of any particular body. In the structure of St. Thomas' system, however, it was necessary to preserve the immortality of the soul and at the same time to assign to the body a far more important role than Plato had given it. Accordingly, St. Thomas worked out a most original theory of the role of matter in the universe which could account for the importance of the body.

According to St. Thomas, who diverged from Aristotle on this point, matter is not simply a potential reality; it is the basis for distinguishing among individuals of the same species; it is a *principle of individuation*. But if this is the case, how can immaterial beings such as angels be distinguished from each other? The reason is that angels differ from each other not as representatives of the same species, but as entirely different species. This idea makes it possible to understand how the gap in the universe between God and man is filled. For St. Thomas, who on this point follows the Neoplatonic and Augustinian tradition, creatures form a continuous series of species from the higher to the lower, and it rests with the numerous species of angels to fill up the infinite interval between God and the most perfect of His earthly creatures—man.

This example of Thomistic thinking illustrates the manner in which Thomas was able to adapt Aristotelian ideas in working out an original philosophy which was to have a profound influence in later centuries.

It was this influence, together with the fact that modern philosophy with its scientific outlook had to do battle with Thomistic scholasticism, which has produced the impression that all medieval Christian thought was Aristotelian. This is not true at all. The imprint of Aristotelian thought came late, was not total, and its influence was not without opposition.

Actually, the most famous representative of Aristotle and his best-known commentator was the Persian philosopher Averroes, who showed that Aristotelian doctrine was inconsistent with several Christian doctrines, such as those of the creation of the world and of the immortality of the soul. For this reason the Aristotelianism presented by Averroes (and known as Averroism) was condemned by the Church in 1277. But little by little Thomistic ideas took hold in the Christian world, and the canonization of Thomas Aquinas in 1323 favored their propagation.

It is unquestionably true that Thomism has become the most influential philosophical doctrine of the Church. Indeed, since the late nineteenth century there has been a revival of Thomism, brought about under the influence of Pope Leo XIII and the Belgian Cardinal Mercier. But let us not forget that other trends, derived primarily from St. Augustine, have also continued to be important in Christian philosophy. While the Dominicans remained faithful to St. Thomas, who was one of their own, and while the Jesuits also propagated his teaching, the Franciscans and the Augustinians have remained loyal to the tradition of St. Augustine and to a somewhat less rationalistic philosophy developed by Duns Scotus (c. 1266–c. 1308). This English thinker, an adversary of Thomism, had great influence in his own country. He died in Paris, where he had come to spread his ideas.

Nicholas of Autrecourt (d. about 1350) and William of Ockham (c. 1295–1349) in France and England respectively, are the most important representatives of nominal-ism, a doctrine which in the fourteenth century stood in opposition to Thomism in a number of European univer-sities—especially on the faculty of Arts at Paris. During the same period in Germany there developed under the influence of Meister Johann Eckhart (1260–1327) a move-ment of mysticism which had close ties with Neoplatonism.

VII

RATIONALISM

Modern philosophy developed in the vernal air of the Renaissance. That great cultural movement, arising first in Italy in the fourteenth century and coming into full bloom in the fifteenth, spread gradually through the whole continent of Europe, bringing a better understanding of ancient culture and a flowering of artistic, literary, and scientific creativity.

The most important philosopher of the Renaissance was Nicholas of Cusa (1401–1464), whose principal work, *De Docta Ignorantia* (*Learned Ignorance*), introduced the idea of the infinity of the universe and dealt a severe blow to the medieval concept of a finite universe with the earth at its center.

The way in which modern philosophy developed was determined by the progress which was made in understanding the phenomena of nature. This progress owed a great deal to the influence of the greatest physicist of antiquity, Archimedes. It was he who inspired the scientific work of Leonardo da Vinci and Galileo, the founder of mathematical physics. What characterizes the new physics is not so much its use of experiment—for Aristotle made experiments, too—but its use of mathematics in conjunction with experiment. Instead of describing natural phenomena as they occur, the scientists of the Archimedean school make an effort to understand them as embodying mathematical relations. This conception of the world is much closer to that of Plato.

Hypotheses are made to answer the problem under investigation, thus creating a kind of intellectual model which is mathematical in nature. The quantitative results of experiment are compared with the results expected by calculation. Then, whenever there is a discrepancy between the two, an effort is made to determine what factors lie behind it.

What is new, then, at this time is the replacement of the *qualitative* science of Aristotle by a *quantitative* science in which methods are sought to express experimental results in mathematical terms.

But this demands a completely new conception of the universe.

The Birth of Modern Science

Before the Renaissance the Greeks and their Christian successors looked upon the world as an ordered universe (*cosmos*) and attached value to order over disorder, to rest over motion; all natural change was regarded as a movement toward order. This is the theory that *everything has its natural place*.

Thus motion was explained by the fact that every body seeks to attain its natural place, and, when it attains it, there it remains. Only through the application of force can it be moved from its natural place or prevented from reaching it. Not all motion can be explained in the same way; motion is understood qualitatively. The downward fall of a heavy body is a natural motion; the upward motion of a heavy body, on the other hand, is not natural and requires explanation.

This whole qualitative idea had to be changed when men sought to explain phenomena quantitatively.

It had to be assumed that there is a certain *law of permanence* which provides that every change be compensated for by a change of an opposite kind. With Galileo, and particularly with Descartes, the reality of such permanence was explicitly affirmed. For Descartes *the quantity of motion is constant* (this law has since been modified). All diminution in the motion of a body is explained by an increase of motion in some other body, so that the total motion in the universe is constant.

This principle of the permanence of motion was dependent on another principle invoked by Galileo and generalized by Descartes: *the principle of inertia.*

For Aristotle a body which is thrown will naturally come to rest. Motion is a transitory and passing state. If motion is natural, it will stop at the end of its course; if it is artificial, it will stop when the force that produces it has run its course.

But this whole idea is contradicted by the motion of the planets, whose course is uninterrupted. This makes necessary the supposition that there are two orders of the universe:

1. The sublunary world, in which the laws of Aristotle's physics seem to be verified.

2. The supralunary world, in which motion is eternal.

Corresponding to these different worlds, there is a difference between the laws of physics (earth) and the laws of astronomy (heavenly bodies).

This theory was modified by Copernicus, who explained planetary motion in a manner very similar to the explanation of the motion of bodies on earth.

Through reflecting on physical motion as analogous to the motion of planets, Galileo came up with an early form of the principle of inertia: Let us suppose a spherical body, neither light nor heavy, which is thrown parallel to the earth. Will it tend to go up or down? It will follow a course at a constant distance from the center of the earth.

Basing his reasoning on a particular example, Galileo sketched out the principle of inertia, which was generalized by Descartes. Uniform motion in a straight line does not require any other force in order to continue. Thus whenever there is any phenomenon in which a quantity of motion disappears, Descartes seeks to explain it by looking for an increase of some other motion.

Any phenomenon is intelligible, according to Descartes, to the degree that it can be explained mathematically—this is the ideal of mathematical physics.

But how can the different sensations which are given in sense experience be explained?

For Descartes the knowledge furnished by sensation is on the same footing with confused knowledge. Clear knowledge is knowledge which corresponds to the data of mathematics.

Descartes worked out a whole new technique for the study of natural phenomena, a technique which depended only on mathematical methods. At that time geometry was still what it had been in Euclid's day, a science of forms with no general method at its disposal. Each problem had to be dealt with by particular procedures. Algebra, on the other hand, had made progress through the contributions of the French mathematicians Viète and Fermat, but it was still handicapped by the lack of a proper symbolism. Descartes improved the symbolism and worked out a liaison between geometry and algebra—*analytical geometry*.

Let us briefly call to mind the basic principles of analytical geometry. It establishes a correspondence between the entities of algebra (numbers) and those of geometry (points, lines, planes).

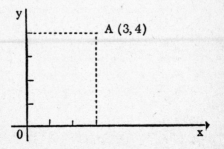

In a plane defined by two perpendicular axes, or co-ordinates (Cartesian coordinates), each point is defined by a pair of real numbers:

The first is the measurement along the abscissa (x- axis).

The second is the measurement along the ordinate (y axis).

These are the Cartesian coordinates.

E.g., Point A in the plane is completely determined by the coordinates x and y [$x = 3$(abscissa), $y = 4$ (ordinate)]. The unit of measurement may be chosen arbitrarily.

The development of this method made it possible to represent lines and curves by equations; that is, by algebraic functions which could be interpreted geometrically and whose properties could be determined.

The application of analytical geometry to the study of natural phenomena, particularly to problems of optics and mechanics, was to make possible an outburst of scientific discovery which provided the basis for the rationalistic philosophy of modern times.

Descartes (1596–1650)

Cartesian philosophy, which marks the beginning of modern rationalism, can be understood only by realizing that it was necessary to make the new physics compatible with the teachings of the Church. Without a demonstration of such compatibility there would be little chance for the new physics to be adopted by the universities and colleges. Descartes risked condemnation by the Church in defending ideas which were opposed to Aristotelian and Thomistic physics. Copernicus had been put on the Index in 1616, and in 1633 Galileo was condemned by the Church for having dared give public support to the Copernican idea that the sun, not the earth, was the center of the universe.

To avoid any such untoward incident, Descartes in 1629 went to Holland, which at that time was regarded the most liberal country in Europe. Followers of several religions had come there and lived together peaceably. (Lest there be any illusions about undue tolerance, it should be noted that in 1642 the city council of Utrecht condemned the Cartesian philosophy "because it is new and turns youth aside from the good old philosophy of Aristotle.")

In Holland Descartes developed the essentials of his philosophic system. He set them forth in the *Discourse on Method* (1637), the *Meditations* (1641), and the *Principles of Philosophy* (1644). Actually the *Discourse on Method* constitutes only an introduction to his scientific views, which are now largely out of date, but that introduction can still be read with great interest.

It was Cardinal de Bérulle, founder of the Congregation of the French Oratory, who showed Descartes where to turn to find a Christian philosophy, different from Thomism, which might be more easily reconciled with the new physics. He advised him to study the works of St. Augustine, which were far from the spirit of Aristotle. Descartes' metaphysics does, indeed, take its inspiration from St. Augustine. Like Augustine, Descartes begins his philosophic reflections with methodological doubt. He begins by rejecting as false whatever seems to him to be in the slightest degree doubtful.

He does not doubt merely for the fun of doubting; through doubt he seeks to test the various ways of knowing to reach a firm basis on which to build his philosophic system.

Still he must find this resting place, and Descartes realizes that the search will take time. Before he is able to establish his knowledge on a solid basis, he must live, he must act. Consequently before working out a rational ethics he must adopt a provisional ethics, which is, for the most part, that of the conventional moral behavior. It consists in conforming to the usages, laws, and customs of the country in which he is living.

This is a point worth noting. If we doubt and we still must act, says Descartes, the best we can do is to persevere to the end with the same attitude we set out with. Descartes compares this choice of a line of conduct to the predicament of a traveler who has become lost in a great forest and does not know how to get out. All he can do is choose, once and for all, a certain direction which he will follow until he reaches the end of the forest. There is no forest so large that one cannot get out by proceeding in a straight line.

CARTESIAN DOUBT

Theoretically Descartes' doubt extended to the whole of knowledge. Practically speaking, he too quickly accepted certain beliefs to have really put them in doubt.

We have seen that the method of doubt with which Descartes began his philosophical reflections consisted in testing knowledge and its sources in order to accept only those things which survived a careful examination. He examined successively three kinds of knowledge:

1. *Knowledge based on authority.* This Descartes cannot accept, since the authorities contradict each other. Some criterion other than authority is needed in order to choose among the assertions that authorities say are indubitable.

2. *Knowledge from sensation.* There is no adequate criterion here. If circumstances differ in the least, the same things are sensed differently; our senses deceive us and we are misled by them. A drunken man sees double; and when we are dreaming, the universe appears quite different from normal. How do we know we are not dreaming now? Must we not undertake a criticism of sense data? Such a criticism, however, would have to be rational. Then cannot rational knowledge supply us with the indubitable criterion we seek?

3. *Rational knowledge.* It is the sciences of a rational character, like algebra and geometry, which seem certain to us, says Descartes. But are they true? To show that they, too, can be doubted Descartes offers the hypothesis of an

evil demon. We believe what the rational sciences tell us because they force themselves on us. Are they therefore true? Some evil demon, as powerful as he is wicked, might introduce false ideas into our mind in the guise of self-evidence.

Must even the ideas which seem best warranted be cast into doubt?

Where can a firm resting place be found, since all sources of knowledge have been thrown into doubt?

At this point, says Descartes, there remains only one thing that cannot be doubted—that is, that we have doubted all the sources of our knowledge. We cannot doubt our doubt, which only seems to confirm it; and if we do not doubt our doubt, we certainly doubt.

Doubting is a form of thinking, which implies existence. Thus Descartes reaches the point of saying "I think, therefore I am"—*cogito ergo sum.* This assertion becomes the starting point of his whole system.

Until now Descartes has used St. Augustine's method, but soon he is to adopt a number of doctrines from Scholasticism and Thomism.

In Descartes' own time various objections were made, and he was forced to reply to them. We shall consider two of them.

1. Why give such importance to thought? Why begin with the fact of thinking? Couldn't it just as well be said, "I eat, therefore I am"? or "I walk, therefore I am"? No, because it is possible to doubt that I am eating or that I am walking; thus we come back to doubt, which is a process of thought.

2. Is not Descartes' *cogito ergo sum* really an inference from a suppressed, but unproved, major premise—*"Whoever thinks is; I think, therefore I am"*? In that case, mustn't the major premise be established? To this Descartes replies that there is such an intimate relation between thought and existence that there is no need for intermediate reasoning; the *cogito ergo sum* is an immediate and self-evident intuition.

THE CARTESIAN METHOD

The criterion which made it possible for Descartes to affirm this intuition was the criterion of self-evidence. It was the self-evidence of the bond between thinking and being that seemed coercive to him.

This is a characteristic trait of Descartes' method. Self-evidence, in the Cartesian view, is rational; it is valid for all rational minds, independent of time or individuality. Being evident is thus essential to the method he adopts to build a philosophic system. Only those propositions which are evident, like the *cogito ergo sum*, are to be accepted.

Here we find an idea which, compared with earlier thinking, is novel. And Descartes is well aware of it. He stands opposed to all the earlier theories of truth which are based on probability. The Cartesian method is to regard mathematical rigor as its model and to look on ideas which are merely probable as false. Self-evidence is a psychological characteristic, but Descartes proceeds to make of it a criterion valid for every rational being.

But how are we to make the step from metaphysical evidence to the assertion of the truth of what is self-evident? We grant that certain propositions are self-evident, but proof of their truth would require some other ground.

Descartes says that if ideas seem evident to us, it is because they possess certain characteristics which account for that evidentness: they are *clear* and *distinct* ideas.

Ideas which are *clear* are those which we can distinguish from other ideas. For example, the idea *dog* is a clear idea; it can be distinguished from that of *horse* or *man*.

Distinct ideas are ideas of such a nature that their elements are clear ideas. For example, it cannot be said that *dog* is a distinct idea, but *triangle* is.

It is apparent here that Descartes' theory of knowledge is based on ideas which, in addition to being clear, cannot be broken down into elements. They correspond to *simple natures*, which by definition are clear and distinct.

This backs up the Cartesian method, which consists in

dividing all difficulties into simple components and building on that basis, taking care not to neglect any of the
components in proceeding from the simple to the complex.

On the whole, the Cartesian method is nothing else than
a generalization of the algebraic method extended into all
areas of thought.

In comparison with St. Augustine this is a great novelty.
The method gives the researcher an important and well-
founded instrument for the investigation of natural phenomena. Its rigor is due to its being modeled on the rigor
of mathematics.

The fact that I think implies the existence of a reality
which is conscious, a soul. I am, says Descartes, a thinking
substance (*res cogitans*). What does this existence consist
in? How are we to conceive it?

Since my existence as a thinking thing is *independent*,
I am a *substance*. Here Descartes adopts a Scholastic notion.
Independent existence (i.e., existence as a substance) is
different from both existence as a property, which depends
on the existence of something else, and existence as an
idea, which depends on a conscious mind.

It should be noted that body is not even considered in
this whole discussion. This fact is not offered as a proof
of the immortality of the soul, but it tends to be one. For
thought is regarded as independent of the body. This constitutes an argument in favor of the philosophy of Descartes
as opposed to that of the Scholastics and the Thomists,
who begin directly with sensation. Sensation cannot be
conceived as occurring without the intervention of the
body.

At this point in the Cartesian system we know nothing
of God or the external world.

THE EXISTENCE OF GOD

The next step is to prove the existence of God. Descartes
offers two proofs:

1. *First Proof.* I know that I am a thinking substance, a
subject who has ideas more or less clear and precise, but

who does not know whether these ideas are the product of his imagination or whether they come from outside.

However, I do know that I doubt, which means that I am lacking in knowledge. Moreover, I am aware of certain needs. This gives me the idea that I am an imperfect being.

But this idea of imperfection would be inconceivable if I did not at the same time have an *idea of perfection.*

Now I cannot believe that I myself am the author of this idea of perfection. It could only come to me from a being which itself is perfect. Descartes assumes that the cause must be as perfect as the effect, and this infinitely perfect being who is the cause of the idea of perfection is God.

This is Descartes' first proof of the existence of God, a proof based on the idea of infinite perfection. Descartes' reasoning comes down to this:

1.   I have in me the idea of perfection.
2.   This idea of perfection is a perfect idea.
3.   The cause of a perfect idea must itself be perfect.

Let us consider the validity of this proof, examining the links in the chain of reasoning.

1.   *I have in me the idea of perfection.* I make the assumption that every negative idea is correlated with a positive idea. Imperfection cannot be conceived without perfection. But is not imperfection, like perfection, a matter of degree? We can start out at first in a state that fails to please us, since it does not fully satisfy our desires, without its being necessary that those desires be based on a knowledge of abolute perfection.

2.   *This idea of perfection is a perfect idea.* This assertion is even more fallacious. Is the idea of perfection a perfect idea itself? What Descartes has done is confuse the properties with the characteristics of an idea. Is the idea of color a colored idea?

3.   *The cause of a perfect idea must itself be perfect.* This notion is part of the tradition of Neoplatonism, a line of thought reaffirmed by Scholasticism, that the cause is always superior to the effect. This idea runs counter to the

idea of progress, since it regards all existence as a descent and perfection as something that can only be found in the past. This concept clearly belongs to a traditionalist society where change is never improvement. It is opposed to the ideal of progressive evolution.

But Descartes does not depend entirely on this proof of the existence of God. He avails himself of another which is a variant of the ontological argument of St. Anselm.

2. *Second Proof.* In discussing the existence of God we must first ask what we mean by God. God is an infinitely perfect being. Now if we are in agreement on the definition, we must agree that God necessarily exists, for He could not be perfect if He did not exist.

But right here there is a difficulty. How are we to understand God's infinite perfection? Is He infinitely good or infinitely powerful? It is difficult to reconcile these alternatives.

If God is infinitely good, He is not infinitely powerful, for He is unable to prevent the existence of evil.

If, on the other hand, He is infinitely powerful, He is not infinitely good, since He has not chosen to prevent evil.

Descartes gives primacy to God's omnipotence. For him God is infinitely free, since freedom and power go hand in hand.

But what does Descartes mean by freedom? For him the term has two meanings:

1. *The freedom of indifference.* This is the freedom we experience when we deliberate, when we believe we possess a freedom of choice. But this hesitation which we interpret as a manifestation of freedom is only the result of our ignorance, without which we would act in a way that left no room for doubt.

We hesitate and doubt only when we are ignorant. Therefore this kind of freedom cannot be an attribute of God, since he does not doubt and since all his ideas are clear and distinct—and therefore self-evident.

2. *Positive freedom, the expression of God's omnipotence.* Everything that God wills becomes real immediately. There is a correlation between God's will and His omnipotence.

God creates the universe by thinking constantly about it. There is an agreement, therefore, between divine thought and the objective existence of the universe. God's freedom consists in the immediate realization of all that He wills. He is truthful because His thoughts always correspond to reality and His thoughts are clear and distinct ideas. That is why our ideas, to the extent that they are clear and distinct, correspond to those of God. And, since His ideas are true, so our ideas, insofar as they are clear and distinct, are true. God does not deceive us.

Such ideas are not derived from experience, since for Descartes experience is confused; they are innate ideas of our reason.

This is how the Cartesian system develops—starting with a thinking subject and arriving at a God who is the guarantor of the truth of clear and distinct ideas.

THE PROBLEM OF MATTER

The universe of matter for Descartes is known through God's thought. Our clear and distinct ideas coincide with the ideas of God, and for that reason they are true.

But the material universe cannot have a direct influence on our mind; it can only be explained by it. Like mind, the material universe is a substance. The qualities of material substance are different from those of thinking substance, which is conscious and thinking. What characterizes matter is extension.

Material substance and thinking substance have nothing in common. This is the metaphysical explanation of why in the Cartesian system the world of matter is separated from the world of mind.

Since matter cannot have any direct influence on mind, any explanation of mental or material events must remain in its proper domain. Motion, for example, cannot be explained by the action of mind on matter.

Knowledge cannot depend on the external world. Descartes' metaphysical premises lead to a rationalist theory of knowledge, not an empirical one. It is through innate ideas, which are placed in us by God, that we can account for our knowledge. The only role of experience is that of concrete verification, not of explanation. Indeed, experimental results require rational explanation.

LIVING BEINGS

If we are required to separate the two aspects of reality, mind and matter, how can the apparent influence of mind on matter be explained?

Descartes deal with this difficulty by first distinguishing between man and animals.

1. *Animals*. He regards animals as very complicated machines. Since language is the expression of thought and animals have no language, they must be deprived of thought. There is no mental factor in them.

For St. Thomas and the Scholastics animals do not possess reason, but they do have instincts which are common to the whole species. As individuals they do not possess a rational means of adaptation.

2. *Man*. What can be said of man? Descartes' view can be expressed briefly: Man is a creature endowed with both mind and body. He is both a thinking thing and an extended thing. And the mutual relation between body and mind cannot be denied:

a. *The influence of matter on mind*. In the case of a fall, the material cause brings about suffering which is mental in character.

b. *The influence of mind on matter*. Movements of the body are directed by an act of will.

A certain interaction between mind and matter must be granted, but such an interaction is very difficult to explain. Indeed, how could two things so different in kind act on each other? How could there be an interaction if all that is mental and conscious is completely divorced from extension, and all that is material is divorced from mind?

The mind cannot be the source of motion. If it were so, even in part, the principle of the permanence of the quantity of motion, so dear to Cartesian physics, could not be maintained. Moreover, in order to act on the physical world, mind would have to be localized; there would have to be some point of contact.

As for the purely physical difficulty here, the influence of mind on motion, Descartes insists that mind is never the creator of motion but merely directs motion which already exists. He compares mind to a horseman who directs his mount without being the source of the motion.

Unfortunately this theory was quickly shaken by one of Descartes' successors, Leibniz, who established the famous principle of the parallelogram of forces. When two forces together bear on a single point, the magnitude and direction of the resultant of the two forces are shown in the parallelogram of forces:

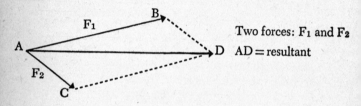

Two forces: F_1 and F_2

$AD = $ resultant

Thus the freedom to alter the direction of motion which is allowed in the Cartesian physics is denied by Leibniz.

But the metaphysical difficulty is even more serious. How can the action of body on mind and of mind on body be understood if the two substances are so totally different in kind?

Seeking to make the point of contact between mind and body as small as possible, Descartes located it in the pineal body within the brain. The problem, however, has nothing to do with the size of the area which is in contact with unextended substance; it is a problem of the nature of the two substances. It is a special case of the broader problem which arises whenever a thinker posits two heterogeneous elements which still must influence each other. It is a problem which is to preoccupy Descartes' two successors, Spinoza and Leibniz.

Spinoza (1632–1677)

Spinoza was a Jew of Spanish origin whose father came to Holland to live; Spinoza was born in Amsterdam and spent his childhood there. After some conflict with the Jewish community, which regarded him as an atheist, he established himself at The Hague.

Spinoza was influenced early by the Cartesian philosophy, but there are two features of his thought which distinguish him from Descartes:

1. Religion does not play the same role in Spinoza's thinking as it did in that of Descartes. Unrestricted by religious dogmas, he was thus able to develop his thought more freely.

2. He was influenced by certain Jewish thinkers who had carried further than St. Augustine the mysticism of Neoplatonism.

In his great work, the *Ethics*, he worked out his philosophical system deductively in the manner of geometry. In the seventeenth century the geometrical method was the ideal deductive method. Since Spinoza came to be regarded as the devil personified, as the Anti-Christ, and since his thought was believed to be dangerous—even to smell of sulfur—the *Ethics* was not published until after his death.

Not until the second half of the eighteenth century, the period of the Enlightenment, did his thought come to be appreciated by those who gave a fundamental place to reason—Lessing, Goethe, and the German idealists who came at the beginning of the nineteenth century.

THE *Ethics*

On opening the *Ethics* one finds what appears to be at first sight a work in geometry. There are definitions, axioms, theorems, and lemmas; each proposition is numbered and demonstrated separately. It must be noted that, despite Spinoza's intention, his proofs are far from having the rigor of geometric demonstrations. This method of presenting the system gives us insight into Spinoza's ideal, which was a geometric, deductive, rationalistic ideal, but Spinoza's failure should not surprise us. A philosophical system cannot be proved like a treatise in geometry.

Descartes' proofs are much less rigorous than those of Spinoza. Descartes was an innovator, but he accepted too many incompatible ideas to have been able to create a thoroughly satisfactory system. The result was that his two greatest disciples—if by disciples one means continuers— developed his thought in two very different directions:

Spinoza gave it a strictly rationalist interpretation.

Leibniz worked out a system incorporating as many traditional elements as possible.

Spinoza begins with eight definitions and seven axioms. Three of the basic definitions are:

1. *Substance:* "By substance I mean that which is in itself and is conceived through itself; in other words, that of which a conception can be formed independently of any other conception."[1]

2. *Attribute:* "By attribute I mean that which the intellect perceives as constituting the essence of substance."[2]

   Thought and *extension* are attributes of substance.

3. *Mode:* "By mode I mean the modifications of substance, or that which exists in and is conceived through something other than itself."[3]

Every figure, every shape, can be conceived as a mode of extension, and every idea as a mode of thought.

On the basis of these three definitions and one auxiliary definition—that of God—Spinoza proves his fundamental theorem: *There is only one substance in the universe.*

This conclusion, of course, is at variance with the Cartesian view that there are several thinking substances (God and individual souls) as well as a material substance.

---

[1] Spinoza, *Ethics* (tr. R. H. M. Elwes), Part I, Def. iii.
[2] *Ibid.,* Def. iv.
[3] *Ibid.,* Def. v.

In this way Spinoza can avoid the difficulties connected with the interaction of substances.

Before proving this fundamental theorem, Spinoza establishes two preliminary theorems:

"There cannot exist in the universe two or more substances having the same nature or attribute."[4]

If there were plurality of substances, each would have a different attribute. If two substances were different, they would differ either in attribute or in mode. Now, they cannot differ in their modes, which are defined in terms of substance (otherwise there would be a vicious circle). They can therefore differ only in their attributes. Consequently if two substances have the same attribute, they must be the same.

This destroys the idea of a plurality of minds having the attribute of thought in common.

"One substance cannot be produced by another substance."[5]

If one substance could be the cause of another substance, the substance which was the effect would have to have a different attribute from the substance which was the cause (since different substances must have different attributes), and the effect would have to be expressed by the attribute of the cause. It would no longer be independent and could be understood only through an attribute of another substance. But this is impossible.

This conception destroys the fundamental doctrine of Cartesian and Christian thought—the idea of God as a creator. God is a substance and cannot be the creator of another substance.

SPINOZA'S PANTHEISM

For Spinoza, God is "an absolutely infinite being—that is, a substance consisting in infinite attributes. . . ."[6] He is

---

4 *Ibid.*, Prop. v.
5 *Ibid.*, Prop. vi.
6 *Ibid.*, Def. vi.

infinite also in His modes. If we understand by attribute a certain way in which substance manifests itself, a certain way of being, God is that to which belong all the ways of being. It follows that the whole of reality looks to God as the ground of its being.

God is the only substance.

If there were in the universe a substance other than God, it would either have an attribute different from the attributes of God—and God then would not be absolutely infinite, since He would lack this attribute—or it would have an attribute of God, in which case it would necessarily be identical with God. Within the attribute of extension, God and the physical universe are the same.

Spinoza's view is thus pantheistic. Everything in the universe exists only as a mode of divine substance; God and Nature are the same: *"Deus sive natura."*

For Spinoza any physical object—a table or a chair—is a mode, a modification of substance in the attribute of extension. It is not God; for God is nature considered in its infinite and eternal aspect. God is "nature *sub specie aeternitatis.*" Particular things are only transitory aspects which are the effects of the unfolding of the eternal structure: it is this eternal structure which is divine.

To know nature in its eternal aspect is to know God.

It can therefore be said that insofar as the physical sciences are concerned with eternal structures, they contribute to the knowledge of God. In this sense scientists are the priests of what Spinoza regards as true religion.

We shall now see how Spinoza's principles make it possible for him to solve the difficulties which had baffled Descartes, and how he was able to construct an ethical theory which might provide a moral ideal for those who devote themselves to scientific research.

PSYCHO-PHYSICAL PARALLELISM

As a consequence of the fact that there is only one substance, and that it possesses infinite attributes, the whole of reality manifests itself in various ways, just as the same thought may be expressed in several languages. Just as different sentences expressing the same thought may be regarded as translations of the same idea, so in the universe the different attributes expressing the same reality must correspond, term for term. To a mode in the attribute of extension must correspond a mode in the attribute of thought.

The analytical geometry of Descartes actually made it possible to define the properties of spatial forms by using algebraic formulas. This is possible only because there is a parallelism between the world of extension and the world of thought.

The correspondence between psychic events and physical events results from the fact that these two forms of existence express the same eternal reality, which is divine.

Since, for Spinoza, there is only one substance, Descartes' difficulty over the interaction of substances is avoided.

The supposed interaction of body and mind is for Spinoza nothing but an illusion. There is a correspondence, not an interaction. To believe that there is an interaction would be to make the mistake of someone who, seeing the same action in a number of mirrors arranged at different angles, believed that what he saw in one mirror was caused by what he saw in another. The true explanation is that there is a psycho-physical parallelism between the phenomena of consciousness and the phenomena which occur in the attribute of extension.

Thus, by reintroducing a unitary theory of reality, Spinoza was able to account for the illusion of the interaction of substances, which in his view does not occur at all.

DETERMINISM

Sense knowledge explains nothing. To understand it we must be able to explain it by making it correspond to rational concepts. What we call experience gives us only confused ideas.

The criterion of knowledge is an internal one—self-evidence. If an idea is clear and distinct there can be no doubt about its truth; doubt is possible only with confused ideas. The confusedness of sensations is the very quality that leads us to doubt them, and our senses deceive us to the extent that we hold confused ideas.

If there is a parallelism between material reality and mental reality, clear and distinct ideas can deal only with particular things; any general idea can only be confused.

If we believe in chance or contingency, it is because our knowledge of the totality of conditions which govern events is imperfect. Doubt and contingency are conceivable only to the extent that our ideas are confused. When we have clear and distinct ideas of the universal order, we know that in nature everything is determined.

Thus, on purely rational grounds, Spinoza for the first time sets forth a *rational determinism.*

Determinism such as that of the Stoics was not the result of a rational analysis but of their conception of the universe as a *macrocosm*, like an enormous animal in which all is tied together organically. Stoic determinism was an organic determinism. Spinoza thought of the universe as a systematic interconnection analogous to that of a mathematical system.

For three centuries after Descartes the deterministic ideal guided mathematical physics, until in 1927 a modification of that conception was introduced by the discovery of the indeterminacy of phenomena on the atomic scale.

Just as we regard contingency as merely a function of our ignorance, so all freedom of choice is removed from Spinoza's universe. What appears freedom is to be explained only by our ignorance of the necessary linking together of all phenomena.

Spinoza compares the freedom we think we have to that of a stone which has been thrown and which might believe that the reason it follows a certain trajectory is that it wills to do so. If the stone reasons in this way, it is because it is ignorant of the fact that its motion does not depend on it. Similarly, in a human being there is a mechanism of which we are ignorant which determines the way we act.

SPINOZA'S ETHICAL THEORY

Though seeming to deny that man be can free, Spinoza is now about to propose the conquest of freedom as an ethical ideal.

How is it possible both to deny and affirm freedom? It is clearly possible only if the idea of freedom is taken in two different senses:

1. Freedom as *the opposite of necessity and determinism.* An event may be called free when it is neither necessary nor determined by fate. This is freedom of choice, free will.

2. Freedom as *the opposite of constraint.* This is the sense in which one can fight for freedom—for freedom from constraint.

But what does constraint mean?

A free act, according to Spinoza, is an act of which we ourselves are the cause; an act is constrained when it is determined by a cause outside ourselves.

At first sight this would seem to agree with common sense, but the way in which Spinoza defines what we are and what it is that is outside ourselves makes it less obvious. There is a fundamental factor which determines the idea of freedom: to know what we ourselves are.

God is perfectly free, for there is no substance other than God which might be external to him or which could constrain him to act in any way.

We are free, says Spinoza, to the degree that our actions are determined by clear and distinct ideas, and, to the extent that this is so, our actions are determined by reason. A free act is an act determined by ourselves, but by ourselves in what we have in common with all men—reason. It is reason, a faculty common to all men, and not our individual character which defines our nature.

Opposed to reason are the passions. The passions are determined by something other than ourselves. Persons or things toward which we experience passions acquire a hold over us; we become slaves to our passions.

In Part III of the *Ethics* Spinoza analyzes the passions in the light of his general philosophical views.

To the degree that we act freely—that is, rationally—we feel that we are active, for we are the adequate cause of our acts. On the other hand, we feel that we are passive to the degree that we are subject to our passions.

On the basis of these ideas of activity and passivity Spinoza defines the feelings of *pleasure* and *pain:*

Our tendency to persevere in our being can be aided or impeded. If it is aided, we experience pleasure; if it is impeded, we experience pain.

"By *pleasure,*" writes Spinoza, "I shall signify a passive state wherein the mind passes to a greater perfection. By *pain* I shall signify a passive state wherein the mind passes to a lesser perfection."[7]

On the basis of these notions of *pleasure* and *pain* Spinoza defines *love* and *hate:*

Love is "pleasure accompanied by the idea of an external cause."[8]

Hate is "pain accompanied by the idea of an external cause."[9]

If we act in conformity to our clear and distinct ideas, we experience pleasure; we feel free to the degree that our clear and distinct ideas coincide with the eternal structure of things—with some aspect of God.

That is why we are more free as we acquire more ideas which are clear and distinct. We are more free as we identify ourselves with God, and we owe this pleasure to God.

Thus the ideal Spinoza offers us is fundamentally the love of God, which coincides with the pleasure resulting from acquiring objective truth.

The passions can be combated only by this other passion—the love of God.

So far as we do not understand the causal connection of the events which have led us to attach ourselves to some

---

[7] *Ethics,* Part III, Prop. xi, scholium.
[8] *Ibid.*, Prop. xiii, scholium.
[9] *Ibid.*

person or thing, we experience pain. If we understand, we are able more easily to combat our passions.

Love for a particular person cannot be shared, with the result that it leads to conflict. On the other hand, the love of God is common to all men, and as a result it is a force for peace.

While the rationalism of Descartes remained attached to religious ethics which could not neglect the individual, Spinoza was able to extend the conclusions of his philosophical thought to the area of moral practice.

Leibniz (1646–1716)

Leibniz traveled a great deal. He lived in France, Italy, and Germany; he died at Hannover, where he was in charge of the ducal library. Almost all his writings were left there in manuscript form, and they were incompletely edited only long after his death.

In terms of his ability to synthesize, Leibniz was perhaps the greatest genius philosophy has ever known. He was a doctor of law, but beyond his juristic training he was well grounded in scholastic learning.

In Paris he became acquainted with a group of mathematicians and became interested in the problems of mathematics and physics. It can be said that in every area of study in which he worked—and there were many—he was an innovator.

Independently of Newton he invented the infinitesimal calculus, and he contributed to the development of physics. But above all he was a philosopher and a theologian who sought to conciliate the various points of view and preserve what seemed to him of value in each.

Unlike Spinoza, Leibniz sought to conserve the value of the individual, his freedom, and what was essential in his religious convictions. In doing so he sought to reconcile these values with a rationalism which was Cartesian in its inspiration.

Leibniz was a scholastic rationalist.

It is most difficult to synthesize all the aspects of his thinking. The works which appeared during his lifetime were occasional writings and dealt with only limited parts of his system. His principal philosophical works were:

Monadology, or the theory concerning monads.

Discourse on Metaphysics, another systematic writing, which appeared after his death; it is perhaps the most coherent exposition of his thought.

New Essays concerning Human Understanding, a polemical work, a reply to the English philosopher John Locke, who had written an *Essay concerning Human Understanding.* Leibniz' *New Essays* was in the form of a dialogue between two persons, one of whom presents Locke's ideas and the other those of Leibniz.

Essays on Theodicy contains Leibniz' views on theology. Here he attempts to reconcile God's freedom with God's goodness (the problem of evil) and to deal with other problems involving the relation between God and man.

THE MONADOLOGY

For Leibniz as for Spinoza, the Cartesian system was a starting point. Yet, although he began from principles nearer those of Descartes than Spinoza's had been, he quickly departed from them.

He raises first of all the question of the nature of matter.

Matter, for Descartes, meant nothing but *extension.* The idea of space was a clear and distinct idea. But the second rule of the Cartesian method advises us to reduce reality to simple elements. This is an idea which in various ways dominated Western thought from the time of Descartes to the end of the nineteenth century. For the last forty or fifty years a contrary principle has been invoked—to explain the simple through the role it plays in a complex whole. There is no doubt, however, that from the seventeenth century on, the dominant principle was to explain things by reduction to the simple. Now, can space be regarded as a simple idea?

For Leibniz and for the geometers, any extended thing

is divisible into parts, and this division can be continued so long as there is an extended surface. As a result, says Leibniz, for space to be understood it must be reduced to its simple elements; by doing this, one arrives ultimately at an indivisible geometric element—the *point*.

Space is therefore a composite reality, and an understanding of it requires an understanding of points.

Leibniz thus introduces a new concept into philosophy: that an infinity of points is required for any extension whatever.

Between the time of Descartes and Leibniz there had been a new development in mathematics, a development in which Leibniz himself had had a hand—the infinitesimal calculus.

Although Pascal had done some work on the concept of infinity, the infinitesimal calculus was not invented until after his death. It was invented by two men working independently, Sir Isaac Newton and Leibniz. (There was a dispute over the question of priority, and charges were made that one had borrowed from the other, but the methods and the symbolism used by Newton and Leibniz were quite different.)

Reduction of extension to a collection of points constituted the first divergence of Leibniz from Descartes.

Moreover, whereas for Descartes extension is the essence of matter, Leibniz insists that there is a difference between empty extension and material reality. Matter offers a resistance to pressure, it exerts a certain force, which is not the case with mere extension.

If a material object exerts force, that force must be derived from constituent elements which cannot be merely geometric points. Somehow force must exist in the elements which make up matter. It is by such reasoning that Leibniz comes to conceive of what he calls *monads*—elements of matter as points endowed with force.

In some sense a monad is an atom, since it constitutes the final indivisible element of material reality.

As early as Descartes' day there had been a revival of philosophical atomism, particularly in the work of Gassendi. There was, however, a great difference between the atomism of antiquity and that of Leibniz. Gassendi's atomism continued the division of matter up to the point where matter ceased to be divisible with the available apparatus of physics. The atom was, in the literal sense of the word, what could not be cut. For Leibniz, on the other hand, the monad is the result of a purely rational division.

Leibniz looks upon every individual thing as an aggregate of an infinite number of monads.

It is difficult for the natural sciences to study the properties of monads because the sciences are concerned with material objects whose properties as aggregates conceal the properties of the individual monads.

But can individual monads be known?

Leibniz tells us that minds as thinking substances are indivisible in space like monads and, like them, have force. Could not each thinking substance be regarded as a monad, and each monad as a thinking substance?

The virtue of this idea would be to conceive the whole universe as made up of substances of the same nature and thus avoid the dualism of Descartes. This idea would constitute a form of *monism*—a concept of reality which reduces all forms of being to one kind. This is a unitary view of the universe, according to which all the particles making up the universe are substances of the same kind.

Leibniz' monism is a spiritual monism; each monad is conceived as a kind of mind, a mental substance.

Having made this reduction, Leibniz must still explain how monads can appear under two such different aspects as body and mind.

To explain it he introduces a new concept into philosophy, that of the *unconscious*. It should be recalled that for Descartes all thought was conscious. But by virtue of the concept of the unconscious, the difference between the universe of consciousness and the material universe becomes one of degree rather than of kind: monads differ in their degree of consciousness.

Each monad is a mirror of the universe. The entire universe is reflected within it. Leibniz compares each monad to God's view of the world; monads differ from each other as the views of a city differ depending on the angle and position of the viewer.

Every monad is a picture of the universe. This means that it is fastened to the whole of the universe by law. This picture of the universe Leibniz calls *perception*.

If every monad has a perception of the entire universe, what is the difference between material monads and mental monads?

These monads are distinguished from each other not only by the fact that they each constitute different points of view with respect to the universe, but also because their consciousness extends over different areas of their perception. This conscious aspect of the monad's perception of the universe Leibniz calls *apperception*.

From this point of view it is possible to arrange monads in a hierarchy based on different degrees of apperception. There is a downward scale from the divine monad, whose perception is entirely conscious—apperception coincides with perception—to the monad which has no apperception at all.

In this respect Leibniz' thought resembles that of Plotinus, who had set up a scale of being descending from the perfect Being, the One. For Leibniz, however, the descent was one of consciousness rather than being.

Leibniz established two principles which applied to this universe in which monads were ordered in terms of apperception:

1. *The principle of indiscernibles:* No two monads are absolutely identical; no two monads have the same degree of consciousness.

2. *The principle of continuity:* This is expressed in saying "Natura non fecit saltus"—Nature has made no jumps. This principle was accepted until the discovery of the discontinuous nature of energy.

The universe is made up of an infinite number of monads —of an infinite number of substances possessed of force— which differ among themselves in their degree of consciousness; between two neighboring monads it is always possible to place an intermediate one. Put another way, reality may be conceived as a series of monads which differ imperceptibly from each other and which constitute a scale extending downward from God, the monad whose apperception is equal to His perception, whose knowledge is completely conscious.

Leibniz gives the term *appetition* to the force which is characteristic of all monads. Appetition expresses the tendency of every monad to maintain its being. This tendency is manifest in the real world in two ways:

1. Since monads are substances they are independent of each other; the changes which occur in them cannot be explained by any external influence, but rather through an internal force—appetition. Change in our perception can be explained on this basis.

2. Insofar as we learn something new, we increase our apperception. This change is also to be explained in terms of appetition.

In this view of the universe each monad is isolated; it is "windowless"; it remains shut up in its own universe; and everything that happens to it comes about as a result of its own internal structure.

But if this is the case, how could Leibniz believe in the existence of many windowless monads? This concept of windowless monads would seem to lead to *solipsism*, a philosophic concept which holds that the only reality in the universe is the self. Yet Leibniz is by no means a solipsist. As a scientist he is too much concerned with the external world and with social questions.

He avoids solipsism by means of an hypothesis which provides an explanation of the relation between monads— even the relation between the soul and the body. Since there can be no direct connection between one monad and another and yet there is an illusion of interaction, Leibniz makes the hypothesis that there must be a pre-established harmony among them.

There exists a harmony among all the monads of the universe, a harmony resulting from the fact that all of them are points of view of God on the same universe. We are to imagine the universe as a huge clock shop and all the clocks in it synchronized by a perfect clockmaker.

For Descartes the movement of one clock had to determine the movement of another in order for them all to show the same time. Spinoza would say that they were all moved by the same machinery. Malebranche, a disciple of Descartes and a priest who sought to enlarge the importance of God, thought that since God was the cause of every event in the universe, He would be the cause of agreement among the clocks. Leibniz' idea was that there was a plurality of synchronized clocks and that God was like a divine clockmaker who had set the clocks once and for all at the same hour.

This hypothesis explains the concordance among the different monads; a divine being is needed to explain the pre-established harmony.

Nevertheless, this explanation was not without its difficulties. If God is a monad whose apperception is equal to his perception, it does not follow that God can be regarded as sufficiently more powerful than all the other substances to regulate their behavior.

LEIBNIZ' THEORY OF KNOWLEDGE

Leibniz' theory of knowledge is a coherent one, but it is far less rigid than that of Spinoza. For the latter, all propositions must express either an impossibility or a necessity; contingency or possibility, in nature, is a function of our ignorance.

Leibniz reintroduces the Scholastic distinction between *necessary propositions* and *contingent propositions*, the latter dealing with events which could have failed to occur.

He explains the difference between necessity and contingency by showing that this difference exists in nature itself. There are propositions which are necessary, like those of logic and mathematics; their denial involves contradiction. To say that they are necessary means that they are valid for all possible worlds—we can imagine no universe in which they would not be valid. Their validity does not depend on the existence of this particular universe. They are so much a part of divine understanding that even God's will could not change them. These necessary propositions do not depend on the existence of any determined entities. What exists in our universe might not exist in a different universe. Except for God, who is a necessary being, all things are contingent.

For Leibniz, who in this respect is a Scholastic and an Aristotelian, all propositions have the structure *subject–copula–predicate* and are rationally explained by the fact that in making the proposition we analyze the subject and make one of its properties explicit. The fact that Caesar crossed the Rubicon could be deduced from the very nature of Caesar. The fact that he was to cross it illustrates the idea that all the events which occur in the universe and which issue from some particular subject belong to the nature of that subject. Everything that happens to a subject is part of his nature.

Since we do not know enough about any subject, we are unable to predict the events which will issue from its nature. God, on the other hand, who knows completely the nature of each monad, could deduce from it all future events. Knowledge of events can come to us only through experience, but God's knowledge is prior to all experience simply through an analysis of the subject.

Our knowledge depends upon experience; we can give an account of events only after they have occurred; but to explain our knowledge rationally we must transform it to explanation a priori.

The proposition "Caesar crossed the Rubicon," theoretically analytical for an infinite being, is not a necessary proposition, for Caesar is not a necessary being. Indeed, it would have been possible for Caesar not to exist at all or to have had such a nature that he need not have crossed the Rubicon. There are therefore propositions which are analytical from God's point of view but which are not necessary, since their truth depends on the existence of something contingent.

THE ROLE OF GOD IN THE UNIVERSE

Leibniz makes a distinction between God's *understanding* and God's *will*.

In God's understanding are to be found all necessary laws and the concept of all possible worlds and all substances whose existence does not involve contradiction.

But not all propositions are possible simultaneously, for possible propositions may be opposed by others which are equally possible.

Thus a universe in which Adam and Eve were not driven from Eden would be incompatible with the fact of their numerous progeny.

To explain the relation between possibles Leibniz introduces the notion of things as being simultaneously possible —*compossible*.

The various possible substances envisaged in God's understanding cannot all coexist. There is a whole pyramid of possible universes, extending from one which might contain only a single possible being to the richest universe in which the greatest number of possible beings coexisted: this is the universe which Leibniz calls "the best of all possible worlds."

It is possible for a real substance in one universe not to exist in another. All these universes are subject to necessary truths, but at the same time truths which hold in our universe might not hold in another.

Contingent substances would not have been called into existence without the existence of a being whose existence did not depend on that of any other being. This necessary being is God.

For Leibniz, as for the other rationalists, the ontological argument is valid in the sense that God's existence can be deduced from His essence; from the idea of an infinitely perfect being a proof of His necessity can be established. But this requires a prior proof that the idea of an infinitely perfect being is not contradictory. For Leibniz not only is this idea not contradictory; it alone makes it possible to explain how a contingent universe—one possible universe among others—could have been brought into existence. And only the existence of a divine clockmaker enables us to explain the pre-established harmony of the universe.

But, since Leibniz is a rationalist, there must be a reason for everything that happens in the universe; the universe is ruled by the *principle of sufficient reason*. This principle is not exclusively logical in nature, for not everything is governed by geometric or deductive necessity; it has another aspect, an explanation in terms of what is best, in terms of *moral necessity*. If one form of necessity is related to God's understanding, the other is related to God's will. Since God is infinitely good, He always acts for the best. Thus He has brought into existence not just some universe or other among those which were possible—for then there would not have been sufficient reason for His choice— but *the best of all possible worlds*.

Rationalism is thus broadened by the principle of the best. The principle provides a sufficient reason for adopting philosophic or scientific theories which, without being necessary, are nevertheless the best that can be conceived. For example, the choice of the simplest hypothesis among various possible hypotheses is justified by the principle of the best.

The introduction of the concepts of time and space, which make possible the study of natural phenomena, can be justified even if time and space are not objectively real; the monads which we attempt to relate to each other in an order of succession or coexistence have in fact no relation to each other. Nevertheless the concepts of time and space provide us with the best means of representing these phenomena and from this point of view are a useful fiction. The role of the scientist, as distinguished from that of the metaphysician, is to provide ideas which are useful in actual practice, even if they are different from reality.

In a word, Leibniz' philosophic ideas make it possible for him to answer in his own way the two great problems of Christian theology—how an infinitely perfect God could have permitted evil and how divine omniscience can be reconciled with human freedom.

Since He is good, God has brought into existence the best of all possible worlds. This does not mean a universe from which evil is excluded, for the best universe is the one in which there is the greatest number of compossibles, and a universe without evil would certainly be poorer in diversity. Only by taking account of the whole can we explain the imperfection of certain details.

As for the second problem, men are free, since their acts result from their own nature. The fact that God knows their acts from all eternity does not make Him the source of human action. Human action is free because it is contingent, because it is possible not to commit it, and because in some other possible world it might not be committed.

Can religious philosophy or ethics be content with a system in which freedom exists only in the understanding of God where also coexist all possible worlds—a freedom which is completely excluded from the world in which we live? There is evidence that at the end of his life Leibniz did not enjoy the reputation of being completely orthodox. In considering his views, it is impossible not to conclude that the reserve with which he was accepted by theologians was amply justified.

VIII

EMPIRICISM

The best-known philosophers of the empirical tradition are:

Francis Bacon	(1561–1626)
Thomas Hobbes	(1588–1679)
John Locke	(1632–1704)
George Berkeley	(1685–1753)
David Hume	(1711–1776)

The writings of these empiricists belong to the seventeenth and eighteenth centuries, and there was a strong interaction between these Bristish thinkers and their continental contemporaries. Bacon, the first of them, antedated Descartes; Hobbes was a contemporary of Descartes and Spinoza; Locke was a contemporary of Leibniz, Berkeley of Malebranche, and Hume of Jean-Jacques Rousseau.

Unlike the rationalists, the empiricists were not primarily concerned with the physical sciences and mathematics; their main interest was in social and political questions.

In seeking to develop a philosophy different from Scholasticism they did not adopt the mathematical method inspired by Galileo, which prevailed on the continent; their methods were inductive, not mathematical. And they were to use these methods in fields other than those of measurable facts.

In a somewhat summary fashion we shall limit our discussion of empiricism to the ideas of Locke, Berkeley, and Hume.

Locke (1632–1704)

In addition to being the great theorist of parliamentary government and the forerunner of political liberalism, John Locke was a student of philosophy, theology, and medicine. He was the spiritual father of the English Revolution of 1688.

Locke was author of the *Two Treatises of Government* and *Letters Concerning Toleration.* The political interests expressed in these works played a part in his metaphysical system. His chief philosophical work was the *Essay concerning Human Understanding.*

Locke's approach is a return to empiricism, in which he makes a relentless attack on Descartes' innate ideas and the Cartesian notion of self-evidence. All we have, says Locke, are purely subjective beliefs in the name of which we assert the objective validity of certain ideas we label as rational. If we think we are in possesssion of objective truth, there is no reason for making concessions to those whose ideas are different from ours.

The tendency to believe oneself the sole custodian of absolute truth was common in religious circles in England, where each of the many sects believed that it alone possessed the true understanding of the Bible.

Locke's philosophy was virtually a philosophy of common sense; few of his doctrines have anything paradoxical about them. But if in Locke empiricism began with common sense, empiricism in the hands of his successors, who sought to give coherence to their ideas, departed from it.

In assigning to experience the fundamental role in knowledge Locke reverted to the old Aristotelian and Scholastic principle *Nihil est in intellectu quod non prius fuerit in sensu*—there is nothing in the mind which has not previously been in the senses. But to grant this function to experience implies a criticism of Descartes' innate ideas.

As examples of innate ideas, Descartes had given the logical principles of identity and noncontradiction, as well as such moral principles as doing unto others as you would they should do unto you.

Locke's reply was that there is no proof that these principles are really universal.

If we ask a child whether he grants the principle of noncontradiction, he will have trouble giving an answer. Nevertheless, it might be replied, even if he is not consciously aware of it, he acts on that principle. This means that there are ideas which govern our conduct without our being aware of them, even though Descartes insisted that all ideas are conscious. According to Locke, those principles believed to be universal do not exist prior to experience, but are derived from it.

Locke likens the human mind to a sheet of white paper or a wax tablet on which experience writes. The mind is formless; it possesses no innate ideas, thus resembling Plato's matter. All our ideas come from experience by which our mind is shaped. And it is Locke's task to show how all our basic ideas come from experience alone.

This line of thinking subsequently underwent a development in France, where Locke's ideas were popularized by Voltaire. Out of them arose the philosophy of the so-called ideologues, who attempted to explain all ideas on the basis of experience. Condillac, for example, with his notion of man as a machine, based his views on the tradition of Locke.

Locke makes a distinction between two kinds of experience. All our ideas come to us through either *sensation* or *reflection*.

1. *Sensation*—derived from observation of external objects.

2. *Reflection*—concerned with "the internal operations of our minds."[1]

The idea of body is derived from sensation, the idea of soul from reflection.

Among the ideas derived from either of these two

---

[1] *Essay concerning Human Understanding*, Book II, Ch. i, §2.

sources Locke makes a distinction between ideas which are *simple* and those which are *complex*.

Simple ideas, which Locke describes as "the materials of all our knowledge,"[2] are derived either from the sensation furnished by a single sense (the idea of *red* or *smooth*), by more senses than one (the idea of *space* from sight and touch), from reflection only (the idea of *will*), or "by all the ways of sensation and reflection" (the idea of *force*, which transfers the phenomena of will to the world of nature).[3]

Among simple ideas Locke makes a distinction between *primary qualities* and *secondary qualities:*

Primary qualities are those used by physicists in describing nature, such ideas as shape, size, density, and motion.

Secondary qualities are those known directly through sensation.

Locke holds that secondary qualities are accompanied by sensations of pleasure and pain, which are themselves subjective.

In making this distinction Locke brings to mind the atomists' doctrine that some qualities actually belong to nature and others are the result of human sensation.

Complex ideas are those which for the rationalist appear simple: substance, mode, and the idea of relation.

1. *Substance.* We do not perceive substance directly. Now, since knowledge cannot come from any source other than experience, how do we acquire knowledge of a reality which is not perceived?

We have sensations, but we do not perceive them separately; they are associated with each other. Shape, color, weight, and the like are all perceived together. A chair, for example, is given as a collection of qualities which are provided by different senses and yet are perceived simultaneously. Substance is what provides the constant relation of these qualities with each other.

2. *Mode.* The idea of mode corresponds to a reality

---

[2] *Ibid.*
[3] *Ibid.*, Ch. iii, §1.

which we do not regard as having independent existence. It depends on other realities. It is a complex idea without substantial existence.

For example, the idea of murder (a mode) depends on the idea of a murderer and a victim (both substances). The idea of a triangle is a mode. What we actually perceive is the triangular object from which we abstract certain properties.

3. *Relation.* It was Locke who first saw the fundamental importance in knowledge of the idea of relation. The notion of natural law is a particular case. The rationalist philosophers had stressed only the relation of inherence that exists between a substance and its attributes; they had not called attention to the idea of relation in its full generality —particularly the relation between correlated phenomena.

Locke is known above all as an advocate of tolerance in religious and political matters. His *Letters Concerning Toleration* were widely read and disseminated in the eighteenth century.

Berkeley (1685–1753)

Paradoxically enough, George Berkeley, the empirical philosopher, became a devout Anglican bishop at Cloyne in Ireland. His principal works date from his youth:

Essay towards a New Theory of Vision (1709)

Treatise concerning the Principles of Human Knowledge (1710)

Three Dialogues between Hylas and Philonous (1713)

Berkeley, like Locke, was an empiricist, affirming that all our knowledge comes from experience, which cannot be doubted. But Berkeley subjects Locke's distinctions to a searching analysis:

1. The distinction between the percept as an immediate datum of experience and the abstract idea derived from experience.

No abstract idea, says Berkeley, can be deduced from concrete experience.

When we say that the sum of the angles of a right triangle equals two right angles, we appear to be talking about some abstract triangle or other. Locke held that this proposition asserted a property derived from the idea of the abstract triangle. But, says Berkeley, there is no abstract triangle. Every triangle has definite sides and angles. A general triangle cannot be imagined. What could it be?

This criticism holds, says Berkeley, for all universals. But if this is true, how can there be abstract ideas?

Berkeley's answer is that what is abstract is not the idea we are reasoning about, but the method we use in reasoning about concrete things. When we reason about triangles we make a mental abstraction from all the properties which are not common to all triangles in order to arrive at propositions which might have a broader application.

2. Berkeley denies completely the distinction between primary and secondary qualities. It is sheer illusion to suppose that primary qualities correspond to objective reality.[4]

Primary qualities and secondary qualities are in fact so closely bound together that there is no way to separate them. If secondary qualities are in the mind of the perceiver, the primary qualities must be in the mind, too. Moreover, there are some secondary qualities which are emotionally neutral. For example, an object may simultaneously have shape (a primary quality, according to Locke), and color (a secondary quality). Beyond this it is possible for shapes, which are primary qualities, to be accompanied by feelings of pleasure or not.

3. The third distinction attacked by Berkeley is much more important. It is Locke's distinction between sensation and reflection. In denying it, Berkeley denies at the same time the distinction between mind and matter.

The whole distinction, says Berkeley, is superficial. All percepts are percepts of a perceiving mind. There are no

---

[4] A primary quality corresponds to an objective reality, while a secondary quality is an impression in the mind of the perceiver produced by a primary quality. Secondary qualities may be accompanied by feelings of pleasure and pain.

material perceptions, and a material substance is inconceivable. Matter is pure fiction. We have perceptions; beyond these the only reality is the mind which perceives them.

There can be only two kinds of reality: minds and the ideas or percepts those minds have. Berkeley thus roots his empiricism in idealism. For an empiricist this is a paradoxical concept: it has reduced the whole universe to a collection of ideas. The paradox derives from the fact that Berkeley accepts simultaneously two propositions which he thinks are based on common sense:

1. What we perceive is real.
2. We perceive nothing but perceptions.

But if the real world is the perceived world, how can imagination be distinguished from reality? What distinction can be made between purely fictitious percepts and those which are real?

Berkeley here reverts in part to Leibniz. An elderly man, for example, can be imagined as seated in a class of students. In what sense is he less real than they? Leibniz would say that the image of the man was less lively and less precise. But there is more to it than that. The image of the elderly man can be made to disappear at will, for the idea depends on us. Perception of the students is imposed on us; we do not control that idea; it is independent of our will.

Berkeley agrees with Leibniz that certain perceptions are stronger, more lively, and more precise than others; these we call real. But the most important thing about them is that they are independent of our will; they are coercive.

But what does this mean? These perceptions are what Berkeley calls ideas, and ideas can exist only in a mind. Since it is clear that they do not depend on our mind, they must exist in another mind, which is the mind of God.

The reality of the external world is thus to be explained by God, in whose mind are the ideas which force themselves on us. This conception of God agrees well with the notion of a God who is the constant creator of reality. He is the warrant that not everything in the universe is sheerly imaginary.

It follows from this that one cannot talk about forces in nature in the way scientists had done before Newton. Forces were merely human concepts framed on the model of the human will. They introduced anthropomorphism into science.

Berkeley's concept of God provides a justification of the scientific method applied to the study of nature. If the universe consists of ideas in the mind of God, science can study the constant relations we perceive in nature. The Newtonian method for seeking permanent relations in nature is justified. The permanence of these relations can be readily understood since God, being all-wise, does not change His mind. He maintains the constant relations of nature.

God manifests himself to us through nature, which is the language by which He speaks to us. It is the business of science to study the signs of that language, and of metaphysics and theology to determine what they mean.

Thus Berkeley's whole system is based on a deeply religious idea: the whole of reality is an expression of divine thought.

Yet there is a certain paradox here; this empiricist, who holds that all knowledge is based on experience, yet argues that the whole of reality depends on a mind which we do not perceive.

However it is this concept which makes it possible for Berkeley to explain the persistence of reality independently of our perceptions. What is it that allows us to affirm that a thing continues to exist even when, for example, we are not actually looking at it? It is God, says Berkeley. God gives reality this persistence of being independent of our perceiving it.

Some of these ideas were extended still further by David Hume, who was to push empiricism to the point of atheism and express skepticism regarding even science.

Hume (1711–1776)

David Hume is generally regarded as the greatest of the English empiricists. His three principal philosophic works were:

A Treatise of Human Nature (1739–40)

An Enquiry concerning Human Understanding (1748)

An Enquiry concerning the Principles of Morals (1751)

In this last work he presents again in a more popular and easy style the basic ideas of the *Treatise*. He was author also of a *History of England*.

Hume pushed empiricism to its final logical consequences. In so doing he reached a number of paradoxical conclusions.

He begins with the basic assumption that we have a spontaneous belief both in the existence of an external world and in the operation of causality. This belief, practically speaking, is the basis of human activity.

Hume's problem is to find out whether this belief is consistent with empiricism. Belief in the existence of objects in nature independent of our experience is difficult to make compatible with empiricism.

According to Hume's empirical doctrine we have:

Impressions, the most forceful and lively sensations (including passions and emotions) as they appear to the mind.

Ideas, "faint images" of impressions in our thinking and reasoning.

Ideas are thus derived from impressions, and we have no knowledge independent of impressions.

Like all the empiricists and rationalists, Hume distinguishes between simple ideas and impressions and those which are complex. This distinction was characteristic, in fact, of seventeenth- and eighteenth-century thinkers, who all attempted to explain the complex in terms of the simple.

It is a feature of Hume's empiricism that for him there

are no simple ideas in the mind which were not originally impressions of sensations. Every simple idea corresponds to an impression; in this sense, then, the mind does not create simple ideas.

If the mind has any power, that power has to do with complex ideas. The mind can modify the magnitude or the order of simple ideas to make a complex idea.

For example, changing the magnitude of an imagined man can give the idea of a giant or a dwarf. Again, by using parts taken from several creatures and changing their arrangement it is possible to form ideas of creatures, like sirens, of which we have had no experience.

Hume was influenced in his theory of mental life by the principle of universal gravitation as it had been developed in Newtonian physics. The laws of the association of ideas were modeled on the laws which governed the attraction of bodies for each other.

Ideas become associated in three ways:

1. *Resemblance.* We associate an idea with some other idea which resembles it.
2. *Contiguity.* Nearness in time and space brings about an association of ideas.
3. *Causality.* We think of the cause or of the effects of an idea.

These laws of the association of ideas have been studied by the Russian physiologist Pavlov in his work on *conditioned reflexes*. He shows not only how ideas can become naturally associated, but also how artificial association may be made. Thus if the sound of a bell is always associated with the feeding of a dog, the dog will eventually secrete saliva at the mere sound of the bell. Here lies a great cause of error. The association of two phenomena can easily lead us to believe that one is the cause of the other. This is the reason, says Hume, that the association of ideas is in large part the source of our errors; these associations provide no objective basis for their application to the future.

But Hume's great contribution was his analysis of this very idea of causality.

ANALYSIS OF CAUSALITY

When can we say that A is the cause of B?

It might be thought that there is a certain internal, occult force contained in the cause which could explain such an occurrence as the germination of a seed to produce a plant. Berkeley had already criticized the notion of force in nature; it is an anthropomorphic idea which reads into nature the concept of will appropriate to mind.

Hume goes even further in his criticism than Berkeley. Just as there is no force in nature, there is no will in the human soul.

When we say we perform an act of will, we perceive an idea followed by an act; but do we perceive the will? When we raise our arm, we have the idea of doing so, then we experience a tightening of the muscles and are aware of the effect; but do we perceive any trace of will?

What then does it mean to say that A is the cause of B?

What we see is the temporal succession A–B. The supposed cause precedes the effect. But is succession in time sufficient to establish causality? What we need in order to establish A as the cause of B is a necessary, not an accidental, connection between the two.

A contemporary Scottish philosopher, Thomas Reid (1710–1796) offered a criticism of Hume. To establish causality it is not sufficient that A be followed by B and that the connection be necessary and constant. Day is always followed by night; yet day is not the cause of night, since night is likewise followed by day. Causality requires an irreversible succession: If A is followed by B, B cannot be followed by A. Causality is therefore an irreversible and constant relation of succession.

But whence comes the idea that a connection between A and B is a constant one?

If this connection has always occurred in the past, we may perhaps believe that it will continue to occur in the future. This hypothesis is based on the idea that the order of nature does not vary. But is this a necessary idea? There is nothing contradictory about assuming that the order of nature can change.

Then how can it be proved that the connection is necessary?

If A precedes B, A may have some specific power to produce B. But (a) we have never perceived this power; and (b) even if such a power be admitted, it is related to the past and at the most explains the past; but must it necessarily hold in the future?

Then where does the idea of necessary connection come from?

Hume's explanation is that it comes from the fact that we have several times observed certain constant successions in the past and this repetition has given us the *habit* of thinking that whenever A occurs we can expect B. It is therefore a purely psychological phenomenon determined by the laws of the association of ideas. But has it any objective basis? The farmer's wife brings grain to the chicken every morning, but one morning she will wring the chicken's neck. There are successions which are not necessary. The recurrence of phenomena in the past is not sufficient to justify believing in an objective succession in the future. It merely brings about a habit of thought.

Moreover, says Hume, if it is only the habit of expecting a phenomenon to be repeated that leads us to believe in causality, and if there is no logical connection between cause and effect, the result is that anything could cause anything.

Beyond this, if we believe that every simple idea (and the idea of necessity is a simple idea) is derived from an impression, what is the impression that could give rise to the idea of necessity?

Indeed, Hume concludes, there is nothing objective which warrants the idea of causality. It is simply a habit of mind, and any science which is based on a causal connection between phenomena has no objective support whatever. The idea of causality appears to be nothing but a prejudice.

Philosophers have been greatly disturbed by this presentation of the *problem of induction*—the enumeration of reasons which justify arguing from an always limited number of instances to the assertion of a universal law applicable both to the past and to the future. Mere empiricism is unable satisfactorily to solve the problem of induction.

Another problem with which Hume deals is that of explaining where we get ideas of objects which are independent of our experience. For example, I look at a statue; I see it, but if I turn my head, I don't see it. What happens to the statute when I am not looking at it?

Berkeley had answered that the statue's existence independent of my perception depended on its being an idea in the mind of God. But if we do not accept this explanation, in what way can the existence of things independent of our impressions be explained?

In the case of an impression which is interrupted and then resumed, there is really a succession of identical impressions. This is what happens, for example, when one repeatedly opens and closes his eyes in front of a picture.

We have, then, to explain how these sense phenomena which are so very much like each other are repeated; it would appear necessary to grant the existence of something which maintained itself in the intervals between our impressions. According to Hume, however, the existence of such an object independent of our perception is nothing but a hypothetical and subjective explanation of the connection between repeated experiences.

There is no logical reason, consistent with empiricism, for believing in the existence of an external world.

While Locke kept fast hold of common sense in developing his empiricism, Hume preferred to be consistent. He showed that some of the ideas of common sense had no real justification, and he wound up with a form of skepticism.

ETHICS—THE IDEA OF FREEDOM

Like Spinoza, Hume did not believe in freedom of the will; but, on the other hand, he did not believe in determinism either—his analysis of causality had made that impossible.

Freedom for Hume consisted in a certain spontaneity of our being which seems to be the source of certain motions. But this spontaneity must not be confused with a freedom of indifference. If anything whatever could produce any action whatever, this freedom of indifference would be identical with chance, and free action would be unforeseeable. Consequently it would be impossible to believe in the existence of a subject responsible for such actions.

Indeed the idea of chance is incompatible with the idea of responsibility. If a "free" action is nothing but the result of pure chance, why should men be rewarded or punished for actions they are not responsible for?

Reward and punishment depend upon a certain consistency of behavior. Those whose behavior is inconsistent and unpredictable—the apparent result of chance—we regard as mad.

To punish a person for some act requires that there be a connection between the person and the act. Otherwise we deny morality, and the idea of deserving or not deserving loses all meaning.

In practice it is the act itself which we reward or punish. The idea of deserving or not deserving is attached to the person. There must be such a connection that there is a reason for the performance of the act. We find this explanation in the person.

After this sketch of rationalism and empiricism in modern philosophy it will probably be agreed that neither of these approaches is completely satisfactory.

In *rationalism* the role of experience is not an important one; all knowledge is explained in terms of ideas which are innate in the knower. But how does it happen that these innate ideas correspond to what is real? How is it that an internal criterion can provide us ideas that correspond to reality?

The rationalists escape from their predicament by assuming the existence of God, who becomes the bridge between thought and the external world. They have, in short, placed the world of Platonic ideas inside the mind of God.

Empiricism, on the other hand, gives to experience the prime role in knowledge. But this leads to a denial of the ideas on which science is based—such as the existence of law in the universe.

Unable to go beyond experience, the empiricists cannot, in fact, establish the validity of scientific laws which bear upon the future as well as the past. Laws which might be admitted as valid for the past cannot be held valid for the future, since it is impossible to know the future by experience.

In whichever direction we turn the situation is unsatisfactory.

Now comes a thinker who was influenced both by the rationalists—especially Leibniz—and by the empiricists—especially Hume. He sought to work out a synthesis. In so doing he inaugurated contemporary philosophy. The creator of this synthesis was Immanuel Kant.

KANT
(1724–1804)

Kant is perhaps the greatest philosopher of all time. He was born at Königsberg in East Prussia; there he carried on his studies, and there he lived his whole life, a life well-regulated and peaceful.

His writings cover the whole field of philosophy. The three which are most important are:

1. *Critique of Pure Reason* (1781), in which he develops his theory of knowledge.

2. *Critique of Practical Reason* (1788), in which he works out his ethics.

3. *Critique of Judgment* (1790), devoted to his esthetics, his theory of beauty.

Since the educated public had made little attempt to become acquainted with the *Critique of Pure Reason*, which was written in a detailed and difficult style, Kant wrote a simpler popularization of his philosophy in the *Prolegomena to any Future Metaphysics* (1783). The very title of this work attests his belief that henceforth no metaphysics could be developed which did not take his thinking into account.

This does not mean that Kant set forth ultimate truth, but so great was the importance of his work and so great his influence on the thinkers who followed him that philosophy since his time cannot be understood without an understanding of Kant's thought. He synthesized the philosophy that had developed since Descartes, and he marked the beginning of contemporary thought.

After Kant the whole character of philosophical problems was altered. Until his time the views of former philosophers had been regarded as opposed to each other. Kant brought about a kind of synthesis of rationalism and empiricism. His philosophical system came to be known as *criticism,* a term which appears in the titles of his principal works.

For the rationalists experience must have a rational explanation. For several years Kant had tried to deal philosophically with Newton's physics. He sought to give a rational explanation of the law of universal gravitation—that bodies attract each other with a force directly proportional to the product of their masses and inversely proportional to the square of the distance between them. Kant had been unsuccessful in his effort to account for this law rationally. In his perplexity he became acquainted with the thinking of Hume, who had affirmed that all knowledge of particular things—which is empirical—is concerned only with the phenomena directly apprehended. We are not permitted by experience to go beyond the particular phenomena of perception. Universal laws, according to Hume, have no objective foundation; they are based only on the habit of repetition, and thus their foundation is psychological. If it were necessary to give a rational account of our beliefs, there would be no alternative but skepticism.

This point of view had a great influence on Kant, who admitted that Hume had awakened him from his "dogmatic slumber." But Kant was led to a conclusion far different from that of Hume.

Critique of Pure Reason

I. INTRODUCTION

Kant grants, with Hume, that experience alone provides no justification for going beyond particulars, which are fixed in space and time, to affirm universal laws transcending experience. There must be a foundation other than experience for our belief in universal laws.

But since there *are* universal laws, such as the laws of mathematics, whose objectivity we cannot refuse to grant (and here Kant parts company with Hume), these universal laws must have some foundation other than experience. Thus, without being an out-and-out rationalist, Kant goes beyond empiricism; he believes that there is some other basis for knowledge.

From a temporal point of view the empiricists are right: knowledge does not precede experience. Kant, however, is interested not in the psychological problem, but in the logical problem. From the logical point of view there is some knowledge which cannot be based on experience alone. Kant is thus led to distinguish between *a posteriori* knowledge and *a priori* knowledge.

A posteriori knowledge is derived from experience.

A priori knowledge, being necessary and universal, must be explained on some ground other than experience.

Kant makes another important distinction, which he derived from Leibniz: the distinction between *analytic* and *synthetic* propositions.

Analytic propositions. Kant accepted the Aristotelian view that propositions have the form *subject–copula–predicate.* On this basis he defined analytic propositions as those the predicate of which is contained in the very meaning of the subject.

For example, in the proposition "All bodies are extended" the idea of body implies the notion of extension; it would be impossible to know what a body is without knowing that it is extended. This proposition is analytical in the sense that it merely makes explicit one aspect of the subject. The relation between subject and predicate is purely logical. It is a development of what the subject connotes.

Synthetic propositions. On the other hand there are propositions in which the predicate supplies something not contained in the connotation of the subject. These Kant calls *synthetic.*

For example, in the proposition "This desk is brown" the

color of the desk cannot be deduced from the idea of desk. The predicate adds something to the subject. There is a relation between the subject and what is asserted about it. This assertion is a synthetic proposition.

Analytic propositions are based on the principles of logic. They do not add to knowledge; they make its implications more specific.

Synthetic propositions are much more meaningful; they do add to our knowledge. So long as synthetic propositions are *a posteriori*—based on experience—it is not difficult to discover their objective basis. But when it comes to synthetic propositions *a priori,* such as "Every change has a cause," the fact of their universality makes it impossible for them to be derived from experience alone. They can be true only because they are necessary; and though experience may tell us what is, it cannot tell us what must be. Since every universal synthetic proposition goes beyond experience, then, insofar as I accept it, it must be universal because it is necessary. Since our belief in necessity is not based on experience, every universal synthetic proposition must be, at least in part, *a priori*. Examples are the principle of causality or the principle of the conservation of matter.

How, asks Kant, are synthetic propositions *a priori* possible? What is their basis? This question the *Critique of Pure Reason* tries to answer.

Before discussing the details of Kant's reply, let us consider an analogy. Let us imagine a machine—such as one which molds an article in plastic—whose function is to impose a shape on its product. Every piece which passes through the machine will have the same shape as every other. Or, to change the figure, let us imagine that we always wear glasses with blue-colored lenses. Everything we see must then be blue.

We know that whatever a person perceives is subjectively influenced by himself as the perceiver, just as the shape of the product is influenced by the machine that stamps it out. Everything the person sees, like everything made by the machine, has a form imposed upon it. Knowing the conditions under which the perception takes place, we also know that everything the person sees must be colored blue.

Might there not be something analogous to this in the structure of the human mind? Might it not be possible to say that the very structure of the mind determines the nature of knowledge?

Consider again the empiricist's idea of the role of mind in knowledge. For Locke, it will be remembered, the mind is like a wax tablet on which experience makes its imprint. But in fact the imprint is not an exact reproduction of reality. It reproduces only the shape, not the color or the material or the heat of the object. There is something selective about the wax: the imprint is not a reproduction of the object as it is in itself.

Considered from this point of view, it is natural to look upon the mind as having a structure of its own. If this is the case, then knowledge is the result of a combination of the impressions derived from the external world and whatever is imposed on them, or selected from them, by the structure of the mind.

A first conclusion immediately follows: We do not know things as they are in themselves (*das Ding an sich*) but as they appear to us. They are, to use Kant's term, *phenomena*.

Just as it would be absurd to ask someone to swim without getting wet, so it would be absurd to ask for knowledge which bore no imprint of the instrument of knowing.

But we do not, for all this, necessarily fall into subjectivism; the structure of the mind, which Kant proceeds to work out, is the same for all human minds, and it is for this reason that objective knowledge common to all men is possible. This is why it is possible to speak of *human* knowledge. Perhaps there are minds which perceive in ways different from men; in this case their knowledge is different from human knowledge. This common structure of the minds of all men is what remains in Kant of the Cartesian reason.

Since we can know only the world of phenomena, and

since this world is the joint product of experience and the structure of the human mind, we can make the Aristotelian distinction between the *matter* of knowledge and its *form*.

The *matter* of knowledge comes from experience; it is supplied by sensation.

The *form* of knowledge derives from the structure of the mind.

Kant thus effects a synthesis of rationalism and empiricism. Rationalism holds that reason supplies both the form and matter of knowledge. Empiricism maintains that the whole of knowledge is derived from experience. Kant grants that experience supplies the matter of knowledge, but insists that the form is due to the structure of the mind.

But all this is an introduction to Kant's philosophy. In his great work he undertakes to determine exactly what part of our knowledge is form and what part matter.

How can we determine what elements of knowledge depend upon the structure of the mind?

We must be guided by the principle that whatever is necessary and universal in knowledge cannot come from experience, for experience is always limited as to the time it occurs and the place we have localized it. The element of necessity must have its explanation in the form impressed on knowledge by the structure of our mind.

Kant compares the philosophic revolution he has brought about to the Copernican revolution in science. Copernicus had put the sun in place of the earth at the center of the solar system, while Kant's revolution, which occurred in a contrary sense, explains the possibility of necessary knowledge by basing it on the very structure of the human mind, not as a function of something external to mind.

Guided by the principle that all necessary synthetic knowledge is derived from the structure of the mind, Kant attempts to analyze those elements in our knowledge which are derived from the structure of the mind. This he terms a *transcendental* investigation. Systematically he analyzes three different faculties of knowledge:

1. *Intuition* (*Anschauung*). Here he seeks the neces-

sary conditions of perception, or what Kant calls *esthetic*. This part of the investigation is known as the *transcendental esthetic*.

2. *Understanding*. Here he seeks the necessary conditions for conceptual knowledge. This part, which corresponds to the "analytics" of Aristotle, he calls the *transcendental analytic*.

3. *Metaphysical reasoning*. Here he seeks to determine the influence of reason when it goes beyond the normal limits of its application. This part constitutes the *transcendental dialectic*.

II. THE TRANSCENDENTAL ESTHETIC

In the transcendental esthetic Kant seeks the necessary components of our faculty of representation.

Are there any necessary elements in sensation? Are there any elements present in all sensation which might rightfully be regarded as *a priori*?

Kant asserts that everything we perceive by the senses must be located in space, and that everything we perceive with our internal sense is located in time. We can imagine empty space, but we cannot imagine an object which is not in space. We might even imagine empty time (that problem had been discussed since Aristotle's time), but for Kant all change must be located in time.

In his discussion of the properties of what he calls "space" and "time," Kant rests upon Euclidean geometry, in which he believes are to be found the *a priori* properties of space. Time he likens to a dimension of space, the only difference being that time is irreversible in its passage from the past to the future.

Space and time for Kant are not concepts, for concepts are formed only by our understanding; here we are operating on the level of perception, whose structure is not supplied by the intellect.

On the other hand, space and time cannot be provided by sensation. Kant shows that they are infinite, and we could have no perception of infinite time and space.

We get the idea of color from perceiving colors (blue, green, red), and each of these perceptions is richer than the idea of color. From the various particular colors we have framed by abstraction an idea which contains their common characteristics. But the same thing is not true of time and space. We do not derive the idea of space by abstraction from perceiving several different spaces. Each perception of a space presupposes space itself.

Space and time, then, are not concepts; they are *a priori* forms of intuition (perception); they are formal elements of experience.

In sensory knowledge it is experience which provides the matter from the external world, while the form is supplied by the structure of our faculty of perception.

Henri Bergson (1859–1941) has undertaken to criticize Kant's conception of time, as being an irreversible dimension of space.

The fact is, says Bergson, that the data furnished by the external sense and the data furnished by the internal sense are different. The spatial elements are regarded as homogeneous, and for that reason we can apply measure and calculation to them. But is this true with the internal sense?

In physics, when time is measured, what is really being measured is space—the space covered by the hands of a watch or by the orbit of a planet. Measurement of time cannot be made except through the measurement of certain spaces passed through in a supposedly uniform motion.

But when we think of the time that is actually lived, psychological time, we see that these elements are not homogeneous at all. Thus a very short time lived intensely may seem very long in retrospect, while a long period during which nothing happens may seem very short.

Bergson thus distinguishes:

1. Physical time.
2. Psychological time—time as it is lived, real time, duration (*la durée*).

As an outcome of Bergson's work, the psychologist Minkowski has written an important book, *Le Temps Vécu.*

At the level of perception we do not really have knowledge, for knowledge requires concepts. To give shape to our percepts we need understanding. As Kant put it, "Thoughts without content are empty, percepts without concepts are blind."

Thus, to develop a science, or even to frame communicable knowledge, concepts are required. This leads us to the Transcendental Analytic.

III. THE TRANSCENDENTAL ANALYTIC

In the portion of the *Critique* known as the "Transcendental Analytic" Kant analyzes the structure of our *understanding*, the faculty of framing concepts in terms of which we think about the objects of sensation.

The Transcendental Analytic is divided into two parts:

1. The Analytic of Concepts.
2. The Analytic of Principles.

The Analytic of Concepts

Kant turns to the investigation of those necessary elements on which we depend whenever we engage in conceptual thought.

If there are such elements, they are not only the most general elements of knowledge; they are a condition for all discursive knowledge. They are the categories. (For Aristotle the categories were the most general of all concepts.)

How can these categories, conceived as Kant conceives them, be arrived at?

Since they must supply the structure of the understanding, the categories cannot depend on the content of consciousness. They are purely formal elements of knowledge. But the science in which the *form* of thought is studied is *formal logic*, and it is logic which provides the means of arriving at the categories.

When we think about science today, we think of it as progressive. We regard it as being capable of development, and consequently do not expect it to provide us with final definitive truth. But in Kant's time, so far as logic was concerned, this was not the view. The logic known to Kant was the logic worked out by Aristotle, and for two thousand years it seemed to have undergone no change. Kant believed it to be made up of eternal and immutable truths. It was for this reason that he turned to logic to find eternal categories.

If our thought has a formal structure, that structure must be manifested in the processes of thought, eliminating all content that applies to some particular experience.

Formal logic, at least in its traditional form, classifies judgments from four different points of view:

Quantity
Quality
Relation
Modality.

Under these four heads Aristotle made a systematic analysis of judgments.

1. *Quantity.* From this point of view three kinds of judgment may be distinguished, depending on the quantification of the subject:

    a. *Universal judgments,* in which something is asserted of the whole extension of the subject.

    All A is B (All men are mortal).

    b. *Particular judgments,* in which the subject is taken in part of its extension.

    Some A is B (Some Americans are students).

    c. *Singular judgments,* in which the subject is a proper name, or refers to some specific individual.

    Socrates is a philosopher.

2. *Quality.* Here Aristotle distinguishes between:

    a. *Affirmative judgments,* which assert a predicate of a subject.

    A is B.

    b. *Negative judgments,* which deny a predicate of a subject.

    A is not B.

To these two Kant adds a third:

    c. *Indeterminate judgments,* which are affirmative in their form and negative in their content.

An angel is immortal. (Formally this judgment is affirmative, but it expresses a negative quality: immortal = not mortal.)

Kant probably added this third type of judgment out of a concern for symmetry, for the other divisions are tripartite. But the distinction is difficult to justify from the point of view of formal logic.

3. *Relation.*

a. *Categorical judgments,* which make an assertion independent of any other judgment.

Socrates is a man.

b. *Hypothetical judgments,* which assert a relation between two propositions such that one is a condition for the other.

If it rains, the sidewalks get wet.

c. *Disjunctive judgments,* which assert a relation of coordination, rather than of subordination, between two propositions.

Either it rains or it does not rain.

4. *Modality.* Judgments may be classified in accordance with the value of the copula *to be* in relation to thought in general. In a judgment of the form *A is B,* the copula may express *possibility*, *reality*, or *necessity*.

a. *Problematic judgments,* which express a possible fact.

Mr. X is standing at the present moment. (This is merely a supposition.)

b. *Assertory judgments,* which express a fact.

I am standing now.

c. *Apodictic judgments,* which express not only fact but also necessity.

A straight line is the shortest distance between two points.

The following table summarizes the results obtained from the examination of judgments from these four points of view:

1. *Quantity:*   a. Universal judgments
                  b. Particular judgments
                  c. Singular judgments
2. *Quality:*   a. Affirmative judgments
                  b. Negative judgments
                  c. Indeterminate judgments
3. *Relation:*   a. Categorical judgments
                  b. Hypothetical judgments
                  c. Disjunctive judgments
4. *Modality:*   a. Problematic judgments
                  b. Assertory judgments
                  c. Apodictic judgments

Kant holds that each of these different kinds of judgment is the expression of a category of our understanding:

Universal		Unity
Particular		Plurality
Singular		Totality
Affirmative		Being
Negative	Express	Not-being
Indeterminate	the category of	Limitation
Categorical		Substance
Hypothetical		Causality
Disjunctive		Reciprocity
Problematic		Possibility
Assertory		Reality
Apodictic		Necessity

Thus we arrive at a table of twelve categories; these forms, according to Kant, are necessarily involved whenever we deal with an object of thought. Whatever may be the object of our thought, we can apply these twelve categories to it.

It might be noted that this whole conception is rather close to Plato: the object participates in an idea which in turn participates in a more general idea, and the most general ideas participate in each other.

As an example, let us systematically apply these twelve categories to a chair:

If we have one chair it constitutes a	Unity
But it is made up of parts	Plurality
And it constitutes a whole.	Totality
It has certain properties, and thus participates in the category of	Being
But it lacks certain properties	Not-being
And from that very fact it is limited.	Limitation
It can be regarded as a	Substance
But its being a part of nature is a result of	Causality
And it is both an effect and a cause.	Reciprocity
Certain properties are possible to it	Possibility
But certain properties it actually does have	Reality
And some of these it has necessarily.	Necessity

It should be observed that these categories have a peculiar characteristic which underwent considerable development in the hands of such later philosophers as Fichte (1762–1814) and Hegel (1770–1831). The four groups of categories are made up of threes, in each of which the second member is the antithesis of the first, and the third the synthesis of the first two.

For example, unity is opposed by plurality, and a unity of pluralities constitutes a totality.

The result is that these notions become more intimately related to each other.

The Analytic of Principles

Under this heading Kant studies the different principles which regulate the application of the categories to experience.

To make use of the categories something more is required. There must be a certain conception of reality which makes their application possible.

1. *Quantity—The Axioms of Intuition.*

We cannot apply the categories of quantity without what Kant calls the *Axioms of Intuition,* which tell us that all phenomena have *extensive magnitude;* they are measurable. The representation of the parts makes possible the representation of the whole, in knowing the parts we know the whole.

But measurement can be applied only to a reality which is homogeneous.

2. *Quality—The Anticipations of Perception.*

Every phenomenon which is the object of sensation has an *intensive magnitude,* a degree. Thus there appears to be a distinction between extensive magnitude and intensive magnitude. Though I can imagine a certain magnitude, such as a surface, by juxtaposing the parts, I cannot imagine a great pain by juxtaposing several lesser pains.

Intensive magnitude is of an entirely different order from extensive magnitude. This distinction of Kant's blazed the trail for Bergson's analysis. Bergson showed that psychological phenomena are qualitatively different from each other and that we cannot apply calculation or measure to them.

3. *Relation—The Analogies of Experience.*

The categories of relation are governed by the "analogies of experience." These are three principles which affirm necessary relations among phenomena.

a. *The Principle of Permanence:* Substance persists through all change in phenomena, and its quantity in nature is neither increased nor diminished.

NOTE: This idea of permanence is one we have already met in Thales and the Milesian school. Indeed, the idea runs through the whole history of natural science. It is expressed in terms of what is thought to be unchanging:

Milesians—air, water, the *apeiron.*

Pythagoras—mathematical structures.

Descartes—the quantity of motion.

Leibniz—the quantity of force.

Eighteenth century—Lavoisier's principle of the conservation of matter.

Present—the conservation of energy.

Thus in the history of the natural sciences some principle of permanence has been consistently affirmed. But there has been variation in the concept of just what it is that remains permanent. The principle of permanence is required for the understanding of nature, but the interpretation of that permanence and the character of the unchanging element have varied with experience as the science of physics has evolved.

b. *The Principle of Causality.* All change occurs in accordance with the relation of cause and effect. When change occurs we ascribe it to a cause.

NOTE: The same observations can be made about this principle as were made about the principle of permanence. The various eras in the history of physics had quite different ideas about how change was to be understood.

Aristotle held that any change of place needed an explanation.

For Descartes the principle of inertia made unnecessary any causal explanation of uniform rectilinear motion; any deviation from this, however, had to be accounted for.

These two principles of permanence and change are related; they are complementary to each other. And when science frames a new principle of permanence it alters its concept of change.

c. *The Principle of Reciprocal Action.* All substances, insofar as they are perceived as simultaneous in space, act on each other reciprocally. This explains how we are to understand the principle of causality in the universe.

4. *Modality—The Postulates of Empirical Thought in General.* These postulates enable us to understand what is meant by the possible, the real (actual), and the necessary.

The *possible* is what agrees with the formal conditions of experience.

The *real* (actual) is what agrees with the material conditions (i.e., sensations) of experience.

The *necessary* is that the connection of which with the real (actual) is determined by the universal conditions of experience.

Kant has made it clear that there is a difficulty in applying the pure concepts of the understanding to the empirical intuitions which are so completely dissimilar to them. Indeed, if phenomena are to be thought about, they must be subsumed under categories and thereby deprived of whatever is unique about them. They must be regarded as capable of repetition and as identifiable in the flow of experience—in the heterogeneity of what Bergson was later to call "duration." To make possible the application of the categories to phenomena—i.e., to think about phenomena— it is therefore necessary to grant the existence of an intermediate representation which in Kant's words "is homogeneous with the category, and on the other hand with the appearance, and which makes the application of the former to the latter possible."[1] "This mediating representation," Kant continues, "must be pure, that is, void of all empirical content, and yet at the same time, while it must in one respect be *intellectual,* it must in another be sensible."[2] Such a representation Kant calls the "transcendental schema." In accordance with the various categories this *schema* involves a diversification in time, which is the *a priori* form of intuition.

This double aspect of time, as a condition for intuition and as an intellectual form, is later to be dealt with by Bergson, who distinguishes between duration (*la durée*) and physical time.

IV. THE TRANSCENDENTAL DIALECTIC

The distinction between *analytic* and *dialectic* goes back to Aristotle. In the *Organon* the two volumes entitled "Analytics" deal with necessary knowledge, while the "Topics" deals with "dialectic." Dialectic deals with what is apparently true, what is more or less probable, and what is therefore more or less doubtful.

Dialectic for Kant is the study of knowledge which, worse than merely having the appearance of truth, is downright deceptive. We have a tendency to reason in the absolute, to go beyond the possibilities which are given in

---

[1] *Critique of Pure Reason* (tr. N. K. Smith), p. 181.
[2] *Ibid.*

experience and to draw conclusions from premises which are by no means established.

This, says Kant, is what characterized the metaphysics of his predecessors, and this he had in mind when he entitled one of his works *Prolegomena to any Future Metaphysics*.

In the latter part of the *Critique of Pure Reason*, under the heading "Transcendental Dialectic" Kant undertakes to show that all purely rational reasoning concerning the soul, God, and the universe consists of *paralogisms*. (A paralogism is an argument in which one is led into error by himself, as distinguished from a fallacy, which aims at leading someone else into error.)

Any attempt to apply the three kinds of judgment based on relation (categorical, hypothetical, and disjunctive) and their correlated categories (substance, causality, and reciprocity) beyond the world of phenomena leads to false reasoning.

The kind of metaphysics Kant is criticizing was very characteristic of the eighteenth century. It was believed that through the use of purely rational arguments a way might be found to form a community of men who would share a knowledge of the truth. Voltaire and Rousseau particularly believed it possible to extract from different religious ideas a solid core of truth common to all men, such as the existence of God and the immortality of the soul, fundamentals that had already been philosophically developed by Descartes and Locke. With some justice the eighteenth century has been called the age of "natural religion."

Kant, who was a profoundly religious thinker, criticized this whole idea of a rational religion and theology. In this connection an interesting comparison can be made with Pascal, who exhibited a religious spirit similar to that of Kant, and who likewise ridiculed any rational theology.

1. *The psychological paralogism*

Kant criticizes the rational psychology which holds that every human being possesses a soul which remains the same throughout the course of his life, a soul which underlies his psychic acts and which is not only invariable but simple (without parts) and cannot be decomposed—immortal, therefore, since death is nothing but the decomposition of a whole into its parts.

According to Kant, even though it were true that the soul is a substance, unique and unchanging, we could not therefore deduce its immortality. Indeed we know the soul only as a phenomenon; we do not know the soul in itself. Any phenomenon can be understood only by applying the categories to it. We must therefore be able to apply all the categories of the understanding to the soul. From this we conclude that the soul is caused by something else (causality), that it possesses various faculties, and that consequently we can apply to it not merely certain chosen categories, but all the categories. The only possible psychology is an empirical psychology.

From this it follows that it is a profound mistake to believe that, since certain categories can be applied to the soul, it possesses in itself, independent of our faculty of knowing, all the properties that rational psychology attempts to attribute to it.

2. *The cosmological paralogism (the antinomies)*

Kant now attempts to prove both the affirmative and the negative sides of arguments about the general nature of the universe. His purpose is to show that rational cosmology ends in antinomies—in contradictory assertions. There are four pairs of antinomies, classified according to quantity, quality, relation, and modality.

A. *Antinomies of Quantity*

1. The *thesis* asserts that the world had a beginning in time and is limited in space.

2. The *antithesis* asserts that the world had no beginning in time and has no limits in space; it is infinite as regards both time and space.

Kant now demonstrates each of these propositions by showing the absurdity of its contradictory.

1. *Thesis:* The world had a beginning in time and is limited in space.

To show that the idea that the world had no beginning

in time is contradictory, Kant makes use of Aristotle's reasoning that there is no way of exhausting a real infinity. If the world had no beginning in time, an infinite time would have had to elapse before arriving at the present. This would require the possibility of passing through an infinite time to reach the present, which is impossible. The world could only have existed for a finite time, and thus it must have had a beginning in time.

If the world were unlimited in space it would be necessary to suppose that, beginning at the place where we now actually are, we would be able to pass through an infinite number of coexistent places in the universe. But just as the infinite cannot be realizable in time, so infinite space is impossible, and thus the world is limited in space.

2. *Antithesis:* The world had no beginning in time and is unlimited in space.

As in the preceding case, Kant undertakes to prove the antithesis by showing the absurdity of its contradictory.

The idea of a world which is finite in time and space is contrary to our intuition. Can we imagine an infinite time which would be completely devoid of all reality and which would continue up to the time the universe began? What would this flow of time mean without anything real, and how could the creation of the universe from nothing be conceived?

The situation is the same with respect to a world limited in space; there would be a whole part of space where no reality ever entered.

These are both incomprehensible ideas, and thus we must grant that the world is infinite in time and space.

B. *Antinomies of Quality*

1. The *thesis* asserts that the universe is made up of simple parts and nothing exists save the simple and what is composed of the simple. (This is the atomistic idea of the universe.)

2. The *antithesis* asserts that there is nothing simple in the universe and that everything is composite.

Kant employs the same method of indirect proof as in the preceding case.

1. If everything in the universe were composite, this would mean that the universe was made up of one composite thing in which there are no simple elements. Now everything which is composite can be decomposed, at least in thought. Let us then in thought do away with the composite. What remains? Nothing. The universe would then be created out of nothing, which is impossible.

2. Everything which is real is located in space, and everything in space is divisible, at least in thought. Therefore there can be no simple reality; every real thing in the universe is composite.

C. *Antinomies of Relation*

1. The *thesis* asserts that there is freedom in the universe.

2. The *antithesis* asserts that everything that occurs is determined in accordance with the laws of nature.

1. Kant makes use of Aristotle's well-known proof regarding the first cause. In seeking the cause of an event we pass from one cause to another, and there arises the problem of knowing whether there is a way of proceeding *ad infinitum* or whether there is a way of exhausting an infinite series. Since this is not possible, we must suppose that a given event is preceded by a finite series of events. We must thus grant that there is a first term which is not determined by any other event. This is what we mean by freedom.

2. To grant that there is freedom in the universe amounts to granting a first cause which would be an exception to the principle of causality; there would be causeless changes in nature, spontaneous occurrences. Such an origin is completely irrational.

D. *The Antinomies of Modality*

1. The *thesis* asserts that there is an absolutely necessary being.

2. The *antithesis* asserts that all being is contingent.

1. If we understand by a contingent being one who could have not existed, such a being exists only because its being has been determined by some other being. Is this other being contingent or necessary? If it is contingent, the same argument must be employed. Thus we cannot do

otherwise than grant that the series begins with a necessary being whose existence is determined by its own essence.

2. If we assume a necessary being, everything that results from it must be either necessary or contingent. Now the necessary effect of a necessary cause is itself necessary. Therefore if we have some contingent element in this necessary being, how was the contingent determined without a contingent being? In fact it is impossible to deduce from a necessary being anything which is not necessary.

This problem is comparable to that of introducing the idea of time into eternity; time is correlative with change, while eternity, which is static, is related to what is unchanging.

What are we to think about these antinomies?

To the rational mind the antinomy raises a problem for which it provides no solution. Thinkers who came after Kant sought solutions which would allow them to escape from the antinomies. With this end in view Kant himself suggested the following solution. He distinguished between two classes of antinomies:

1. *The mathematical antinomies.* These are the first two, which deal with the properties of space and time. Here we treat space and time as if they were objective realities, whereas they are really nothing but forms of the intuition and have no existence in the external world. This explains the contradictions into which we are led.

2. *The dynamic antinomies.* These, which deal with the ideas of freedom and necessity, lay the ground for the Kantian solution in the area of religion. Kant was actually a devout Protestant. He needed to provide a place for human freedom and for the existence of God as a necessary being. He had to do this in a manner consistent with his scientific beliefs.

This he achieved by providing a radical distinction between the world of *phenomena* and the world of *things in themselves.* The antitheses deal with the world of phenomena, the world which is the object of science, but this does not mean that the theses cannot be true in the realm of *things in themselves.*

3. *The Theological Paralogism (The Ideal of pure reason)*. The theological paralogism, according to Kant, consisted of those arguments which the eighteenth century regarded as rational proofs of the existence and nature of God; but in reality they present only the Ideal of pure reason.

Kant made a savage attack, recalling that of Pascal, on rational theology. Both men criticized the attempts of the rationalists to prove the existence of God, and they both showed that faith could be supported only on grounds which were purely ethical.

Kant shows that the various rationalist arguments for the existence of God are all inadequate. He distinguishes three principal arguments: (1) The *teleological argument,* based on the harmony of the universe, on final causes; (2) the *cosmological argument,* based on efficient causality; and (3) the *ontological argument.*

He undertakes to show that each of the first two of these arguments depends on the argument that follows it.

1. The *teleological argument* asserts that the harmony of the universe cannot be understood without the existence of a creator of that harmony.

Kant's objection is that the creator of a universal order might be an architect without necessarily being the creator of matter. Further, if God be compared to an architect, His perfection must be proportional to the harmony of the edifice He has designed. That harmony is not perfect, thus the designer must be imperfect.

Thus we move from the nature of the universe to God as the cause of the universe—to the cosmological argument.

2. The *cosmological argument* is Aristotle's old argument that there must be a first cause for every event and that first cause is God.

But this idea of a first cause who is also a necessary being forms part of the fourth antinomy, whose thesis asserts the existence of a necessary being. We have already seen that the antithesis can be perfectly proved.

Kant calls attention to the fact that in order to establish that this necessary being is God, it must also be proved that it is perfect. Otherwise we might have proved the existence of some primitive atom, for example, without having proved the existence of a perfect being. It must be proved that necessity and perfection belong to the same being. Suppose the order of the terms be changed: the perfect being is a necessary being. In that case we have the ontological argument, which seeks to deduce necessity from perfection.

3. The *ontological argument*. This argument, employed by St. Anselm, Descartes, and Leibniz, is the keystone of the arch.

We hold that God is a perfect being; we cannot conceive a perfect being without granting that he necessarily exists; for if he did not exist, he would not be perfect, and we would have fallen into a contradiction.

Against this argument Kant raises three objections:

1. *First objection:* In order to deduce the existence of God from His perfection, it must be established that existence is a perfection. But can pure existence be regarded as an independent property? Existence cannot be regarded as a property in itself. It is always attached to the properties of what is. Thus, I can minutely describe a hundred dollars, but if they lack existence they are of no use in paying my debts. There is a clear separation between essence and existence. Essence does not include existence, and therefore existence cannot be deduced from it.

Let us note that the supporters of the ontological argument could reply that in the case of God, who is a perfect being, essence and existence do coincide.

2. *Second objection:* In order to reason about a concept one must first prove that it is not contradictory. To prove that it is not contradictory one must exhibit an example of the concept. To prove that the concept of God is not contradictory it would be necessary to exhibit a being which possessed all the properties attributed to Him. Therefore God's existence cannot be proved without actually pointing Him out.

3. *Third objection:* This is the fundamental objection; it is purely logical in character.

The ontological argument begins with a definition: God is a perfect being. Therefore if the name *God* is to be applied to any being, the property of perfection must be predicated of that being. In other words:

If *x* is God, *x* is a perfect being.

But if *x* is a perfect being, *x* necessarily exists.

From these two syllogistic premises the conclusion may be drawn:

If *x* is God, *x* necessarily exists.

In order, however, to assert the conclusion categorically it must be established that *x* is God; thus it must be proved in some other way that God exists. (St. Thomas did not accept the ontological argument.)

From the point of view of religion and ethics the outcome of the *Critique of Pure Reason* is negative. It proves that the fundamental dogmas of religion are all indemonstrable by means of pure reason and logic alone.

Critique of Practical Reason

In the *Critique of Practical Reason* Kant is primarily concerned with understanding and explaining the problem of moral good.

How is the good to be defined?

Kant disagrees with the ancient Greek notion that the good is to be identified with some end, such as happiness, health, riches. These different ends may be used either morally or immorally, since we can gain them independently of morality. Indeed, says Kant, we cannot define morality in terms of an end to be attained, since in this world there is no necessary connection between morality and an end.

The quality of a moral act must be affirmed independently of the end to be attained. *An act is moral when it is determined by a good will.*

Kant thus takes his stand in the age-long debate between two positions:

1. Morality depends on the moral agent (the intent).
2. Morality depends on the act (utility).

Kant's view is linked with the Lutheran position, which gives primacy to faith, not to works.

When can it be said that a will is good? Kant replies: When it is a will to act in accordance with duty.

But mere conformity to duty is not enough, for many useful and pleasurable acts can be in accord with duty. What is necessary is that the act be willed for duty's sake; that is, that it cannot be explained by any other motives such as pity or compassion.

For Kant an act is performed for duty's sake when it is performed out of respect for the moral law.

But what is the nature of this moral law?

Here Kant is faced with a problem. We know that historically there have been different moral laws and that they have evolved in such a way that any definition of moral law in terms of its content would have no universal validity.

Kant's answer is that the principle or maxim which serves as a rule of action is a moral law when we can give it the status of a universal law, valid for all men.

It is our conscience which defines the content of the moral law, but it is reason which makes it possible to define its form.

A moral act is an act which obeys the categorical imperative: "So act that the maxim of your will could always hold at the same time as the principle of a universal legislation."[3]

This rule is purely formal. It does not tell one how to act; it merely specifies the form. On the other hand, it is universally valid. This double character shows its rational origin; it is not derived from experience. The categorical imperative is an example of reason at work in the area of the practical.

The categorical imperative is an obligatory imperative. It imposes duties which can either be respected or denied. It is correlative with human freedom.

Freedom can be understood only in relation to an obliga-

---

[3] *Critique of Practical Reason* (tr. Lewis White Beck), Book I, ch. i, §7.

tory moral law, an imperative which it is possible to obey or disobey. Such a law is not to be confused with the necessary laws of nature, which are independent of the will.

This possibility of choosing between obedience and disobedience carries with it moral responsibility on the part of those to whom the imperative is addressed. Men are free and responsible.

The categorical imperative is not simply an imperative; it is also categorical. As such it is to be distinguished from hypothetical imperatives and hypothetical laws (If you wish to attain such-and-such an end, you must act in such-and-such a way). With hypothetical laws the command depends on the result desired. The value of a moral act, on the other hand, does not depend on the end to be attained.

This is why Kantian ethics is called an *ethics of duty* as opposed to an ethics of utility.

A moral being deserves to be happy, but he is not necessarily happy because he is moral. We are all familiar with instances where there is no correlation between virtue and happiness. Life on this earth gives no guarantee of such a correlation.

Our sense of justice leads us to hope for the achievement of the highest good, the identity of morality and happiness. That is why we must believe in the immortality of the soul and in the existence of a Being who will bring about the identity of morality and happiness; we must believe in a just God.

Belief in the immortality of the soul and in the existence of God is thus based on our wish to achieve the highest good.

A Critique of the Philosophy of Kant

The philosophy of the nineteenth century cannot be understood apart from Kant's philosophy. What we see after Kant among the various philosophers is an attempt to deepen, to criticize, or to modify the principles of the Kantian philosophy.

Post-Kantian philosophy deals principally with three basic problems:

1. Kant's concept of things-in-themselves.
2. His concept of the structure of human thought.
3. The relation between human thought and the reality which it has to understand and explain.

1. Kant adopts a point of view which is difficult to understand: He insists that things-in-themselves are unknowable, and yet he makes them the basis of his ethics and his religious philosophy.

On the other hand, he asserts their existence. His principal argument is the fact that since we know phenomena and perceive appearances, it would be impossible to do so without there being something that appears, a cause which produces them.

Two contemporaries of Kant, F. H. Jacobi (1743–1819) and Salomon Maimon (1754–1800), criticized these views.

Jacobi argued: "To affirm the existence of things-in-themselves you start from phenomena and you seek their cause. Can you reason in this way? You apply the principle of causality to the relation between phenomena and their supposed cause. But have you any right to apply this principle which binds phenomena to things-in-themselves, which lie beyond the world of phenomena? Don't you really go beyond the domain in which the principle of causality is applicable?"

This criticism was supplemented by Maimon. The things-in-themselves, he argued, which you call the "matter of knowledge," are really intellectual constructs made in order to explain the possibility of knowledge. To these things-in-themselves you ascribe what you do not put into the form of knowledge. Instead of being prior to knowledge, they are constructs of the mind, intended to make your system coherent.

If we hold that the matter of knowledge is a construct of our mind, the equilibrium which Kant sought between the contributions of experience and the contributions of the mind is destroyed. The mind is the master of the field of battle.

If we adopt this point of view, we take leave of criticism and land in a quite different doctrine—*speculative idealism* (distinguished from the realistic idealism of Plato). Speculative idealism was preached by the three great post-Kantian philosophers, Fichte, Schelling, and Hegel.

To the degree that we tip the balance of the scales toward reason, reason will make use of the dialectical laws of the development of thought and undertake to reconstruct our whole conception of the universe. It will tend to pay scant attention to experience.

Thus it was that Schelling and Hegel attempted to construct a philosophy of nature, an enterprise perfectly understandable in pre-Socratic times, but rather ridiculous in the nineteenth century.

We witness therefore the development of Hegel's huge system of natural philosophy, a philosophy which had to compete with science. It was in reaction to this sort of thing that the scientific world came to feel a kind of disgust with metaphysics, a disgust which was expressed by Auguste Comte, the father of *positivism*.

2. The second criticism arises out of a development within the mathematical sciences. It deals with Kant's doctrine concerning the structure of the mind.

Kant based his doctrine on certain presuppositions which were accepted in the mathematics and logic of his own day. These he regarded as necessary.

Thus, when he argued that space is a pure form of intuition, he gave it the properties described in Euclidean geometry.

One of the fundamental postulates of Euclidean geometry is that through a point outside a given straight line one and only one line may be drawn parallel to the given line. Since the time of Euclid unsuccessful attempts had been made to demonstrate this postulate as a theorem. In 1826 the Russian mathematician N. I. Lobachevski (1792–1856) worked out an ingenious method for proving the postulate. If Euclid's postulate is true, it must be possible to establish it by a *reductio ad absurdum,* an indirect proof, by showing that the assumption of its falsity leads to a contradiction. "Through a point outside a given line," he assumed, "an infinite number of lines may be drawn parallel to the given line: these are included within two limiting parallels which form the angle *a,* known as the parameter of the system."

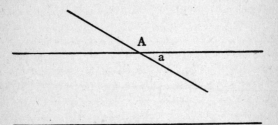

Constructing a new geometry based on this postulate, Lobachevski reported that, to his own astonishment and contrary to his expectation, he had not found any contradiction. To be sure, the theorems he arrived at in his geometry were quite different from those of Euclid, but his system was nonetheless a consistent and coherent one. For example, in place of the Euclidean theorem that the sum of the interior angles of a triangle is equal to two right angles, he found that the sum was less than two right angles.

In 1854 the German mathematician G. F. B. Riemann (1826–1866) chose a different postulate: through a point outside a given straight line no line may be drawn parallel to the given line. On this basis he, too, was able to develop a perfectly coherent non-Euclidean geometry. This time, for example, the sum of the interior angles of a triangle was found to be greater than two right angles.

The first conclusion that can be drawn is that once there have been developed several systems of geometry, it is no longer possible to say simply that geometry is applicable to the world of physical phenomena.

When, for example, it is said that light travels in a straight line, is this straight line a straight line in Euclidean geometry or in some other geometry? Something else than purely rational concepts is needed in order to describe natural phenomena. Pure geometry is one thing; the geometry of physics is another.

For Descartes pure geometry and the geometry of physics were the same thing. But this is no longer the case. There must be a separation between purely rational systems and the description of the physical world which they make possible.

Several rational systems are available, not all of which are suited to describing the physical world. There exists no rational principle which would make it possible to say that this system of geometry rather than that really applies to the world. Each of the three systems we have mentioned is a completely coherent system. The French mathematician Henri Poincaré (1854–1912) even showed that if there were a contradiction in Riemann's geometry there would also be one in the geometry of Euclid.

One of the greatest mathematicians of the nineteenth century, Carl Friedrich Gauss (1777–1855), sought to determine experimentally which geometry must be applied to phenomena. He selected three mountaintops on which he placed goniometers. From each of the three summits he took bearings and thus measured the three angles of the triangle formed by the mountaintops. He then found the sum of the three angles. However, the conclusion was in-

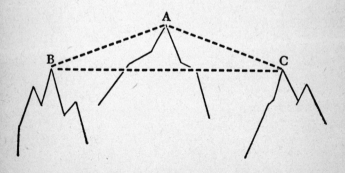

decisive. The errors inherent in all physical measurement were such that it was possible to interpret the results as being compatible with all three geometric systems. (In the universe described by Einstein's theory of relativity space is Riemannian.)

From the moment that it is possible to work out several coherent systems of geometry, the whole Kantian account of geometric space falls apart. It is no longer possible to view geometry as the result of the structure of the mind.

Moreover, these findings require a modification of the idea of truth. A true proposition, it was formerly held, is a proposition which agrees with reality. Now we find ourselves faced with three systems of geometry, each as coherent and rational as the others, without being able to say which corresponds to reality. It appears from this that truth must be understood as coherence within a given system. Under these conditions can it be imagined that a proposition is true in itself? Truth is no longer a property of isolated propositions, but is correlated with the system of which the propositions form a part.

From this it also follows that the idea of *a priori* truth acquires a new character.

On the other hand, since truth and reality do not necessarily correspond, there is no longer any need to invoke the divine mind to explain such correspondence or to talk about reason as imposing its structure on the real.

3. The third criticism deals with the relations between reason and nature, between thought and reality.

Both the rationalists and the empiricists had found solutions to this problem, solutions which were radically opposed but which were capable of compromise.

For the rationalist the laws of nature are nothing but the laws of reason: they are laws of the divine reason which correspond to our innate, self-evident ideas.

For the empiricists our mental concepts are a tracing of the structure of nature, and it is experience which determines the categories.

With Kant there is no sharply defined primacy either of reason or of nature; there is a kind of equilibrium between the two factors. One of them (nature) provides the matter of knowledge; the other (reason) provides the form.

But what can be the relation between these two elements? How can matter and the form supplied by our understanding work together? If they are completely independent factors how can they be related? And if they are not independent, how can the limits of their independence be determined?

Toward the end of the nineteenth and the beginning of the twentieth century it began to be wondered whether the categories of the mind might not be influenced by experience. Could not the relation of matter and form be understood analogously to the relation between the water and the bed of a river? Though it is true that the shape of the river bed determines the shape of the water, the action of the water modifies the bed of the river. If reason imposes its structure on experience, does not experience likewise modify the categories of reason?

About the middle of the nineteenth century the English scientist and philosopher William Whewell (1794–1866) did some interesting work on the historical evolution of the inductive sciences. He showed how ideas and facts had a reciprocal influence on each other.

At the end of the nineteenth century and the beginning of the twentieth it was the principal task of the historians of science to study the correlation between scientific categories and the phenomena they dealt with. Among the most important thinkers who investigated this problem were Federigo Enriques (1871–1946), Leon Brunschvicg (1869–1944), and Gaston Bachelard (1884–1962).

The same problem was also explored by a pupil of Brunschvicg, Jean Piaget (1896–   ), in the realm of genetic psychology. He studied the manner in which the categories of thought develop from infancy to adolescence.

One group of scientists and philosophers associated with the journal *Dialectica*, edited by Professor Ferdinand Gonseth of Zürich, took up the same problem in the evolution of contemporary science.

Instead of the idea of an eternal and unchanging reason

we find the idea of a reason modified by experience, by historical and social conditions. The concrete problem of the theory of knowledge is to study the means which make it possible to describe and explain phenomena and to determine the influence which the objects of our knowledge exercise on the processes that make knowledge possible.

BIBLIOGRAPHY

GENERAL HISTORIES OF PHILOSOPHY

Copleston, Frederick, *A History of Philosophy* (7 vols. published to date), London, Burns Oates & Washburn, 1946– . Vols. 1–5 also available in Doubleday Image Books.

Fuller, B. A. G., *A History of Philosophy* (3d ed., rev. S. A. McMurrin), New York, Holt, Rinehart & Winston, 1955.

Gilson, Étienne (gen. ed.), *A History of Philosophy* (4 vols.), New York, Random House, 1962– .

  Vol. 1. Anton Pegis, *Ancient Philosophy* (to be published)
  Vol. 2. A. A. Maurer, *Medieval Philosophy* (1962)
  Vol. 3. E. Gilson and T. Langan, *Modern Philosophy* (1963)
  Vol. 4. E. Gilson, T. Langan, and A. A. Maurer, *Recent Philosophy* (1965)

O'Connor, D. J. (ed.), *Critical History of Western Philosophy*, New York, The Free Press of Glencoe, 1964.

Russell, Bertrand, *A History of Western Philosophy*, New York, Simon & Schuster, 1945.

Windelband, Wilhelm, *A History of Philosophy*, tr. by James H. Tufts, New York, The Macmillan Co., 1901. Also available in Harper Torchbooks.

ANCIENT PHILOSOPHY

General Works

Cornford, F. M., *Before and After Socrates*, Cambridge, Eng., University Press, 1932. Also available in Cambridge paperback.

Guthrie, W. K. C., *A History of Greek Philosophy* (5 vols.),
    Cambridge, Eng., University Press, 1962–   .
Jaeger, Werner, *Paideia: The Ideals of Greek Culture*, tr. by
    Gilbert Highet (2nd ed., 3 vols.), New York, Oxford
    University Press, 1945.
Robin, Leon, *Greek Thought*, tr. by M. R. Dobie, London,
    Kegan Paul, Trench, Trubner & Co., 1928.

Greek Philosophy Before Plato

Burnet, John, *Early Greek Philosophy* (4th ed.), London, Adam
    & Charles Black, 1930.
Kirk, G. S. and J. E. Raven, *The Presocratic Philosophers*, Cam-
    bridge, Eng., University Press, 1957.
Taylor, A. E., *Socrates*, London, P. Davies, 1933.

Plato

The Dialogues of Plato, tr. by Benjamin Jowett (2 vols.), New
    York, Random House, 1937.
The Collected Dialogues of Plato, ed. by Edith Hamilton and
    Huntington Cairns, New York, Pantheon Books, 1961.
Friedlander, Paul, *Plato: An Introduction*, tr. by Hans Meyer-
    hoff, New York, Pantheon Books, 1958. Also available
    in Harper Torchbooks.
Gould, John, *The Development of Plato's Ethics*, Cambridge,
    Eng., University Press, 1955.
Ross, Sir David, *Plato's Theory of Ideas*, Oxford, Clarendon
    Press, 1953.
Taylor, A. E., *Plato: The Man and His Work* (6th ed.), London,
    Methuen & Co., 1949. Also available in Meridian Books.

Aristotle

The Works of Aristotle, tr. under the editorship of W. D. Ross
    (12 vols.), London, Oxford University Press, 1908–1952.
The Basic Works of Aristotle, ed. with an introduction by Richard
    McKeon, New York, Random House, 1941.
Jaeger, Werner, *Aristotle, Fundamentals of the History of His
    Development*, tr. by Richard Robinson (2nd ed.), Ox-
    ford, Clarendon Press, 1948.
Randall, John Herman, *Aristotle*, New York, Columbia Univer-
    sity Press, 1960.
Ross, W. D., *Aristotle* (2nd ed.), London, Methuen & Co., 1930.
    Also available in Meridian Books.

The Stoics, Epicureans, and Skeptics

Bailey, Cyril, *The Greek Atomists and Epicurus,* Oxford, Clarendon Press, 1928.

Bevan, Edwyn, *Stoics and Sceptics,* Oxford, Clarendon Press,
1913.

Neoplatonism

Plotinus, *The Enneads,* tr. by Stephen McKenna (3rd ed.), New
York, Pantheon Books, 1958.

Bréhier, Émile, *The Philosophy of Plotinus,* tr. by Joseph Thomas,
Chicago, University of Chicago Press, 1958.

Inge, W. R., *The Philosophy of Plotinus* (3rd ed.), London,
Longmans, Green & Co., 1929.

PATRISTIC AND MEDIEVAL PHILOSOPHY

General Works

*Medieval Philosophy: Selected Readings from Augustine to
Buridan,* ed. by Herman Shapiro, New York, The Modern
Library, 1964.

Selections from Medieval Philosophers, ed. by Richard McKeon
(2 vols.), New York, Charles Scribner's Sons, 1929.

Copleston, Frederick C., *Medieval Philosophy,* London, Methuen
& Co., 1952. Also available in Harper Torchbooks.

Gilson, Étienne, *History of Christian Philosophy in the Middle
Ages,* New York, Random House, 1955.

Leff, Gordon, *Medieval Thought: St. Augustine to Ockham,*
Harmondsworth, Penguin Books, 1958.

St. Augustine

The Confessions of St. Augustine, tr. by E. B. Pusey, New York,
E. P. Dutton and Co., 1951.

The City of God, tr. by Marcus Dods, New York, The Modern
Library, 1950.

St. Thomas Aquinas

Basic Writings of Saint Thomas Aquinas, ed. by Anton C. Pegis
(2 vols.), New York, Random House, 1945.

On the Truth of the Catholic Faith (*Summa contra Gentiles*),
tr. by Anton C. Pegis (5 vols.), Garden City, N.Y.,
Doubleday Image Books, 1955.

Copleston, F. C., *Aquinas,* Harmondsworth, Penguin Books, 1955.

Maritain, Jacques, *Saint Thomas Aquinas,* tr. by J. F. Scanlan, New York, Sheed & Ward, 1931. Also available in Meridian Books.

MODERN PHILOSOPHY

General Works

Burtt, E. A., *The Metaphysical Foundations of Modern Physical Science,* London, Routledge & Kegan Paul, 1924.

Cassirer, Ernest, *The Philosophy of the Enlightenment,* tr. by F. C. A. Koelln and J. P. Pettegrove, Princeton, Princeton University Press, 1951. Also available in Beacon Paperback.

Høffding, Harald, *A History of Modern Philosophy,* tr. by B. E. Meyer (2 vols.), New York, The Macmillan Co., 1900. Also available in Dover Books.

Wright, W. K., *A History of Modern Philosophy,* New York, The Macmillan Co., 1941.

Descartes

The Philosophical Works of Descartes, tr. by E. S. Haldane and G. R. T. Ross (2 vols.), Cambridge, Eng., University Press, 1911. Also available in Dover Books.

Philosophical Writings, ed. by Norman Kemp Smith, New York, The Modern Library, 1958.

Discourse on Method and *Meditations,* tr. by Laurence J. Lafleur, Indianapolis, The Bobbs-Merrill Company, 1960.

Gibson, A. Boyce, *The Philosophy of Descartes,* London, Methuen & Co., 1932.

Kemp Smith, Norman, *New Studies in the Philosophy of Descartes,* London, Macmillan & Co., 1952.

Spinoza

The Chief Works of Benedict de Spinoza, tr. by R. H. M. Elwes (2 vols.), London, George Bell & Sons, 1883. Also available in Dover Books.

Earlier Philosophical Writings, tr. by Frank A. Hayes, Indianapolis, The Bobbs-Merrill Co., 1963.

Hampshire, Stuart, *Spinoza,* Harmondsworth, Penguin Books, 1951.

Wolfson, Harry Austryn, *The Philosophy of Spinoza* (2 vols.), Cambridge, Harvard University Press, 1934. Also available in Meridian Books.

Leibniz

Philosophical Papers and Letters, ed. by Leroy E. Loemker (2 vols.), Chicago, University of Chicago Press, 1956.

Philosophical Writings, tr. by Mary Morris, New York, E. P. Dutton & Co., 1934.

The Monadology and Other Philosophical Writings, tr. by Robert Latta, London, Oxford University Press, 1898.

New Essays concerning Human Understanding, tr. by A. G. Langley (3rd ed.), La Salle, Ill., Open Court Publishing Co., 1949.

Russell, Bertrand, *A Critical Exposition of the Philosophy of Leibniz,* London, George Allen & Unwin, 1900.

Saw, Ruth Lydia, *Leibniz,* Harmondsworth, Penguin Books, 1954.

Locke

An Essay concerning Human Understanding, ed. by John W. Yolton (2 vols.), New York, E. P. Dutton & Co., 1961.

Two Treatises of Government, ed. by Thomas I. Cook, New York, Hafner Publishing Co., 1947.

Aaron, R. I., *John Locke,* London, Oxford University Press, 1937.

Morris, C. R., *Locke, Berkeley, Hume,* Oxford, Clarendon Press, 1931.

Berkeley

A Treatise concerning the Principles of Human Knowledge, ed. by Colin M. Turbayne, Indianapolis, The Bobbs-Merrill Co., 1957.

Three Dialogues between Hylas and Philonous, ed. by Colin M. Turbayne, Indianapolis, The Bobbs-Merrill Co., 1954.

Works on Vision, ed. by Colin M. Turbayne, Indianapolis, The Bobbs-Merrill Co., 1963.

Warnock, G. J., *Berkeley,* Harmondsworth, Penguin Books, 1953.

Hume

The Philosophy of David Hume, ed. by V. C. Chappell, New York, The Modern Library, 1963.

A Treatise of Human Nature, ed. by L. A. Selby-Bigge, Oxford, Clarendon Press, 1888.

An Inquiry concerning Human Understanding, ed. by Charles W. Hendel, Indianapolis, The Bobbs-Merrill Co., 1955.

An Inquiry concerning the Principles of Morals, ed. by Charles W. Hendel, Indianapolis, The Bobbs-Merrill Co., 1957.

Dialogues concerning Natural Religion, ed. by Norman Kemp Smith (2nd ed.), London, Thomas Nelson and Sons, 1947. Also available in Library of Liberal Arts.

Kemp Smith, Norman, *The Philosophy of David Hume*, London, Macmillan & Co., 1941.

Passmore, J. A., *Hume's Intentions*, Cambridge, University Press, 1952.

Kant

The Philosophy of Kant, ed. by Carl J. Friedrich, New York, The Modern Library, 1949.

Critique of Pure Reason, tr. by Norman Kemp Smith, New York, The Macmillan Co., 1929.

Critique of Practical Reason and Other Writings in Moral Philosophy, tr. by Lewis White Beck, Chicago, University of Chicago Press, 1949.

Critique of Judgment, tr. by J. H. Bernard, London, Macmillan & Co., 1892. Also available in Hafner Library of Classics.

Prolegomena to Any Future Metaphysics, tr. by Lewis White Beck, Indianapolis, The Bobbs-Merrill Co., 1950.

Foundations of the Metaphysics of Morals, tr. by Lewis White Beck, Indianapolis, The Bobbs-Merrill Co., 1959.

Beck, Lewis White, *A Commentary on Kant's Critique of Practical Reason*, Chicago, University of Chicago Press, 1960. Also available in Phoenix Books.

Kemp Smith, Norman, *A Commentary to Kant's Critique of Pure Reason* (2nd ed.), New York, The Macmillan Co., 1923.

Körner, S., *Kant*, Harmondsworth, Penguin Books, 1955.

Paton, H. J., *Kant's Metaphysic of Experience* (2 vols.), London, George Allen & Unwin, 1936.

de Vleeschauwer, Herman J., *The Development of Kantian Thought*, tr. by A. R. C. Duncan, London, Thomas Nelson and Sons, 1962.

Wolff, Robert Paul, *Kant's Theory of Mental Activity*, Cambridge, Harvard University Press, 1963.

INDEX

STUDIES IN PHILOSOPHY

ISLAND INTRIGUE

ISLAND INTRIGUE

WENDY HOWELL MILLS

W🌐RLDWIDE®

TORONTO • NEW YORK • LONDON
AMSTERDAM • PARIS • SYDNEY • HAMBURG
STOCKHOLM • ATHENS • TOKYO • MILAN
MADRID • WARSAW • BUDAPEST • AUCKLAND

Island Intrigue

A Worldwide Mystery/May 2016

First published by Poisoned Pen Press.

ISBN-13: 978-0-373-26993-8

Printed in U.S.A.

For Zackman

ONE

"IT's DEFINITELY TIME I got out of the cottage," Sabrina Victoria Dunsweeney said to herself as she walked down the sandy street. "I need to meet some of the locals. After all, what in the world am I going to tell my kids when I get back home to Cincinnati? 'Children, I had a wonderful time on Comico Island while you worked on synonyms and antonyms. I stayed in my rental cottage the whole month and talked to the walls!' Granted, the locals haven't been very friendly, but they just haven't gotten the chance to meet the new me yet."

Across the street, loud voices were coming from the post office as Sabrina hurried up the steps of the dilapidated Tubbs General Store. On the wall beside the battered screen door of the store was a chalkboard reading: "Bill and Patty had 7 lb. Boy, named after Uncle Will."

"Hello," Sabrina said to the old grizzled man dressed in a frayed plaid shirt and overalls who was sitting on the front porch of the store. She also smiled at the skinny man holding a paper bag who was sitting on the stairs.

Accompanied by a scream of rage, a paperweight came flying though the screen door of the post office across the street.

"Hello." The man in the rocking chair didn't look at her.

"Yep," said the skinny man.

Sabrina sat down in a rocking chair. The walk from her cottage had worn her out.

"I'm Sabrina Dunsweeney," she said after a moment.

"You're the one staying in Lora's cottage and feeding her cats. Drive a red convertible, don't you?" The old man nodded. He wore white boots stained yellow with age, and sporadic cinnamon-and-sugar hair dotted his cheeks and head, a poor testimony to his once fiery red hair. A twinkle of amused blue peered from under shaggy eyebrows and a large nose dominated the rest of his face.

Sabrina was taken aback. After a minute, she asked, "And you are?"

"Lima."

They sat in silence except for the crinkle of the paper bag as the skinny man took a drink from the bottle inside.

The screeching across the street had reached Cat Fight proportions.

"What's going on?" It was apparent that neither Lima nor the other man was going to say anything about the commotion.

"What do you mean?" Lima asked, as if the noise from the post office wasn't almost deafening.

"That," Sabrina said, as a stapler followed the paperweight into the street.

"Yep."

Sabrina looked at the skinny man more closely. From a distance, in his baseball cap and T-shirt that looked as if it had never seen water, much less soap, she had thought he was a teenager. Now she saw by the lines bunching up around his eyes and mouth and the sterling glint to his otherwise brown, messy hair that he was close to fifty. There was something uncomplicated in his eyes that made her think he probably lived a simple life, one unencumbered by much thought or motivation.

"Oh, that." Lima slowed his rocking. "It's just Mary Garrison Tubbs and her niece, ain't it, Bicycle Bob?"

Bicycle Bob closed his eyes and leaned his cheek against the splintery wood of the stair rail.

"It sounds as if they're killing each other," Sabrina said.

"Nah. Mary just won't let Roxanna alone."

"Why?" Sabrina asked, when it was obvious Lima wasn't going to explain. She ran her fingers through her rambunctious blond curls, still surprised to not find them bound in a tight bun.

"Weeell," Lima said with satisfaction, and Sabrina realized with amusement that he had just been waiting for her to ask. He sat back more firmly in his chair, and prepared to spin his story. "You see, Mary has been running that post office by herself for almost thirty years, but the postal author-i-tees finally made her retire. Her niece Roxanna took the exam so she could be postmistress and at first Mary was thrilled to pieces about Roxanna being postmistress—keeping it in the family, and all that. But now, Mary won't let Roxanna have any peace. She just can't help but go in there and tell Roxanna how things ought to be done, and well—you know the Tubbs, they can be hot-blooded."

A few moments later an older woman in sensible shoes and a very red face came storming out of the post office. She stopped to pick up the paperweight and stapler and tossed them right back through the torn screen of the post office door. She marched toward the store porch.

"Good Lawd," Lima muttered.

"Bob McCall, you should be ashamed of yourself, sitting here getting all tanked up for all and sundry to see. What would your brother say?" She addressed her comments to Bicycle Bob, who had slipped down so he was almost lying on the stairs.

Sabrina realized Bicycle Bob was plastered out of his skull. She should have known, she'd seen her mother like that enough times, but her mother was more of a genteel drunk, sipping her stingers in her fancy silk housecoat in the dusty parlor.

"His brother's the police chief," Lima said to Sabrina, out of the corner of his mouth. "Sergeant Jimmy McCall."

"And you, Lima Odell Lowry, don't you have anything better to do than sit here rocking the porch all day long?"

"Nope."

"You should be out helping your nephew campaign for president. How do you expect Brad to win if his own family won't support him?"

"I helped 'em. I stuck up some of them posters the other day."

"Your nephew is running for president?" Sabrina wondered just how much she had missed in the last week while she sat in her cottage.

"President of the Sanitary Concessionary," Lima said. "It's the most important position on Comico, 'cause he controls where people can build, if he lets 'em build at all, and he can close businesses down if their septic system ain't sustainin' them."

"Goodness," Sabrina said.

"Do I know you, young lady?" Mary Tubbs asked Sabrina, lifting a heavy gray eyebrow in disapproval.

But Sabrina had been a school teacher for many years and was well-versed in eyebrow lifting and look-

ing down her, unfortunately for her purposes, pug nose.
"My name," she said, drawing herself up, "is Sabrina
Victoria Dunsweeney. And you are?"

The woman gazed at her as if she couldn't believe
Sabrina didn't know who she was. "I don't think you're
related to Helen Dunsweeney." She said it with the mat-
ter-of-factness of a person who knows all of her neighbors' lineage intimately.

"No, I don't believe I am."

"Are you from New York or New Jersey?"

"Please?"

"All of you are from New York or New Jersey," Mary
said, and then turned back to Lima, dismissing Sabrina.
"Anyway, Lima, Elizabeth is holding a tea party to raise
money for Bradford. You need to go and contribute."

"I knew about the dang tea party. I'd sooner beat myself with a sack of wet catfish than make a pot of tea.
Why in the world do I want to buy a teapot?"

"To raise money for your nephew! You know how
hectic everything has been since Bradford's office burnt
down. I've got to go supervise the setting up of booths for
the Regatta. If I'm not there, nothing gets done right." She
turned and marched down the street toward the docks.

"She is the bossiest old woman I have ever met," Lima
said. "I'm glad I never married her."

"You were going to marry her?" Sabrina tried to hide
her surprise.

"Everybody thought we were," Lima said, "back when
we were in high school. She was valedictorian of our
class, and I was at the bottom, but we always got along.
Of course, there were only five of us graduated that year,
but never you mind that. But then the war started, and

of course I signed up for the Navy. By the time I came back, she was already married to Justice Tubbs, the flat-footed shirk."

"Well, I think you probably got off lucky," Sabrina said under her breath.

"Yes, ma'am, Ah think you may be right." Sabrina had the awful feeling that Lima was attempting a John Wayne drawl. He subsided back into his normal voice. "So I never got married at all."

"Me either," she agreed cheerfully.

"You on vacation?"

Sabrina considered that. A vacation? That didn't seem the right word to call it.

"I've taken a month off teaching to come here, yes," she answered.

"In October? That seems a right strange time for a school teacher to take a vacation."

Sabrina just smiled.

"Have you seen the ghost yet?"

"The ghost?"

"The one of Walk-the-Plank Wrightly, the pirate who was killed almost three hundred years ago. His house used to be right where you're staying, and people have been seeing him right and left lately."

"No ghosts," Sabrina said. "Though somebody with very large feet is walking on the beach every morning. Maybe it's the ghost!" She was joking, but Lima just nodded.

"Maybe it is."

There was a moment of silence, unbroken except for the crackle-crackle of Bicycle Bob's paper bag.

"Is your nephew really running for president of the Sanitary Concessionary?"

"You not being from around here accounts for your not understanding." Lima gave a little nod of his head as if she had just confirmed his opinion of her lackluster intelligence. "President of the Sanitary Concessionary is the biggest thing you can be on Comico Island. The last president of the Sanitary Concessionary just got elected to the Senate."

"The Comico Senate?"

"No. The State Senate."

"I see." Sabrina thought for a moment. "Who is running against your nephew?"

"Do you hear her, Bicycle? She's asking who would be dumb enough to run against Bradford." He snorted in disgust. "Everybody knows better than to run against a Tittletott. They've been running things around here for as long as I can remember. Own half the land on the island, they do. Doesn't pay to get in their way. Thought things were going to change a while back when Dock Wrightly was president, but everyone knew that wasn't going to last. But you got to get one of those quorum things, even if you are running unopposed. Say not enough people get out and vote, or they all write in 'Mickey Mouse,' and then Brad won't get to be president, and probably he'd never get into the Senate either. So he's got to campaign."

"Hmmm," Sabrina said.

"Bye, Bicycle," Lima said, struggling to his feet and stomping his white boots sharply on the porch floor. He looked at Sabrina. "Are you coming?"

"Please?"

"I figure if I take you to the tea party everybody will get off my back about not staying the whole time," Lima said without looking at her.

"WHAT'S THE NAME of this road?" Sabrina asked as they followed the dirt road toward the mirror shimmer of the harbor. "Street signs seem to be few and far between on this island."

"We took them all down during World War Two. Didn't want to make it easy for the Germans to get around. This is Post Office Road," Lima said. "It runs from the harbor all the way to the ocean. The mail boat used to come every day or so, and the postmaster would be waiting on the dock for him, along with about every other person on the island."

Post Office Road concluded at the ferry docks, which stood stolidly on the edge of the large, natural harbor nestled on the north end of Comico Island. Sabrina paused to enjoy the view, the pale blue sky and water melting into mutual anonymity in the distance, the sun raining down on fishing boats and sailboats. A couple of cars were waiting in front of the ferry dock, and Sabrina glanced at her watch. Eleven-thirty. The twelve o'clock ferry would be here soon.

Along the gentle curve of the harbor, restaurants in ramshackle, paint-lacking buildings leaned over the water and large, island-style cottages with aggressive white trim had been converted into B & B's and motels. One large monstrosity of a building, five stories tall and all brick, towered over every other structure on the harbor front, ruining what otherwise would be a perfect postcard picture of a charming, waterside town.

There was excitement in the air, and people were out along the harbor front, putting up banners and balloons and setting up booths. Mary Garrison Tubbs was very much in evidence as she called out orders through a bullhorn.

"Is this all for the campaign?" Sabrina asked in surprise.

"Nah," Lima said. "It's for the Regatta. Every year a bunch of sailboats stop by here on their way up the coast."

They turned left onto the sand-swept, paved road that circled the harbor, while all around them the people setting up the celebrations for the Regatta waved and called hello to Lima.

"How are you settling into Lora's cottage?" Lima shot Sabrina a speculative glance.

"Lora? I was wondering about the lady who lived there. There are pictures of her and children all over the place. It's very cozy."

"She used to be a school teacher."

"Like me," Sabrina said, realizing why she had felt instantly at home in the little cottage.

"Lora was a good woman," Lima said ruminatively. "How she loved to dance, before her stroke. That happened years ago, but she managed okay until she finally up and fell a couple of months ago and broke her head. She wouldn't hear about going to stay with her daughter-in-law, Nettie. Wouldn't have made a difference anyway, I 'spect. At least she died in her home, where she was happy."

"Hmmm." Sabrina wasn't sure she liked the idea that someone had died in her rental cottage. How creepy. But at least the woman hadn't been murdered or anything.

"Where are we going?" she asked, to change the subject.

"Tittletott House." Lima gestured at a large, insipid, blue house with white shutters and the inevitable white verandah. "Brad's a Tittletott. Mrs. Elizabeth, Brad's mother, runs it."

"It's a hotel?" Sabrina looked up at the large house.

"One of those bread and breakfast places."

"Bread and breakfast?"

"Yeah, they serve a lot of toast with breakfast," Lima said knowledgeably. "Anyway, the Tittletotts have owned this island since the 1700's, and they've never let any of us forget it. 'Specially Elizabeth Tittletott, that old biddy. When old CQ Tittletott died, we thought things might change but he passed everything on to Brad, and he's a Tittletott through and through."

"Lima!" An older gent in the ubiquitous white boots grabbed Lima by the arm. He immediately launched into a long-winded description of the length, width, and stamina of the fish he'd caught that day. Sabrina thought he had perhaps caught a whale by mistake.

"That ol' fish was slicker'n eel snot, let me tell you—"

Sabrina turned and looked up at the big house. The yard was a lush carpet of green, impeccably landscaped, and the sweet smell of roses lured her around to the side of the house where an impressive variety of the species grew in abundance.

"How beautiful!" she said, and stooped to press her face against a glistening silvery-pink bloom. Voices from the open window above her caught her attention.

"What's he doing back in town?" It was a man's voice, whiny and frustrated.

"Keep your voice down," a woman hissed in a cultured southern accent as thick as honey-butter. "Do you want the whole town to know? My God, why can't you be more like your brother?"

Sabrina glanced up at the window, but she couldn't see who was talking.

"What is he doing back in town?" the man repeated in a lower voice.

"How should I know? Bradford said he contacted him a couple of days ago and started talking about what happened. Bradford said he was almost *threatening* him." The woman's voice dropped.

"Why should my dear brother worry? He's got nothing to fret about, does he?"

"But it's almost election day! Who knows what he'll say? Those Wrightlys will do anything to get at us, you know that!"

There was a long silence.

"Gary, are you listening to me? We don't have much time, I need to get back to the party."

"Yes, Mother." His voice was weary.

"If he should approach you, don't say anything. Don't tell him anything that he can use against your brother, do you hear me?"

"Yes. I hear you."

"He's dangerous. He could ruin all of us!"

TWO

"SABRINA!" LIMA CALLED, and she started guiltily. Above her there was an abrupt silence and then a door slammed.

"Right here!" She hurried back around to the front of the house.

"Where did you go? Never mind, let's go in," Lima said, stomping up the stairs to the front porch of the house.

The door opened, and a large woman of about sixty in a peacock silk dress and an elaborate beehive hairdo stood in the doorway.

"Lima Lowry, I declare," she said, with a coquettish flutter of her mascara-encrusted lashes. Her voice had a distinctive southern strum, a drawling lilt that Sabrina recognized. Sabrina studied her with interest, wondering who the woman was, and why she had sounded so angry just moments before.

"Elizabeth, darling," Lowry said in a courtly voice, bending at his waist and kissing the hand that Elizabeth proffered. Two people squeezed out of the door from behind her, and with expressions of profound relief they hurried down the driveway. Both clutched strange multicolored sculptures in their hands—after a second look, Sabrina decided that the neon sculptures were most likely the famous teapots.

"Lima, Lima," Elizabeth said in a flirtatious voice, "where did we go wrong?"

"Elizabeth, two shining stars like ourselves are not meant to marry. Our neighbors would have had to wear sunglasses," Lima said grandly.

Elizabeth deigned to glance at Sabrina with eyes which were face-lifted into a permanently aghast expression. "And who, may I ask, is this?"

"Sabrina Dunsweeney," she said in a friendly voice.

"Aaaall right." Elizabeth sighed, as if she was a maitre d' just barely allowing a marginal customer into the building. She opened the door wide and Sabrina followed Lima into the house.

The large front living area had been converted into a lobby, decorated in casual, artfully stressed wicker and bright cushions. A rainbow array of fresh roses crowded every available surface. Displayed on the walls were campaign posters showing a handsome young man, and many of the people milling around the room sported buttons that read "Brad's the Lad for President!"

"Don't mind Elizabeth, she's like that with everybody. Went to school on the mainland and came back with some exaggerated ideas about her own importance in the grand scheme of things, if you know what I mean." Lima winked at Sabrina and then made a beeline for a little girl in a fancy pink dress carrying a tray of what could only be scones.

Sabrina went over to look at the teapots which were arranged on long tables. She never knew teapots came in such shapes and sizes. Silver pots, bronze pots, cast iron pots, ceramic pots, clay pots, pots big enough to serve a family of forty-six, miniature teapots suitable for Barbie and her pals, pots in fanciful shapes painted crazy neon colors, pots shaped like farm animals…many, many pots.

Around her, several conversations were going on at

once: "After the tea party, we need to go down to the dock and watch the Regatta come in…" and "I guess I need to buy a dern teapot or Mrs. Elizabeth will never invite me to another party…" and "You seen the ghost yet? Hear he's been hanging around by the Old Wrightly house…"

Sabrina glanced surreptitiously at the price tag on one of the crude clay pots, painted with a childish sunflower, and tried not to gasp at the price.

"Do you like that one?" asked a woman dressed in a chic green wrap-around dress and wearing very high heels to emphasize her slender ankles. She looked to be in her mid-thirties and her golden hair was brushed into a sophisticated French twist. Sabrina fought the urge to smooth down her own unruly gold curls which bounced around her head no matter how hard she tried to repress them.

"Please?"

The woman looked confused, but continued on. "It's shaped after an ancient pot which was made by the local Irrocottilo Indians hundreds of years ago. Would you like to buy it?"

"It's very nice, but no." Sabrina hastily replaced the ugly pot.

"What about one of these? These are made by a talented local artist, Bob McCall." The woman picked up one of the strange, misshapen, neon pots and held it out to Sabrina.

"Bicycle Bob?" Sabrina asked in surprise. "He makes those?"

"I didn't realize—" The woman broke off in confusion. Recovering, she offered her hand.

"I'm Virginia Tittletott. And you are…?"

"Hello, nice to meet you, Virginia. I'm Sabrina Dunsweeney." Sabrina extended her hand.

"Ms. Dunsweeney! You're the one who always wears such pretty, bright clothes and drives the red convertible." Virginia's pretty face smoothed in satisfaction. "I covet that car."

"It's a rental."

"How nice to meet you. I had thought that you were one of the people staying in a local hotel." Virginia tactfully avoided the word "tourist."

"Lima asked me to come with him," Sabrina said shamelessly.

"You better watch out for him." Virginia laughed. "He's had every woman on this island in love with him at least once sometime in the past eighty years."

"I noticed that."

"Are you enjoying your vacation?"

Sabrina hesitated. "I am now."

"Virginia, do you know where Missy put the extra scones and muffins?" A thin man wearing a petulant scowl and glasses pulled at Virginia's arm.

"Yes," Virginia said. "I do. Gary, this is Sabrina Dunsweeney, no relation to Helen. Sabrina, this is Gary Tittletott, my husband. If you will excuse me." Virginia disappeared through an archway in the back of the room.

"This is a very nice party." Sabrina studied the man with interest. He must be the Gary to whom Elizabeth was speaking. Who were they talking about? Why were they so afraid this mysterious "he" was back in town? All in all, very strange.

"Do you think so?" Gary's nervous gaze roamed the room. He looked very uptight, as if expecting Sabrina to shout "boo" at him at any moment, and somehow insubstantial, as if he was accustomed to fading into the woodwork. He kept scratching at his neck, so hard that red welts were rising, and pulling at the sleeves of his too-large sports coat.

Sabrina looked over Gary's head at one of the campaign posters. Bradford, the man on the poster, was a bolder, bigger version of Gary Tittletott. They were brothers, though Gary had been cheated of the basic vitality that imbued his brother.

"Listen up, everyone," Elizabeth Tittletott called stridently. "If anyone would so desire, the bar is now open for those who would like a drink."

Sabrina was unprepared as Gary bolted for the open French doors at the far end of the room.

"Please don't let me stop you," Sabrina said to Gary's retreating back.

"And who is this?" asked a warm, enthralling voice.

Bradford Tittletott stood behind her with a smile pinned to his handsome mouth. Lots of practice, she mused, to have a smile that consistently wide and even. He wore a perfectly fitted lightweight suit and his dark blond hair curled rakishly on his forehead. Rakish. She'd always liked that word, and it applied very neatly to the candidate.

"Bradford Tittletott," he said, proffering his hand. "Call me Brad."

"Hello, Brad." Sabrina shook his hand. "I'm Sabrina Dunsweeney."

"Yes, Helen is a wonderful woman. I'm glad to meet you. How long have you been on the island?"

"I've been here for about a week." She stared up into his blue eyes. Lord, they shouldn't make men this handsome. Who would be threatening this attractive, pleasant man?

"Well, I hope to meet you again." Brad squeezed her hand and dropped the smile down a notch from personal to intimate.

"That would be nice," Sabrina said, and then realized she was grinning like a smitten schoolgirl. She cleared her throat. "Good luck with your campaign."

"Thank you, Sabrina." He touched her arm and walked off.

Hoping to hide her blush-stained face, Sabrina turned to study the ancient document framed in a varnished picture frame which hung over the fireplace.

"I see you've found the Tittletott pride and joy." Virginia came up beside Sabrina. "It's the Tittletott deed to Comico Island."

"Really?" Sabrina looked at the framed document more closely. It was yellow and cracking, and the ink was faded and almost unreadable, but Sabrina could read the date: 1720.

"The island was deeded to my husband's ancestor Lord Russell Tittletott back in 1720. He had to clean up all the riffraff first—this island was notorious for harboring pirates—but once he cleaned them all out, he built a house and came here to raise his family. This building is built on the foundation of Lord Tittletott's first house."

"How fascinating."

"It's all a bunch of bunk," Virginia said, smiling sidelong at Sabrina. "Of course, my mother-in-law is in love with that story, and so is the rest of the island, actually, but who really cares about something that happened almost three hundred years ago? God forbid, don't let Elizabeth hear me say that."

"I won't tell her," Sabrina promised.

They stood in comfortable silence, watching as Elizabeth browbeat a hapless tourist into buying one of Bicycle Bob's monstrous teapots.

A couple walked out onto the terrace, holding tea cups gingerly. The woman suddenly thrust her tea cup at her husband and came back inside. A moment later, the man's eyes widened and he followed his wife.

"And sometimes right when I get fed up with this place," Virginia said softly, almost to herself, "something happens to make me realize that Comico Island is in my blood. I could never leave here."

She was looking out the window overlooking the water lying like crumpled gray silk across the harbor. Sabrina followed her gaze to see a parade of boats with colorful sails aloft glide through the inlet.

"The Regatta," Virginia said. "Every year the sailboat race stops over here for the night. It's always a whole lot of fun."

Virginia looked around as raised voices drifted from the front of the lobby.

"What's going on?"

"Momma, I don't feel so good." The little girl in the pink dress was painfully flushed.

"Calm down everybody, calm down! There's nothing to be concerned about!" Elizabeth's voice was shrill, but nobody appeared to be paying her any attention.

All around, people were clutching their stomachs and looking around wide-eyed. Sabrina noticed a line of people in the hall beside the reception desk, fidgeting from foot to foot. A man came out of the bathroom, paused, and then went back in. The next person in line beat angrily on the door.

"Like it's something I ate." An old man leaned on the arm of his wife. "Haven't felt this bad since I ate that raw squid when I was a kid."

"We should have known something would happen," Virginia murmured. She hurried over to Elizabeth and the two conferred in low, urgent tones.

"I assure you, the food at the Tittletott House is, as always, of the highest quality." Elizabeth was almost yelling as more people headed for the lengthening bathroom line, and others hurried out the front door.

"Don't forget to buy a teapot!" she shouted at their retreating backs.

"Hee, hee," Lima chortled as he came up to Sabrina.

"What in the world is going on?"

"Laxatives, I do believe. In the tea, or maybe in the chocolate scones, but I recognize the signs. Should, since I did it to my fourth grade class back about a hundred years ago."

Sabrina put down her cup on the nearest end table. "You're saying someone put laxatives in the tea or the scones? Why would they do that?"

Lima shrugged. "Maybe it was an accident, maybe it was someone who doesn't like the Tittletotts. Plenty of 'em around. All I know is Brad Tittletott has got worse luck than a fish caught twice the same day. He's a golden boy, don't get me wrong, but things just don't ever go right for him. This campaign has been jinxed since he started it. First his office burns down, and now this."

People were beginning to yell back at Elizabeth as she tried to cajole them into buying a teapot as they stood in line waiting to get into the bathroom.

"Let's get out of here," Lima said as Elizabeth spotted them.

"I didn't drink any of the tea, because it was too hot," Sabrina said, allowing herself to be ushered toward the door. "But I saw you drinking it. And eating the scones. How come you're not affected?"

"Got a stomach like steel," Lima said complacently. "Always have. Nothing can upset this ol' tummy."

"Miss Dunsweeney." Elizabeth clamped a taloned hand on Sabrina's shoulder. "You must have forgotten to buy a teapot."

Ten minutes later, Sabrina left the Tittletott House clutching a teapot shaped in the form of a smiling pig. Her only consolation was the look on Elizabeth Tittletott's face moments after Sabrina bought the teapot and just before Elizabeth beat a hasty but very dignified retreat toward the bathroom.

"Hee, hee, hee," Lima said.

Smothering a smile, Sabrina followed him down to the docks where the small rubber boats were bringing in the crews from the great sailboats.

The rich smell of fried seafood, big soft pretzels, and griddle cakes floated through the air, and the school band, all six of them, were playing a lively tune involving several missed notes and an out-of-tune trumpet. The crews of the sailboats, big, hearty people with red faces and white smiles, circulated among the crowd in their team-color windbreakers. The islanders slapped them on the back, and handed them cups full of draft beer.

"Lima, we need you to pump the keg." Mary Tubbs pulled Lima toward a booth.

Sabrina found herself holding a plastic cup full of beer, roaming alone through the growing crowd. She had not had beer in—she searched her memory. Well, it had been a good long time.

The smell of griddle cakes was becoming almost intoxicating, and Sabrina made her way over to the appropriate booth. She was surprised to find Virginia Tittletott behind the counter.

"Sabrina!" Virginia's crisp, green eyes widened as she saw Sabrina. "I see you survived the tea party unscathed. Frankly, I was glad I promised to help out with the Regatta so I could get out of the cleanup. Would you do me a favor? I took over from Missy Garrison, who had taken over from Katie Garland, who had relieved Sondra Lane…anyway, I really must use the ladies' room, if you wouldn't mind…?"

Sabrina nodded uncertainly and Virginia hurried out from behind the booth, untying her apron and thrusting it at Sabrina. Sabrina watched in bemusement as the slim woman made her way to where the crews were congregating. Virginia stood on tiptoe, trying to see over the heads of nearby people, and then made her way to a blond giant with young Robert Redford looks. The man was surrounded by islanders, but Sabrina caught the furtive, shared smile between the two of them.

Hmmm.

A moment later, people were clamoring for more griddle cakes, more griddle cakes, and Sabrina was busy distributing the hot, fragrant delectable and collecting the two-fifty for each.

The afternoon flew by. A pretty, stocky woman with long black hair who introduced herself as Sondra Lane eventually relieved Sabrina, and she walked around looking at the island-made crafts and watching the musicians and an inept magician. For the first time since she had arrived on the island she felt welcome.

After dark, Sabrina found herself in the Walk-the-

Plank Pub, a shabby building right on the edge of the harbor, with outside seating featuring plastic lawn furniture and paper towel rolls on the tables. The place was packed, and Sabrina was clapping along to the catchy tunes played by an old man with a guitar. Some type of contest involving walking the porch rail ended with one man in the water, the other sprawled across a table with his face in a plate of fried flounder and hush puppies.

"Salt, salt, salt!" Sabrina yelled along with the crowd, grinning at her nearest neighbor who was tossing a shaker of salt over her shoulder. She felt part of the crowd and invisible all at the same time. She could do whatever she wanted and no one would think to care. She finished her beer as the song ended and decided it was high time she took herself home, before she was too tipsy to *find* home. She left the bar and turned down the dark street toward her end of the island. She was suddenly so tired she could barely see straight.

She felt a headache coming on, and she hoped it wasn't anything serious, like an aneurysm or an embolism. She could hear music and voices, but they faded as she crossed a rickety bridge and entered the embrace of shadowed trees. She crossed her arms across her chest, thankful there wasn't any violent crime on the island.

Fireworks lit the night sky above the trees, illuminating the huge, bearded man standing not ten feet from her.

THREE

"WHAT AM I supposed to say again?" Sid Tittletott hissed, grappling with the big white box.

"Don't say anything. You'll say something stupid and then she'll know we're lying," Terry Wrightly said.

The two boys stopped at the edge of the stairs and gazed up at the small gray cottage where Lora Wrightly had lived for sixty years. Terry had been in this house hundreds of times in his short life, but right now the house seemed menacing and foreign.

"Do you think he's in there? Do you think Walk-the-Plank Wrightly is really staying here?"

"I don't know. I don't think ghosts need a place to sleep. But I'm not sure." Terry tapped a clipboard attached to several official-looking papers against his thigh.

"But this is *his* house. Walk-the-Plank Wrightly built this house almost three hundred years ago." Sid was convinced the ghost of the famous pirate was staying in this house. Everyone was talking about him, after all, and several people had seen him.

"Not this house, stupid," Terry said. "It's in the same spot, that's all."

"Well, let's do it. It'll be Mitchell's Day before we get in there." Sid tried to act nonchalant, but his knees were feeling weak, like the time he and Terry had snuck a pack of cigarettes from Tubbs Store and tried smoking one.

"Okay, here goes." Terry took a deep breath and advanced up the stairs.

He knocked on the door.

"Harder!" Sid whispered. "She'll never hear you."

Terry knocked so hard his knuckles hurt.

There was silence for a moment, and then an ungodly shrieking noise sounded from inside.

"Oh jeez." Sid took a step backwards.

Terry knocked again, trying to look confident.

The unearthly noises came again, and Terry found himself on the very edge of the steps with Sid halfway across the yard when the door swung open.

It was the blond lady, blinking in the vivid morning sunlight. Her hair was a mess of blond curls and she was dressed in orange and red and purple.

"It's okay, Calvin," she said in a soothing voice. "Don't be scared."

Terry and Sid looked at each other, and then craned their necks to see behind the woman. There was no one there. Sid gulped.

"Hi, ma'am," Terry said in an unnaturally high voice, and stopped, unable to continue.

"Hello, how are you two boys doing this beautiful Sunday morning?" Terry found himself relaxing when the woman smiled. Something about her smile was very nice.

"We're fine," Terry said.

"I'm Miss Sabrina Dunsweeney, but you may call me Miss Sabrina," the woman said. "What are your names?"

Her voice was compelling, and Terry and Sid stood up straight, puffing out their chests and lifting their chins.

"I'm Sid Tittletott," Sid blurted. "You can call me Sid." He elbowed Terry, smirking.

"Sid Tittletott," the woman said thoughtfully, putting

her hand up to stroke the back of her neck. "Let's see. Would you be Virginia and Gary's son?"

Sid nodded. "Elizabeth Tittletott is my grandmother," he said, and Terry knew he was trying to impress Miss Sabrina.

"I see." She turned big blue eyes on Terry and he tried not to blush.

"I'm Terry Wrightly." He looked at his feet.

"Ah," Miss Sabrina said. "I'm guessing Roland Thierry Wrightly the Tenth, the owner of this house, is a relation?"

"Grandpa Dock."

"I don't suppose either of you have been clipping my roses, have you?"

The boys avoided looking at each other. She seemed so normal, and then she beamed over into Bonko Zone.

"Will you buy some cookies?" Sid was unable to hold back any longer.

"Please?"

"Would you buy some cookies, please?" Sid corrected himself. "We're selling them to raise money for—" He broke off, looking at Terry.

"To raise money for a school play," Terry finished, having practiced this line beforehand.

"Really? How nice. What play?"

"Uh—" Terry floundered, looking at Sid for help. *This* he hadn't anticipated.

"*Romeo and Jello!*" Sid smiled broadly at Terry. See, he did remember something from Mrs. Piggy Perkin's English class.

"Ah." Miss Sabrina smiled her nice smile. "Do you have someone to help direct this play?"

"Well, no, not yet," Sid said, and Terry kicked him, hard. "Ouch!"

"Well, you're in luck. I happen to know *Romeo and—* uh, *Jello* pretty well. When do you begin rehearsing?"

Terry and Sid stared at each other.

"How about tomorrow? Would you like to rehearse here? Good. Three-thirty tomorrow afternoon, then, right after school." Miss Sabrina beamed at the two of them. "Oh, and you needed me to buy some cookies? Let me get some money."

She left the door open and went inside to find her purse. Terry and Sid were in shock, and didn't even remember to peek inside the house which was the entire reason for their visit.

Miss Sabrina came back with her purse, took the clipboard from Terry, and signed her name on the top line. "Haven't had much luck yet, have you?"

"You're the first house we've been to," Terry recovered enough to say.

"I'll take a big bag, then," she said. "Here's five dollars."

Sid opened the top of the big box and brought out a bag of cookies and handed them over.

"How nice." She opened the top of the bag and peered inside. "Calvin, don't these look yummy?"

This time Terry could have sworn he heard someone answer. Someone with a very high, chirpy voice.

"What kind of cookies are these?"

"They're my grandma's special, her Millionaire Cookies. She owns Nettie's Cookie Shop down the road." And he had better get this box of cookies back before Grandma Nettie returned to the shop or there would be heck to pay.

"Okay, gentlemen," Miss Sabrina said, closing the top of the bag. "I expect to see you here at three-thirty sharp tomorrow afternoon."

"Yes, ma'am," Terry and Sid muttered and started inching their way backwards down the steps while Miss Sabrina smiled at them.

"Wonderful, I'll see you tomorrow."

"Yes, ma'am."

"And, boys?"

They looked up at her, not aware of the pure desperation written all over their faces.

"Don't forget to bring the rest of the cast."

SABRINA CLOSED THE door behind the two boys and smiled to herself. They seemed like nice young men.

"What do you think, Calvin?" She reached up and stroked his warm body cuddled behind her neck.

"Cheep, cheep, cheep," the parakeet said, mimicking the sound of her voice. He imitated everything, from the sound of the telephone to the beeping of the microwave.

"Do you think they'll show tomorrow?"

Before Calvin could answer, Sabrina tripped over something under the Oriental rug and Calvin screeched with indignation.

"Sorry, boy."

Sabrina put the small yellow parakeet on the floor and went into the kitchen. She looked out the window and wasn't surprised to see Apples grazing the back lawn. The shaggy brown pony seemed as much at home in her yard as the two cats curled up on the porch. She stood for a moment, watching as the sun poured through a chink in the clouds, spilling iridescent light over the sound. The splash of an osprey hitting the water generated an explosion of dancing diamonds that sparkled and glittered atop the waves even as the osprey flew away with the fish wriggling in its grasp.

"What do you think, Calvin?" She turned to find the small bird climbing the miniature palm tree to reach his favorite new perch on the windowsill. "Who's trimming the roses?"

Sabrina picked up her cup of hot tea and dug into the white bag for a cookie. When she had left to go on her walk this morning, she noticed the roses around her rental cottage were freshly pruned. When she checked the small shed where she kept her bike, she found a large pair of lawn shears, neatly oiled and sharpened, with the remains of a rose bud in the hinge of the shears.

"Maybe it's the person with the big feet who's walking on the beach every morning." The footprints were there again this morning, an unbroken string of very large footprints down the clean expanse of sand. She'd followed them until they veered off into the marsh.

She couldn't help feeling a little spooked. After seeing that man last night just standing there in the dark woods, his eyes fixed on her, she ran home and closed the door, for the first time fervently wishing that the doors had locks.

In the bright light of day, she wondered if maybe she was overreacting. The man could very well have a good reason for standing in the woods. Maybe he was hunting, or looking for something.

"Maybe it's that ghost—what's his name? Walk-the-Plank Wrightly."

She laughed, munching on the cookie—they were mouth-tingling good—and went back into the living room.

"For heaven's sake!" Sabrina said, as she tripped over

the thing under the Oriental rug once again. She'd been meaning to see what was under there, but it never seemed worth the effort. As she hopped on one foot, rubbing her stubbed toe, she decided it was high time to see what was under that rug.

Calvin followed her into the living room and watched with interest as she took the corner of the somber rug, so out of place in the cheerful room. She pulled it back to reveal what looked like a hatch in the varnished wood floor.

Calvin chirped in delight and waddled over to peck at the door.

A metal ring for opening the hatch was what she had been tripping over. There was a large stain covering the hatch, almost as if someone had spilled grape juice on the wood floor.

"Why in the world would someone put a door in the floor?" Sabrina mused.

Calvin pecked at the metal ring.

Sabrina shrugged, grasped the metal ring, and gave it a hearty pull. The door hesitated, and then swung upward and stood upright. Sabrina peered down inside the hole, wrinkling her nose at the smell of old, dry dirt.

Calvin chattered in excitement, and Sabrina nudged him back from the opening.

The cottage sat on four-foot-high pilings to protect the house against sudden storm surges. The hatch simply opened on the empty space under the house. But why?

"What's this?" Sabrina leaned forward, her eyes adjusting to the gloom. Something colorful lay on the ground under the hatch.

Sabrina reached inside the hole, but could not quite reach whatever it was.

Calvin cheeped impatiently, and Sabrina sighed. She

lay down on her stomach, and reached down into the hole, very conscious of spiders and snakes and lizards, oh my, and grasped the edges of several pieces of paper. She sat up with difficulty and studied her prize.

Bright green, yellow and blue construction paper was scrawled with angry crayon pictures. Stick figures of people and dogs and houses, engulfed in brilliant orange, red and yellow flames.

More disturbing than the furious pictures were the red spots spattered all over the construction paper.

Red spots. Blood spots. Blood was spattered all over the childish, furious pictures.

FOUR

SABRINA TURNED THE top picture over, and saw that some-one, an adult, had written the date in the top right-hand corner. The pictures were almost twenty-five years old.

"Calvin, what child would have drawn these?" Sabrina thumbed through the crayon pictures once again. They were angry, vivid pictures. A puppy hanging from a noose. A large house burning while a stick figure waved its hands from a top window. A person lying on the floor, bright red blood spreading in a pool around the body. A person dancing around with his clothes on fire. A half-wolf, half-human creature with a human arm in its jaws. A figure being burned at the stake. Six pictures, all de-picting scenes of violence and hate.

Sabrina shook her head, upset. She believed she was looking at pictures drawn by a seriously disturbed child, most likely under the age of ten. Only one other time had she seen pictures this brutal and bloody. That child had tried to kill his baby sister when he was eight years old. Her heart still twinged when she thought of her inabil-ity to help that poor, abused child. She tried, goodness, she tried, but the mother resisted her efforts and the chil-dren's services people were so overworked they barely even looked at the pictures.

"It's too late now, Calvin. Whoever drew these pic-tures is all grown up. I wonder if anybody tried to help? I wonder if it was just the pictures, or if there was more?"

She knew that disturbed children often act out in more than one way. He or she could very well go from drawing pictures of fires and torturing animals to arson and acts of cruelty against real animals.

Calvin pecked at the one of the blood spots speckling the top two pictures.

"I'm not sure where that came from." Sabrina looked down into the hole, but the dirt looked dry and undisturbed except for a few dark spots. Sabrina laid the hatch door down flat and looked at the large grape juice stain on the cover of the door.

Sabrina traced the stain with her fingers.

"This must have been where old Lora Wrightly fell, and the blood from her cut head dripped though the edge of the hatch onto the pictures." Sabrina studied the pictures. "But why were the pictures under there? They couldn't have been in there for twenty-five years. They're not dusty or dirty at all."

Sabrina stood up. "Well, perhaps someone knows something about these pictures. Maybe there's an innocent explanation."

"Whhhr," Calvin said doubtfully.

"I know, I know," Sabrina said, because she couldn't get rid of the gut feeling that something was very wrong. She just didn't know *what.*

A half an hour later, she started down the sandy driveway, past her bright red convertible rental car. It hadn't taken her long to discover that the only people who drove on the island were the tourists. In a town less than a mile square from sound to sea, who needed to drive?

The two cats, which she had named Gray and Grayer, were curled up together in a patch of sunlight on the lawn. They looked up, yawned at her, and closed their eyes.

"I'll feed you when I get back," she called to them.

It felt good to have purpose again. The first couple of days she wallowed in solitude. It was the first time she'd really spent time by herself for as long as she could remember. She slept a lot, and sat on the back porch and looked at the water. But the guilt was there, stinging the back of her mind. How could she enjoy being alone when the only reason she *was* alone was because her dear, sainted mother was gone?

If her best friend Sally hadn't insisted, she never would have agreed to this trip, or vacation, or whatever it was. Sally called it a "recovery interlude," but that was just Sally being Sally. The whole ugly incident with Mr. Phil had been the deciding factor. Sabrina had decided she needed a break, to get away. The rest had done her good, though she could not remember sitting still for such an extended length of time in all her life. The idea of finding out more about the pictures under the hatch was tantalizing. It seemed the perfect remedy for what ailed her.

Speaking of ailments, she needed to check her medical book to make sure the bug bites she found on her ankle this morning weren't anything serious. You never knew, it could be the bite of a brown recluse spider and her flesh was slowly rotting away and she didn't even know it.

Sabrina passed an apple orchard enclosed by an aging fence, and continued down the private dirt road that meandered along water as still and solid as a marble dance floor. A dilapidated dock was nestled among the oaks and loblollies, anchoring an equally dilapidated boat that looked as if each day it continued to float was a good day. Almost hidden in the woods were several out-of-plumb sheds and a menagerie of rusted old cars. Sabrina saw the two little boys she met this morning duck out of sight behind one of the old Ford trucks. The subsequent frantic rustling and muffled cries of "Get it off me! Get it off me!" seemed to indicate that their hiding place was already inhabited.

The "New Wrightly House," as the sign over the front door proclaimed, was much bigger than the house she rented, the "Old Wrightly House." It was painted a dull green and surrounded by a white porch, on which a chair was rocking madly, as if someone had been sitting in it just moments ago. It was the home of Sabrina's land-lord, Thierry Roland Wrightly the Tenth according to her rental papers, though she'd yet to meet him.

"Hello!" She knocked on the wooden edge of the screen door. As her eyes adjusted to the dimness inside, she could see an ancient living room and an old man huddled on the couch staring at her.

"Hello, Mr. Wrightly?"

The man looked at Sabrina for a moment, and then opened his toothless mouth and screamed.

Since Sabrina hadn't looked in the mirror this morn-ing—her eyes had been half closed when she brushed her teeth—she was a little concerned that maybe the old man's screaming had something to do with her appear-ance. But she was wearing her pretty new pink dress, the emerald scarf with streaks of orange, and the just-out-of-the-box purple pumps. She had brushed her golden curls this morning—she remembered distinctly because the brush had gotten caught in her hair and it had taken her five minutes to get the tangle undone. She thought she looked pretty snazzy.

"I'll have none of that, do you hear me, none of that!" the old man yelled, and jumped from his chair to slam the door in Sabrina's face.

"HERE SHE COMES AGAIN," Lima Lowry said, rocking his chair a little bit faster. His large feet, encased in white rubber boots up to his knees, were firmly planted on the front porch of Tubbs General Store. After eighty years of tromping through the mud flats and marshes of the sound, he wasn't about to get rid of his favorite boots just because he didn't do much of that stuff any more.

"Yep." Bicycle Bob took a liberal swig of his Rot Gut 20/20. He sat on the first step because the rocking chairs made him woozy and he liked to keep close to Trigger, his gleaming yellow beach bike.

"Always wearing them bright colors." Lima leaned back in his chair and contemplated Sabrina Dunsweeney—no relation to Helen, apparently—who was striding briskly down the street. "If'n I close one eye and squint, she kinda looks like a psychedelic Easter egg, all painted up, just arollin' down the street." He sputtered with laughter, pleased with his observation. He prided himself on his keen eye and quick wit, even if Bicycle didn't appreciate it much.

"Yep," said Bicycle Bob, who rarely had anything else to say, except maybe "nope."

"May's been cleaning her house. Said the woman burns up more pots than anybody has a reason to. May also said she saw both Lora's ghost and Walk-the-Plank Wrightly one day last week when she was cleaning. I shouldn't wonder the two of them aren't dancing a waltz somewhere. Lora always did like to dance," Lima said wistfully, conscious of the passing years and how few of his friends remained in this world. Lora had been one of his favorites, and he preferred to think of her before she suffered her stroke and her graceful body became twisted and slow.

"Nope," said Bicycle, who sometimes got confused about what exactly was expected of him in a conversation. He rocked a little on his stair seat, as if maybe the whole world was rocking for Bicycle Bob.

Bicycle was a good guy, Lima thought affectionately, even if he did drink too much. Why, Lima could remember in his younger days when he drank more than Bicycle. Well maybe not *more*, but he did drink a lot. There was that one time when he was about fifty when he tied on a good one and took his boat out and sank it. Barely made it to shore alive.

But that was on Mitchell's Day, and he should have known better than to go out on the water on Mitchell's Day.

As Miss Sabrina approached, Lima assumed the pose of "The Thinker," that famous statue out of France, or one of those states over in Europe. He figured it was an apt position, considering the sheer magnitude of his brain power.

"Hello, Lima," Sabrina said as she reached the porch. It was nice to see a friendly face after her run-in with the old man at the New Wrightly House. Lima was resting his chin on his hand and seemed to be contemplating his belly button. "Is everything all right?"

He held the uncomfortable-looking pose for a moment more and then sat back in his chair. "Hello, Miss Sabrina. You seen the ghost yet?"

"You mean Walk-the-Plank Wrightly? No, I haven't, though I'd love to hear his story. Do you know it?"

"It's a long one," Lima said, rocking faster.

"I've got some time." Sabrina sat down in the rocking chair next to his. She was breathing hard and her chest hurt, but she was anxious to hear the story of this notorious ghost.

"Weeeell, let's see." Lima settled back into his chair. "Walk-the-Plank Wrightly was one of the meanest pirates ever seen around these parts. Meaner than Blackbeard, more vicious than Bloody Hands Bartly. He terrorized these parts for more than five years back in the 1700's, raidin' ships and killin' people. Not a single person survived one of his attacks 'cause he made every one of the crew walk the plank when he captured a ship. Didn't want to leave any witnesses, you see. Even when the authorities told the pirates if they came clean and stopped pirating they'd be pardoned, Walk-the-Plank Wrightly kept right on doing what he did best.

"Back in those days, they didn't call him Walk-the-Plank Wrightly, though, they called him Walk-the-Plank Jack, 'cause no one knew who he was. After he had raided a ship, they'd find the ship floatin' completely empty and a couple of days later the bodies would start washing up on shore.

"After a while, people started to think that maybe Walk-the-Plank Jack was someone who lived on Comico Island, because the attacks always took place right around here. People on the island started lookin' at their neighbors closely, wondering if this evil man was someone they knew. And there wasn't a whole lot of people on the island back then, just a few hard-working fishermen and their families and a few exiled noblemen from England.

"Roland Thierry Wrightly was a merchant trader with several big ships, and he sailed from the colonies up north down to the Car-ribbon with cargo. Everybody liked Roland Wrightly, he was a nice man and was known for helpin' out his neighbors on Comico Island. Even the governor was fooled by him, and he gave Wrightly the deed to this island as a gift. But nobody knew what secrets Wrightly held in his black heart.

"Nothing much changed after Wrightly got the island, except the pirating got worse. Wrightly pretended like he was tryin' to hunt the pirate down, but of course he never was going to find him, 'cause *he* was the pirate! But no one knew that, and bodies kept washing up on shore and ships were found floating with no one on board.

"A couple years after Wrightly got the title to the island, people started sending petitions to the governor, asking him to help 'em get rid of the pirate. He called on his friend Lord Russell Tittletott, who was a well-known retired naval man from England, and he asked Lord Tittletott to get rid of Walk-the-Plank Jack. If he did it, the governor would give him whatever he wanted, short of the moon and stars.

"It was a challenge-like, and Lord Tittletott took up the gauntlet. He started hunting for that pirate, and it was like Walk-the-Plank Jack was thumbing his nose at Lord T because the pirating just got worse for a couple of months. Bodies were floating up onto the beach and it didn't seem like Lord Tittletott would be able to catch that evil pirate.

"But one day, Lord T went out onto the high seas and he caught Walk-the-Plank Jack right in the act. He was too late to save the crew of the beleaguered ship, but he came up beside the pirate ship, and the crews fought it out, hand to hand. All but five of the crew were killed, and Walk-the-Plank Jack was captured.

"Imagine Lord Tittletott's surprise when he discovered that it was his good friend Roland Wrightly! He and Wrightly had been friends for many years, and both had petitioned the governor for the title to Comico Island. Lord Tittletott was shocked and sad, but he knew what he had to do. Right then and there he made Wrightly and his five remaining crew men walk the plank on the dread charge of piracy. He had to do it, you see, even though Wrightly was a good friend.

"And that's how Walk-the-Plank Jack became Walk-the-Plank Wrightly. When Lord Tittletott got back to Comico Island with Wrightly's empty ship in tow, all of the islanders were happy the pirate had been caught, though sad it turned out to be Wrightly. And when Lord Tittletott asked the governor for the title to Comico Island as his price, the governor was happy to agree. So that's how Lord Tittletott won Comico Island. Old Walk-the-Plank Wrightly still walks the beaches of this island, you know, looking for the treasure he buried right before he died."

Lima finished his story and rocked his chair contentedly.

"What a double life that man must have led," Sabrina said. "Did he have a family?"

"He left behind a pregnant wife who always swore her husband was unfairly accused. On account of her condition, Lord T let her keep the house and a little land, which everyone thought was mighty chilvy-rus of him. That's where you're staying, or at least the Old Wrightly house is on the same spot where his house used to be. May saw him from one of your upstairs windows the other day. Big hulk of a man, dressed all in black and carrying a sword."

Sabrina was having trouble keeping a straight face. She was a rational person, and she certainly didn't believe in ghosts, even though the islanders seemed to take his presence for granted. But she had seen a man standing in the woods last night, and someone was walking on her beach.

Would a ghost leave footprints?

Stop it! she told herself. There were no such things as ghosts.

"This Lord Tittletott is an ancestor of your nephew running for president, Brad?"

"Lord, yes. Didn't you see the deed on the wall at the Tittletott House? The Tittletotts don't never let anybody forget that they are related to the savior of the island."

"And Walk-the-Plank Wrightly is an ancestor of the Wrightlys who live on the island?" Sabrina was curious about the familiar names in the story.

"All the Wrightlys got that bushy black hair and are crazy as coots, but all of 'em with hearts big as all the sea, even if they are Wavers."

"A what?"

"A Waver. The Wrightlys live on the other side of the crick, so they're Wavers. I'm a Towner, 'cause I live on this side of the crick."

"You've got different names for yourselves, depending on which side of the creek you live on? What does it matter? It's a very small town as it is."

"You'd be surprised," Lima said darkly. "Those Wavers can be real sneaky characters. They'll smile at you when just that morning they were ripping off your line. They talk funny, dress shabby, drink a lot and have loose women."

"Perhaps a leash would be helpful?"

Lima just stared at her.

"But all of you live less than a mile from one another." She understood how a city could be divided up into cliqu-ish sections depending on cultural and financial differences—even Cincinnati had its East and West sides—but she found it hard to believe that the people living just on the other side of the twenty-foot wide "crick" could be so different.

"It used to be further. That bridge ain't that old."

Sabrina said nothing, because the bridge had looked ancient to her.

"Not too long ago, back in the fifties, there was no bridge. Before that, you had to go by boat to get over to the other side. I remember when I was a kid, we used to go visit relatives on the Waver side for the weekend. That was when the feuds stopped for a spell, Tubbs against McCalls, Tittletotts against Wrightlys. Those feuds could get real bad. Burnin' down houses, murderin'. It was ugly. Never come to much good for a Towner to be friends with a Waver. Look what happened to Rolo Wrightly and Bradford Tittletott."

He nodded as if the feud between an unknown Wrightly and a Tittletott was proof positive that Wavers and Towners just couldn't get along.

Sabrina tried to understand. "You're a Towner, and it sounds like I need to be careful since I'm staying over on Waver side of town. What does that make me?"

Lima snorted. "You're worse than any Waver. You're a tourist."

FIVE

"THAT'S PRETTY HARSH, don't you think?" Sabrina kept her voice pleasant, though really she was more inclined to laugh than be angry.

"Nope." Lima kicked at the porch planks. "All you tourists are ruining the island. Have been for years, 'cept it's just been getting worse. I've lived here for eighty-some years. I remember what it was like when the only boat coming to the island was the mail boat, and it only came once every couple of days. The only outsiders we saw were the hard-core hunters and fishermen, and the only place for them to stay was at the Tittletott House, which was also the only place they could eat. And if they didn't get their butts to dinner on time, then they just wouldn't eat."

"I imagine the tourists must bring quite a bit of money into the island's economy," Sabrina said carefully. "Before that, the island's only economy was what you gleaned from the sea, I'd imagine."

"Yeah, and all those tourists buying up the little real estate we got left raised property values so high that us that's been living here for years can barely afford our taxes! Us fishermen ain't making a dollar more, I tell you that! They spend all this money to come here, a beautiful, unspoiled island away from the beaten track, and then they complain that we don't have a movie theater or a Wal-Mart! I always wondered why they call it 'tourist season' when I can't shoot the—"

"Lima, stop getting all riled up," a woman's voice said through the screen door of the store. "Don't forget your blood pressure."

"You have high blood pressure?" Sabrina asked with interest, always curious about other people's health. "I hope you don't smoke, you have a much greater risk of developing complications. You don't look overweight, but you want to make sure you don't eat salt, and definitely avoid alcohol!" She beamed at the old man.

"What are you, a doctor?"

"No, I'm a teacher." Sabrina was puzzled at his cantankerous reaction.

"Anyway, Lima." The slender young woman pushed the screen door open, and leaned a blue jean clad hip against the door sill. "You don't need to be getting all excited."

Lima waved a hand at her. "I'm fine, I'm fine, Stacey."

"And don't you listen to him, ma'am." Stacey turned to Sabrina. "Some of us are happy the tourists are here. There's good and bad in it, but most of us realize that change was going to come, and we've accepted it."

Sabrina smiled at Stacey, who couldn't have been more than eighteen. "I'm surprised you're not in school."

"I'm going to go," Stacey said, "but my dad needed some help with the store, so I decided to start college next year instead."

"What are you going to study?"

"Environmental engineering," the girl said proudly. "Then I'm going to come back to the island and join the National Park Service."

"The Nazi Park Service," Lima muttered.

An old man reeking of the sea and less pleasant things wandered up and sat in the rocking chair on the other side of Lima. The two of them engaged in an intricate conversation about crabbing and "jimmies" and "peelers" which left Sabrina feeling as if she was hearing a different language. The islanders had a dialect all their own, Sabrina had already noticed, but she wondered if perhaps they didn't also have a *language* all their own.

The wind was rising, gently rocking the empty chairs on the porch and taking little sweeps at the sand and grit on the road. Sabrina chewed on her lip, unable to enjoy the uncomplicated talk and picturesque view. She couldn't help thinking about the child who drew those pictures twenty-five years ago.

Rationally, she knew the child who had drawn the pictures was all grown up. There was nothing she could do to help the child now. But still she worried…why had the pictures been under the trap door? What was the trap door *for* in the first place? And was it really old Lora Wrightly's blood on the pictures? Somehow that bothered her more than anything.

After exhausting the talk about Leroy's bad luck crabbing that day, and the tourist who had backed his brand-new boat into the water without putting in the drain plugs, Leroy took his leave. Sabrina was left alone with Lima, except for Bicycle Bob who was snoring softly on the steps.

"Ahem. Lima, I was wondering…" Sabrina coughed. "That is, I've been thinking about Lora Wrightly. She was a teacher you said?"

"Oh yes." Lima settled back into his rocking chair, but not before shooting Sabrina a sharp look. "Best teacher we ever had before her stroke. It was a shame that happened."

"I'm sure that must have been hard for her."

"It just shouldn't have happened, that's all I'll say about it. It was just sheer heartbreak, and the person responsible better know good and well that it's *his* fault that his grandmama had that stroke."

"How long ago did she stop teaching? When did she have her stroke?"

"Fifteen years ago, she heard the news and keeled over. They had to take her to the mainland, but as soon as she could she was back in her little house. Poor thing. Couldn't teach after that, though."

"What grade did she teach?"

"Grade?" Lima snorted. "Miss Sabrina, we didn't have grades back then. At least not like you're used to them. Everybody in one class was the way it worked up to ten years ago."

Sabrina shook her head, frustrated. She wasn't getting anywhere like this. She took a deep breath, strangely reluctant to talk about the pictures, as if acknowledging them would release their evil. "Lima, I found some awful pictures under the floor in the living room. They were dated twenty-five years ago, and they were drawn by a disturbed child, I just know it."

Lima looked at her sharply. "A tiddly-winked kid drew some sick pictures twenty-five years ago? Here on the island? That could have been anyone! We got us some hellraisers on this island, let me tell you. I wouldn't worry too much about some pictures drawn twenty-five years ago, if I were you, Miss Sabrina."

"But I think Lora might have been looking at them recently," Sabrina persisted. "I was just wondering why.

Do you remember anything…strange going on twenty-five years ago? Were there incidents of animal mutilation, of arson, or—"

"Arson?" Lima sat up straight in his rocking chair. "Fires…hmm." He stared past Sabrina down toward the sound. "Yes, I do remember when someone was setting fires to the trash cans. That was when he was a boy. If only we had known it was him, maybe we could have slapped some sense into him before he did what he did. Hi, Loretta! Any luck fishing this morning?"

Lima seemed inordinately pleased to see the man—was his name really Loretta?—and it was clear he didn't want to talk about disturbed children and arson any longer. Sabrina's stomach grumbled, and she got to her feet.

"Well, it was nice talking to you, Lima," she said. "I promise if I see Walk-the-Plank Wrightly I'll ask him what he's doing back after all this time."

"Don't mean no good, I know that much." Lima waved cheerfully and turned back to Loretta.

Sabrina waved and went down the steps, trying to avoid stepping on a snoring Bicycle Bob.

The clouds had taken over most of the sky, and Sabrina shivered as a cool breeze slithered past her arm and hissed across the nape of her neck. She was glad she had her raincoat with her. Fall weather on the island was fickle.

She hurried down the street and turned left onto the road that circled the harbor. All of the sailboats from the Regatta were gone, and people were cleaning up from the celebrations. Several people waved at her, and she waved back, feeling pleased to be accepted.

Virginia was on the front lawn of the Tittletott House,

picking up beer cans and trash. She looked up as Sabrina came up the walk.

"I thought I'd have some lunch," Sabrina said.

"How nice. Go on in. I'm just finishing up."

The front door was open, and Sabrina went inside. The lobby was deserted, the traces of yesterday's disastrous tea party already gone.

Sabrina went through the double doors into the small dining room. Three tables were occupied, and a plump woman in jeans smiled at her from where she was pouring coffee at one of the tables.

"Seat yourself," she called.

Sabrina chose a small table next to a window. The dining room was pleasant, with light green walls and flower stenciling near the ceiling, and fresh flowers in baskets all around the room.

The plump woman, wearing a T-shirt proclaiming "The gene pool could use a little chlorine," hustled over with ice water and a menu.

"Our special today is a grilled tuna sandwich and fries," she said. "I'm Missy, I'll be right back."

Sabrina glanced over the menu's selection of sandwiches and seafood. She longed suddenly for a cheese coney, a hot dog topped with good old Cincinnati chili, mustard, onions and cheese. Her stomach grumbled again. She thought about her monthly visit to the Maisonette, where she treated herself to lunch at one of the best restaurants in the country.

Sabrina sighed, and glumly ordered the special and some ice tea when the cheerful woman came back to the table. She then settled back in her chair and thought about what Lima revealed. She had the distinct feeling that he knew who drew those pictures.

Bradford Tittletott and another man came through the dining room and headed for the small bar at the back of the room.

"Miss Dunsweeney." Brad paused by her table as the other man continued to the bar without even glancing at Sabrina. "How nice to see you. Did you enjoy the Regatta?"

"It was wonderful." She noticed that he did not mention the disastrous end to his tea party.

The man was undeniably handsome, with his light hair brushed away from his forehead, and his clean, unblemished features. His lively eyes and the mischievous twist to his lip saved him from an unfortunate resemblance to a Greek statue.

Missy reached a long arm around Brad and set Sabrina's plate in front of her. "Tartar or ketchup?"

"Tartar, please."

"Missy, just the person I wanted to see." Brad put an arm around the other woman. "Missy, have you met Sabrina Dunsweeney? She's staying at the Old Wrightly place. Sabrina, this is Missy Garrison. She's the island's Jane of all trades. She does everything: waitress, cab driver, teacher, registrar of taxes…"

"Oh you." Missy laughed and hurried away to seat a couple waiting at the door.

"I'll let you get to your food," Brad said. "It was good seeing you."

"Same here," Sabrina said as he joined his friend at the bar.

She took a bite of her sandwich piled high with a slab of blackened tuna, tomato and lettuce and closed her eyes as the flavors tingled her taste buds. She was surprised to discover that it was quite good.

The dining room was filling up, and Virginia came in to help Missy with the tables. Sabrina ate her sandwich and watched the people around her while pretending not to. There were two distinct types of people in the room: the tourists, well-dressed pale people who talked loudly and spread maps over the tables as they ate; and the islanders, taciturn people in flannels and old dresses who made a point of sitting with their backs to the tourists.

Bradford Tittletott stood out from the crowd. He looked casual and relaxed in his pressed blue pants and sparkling white shirt that matched his flashing teeth. He smiled a lot as he talked, and greeted tourists and islanders alike as they came into the dining room. His companion, who had already downed three shots, was as unlike him as the cool winter night is to the brilliant summer day. He looked younger than Brad by perhaps a couple of years, and was very tan, with dark bushy hair pulled back into a ponytail and blue eyes that were always sliding away from direct eye contact. He was dressed in island wear, ragged blue jeans, sandals, and T-shirt, and he reminded Sabrina of someone.

She decided that the man could very well be handsome, but as it was he looked sullen and discontented. If he had been a student in one of her classes, Sabrina would have sat down with him and found out whether maybe he was having trouble at home. She wondered about the relationship between the two so obviously different men.

Brad was talking on a tiny cell phone when Sabrina paid for her tuna sandwich and left a generous tip for the smiling Missy. In the lobby, Gary was sitting behind the registration desk, looking over his shoulder as she came through the door from the dining room.

"I don't think so," he said to someone through the doorway leading to the back room.

He turned and stared at Sabrina, as if trying to remember who she was, and then evidently shucked her into the mental file labeled: "Tourist—potential money" and smiled.

"Hi Gary, I'm Sabrina Dunsweeney. I met you yesterday?"

"Oh, yes." Gary smiled again, if anything more mechanically than before. Sabrina wondered what in the world was wrong with the man. His shoulders were hunched, his blond hair lank and even a bit greasy. He looked like he did everything possible to make himself look different from his brother.

"Like I was saying, Gary," said an imperious female voice from the doorway of a room directly behind the registration desk. "It's unbelievable that Bradford brought that horrible Thierry Wrightly in here again. I never understood what Bradford saw in those Wrightly boys anyway. I told him, fine, if he wanted the man's help for the Waver vote, that's one thing, but not to bring him into this house. You'll never know what he'll walk out with. You know those Wavers." She finished the sentence as she swept into the doorway, and stopped as she saw Sabrina.

"Hello," Sabrina said.

Apparently Elizabeth Tittletott's extravagant attire from yesterday had not just been a fluke for the tea party. Today her wardrobe consisted of a bright red silk kimono and matching pumps, her ashy blond hair piled high on top of her head. Sabrina was quite jealous.

"Hello. Mrs. Dunsweeney, I think it was?"

"I'm not married."

"Ah." Elizabeth nodded knowingly.

"Did you ever find out who put the laxative in the tea?" Sabrina asked, with a touch of malice.

"It was one of those nasty Wavers." Elizabeth's eyes narrowed. "I told the sergeant I wanted to press charges but he said it was just a prank and we'd be better off ignoring the whole thing. I mean, *really*." She sniffed.

Brad came around the corner and saw the three of them. His face was flushed and he looked excited. "I got a call from Ninja—my uncle just got elected to the Senate, but he used to be the president of the Sanitary Concessionary—" he added as an aside for Sabrina's benefit. "He says he'll definitely support me. He's going to try to make it to the rally on Wednesday night."

"How wonderful!" Elizabeth gushed, rushing over to her son and patting his arm.

"How wonderful," Gary echoed, but with a touch of sarcasm. His eyes glittered with something other than brotherly love. Bradford was oblivious, basking in the praise from his mother.

"I just came in for some lunch," Sabrina said, as she turned to leave. "Congratulations, Brad."

Surprisingly, Gary called after her in a pleasant voice: "Miss Dunsweeney, please come back any time."

Sabrina left the Tittletott House feeling uneasy. Something strange jittered beneath the Tittletotts' conversation, something dark and ugly, like hate and jealousy.

Sabrina shivered and hurried out into the stormy afternoon.

SIX

MURKY CLOUDS HOVERED, fat and heavy with rain. Lightning glimmered in their depths, like a faulty light bulb ready to blow. Though it was only early afternoon, the thick air was so dark it could have been dusk.

Sabrina turned left along Hurricane Harbor Circle. Boats of all sizes were scurrying home across the flat pewter water, leaving contrails of foaming water in their wakes, and waitresses were closing the mismatched umbrellas over the outside tables at Walk-the-Plank Pub.

The young, dark man with Brad was a member of the infamous Wrightly clan, she thought as she walked down the deserted street. A family descended from a vicious pirate and reputedly proud of it.

She passed the Ride the Big One Surf Shop and Bar and followed the curve of the road away from the harbor toward the rickety bridge. She paused on the bridge and looked up at the sky, marveling at the dense purple-black of the clouds. A slight wind began pushing at the heavy air, stirring the drooping leaves on the trees.

"I think I'd better hurry," Sabrina said out loud, and suited action to words. Her cottage was still five minutes away and as she tottered down Lighthouse Road in her heels, another gust of wind rushed from the sky, bending the trees and swirling leaves through the air. She hugged her bare arms and increased her speed.

She was in the run-down part of the island that Lima

called "Waver Town." Old ramshackle houses and shops leaned haphazardly on either side of the street, and a weather-beaten dock stretched out into the harbor. Rusty work boats chugged homeward in great clouds of black smoke.

This was definitely not the tourist part of town. Old cars and pickup trucks with no tires and very little paint were reposing on blocks in front yards, and crab pots and nets were stacked in every available space. Bearded men dressed in rubber overalls hurried past her, carrying buckets and rakes. She was rounding the curve by the High Tide Baptist Church when the next gust of wind brought with it cold, stinging raindrops, which quickly increased to a downpour.

"Just wonderful," Sabrina said, and then spotted the bright welcoming lights of a shop through the hammering rain. She slipped in the muddy street and lurched against the door, falling through it onto her knees.

"Ooooh, child, what in the world have you done to yourself?" asked a low, melodious voice. Little hands helped her off the floor, and closed the door decisively on the howling wind.

"Thank you," Sabrina mumbled, swiping heavy curls out of her eyes, and blinking as she saw the apparition in front of her.

A tiny, elderly woman dressed in a long white robe stood with her hands on her hips. Elaborate designs in green and gold were embroidered on her immaculate robes, and some sort of symbol was drawn in what looked like a black magic marker on her forehead.

"You're the girl staying in our old house," she said, surveying Sabrina from head to foot. "Dunsweeney. Sally, or Sarah. No, wait. Sandra, Samantha, Savannah—"

"Sabrina." Sabrina tried to wipe the mud from her knees and discovered with a wince that blood was mixed with the mud.

"Look at you, child, you scraped your knees. Sit down, and I'll fix you up." The woman pulled Sabrina over to a chair, and then disappeared into a back room.

Sabrina caught her breath as she looked around the store. Though the exterior of the store was unfinished and rough, the inside was bright and cheery, with white tile and walls, red checkered tablecloths on the two tables, and long gleaming display cases displaying various types of cookies, cakes and bread. And the smell! The smell was intoxicating.

Outside, it was impossible to see more than a few feet past the windows. The rain was drumming on the roof, the wind picking at the edge of the door, threatening to throw it open. Sabrina looked around, wondering what the old woman was doing.

"It's a regular devil's blow out there," the diminutive lady said as she came out of the back room and carefully closed the door behind her.

"You're right. I thought I could beat it home. Should we be worried about tornadoes?" Sabrina glanced out the window as a hard gust of wind smacked the building.

"I'd be more worried about water spouts if I were you."

The woman crouched in front of Sabrina and, using a wash cloth, wiped the blood and mud from her knees.

"Water spouts?" Sabrina winced despite the woman's gentle touch.

"Tornadoes on the water. They normally stay out on the water, but you never know, sometimes they'll come ashore. Like that one." She gestured at a picture on the wall. "That one came ashore 'bout ten years ago and wiped out a row of houses."

Sabrina looked where she was pointing and saw a picture of a white lighthouse, dwarfed by a large black funnel cloud, stretching from the water to sky.

"You got a picture of it? Weren't you scared?"

"I just happened to be volunteering at the lighthouse that day, and here comes a storm, from slick cam to devil's blow, in a matter of minutes. And there was the water spout, just getting bigger and bigger and coming closer and closer. Nowhere to go, really, so I just took pictures of it, until it veered to the side and came ashore where Lighthouse Estates is now. Killed one old tourist fellow, picked him up and dropped him down slam bam on top of the recycling center. Scared the helius out of Missy Garrison, who was working there. I always wondered what it felt like, to be picked up by that big old wall of wind and water, and flown through the air. I'd say it wasn't a bad way to die, flying through the air. There, how does that feel?"

Sabrina realized that she had been so fascinated by the woman's story that she hadn't paid any attention as the woman smeared on brown ointment and taped soft white bandages across her knees. Now, she peered with interest down at the bandage and saw that it had been professionally applied. Sabrina made a mental note to apply antibiotic cream when she got home, and to look in her medical book to make sure there was no exotic germ or fungus she might have picked up in the mud.

"Thank you. I feel like a kid at the nurse's office." She flexed her knees, ouching a bit as she did.

"I'm Louise Nettie Wrightly." The woman thrust

out her hand, smeared with the brown ointment. "Call me Nettie."

"I'm Sabrina." Sabrina shook her hand. This was the matriarch of the infamous Wrightly family? "What kind of ointment is this?" She smelled the pungent stuff on her fingers.

"My own special recipe," Nettie said, getting to her feet as agile as a child. "Raccoon's blood, turtle's teeth, bat dandruff…" She broke off, her eyes gleaming.

"How nice. Your broom's in the closet, I presume?"

Nettie burst out laughing. "No broom. I'm not a witch, though Wicca has always fascinated me. I call myself an Experimentalist. I experiment with religions. I've got a real talent for them. I embrace all religions, all denominations, and I plan to start my own one of these days."

The wrinkled face was set in earnest lines, a slight hunch to her shoulders giving her a coquettish upward tilt to her face, as if she was always peering toward the sky. Her bright cinnamon eyes were small and lively, an impish gleam in them as she waited for her visitor's reaction.

Sabrina wasn't quite sure what to say. She decided to stay on the safe side of the slippery slope of religion. "I love your shop. It must be a wonderful place to come to work every day."

"It's nice all right." Nettie looked around and nodded in approval. "I just wish those infernal Tittletotts would sell it to me so I wouldn't be beholden to them for my livelihood."

"You don't own the shop?"

"No, the Tittletotts own this building, and most every building in Waver Town. They lease them to us, but it sticks in our craw to have to pay them rent every month.

And if they ever decided to take against a body...well, they would have us over a barrel, let me just say that."

"Well." Sabrina floundered for yet another safe subject. "I wanted to tell you how much I've enjoyed staying in your cottage."

"My husband grew up there." Nettie was easily diverted, Sabrina was thankful to see. She sat in the chair opposite Sabrina and smoothed her white robes. "He built the New Wrightly House for me when we got married forty years ago, but I always liked the old one best. So many people lived and died in that house. It's over a hundred years old."

"I never would have guessed." Sabrina kept a straight face.

"We never expected to rent it out like this, but that real estate friend of Thierry's told us how much money we were missing out on every week we let it sit empty, so we thought...why not?"

"I'm certainly glad you decided to. I think I may have seen your son, Thierry, today."

"That boy." She sighed. "Sometimes it's a real trial being a parent. You don't have children, do you? No, I didn't think so. You love your children no matter what, no matter how much they disappoint you. Thierry's been following after a bad man—he's always been easily swayed by pretty talk, you understand. Thierry's like that, never thinking much before jumping into something. He means well, but sometimes I think he's not so smart. But you love them no matter what, you have no choice." She sighed again, then smiled. "May says you've made yourself quite at home, with your little sparrow. I'm glad. Lora is happy to have you there, I think."

"Calvin's a parakeet."

"A parakeet? You should bring him over to meet Horatio." Nettie beamed a crinkled smile at Sabrina.

"Horatio?"

"My cockatoo. I'm glad you're a bird person, so few of us are. You've got your cat people, and your dog people, of course, and some people are even rodent and reptile people, though I've never really understood that. And then you've got your bird people. We're a special breed, my dear."

"Really? I didn't know." Sabrina found herself relaxing with this sweet, slightly batty matriarch of the Wrightly clan, and barely able to get a word in edgewise.

"My, yes. A special breed. Now, if you were a twelve twelve person as well, that would be a real coincidence."

"Twelve twelve person?"

"Yes. I'm attracted to the number twelve twelve. Have been my whole life. I always look at the clock at twelve twelve, my first child was born at twelve twelve, the last four digits of my phone number are twelve twelve. I could go on and on. It means that I'm one of the special people who will help lead the people of the world to the light after Armageddon. Though it better happen soon, or I'll be dead, and all those people will wander around aimlessly without me."

"Sometimes I look at the clock at 3:04," Sabrina said. "Does that mean anything?"

Nettie cocked her head to one side like a bird, and thought. "I'm not sure. I'll have to look it up. It may mean that you have some small task after Armageddon, like leading the birds to safety, or helping clean the roads that lead to the light. Something like that. The good thing is that you're a numbers person. That means we have even more in common. Well, it looks like the rain has stopped." She got to her feet. "It's been wonderful talking to you, why don't you bring your parakeet over tonight, maybe around eight? Good. I'm sure Horatio would love to meet him. Here's some cookies to take with you, my specialty, Millionaire Cookies. Good-bye."

A moment later, Sabrina found herself outside the shop, holding a fragrant white bag, and wondering at Nettie's version of "Here's your hat, what's your hurry?" She hadn't been able to ask any questions about Lora.

"SHE'S GONE," NETTIE WRIGHTLY said as she came into the back room of the shop. "I don't think she suspected anything. You have to be more careful. If anybody sees you…" Nettie lowered herself to a chair, feeling the pain in her joints. Well, why not? She was almost sixty-five years old. Or was it seventy-five? Anyway, she was old enough to know better, that's for sure.

"No one saw me," the man said. He was seated in the back corner of the store room, his black clothes blending into the shadows. A black hat was pulled low over his eyes, and a long sword in a black sheath rested by his side.

"You're just lucky then," Nettie snapped, but then her tone softened. "It was a bad storm. I don't blame you for wanting to get out of the rain. Now you better stay here until it gets dark, and then slip out the back. I'll pack you some more sandwiches, and I've got a bag of shrimp I boiled up after Dock brought them in yesterday. This can't go on too much longer."

"It doesn't have to," the man said in a low voice. "It'll all be over Wednesday night."

SEVEN

WHEN SHE GOT HOME, Calvin was chattering darkly in his cage.

"Varooom, varooom."

Sabrina saw the vacuum cleaner in the corner of the living room, and understood the noise Calvin was imitating. He hated the vacuum cleaner.

"Hallo, Miss Dunsweeney," May Mitchell said as she came out of the kitchen. May was dressed in her usual shapeless faded dress, her gray hair pulled ruthlessly away from her tanned, skeletal face. Sabrina had forgotten the woman was coming today. In fact, she'd accepted that the dour island woman pretty much came whenever she wanted.

"Hello, May. That was some storm, wasn't it?" Sabrina said, prepared for the little smile and the frosty dismissal May always delivered. May had been very proper and polite the two other times she cleaned the house, but never friendly. But this time May surprised her.

"See you bought a teapot," she said, gesturing into the kitchen where Sabrina had dumped the pig-shaped teapot on the stove from lack of anywhere else to put it. The thought of making tea in the smiling, bloated pig was vaguely unsettling.

"Please? Yes, I bought it yesterday at the Tittletott House."

"I got one too," May said. "I must have gone to the

party earlier than you, because I didn't see you. Mine's shaped like a cow in a wedding dress."

"It was a nice party." Sabrina brought Calvin out of his cage and set him on her shoulder. She wondered if she should mention the laxatives in the tea, but it seemed gauche somehow.

"He didn't like the electric broom much," May said, nodding her head at Calvin. She was obviously struggling to find something to talk about. Sabrina wondered why she was bothering, but she was happy to oblige.

"No, he's always hated vacuum cleaners. Back in Cincinnati, he used to try to attack mine, and one day I ran over his tail and sucked off most of his tail feathers. He looked funny waddling around with no tail."

May and Sabrina laughed together, and the laughter trailed off into uncomfortable silence. May stood, twisting her hands in the dishcloth she held.

"Did you meet Bradford?" she blurted.

"Bradford Tittletott?" Sabrina asked. "Yes. He seems like a nice man. I'm sure he'll make a good…uh, president."

"Sure." May nodded her head briskly. "He will. Ninja Tittletott did a good job too, but he was getting old. He started forgetting things, talking to electric poles, shaking hands with the little flags on the mailboxes. We were all relieved when he got it into his head to run for the state senate and got elected." She paused. "Bradford is the cream of the crop. The best this island's got to offer and we're all proud of him. I'm making flounder fritters for his rally Wednesday night." Her eyes were dreamy, and her tone ranged between that of a proud aunt to a giddy school girl. Sabrina half expected May to ask her if she'd noticed how nice his buns were.

"Are you related to Brad?"

"My sister Greta is married to Haleb, who is fifth cousin to Lima Lowry, who of course is Brad's relation on his mother's side, so yes, I am related." Her tone seemed to imply that she was related enough to have a hold on the boy, but not close enough for consanguinity to be a problem if the boy chose to look her way. Sabrina struggled not to laugh. May was a leathery, wind-blown woman in the throes of passion for a man twenty years her junior.

Brad Tittletott seemed to have that effect on a lot of women. It was something about the way he pitched his voice lower when he talked to a woman, and leaned close as if he had something private to say, and looked straight in her eyes as he talked as if she were the only person in the world.

Sabrina shook her head. Goodness. If she didn't watch out, next she'd be thinking about his buns.

"Have you heard about the ghost?" May asked matter-of-factly.

Ah ha, Sabrina thought, this was what she wanted to talk about.

"Walk-the-Plank Wrightly?" Sabrina asked. "Yes, Lima told me about him."

May's eyebrows rose, and Sabrina saw that her stock with the woman had risen as well. Not only was she hobnobbing with Queen Elizabeth Tittletott, she was talking to Lima Lowry. How bad could the crazy blond tourist be?

"I was just wondering." May attempted nonchalance but failed. The tiny gray hairs on her hairline, which had fought their way free from the confines of her bun, almost quivered with eagerness, and she kneaded her hands in the dishcloth. "I was just wondering if maybe you had seen him? You *are* living on his land…"

"No," Sabrina said regretfully. "I haven't seen him, I'm afraid."

"'Cause I could have sworn I saw him when I was cleaning the upstairs bedroom and looking out over the marsh. Could have sworn I seen Walk-the-Plank Wrightly dressed all in black walking through the marsh right before it rained. And what's more, I saw his wife, Sarah Wrightly, blond and golden, walking at his side! And then they disappeared right into the marsh. It was the strangest thing I've ever seen." May was caught up in her story, her bland face twisted with excitement, her boggy eyes closed as she tried to memorize exactly what she had seen.

"Well, goodness, it sounds to me like you may have seen a ghost then," Sabrina said, wondering if it was the same man she had seen in the woods. Even so, you didn't see her going around talking about seeing ghosts. In Cincinnati, that was a recipe for a tiny, locked room and a nurse named Hilda who force-fed you applesauce.

"I might have, at that. It's the second time I've seen 'em in that marsh. I'd look out if I were you. Who knows what a ghost might be up to?"

"Thank you, I will." Sabrina looked around at her spotless house. "And thank you for doing such a good job cleaning. Everything looks wonderful. Let me get you a check."

"I'm almost done," May said. "I've got to get to my restaurant anyway, and get ready to open for dinner."

Sabrina followed as May headed back to the kitchen. "Your restaurant?"

"I own Blue Cam over on the Towner side of the harbor. Used to be Nouveau Island Food With a Twist, but nobody could ever figure out the menu—like it was written in another language except you recognized some words, the small ones. If you wanted to eat there you just ordered by number and prayed whatever came wasn't seaweed or raw fish. I changed the name when I took over from those slick New Jersey fellas. Been trying to make a go at it, but I don't think I'm cut out for the restaurant business. I'm about ready to get rid of it and do something else. Maybe I'll set up a booth and sell conch shells. Missy Garrison made a living at that one year, I hear." May had turned back to washing dishes as she spoke.

Goodness gracious, get the woman talking and she wouldn't shut up! "The Blue Cam," Sabrina said, searching her memory. "I don't think I remember seeing it."

"Yeah, well, that's what everybody says. It's right next to the Ride the Big One Pub, and no one has trouble remembering *that* place." May's face twisted. "Anyway, I'm just going to finish up here in the kitchen. What do you do to these pots, anyway? Looks like you're burning glue in them." She held up a pot to show the black crust on the bottom of the pot.

"Risotto," Sabrina said cheerfully. "It was great."

May stared at her, and then shook her head as she stacked washed dishes into the dish rack with unnecessary force. It bothered Sabrina to have someone else wash her dishes—she had always cleaned the house she shared with her mother. But this month was different, and Sally insisted she get someone to clean her house so she wouldn't have to worry about it.

May left while Sabrina was perusing *Romeo and Juliet*. Calvin was sleeping on the windowsill, his head hunched forward and his eyes closed. It had been a while since she had read over this, one of her favorite plays, and she smiled in contentment as she read, savoring the magnificent wordplay.

"I hope the boys bring the entire cast tomorrow," she said out loud as she considered the cast of characters. Even in a pinch, they would have to have at least eight or nine children. Of course, Romeo and Juliet, but what about the Friar and Mercutio and Benvolio and the nurse? And the feuding lords, Montague and Capulet?

Somewhere in her ruminating, she fell asleep and dreamed that she heard the back door open and someone come in. A big, shadowy figure stood in the doorway from the kitchen, but she could not see his face and she could not move, and she opened her mouth to scream—

It took several moments to register that someone was knocking on the front door. When she opened her eyes she was surprised to see that the sun had set, though the water gleamed with an incandescent pink light, as if the glowing orb was buried in the depths of the sound. The storm clouds had moved away, and the moon hung, massive and orange, low on the darkening horizon.

Calvin was stirring on his cooling windowsill, looking around as the knocking continued.

"What a dream! My heart is still pounding. I wonder who that could be?" Calvin chirped in irritation as she got to her feet and went to the door.

"Hello, Ms. Dunsweeney," Bradford Tittletott said. "You left this at the house today." He held out her coat.

"Goodness." Sabrina took the coat. She must have forgotten it at the table where she had lunch. "I appreciate you bringing it to me." She looked up at him, wishing she was wearing heels because she was getting a crick in her neck.

"No problem," he said easily. "It's the neighborly thing to do." He slouched against her door frame, sexy in his immaculate suit with his rumpled blond hair.

"Would you like to come in?" Sabrina asked after a moment.

"No, no. I just thought—well, I just don't want you to get the wrong impression of my family. My mother and brother can be rather—outspoken at times. I just don't want you to misunderstand anything they said this afternoon."

Sabrina thought back on the conversation she had overheard that afternoon at the Tittletott House. Gary and Elizabeth had been talking about Thierry Wrightly in a rather derogatory fashion, but surely that could not be what Bradford was worried about her overhearing? What juicy tidbit did she just miss overhearing?

"No, I don't think I misunderstood anything," she said. "It *was* rather—um, shocking." She hoped she hadn't overdone it.

"Well—" Bradford hesitated, studying her with guileless eyes. "Yes, I imagine it might have been. Of course, none of it was true. Just people trying to discredit me."

"Yes, ahem," Sabrina said, wondering how in the world to draw the secret, whatever it was, out of him.

"Well, I hope you didn't miss the jacket too much. You have a nice night."

"You too, and thank you," she called after him as he went down the steps and into the night.

Sabrina stood staring after him, until a stirring in the bushes made her slam the door. Why in the world didn't this house have any locks?

She turned to find Calvin right behind her, head cocked in curiosity.

"Now what was that all about?"

He cheeped, and waddled toward the kitchen.

"I know, I know," Sabrina said. "It's supper time."

She got Calvin his food and opened the refrigerator to stare at the contents unenthusiastically. She liked to pamper her stomach, she always had. Each meal was an adventure to her. But the island did not have the gourmet items that she enjoyed, like portabella mushrooms, couscous, and saffron. How was she supposed to create culinary masterpieces with a small can of pork and beans ($4.95), creamed corn (two cans for $6.00) and a bag of tortilla chips ($5.50—the salsa had been too expensive to even contemplate). She wondered how the locals could afford to live on this island.

She moved aside a loaf of bread ($3.99) and was surprised to see a bag of boiled shrimp shoved into the back corner of the refrigerator. Where had that come from? She searched her memory, trying to remember if she had picked it up at one of the several fresh seafood marts around the island. Now *that* was a plus about island living, all types of seafood fresh off the boat. But the last thing she had picked up was some scallops the other day and she made scallop carbonara with that. So where did the shrimp come from?

She opened the bag and sniffed cautiously. It was fresh.

"Ah ha!" Sabrina said out loud, and Calvin glanced up at her. "It must be from May, Calvin. It's a gift. These islanders are really coming around."

Calvin chirped around a mouthful of birdseed.

Rubbing her hands in excitement, Sabrina checked to see if she had the necessary ingredients. Tomatoes, no angel hair pasta, but here was some spaghetti, garlic—

unfortunately, not fresh garlic, but the stuff in a jar—and white wine…too bad, no French bread, but…

AN HOUR LATER, the smoke finally dissipating out of the kitchen, her stomach full of shrimp scampi pasta, she and Calvin traveled down the dark road toward the New Wrightly House. Daylight saving time had recently reverted to standard time and darkness fell early. The orange globe of the moon had risen and shrunk to a pale silver orb, illuminating a narrow, glittering path across the restless water. Sabrina shifted her gaze from the moon to the stars, twinkling like a million fireflies in the lustrous black sky. She couldn't remember ever seeing so many and so bright. She picked out the Big Dipper, and with more difficulty located the Pegasus in all its autumn glory.

Calvin scolded as she tripped over a rut in the sand road.

"Sorry, Calvin. I just can't believe how clear the stars look."

He settled back down on her shoulder, his little head swiveling as an owl hooted from the apple orchard. Sabrina heard the rumble of hoofs, and out of the shadows came two island ponies, shaggy and brown, snuffling and blowing a bit when they saw her. Sabrina stood still as they trotted by her and effortlessly jumped over the fence into the orchard. A moment later, Sabrina almost tripped over a possum. He turned and stared at her, his long nose twitching, then hurried off into the underbrush.

Sabrina could hear the water lapping against the side of the old dock, the susurration of the silky water tickling at her ears. Up ahead, the lights of the New Wrightly

House shone, and Sabrina hoped that Nettie Wrightly remembered the invitation she had issued.

Sabrina climbed the wood stairs and knocked on the door. She wasn't really surprised when the door was flung open by the old withered man. He stared at her, working his toothless gums, his face twisting into a scream.

"No, no, I'm harmless," Sabrina said, stepping forward and putting her hand out to the old man. "Please don't scream."

But it was too late. He shook her hand off as if it were a big, hairy spider and, still screaming, slammed the door in her face.

Sabrina stood in the cool night air, staring at the door. She had an incredible feeling of déjà vu.

EIGHT

SHE WAS DEBATING knocking again when the door swung open. Nettie still wore her embroidered white robes, and tonight she wore a flashing...*thing* on her head, silver like a tiara, blinking with multi-colored lights.

"Come in, come in." Nettie opened the door wider so she could enter. "Good to see you. I just got this today." She touched her twinkling headgear. "It's supposed to enhance my ability to receive messages from the other world."

Sabrina glanced past the woman at the old man huddled in a chair, glaring at the TV, his shoulders hunched. "Hello, Nettie. I don't want to offend anybody..."

"Who? Dock? He's harmless. Crazy as a Mitchell's Day sailboarder, but he's harmless." With that ambiguous statement, Nettie pulled Sabrina inside.

"This must be Calvin!" Nettie reached up and scooped the tiny bird off Sabrina's shoulder as Calvin twittered in surprise. "Good bird," Nettie crooned, stroking him. He gazed up at her, mesmerized by the sound of her voice.

"Please tell me you're not getting another flying rat," Thierry Wrightly drawled as he strolled into the room. He was still wearing the same dingy blue jeans and T-shirt and showed no sign that he recognized her from the Tittletott House. He held a Budweiser in one hand and a cigarette in the other.

"This is Calvin, Thierry." Nettie held up the bird so her son could see him.

"He's a budgerigar, more commonly known as a parakeet," Sabrina said. "He's very rare because he's buttercup yellow, just like a little chick, except for the bit of white on his forehead and underside. He was a gift from a friend of mine who is a bird breeder."

Thierry snorted. "And who's the tourist?"

"Thierry!" Nettie scolded. She was so tiny that she had to crane her head all the way back to see his face, and he grinned down at her from his six-foot-two height, not in the least repentant. "You're not too old for me to put over my knee, you know," she said, and he smirked. Nettie turned back to Sabrina. "Sabrina, this is Thierry Roland Wrightly, my no-good son. Thierry, Sabrina Victoria Dunsweeney."

Thierry sketched a wave at Sabrina which she returned with a small smile. She was trying to remember when she had told Nettie her middle name. She was sure she had not put it on her rental application.

"It's all right, Dock," Nettie was saying to the old man still crouched on the couch. "It's the girl staying down the road, not one of those nasty people. Calm down." She patted his shoulder, and Calvin mimicked her murmur.

The old man cast a wary eye on Sabrina and quickly turned his head away. He was wearing baggy pants and a stained white undershirt, and his thin, sunken face was covered with stubble and a large pair of glasses.

"Hello, Dock," Sabrina said, but the old man refused to look at her. Nettie continued to soothe him, and Sabrina turned questioning eyes on Thierry.

"Thinks you're one of those insurance salesmen," he explained. "One came along last year and scared him half to death. He talked about strokes and heart attacks for weeks, until he stopped talking. Now he's scared to answer the door."

"Goodness."

"Dock, honey, you can go out in your boat tomorrow. I think it's supposed to be nice. Would you like that?"

Dock ignored her, his eyes riveted on the TV.

"Is that his boat docked down the street?" Sabrina asked.

"Yes. Sometimes I think I shouldn't let him out on the boat, but he always finds his way back, and it's the only thing nowadays that makes him happy. Let's go into the other room and let Dock watch his show."

As they left the room, Sabrina noticed that Dock was watching MTV.

At the back of the house was a long, high-ceilinged room, kitchen and family room combined, with a large fireplace at one end of the room. A boy was seated at a table, poring over a book.

"Why, hello, Terry!" Sabrina exclaimed as she came through the door. He looked up, utter surprise and then apprehension crossing his face.

"Miss Sabrina," he stammered.

"You've met my grandson?" Nettie asked, crossing to the boy and putting her hand on his shoulder. "Spell 'onomatopoeia,'" she instructed.

"That's not one of my words!" Terry protested.

"Doesn't matter. Ask Miss Sabrina, a spelling bee isn't complete without 'onomatopoeia.' She should know, she's a teacher."

"She's right," Sabrina agreed. When had she told Nettie she was a teacher? "When's your spelling bee?"

"Wednesday night," Terry said. "It was supposed to be

just a spelling bee, but then Mr. Tittletott wanted to use the school gym for his rally, so they decided to combine the spelling bee with the rally. Mr. Tittletott is going to give away the prize, a fishing pole."

He glanced at his grandmother as he spoke, his face full of furtive excitement. Sabrina looked up to see the old woman purse her mouth in dislike.

"I wish you'd shoot the freak, oooh, oooh," said a squawking, querulous voice, and Sabrina turned to see a large white bird in a cage behind her. He was halfway hidden by the door, which is why she had missed him when she came in.

"Horatio." Nettie crossed to the cage as the bird dipped up and down in excitement, unfurling the yellow and white plumage on his head.

"I wish you'd shoot the freak, oooh, oooh," he said again, dipping up and down.

"Cheep," Calvin said in dismay as Nettie brought him closer to the other bird. "Cheep!" He twisted his little head and looked desperately at Sabrina.

"Horatio, this is Calvin. Calvin, this is Horatio," Nettie said. The two birds stared at each other in mutual dislike. Horatio reached out a clawed foot, mutely begging to be taken onto Nettie's arm. When she kept out of his reach, he threw a temper tantrum, shaking his head and squawking at the top of his lungs.

"Mom!" Thierry bellowed as he came into the room and went straight to the refrigerator for another beer. "Do something about him!"

Horatio continued to squawk, and Calvin fluttered his wings at the other bird, puffing up his feathers so he looked imposing, and said emphatically, "CHEEP!"

"I WISH YOU'D SHOOT THE FREAK, OOH, OOH," Horatio screeched.

Terry put his hands over his ears, and Sabrina felt like doing the same. She crossed to Nettie and rescued Calvin, who gratefully crawled up to her neck and hid under her hair. Nettie was able to pick up Horatio, and he subsided into contented clucking, happy at getting his own way.

"Horatio, you've been watching MTV again," Nettie scolded. "He picks up the strangest things off the television. I really wish Dock wouldn't let him watch it."

"*I'll* shoot the freak." Thierry crossed over to his son and shot a dark look at the bird. "What can you spell today, kid?" He looked down at the boy, and Sabrina realized that this was father and son. Somehow, Thierry had struck her as too young to have a son, but he must be at least thirty, plenty old enough to have a son Terry's age.

"Uh, I can spell 'anarchist,'" Terry said, and proceeded to do so.

"Christ, what kind of words are they teaching kids nowadays?" Thierry said, when Terry was done. "Did they teach you how to spell 'commie' and 'lily-livered,' too? You know what they say, knowledge is power and power corrupts. Right?"

Terry's face fell and he nodded in incomprehension.

"So study hard, little man, be evil!"

Laughing at his cleverness, Thierry went back into the living room, where the insistent beat of rap music was pounding through the walls.

"Please sit down," Nettie said, pointing at a stool and whispering to Horatio. She looked up at her grandson. "Terry, get the lady one of my special drinks."

Sabrina started to protest, but then decided it might be construed as rude. She held her tongue as the boy ambled over to the freezer and poured thick, red liquid out of a pitcher into a glass.

"Here," Terry said, banging the glass down onto the counter in front of Sabrina and slopping quite a bit of the sluggish liquid onto the wooden surface.

"Thank you." Surely Nettie wouldn't serve blood as her "special drink"? She stole a look at the other woman, who was murmuring nonsense words to her big white cockatoo, the tiara blinking cheerily on her head.

Maybe she would.

Nettie looked up, her little eyes twinkling as she caught Sabrina's gaze. It was a challenge, plain and simple, so Sabrina steeled herself and took a small sip.

"It's good!" she exclaimed, and turned to find Nettie gurgling with laughter.

"You sound surprised." Nettie put Horatio back on top of his cage and came over to the counter.

"I just—it looked like—" Sabrina broke off, realizing she had just opened her mouth to switch feet. "It's very good," she said lamely.

"I'm glad you like it." The old woman climbed up onto the stool beside Sabrina. "It's fresh fruit punch. I keep it very cool, so it's almost slushy, which is why it looks so thick."

Sabrina took another sip of the delicious drink. Nettie was swinging her bare leathery feet back and forth.

"You're a talented cook, Nettie," Sabrina said. "Your Millionaire Cookies are wonderful."

"You think so? Thank you." Nettie smiled, her face crinkling with amusement. "People from the mainland are always telling me I should market my cookies. Tell me I'd make a mint."

"They're right," Sabrina said, thinking about the rich, delicious cookies.

Nettie shook her head. "I don't think so. Those mainlanders are just about as sneaky as the Towners. I'm sure they'd find some way of ripping me off."

She smiled at Sabrina without malice. "Of course, you know I'm not talking about you. I've never met anyone from Cincinnati before. Why are you here? You don't feel like someone on vacation. Have you been ill?"

"My mother died not too long ago. We were very close. I decided to get away for a while," Sabrina said instead, which was all true. She didn't mention what had happened with Mr. Phil.

"I'm so sorry. How terrible for you."

"It's been hard. She was a wonderful woman."

"How brave of you to come all this way by yourself! I've only been off the island twice, myself."

"You've only been off Comico Island *twice*?" The island was only twelve or thirteen miles long, and a couple of miles wide.

Nettie shook her head and gave one of her uncomplicated smiles. "The last time was when Terry's mother had to be flown to a mainland hospital to have Terry, because he was inside her upside down and backwards, poor thing."

"What about when you had your own children? Didn't you go to a hospital on the mainland?"

"The girls these days. They run to the doctor at the drop of a hat. I never saw a doctor in my life. Angel Tubbs, she was the midwife for this island for fifty years. She delivered my two children, and most of the people on this island."

"You cut out my heart with a pitchfork," Horatio

crooned, and Sabrina recognized the lines from a current song playing on the radio.

"The bird used to say things like 'Horatio wants a cracker' and 'pretty bird.' Now that Dock watches that music station all day long, Horatio talks about shooting and dissecting people. It's horrible."

Sabrina nodded in agreement. She had listened to the CDs her students brought to class for recess and was appalled at some of the lyrics.

"It's only recently that we got cable here. Before that, all we had was what we could pick up with our rabbit ears. Not much, so most people used their TVs for an end table. Then they got cable out to us, and now people sit inside all day and watch TV. Instead of being social, and having Mullet Tosses and Quilting Circles, instead of going over to their friends' houses and gossiping over a cup of coffee, they sit at home in front of their TVs and dial their friends on the telephone." Nettie shook her head in disgust and reached over to take a swig of Sabrina's drink.

"No one wants to come to my séances anymore," she continued mournfully.

"You do séances?"

"Oh yes." Nettie brightened. "I talk to Hichacokolo, he's one of the original Irrocottilo Indians who used to live on this island. He's always full of gossip about the afterworld, says it's pretty much like here, except no one can do evil, so it's pretty boring. Hichacokolo is a character, let me tell you." Nettie lowered her voice. "I think he's probably a homosexualist, if you want to know the truth. Always talking about the clothes people are wearing, and he talks with a 'bith of a lith', if you catch my meaning." Nettie winked at Sabrina. "Then there's English Jane.

She was one of the first English women to come to the island, but she's a whiner. Always talking about how bad it was back in those days, how cold it was, how sick she got of fish, how she hated the Indians. She and Hichaco-kolo definitely do *not* get along. Sarah Wrightly, the wife of Walk-the-Plank Wrightly, she's not like English Jane at all. She always wears a long white dress, with a red rose fastened to her bosom, and she carries her lantern as she searches for her lost husband's treasure. She's a nice woman, I've always liked her."

"What about Walk-the-Plank Wrightly? Do you ever talk to him?" Sabrina smiled, humoring the woman.

Nettie cocked her head and peered at Sabrina out of one of her tiny eyes. "Funny you should ask," she said. "I was talking to him just the other day."

"Did he tell you why he was back after so long?"

Nettie pursed her mouth. Sabrina felt eyes on her back and turned to find Terry openly eavesdropping.

"He said he has some things to take care of," Nettie said.

"Is he still mad at Lord Tittletott for exposing him as a pirate?"

"He's mad at the Tittletotts for being the sneaky, lying Towners that they are."

"But, Grandma, Sid's a Tittletott, and he's not all bad," Terry protested. Nettie's face softened as she turned to look at her grandson.

"His mother took off when he was two," she murmured to Sabrina. "Raised him like my own." She smiled mistily at Terry, and raised her voice so he could hear. "Sid's not old enough to have picked up all the Tittletott traits. Give him time."

Terry looked rebellious and closed his book. "I think

he's nice. And I like his Uncle Bradford, too. Dad likes him, so why shouldn't I?"

"Your dad's been playing with the devil," Nettie muttered.

"Ahem," Sabrina said, trying to break the tension in the air. "I wanted to thank you for letting me stay in your mother-in-law's house. It's very homey, she must have been a wonderful person."

Nettie turned and appraised Sabrina. "Ah ha, I see you've already picked up the vibes. Just enough to make you curious, right?"

Sabrina shook her head and smiled. "All right. I'll admit it, I'm fishing for information." And she proceeded to tell Nettie about the pictures she had found under the hatch in the floor.

"Pictures?" Nettie lowered her voice, but Terry was leaning forward so he could see the TV in the living room. "From twenty-five years ago? But what would they have been doing under...? Goodness." Nettie stood in thought, her finger tapping her leathered face. "Goodness, goodness. I wonder if *that's* why, but no... I don't understand."

"What do you remember?"

"A week before she fell and hit her head, Lora had me go up into the attic and pull down a crate where she kept some files. I asked her what they were, and she said she had kept work from her favorite students all through the years."

"You think she might have pulled those pictures out of one of those file folders?"

Nettie shrugged. "It makes sense, doesn't it? Why else would she have had pictures from twenty-five years ago?" Something was troubling Nettie, and she avoided Sabrina's eyes.

"Nettie?" Sabrina questioned softly.

The older woman was silent for a moment. "It's just that… I saw some of the file folders she pulled out. We called them the 'rat pack' when they were kids, they were that inseparable. I remember wondering why Lora was looking though their folders."

"The rat pack?"

"Yes. Of course, they're all grown up now. Brad and Gary Tittletott. Virginia Garrison, now a Tittletott. And…my sons. Thierry and Rolo Wrightly."

There was silence in the room, broken only by the pounding beat of the TV.

"If she was looking for those pictures—and why would she be after all this time?—why would she pull out all their folders? Surely she would remember which one of them had drawn those pictures. It's not something you forget."

But Nettie was shaking her head. "Lora's memory had been spotty since her stroke. I wouldn't be surprised if she remembered that one of the rat pack drew those pictures, but not which one. As to why she was looking for them after all this time… We may never know." She paused. "I want to see the pictures. I'm afraid…yes, I want to see those pictures. Do you mind if I come by tomorrow?"

"That would be fine." Sabrina stood. She could see how shaken Nettie was, though she wasn't sure why. Something else was going on here, something she didn't understand. Calvin scratched at her neck as he woke.

"I think I'll be heading along," she said and Nettie didn't protest. "Thank you for inviting me over."

"I'll see you tomorrow." Nettie ushered Sabrina through the living room to the front door. "Maybe next time you come over you can meet Hichacokolo and English Jane." She seemed to be making an effort to change the subject.

"That would be nice," Sabrina said, and tripped over something under the living room rug. Dock glanced over at her, and then back at the TV. Thierry laughed out loud.

Sabrina looked down and saw the outline of another hatch under the rug, like the one in her house.

"Watch out for the hurricane hatch," Nettie said. "It'll get you every time until you get used to just where it is. Then you kind of unconsciously avoid it without thinking about it. I call them the island's version of a burglar alarm."

"What is it for?"

"A hurricane hatch," Nettie said. "When the waters come up high enough, you open the hatch and the water comes up through the hatch instead of washing the house away. Don't you have hurricane hatches in Cincinnati?"

NINE

"TELL THEM THE TRUTH, BRAD! Tell them what really happened!" Rolo's voice cracked, wavered upward into a falsetto as he leaned forward to grasp the shoulder of his best friend.

Brad's eyes burned, but he tried to keep his voice steady. "I can't, Rolo, please, don't you understand? I can't help you."

The wind rushed through the marsh grass, rustling the crimson leaves of the huge oak tree above their heads—why did he remember that so vividly?—and a seagull called, high and accusing.

"I can't believe this," Rolo said, his voice low. His dark, bushy hair was tied at the base of his neck with an old piece of leather, and his blue eyes were shining with tears of anger and disbelief. "I just can't believe this."

"I brought you some food, and some money. Here. Stay here at the treasure tree until tonight, and then you can take a boat and get across to the mainland."

He was proud that he managed to keep his voice calm. It was amazing what you could do if you had to. His mother's favorite saying, usually so annoying when she said it over and over again in that self-righteous tone of hers, was oddly comforting today. *Take care of today and tomorrow will take care of itself.*

Rolo straightened. He understood now. "You won't tell the truth even if I do? Is that what you're saying?"

Brad looked down. His throat constricted, and he tried to forget the pain he had seen in his best friend's eyes, the disappointment and the rising hate. Tomorrow will be just fine and dandy, he told himself with desperate determination.

"You know I can't."

Rolo was silent and Brad did not look at him.

"All right, I'll do it. Who would believe a Wrightly anyway? I would ask you to tell Virginia good-bye for me, but I guess I can't trust you to do that either. You're probably glad to get me out of the way so you can have her." Rolo's voice was cold and hard, all emotion suppressed fiercely.

He stared at Brad for one long moment. "I'll be back, Bradford Tittletott, and I won't forget this as long as I live." He turned and disappeared into the whispering marsh grass.

Brad gazed after him, unable to shake the feeling that he had just made the biggest mistake of his life.

BRAD TITTLETOTT AWOKE with a start, struggling against the sweaty sheets wrapped around his arms and neck. His heart was thrashing inside his chest and for a moment he worried that he might be having a heart attack. He took several deep breaths and tried to sort dream from reality. He was safe in his bed. Fifteen years separated him from that terrible day when he had betrayed his best friend, and tasted the first bitter fruits of being an adult. It was all over, the past dead and buried.

Then he remembered what was happening and stiffened with fear.

It wasn't over. No, it wasn't over by a long shot.

SABRINA WALKED ALONG the edge of the sound the next morning, shivering in the cool morning air as thin and clear as ice water. Clumps of spindrift like white cotton candy rolled along the edge of the shore, and waves of scrabbling fiddler crabs scattered at her approach.

Ahead of her, the familiar footsteps marched in front of her in the drying sand left by the retreating tide. Once again, the man who left the footsteps, or the ghost of Walk-the-Plank Wrightly as she had grudgingly begun to think of him, had been before her.

"It's a beautiful day, isn't it, Calvin?" She savored the choppy blue water topped with luscious whitecaps, and the sun-brightened marsh grass *shuuushing* in the breeze. The wind was a constant companion on Comico Island, she had noticed, and today it was running friendly fingers through her hair, tugging at her clothes and tickling at her ears.

Calvin's eyes were on a flock of geese floating in the shallows farther down the beach. There were hundreds of them, honking and splashing their wings at each other. Sabrina stopped at a fallen tree and sat down to watch the birds. They hadn't noticed her approach, and were busy feeding, grooming, resting, and doing whatever else a bird does on an impromptu pit stop.

"Cheep, cheep," Calvin called to them, but his little voice failed to reach the large, graceful birds.

"And what would you do if they came for you?" Sabrina asked. "You probably would look like a pretty good appetizer to them."

Calvin cheeped indignantly and Sabrina laughed.

Today, the footprints had veered off into the marsh a little ways back, and Sabrina considered following to see where the footprints led. But one look at the marshy, muddy ground inside the tall marsh grass and she changed her mind.

"He must be part duck to get through that mess."

She glanced at her watch, considering what she had to do today. At three-thirty, the boys would be coming over for the play rehearsal.

Nettie was pleased, though surprised, at her grandson's interest in the theater. Sabrina wondered that she hadn't heard anything about the play before. Thierry Wrightly just laughed and clapped his son on the back.

"Gone and got yourself into it this time," he said and Terry threw him a desperate look.

"I'll make sure he's there on time," Nettie promised. "I'll send him right after school."

Sabrina decided she liked Nettie, though the old woman was a bit strange. But who didn't have their little foibles? Sabrina's mother used to wash her hair ten times a day, and insisted that Sabrina wash the bed sheets every day. One day she came home to find her mother trying to stuff Grandma's antique clock into the washing machine, along with the toaster. And Mama was a sweet, wonderful woman. Just goes to show that you can't judge people.

Sabrina thought back to Nettie's comments the night before about the pirate Walk-the-Plank Wrightly: *He's mad at the Tittletotts for being the sneaky, lying Towners that they are.* It sounded as if the grudge she bore was personal. What was behind the bad blood between the Tittletotts and Wrightlys? Sabrina remembered that Lima spoke about a feud between the two families, but that must have been over years ago. Feuds in this day and age were obsolete.

But the animosity was there, dark and strong, in both the Tittletotts and the Wrightlys. Despite this, Brad and Thierry were as thick as thieves. What was that all about?

More importantly, Sabrina was puzzled over what Nettie revealed about Lora. Why was the old woman looking at pictures drawn by a disturbed child twenty-five years ago? Why did she put the pictures under the hurricane hatch?

"I'll just have to wait and see what Nettie has to say today," Sabrina said.

The beach petered out into a bulkhead that surrounded the property of the Old Wrightly Cottage, and Sabrina climbed the sand path to the backyard of the cottage. The phone was ringing as she fed the two gray cats and she rushed to answer it.

"Never retire, Sabrina," said a gravelly, oh-so-familiar voice over the telephone line.

"Sally, don't say that." Sabrina was used to her best friend's flights into depression since she retired from teaching.

"It's not that I even want to teach anymore. Sometimes I think I'll be happy if I never see another snot-nosed brat again. But then I'll see them at the bus stop, and I miss every one of my children, even the pain in the butt ones."

"I know what you mean," Sabrina said. "I miss mine."

"You may miss your kids, but you're not missing the weather, that's for sure. They're calling for sleet tonight."

"Goodness, already?" Sabrina glanced out the window where the sun was shining warmly.

"This is Cincinnati, remember? Maybe I'll come visit you. It's not as if the Helpful Ladies Group will miss me, or the comatose patients I visit at Good Samaritan Hospital. They gave me the comatose ones because they said if anyone could talk a person out of a coma, I could."

Sabrina smothered a smile. "What else has been going on?"

"Well, I took some of the kids from my Monetarily Challenged Kids Club to the Boofest at Union Terminal. I swear all these kids want to see anymore is blood and guts. If someone doesn't get decapitated or burned alive, then they're just not interested. And then Jean Kirkle has decided to try out for the May Festival Chorus, and you know she sounds like a howling banshee when she sings, but of course we all tell her she sounds *wonderful*."

Sabrina sighed, feeling homesick.

"Sabrina," Sally's gruff voice was gentle, "how are you feeling?"

"Well... I'm not sure, Sally. My ankle's been hurting a little, I think I twisted it running in my heels, and my knee is scraped, and I've got this bite on my foot..."

"Sabrina. You know what I mean. You've just had a tumor removed from your breast. I know you like to avoid the subject, but..."

Sabrina twisted the phone cord tightly around her fingers. Mr. Phil, or the smooth, firm lump in her breast that her doctor had identified as a Phyllodes tumor, was gone, but the fear would remain with her the rest of her life. This time it wasn't malignant, but what about next time?

"I'm tired, that's all. So much has happened, it just seems easier sometimes to sleep."

"That's to be expected, honey. You've been through the wringer the last couple of months. First your mother dies, and then you're diagnosed with that tumor. You need to rest and get back your strength."

"Sometimes I wake up and wonder what in the world I've got to live for."

Sally snorted. "You just need some time to recover and decide what you're going to do now that you don't have to think of that old woman every minute of your life."

"It's like I don't know how to act anymore. All these years, I knew exactly what I was doing and who I was. And now…"

"Your mother died just three months ago, honey. You've spent your entire adult life taking care of her. And I know she was a tyrant, honey, don't you contradict me! You did everything for her, and all she could do was criticize you. You're just feeling a little bit of relief and a lot of sadness. It's to be expected." Sally's voice was no-nonsense.

"The more I've thought about it, the more I realize I'm just a string of halfhearted failures. I've never cared about anything much. I go through the motions when I'm teaching—"

"You're a good teacher! A little distracted, maybe…"

"Every date I've gone on has been lukewarm and I didn't care—"

"That's because your mother would scream at you every time you went on a date. It wasn't worth it and you knew it."

"I've tried writing poetry, I've tried acrobatic swimming. I took that 'Self Improvement Through Useless Bits of Knowledge' class and all I learned was that the dot over the letter 'i' is called a tittle and that a housefly hums in the middle octave, key of F. I even tried to get my medical degree through that 'Be-a-Doctor-in-Five-Weeks' program and I didn't last two weeks! The only thing I'm good at is my cooking—"

The silence was deafening. Sabrina forged on. "I guess I'm saying I want to care about something, follow through with it. Does that sound strange?"

"No, honey. I think if you cared a little more about yourself—"

"I take six vitamins a day and brush my hair five hundred times nightly!"

"Cared about yourself a little more," Sally repeated, "you'd see that the rest of it comes naturally. You've been acting like an old woman your entire life. You've made a good start buying all those bright new clothes and changing your hairdo. If you didn't do something, you were going to end up in an insane asylum."

"Is that such a bad thing? Sometimes I think it would be a relief to be insane. There are no expectations. Sane people are boring."

"Listen to you! You already sound better than you did. I guess going out to that backwoods little island was a good idea after all, as much as I was against it at first."

Sally was horrified when she learned Sabrina planned to go to an isolated island nobody ever heard of, in the middle of nowhere. When Sabrina found the tiny speck of land labeled "Comico Island" on the map, she had known one thing for certain: it would be nothing like Cincinnati. That was all that really mattered.

They talked for a few minutes longer and then the two friends said their good-byes. For a few minutes, Sabrina wished with all her heart she was back at home, putting together her lesson plan or grading papers. What kind of teacher was she, taking off in the middle of the school year?

A very tired and confused one, she decided. She realized that she missed Sally, but she wasn't really homesick. After all, she had a new place to explore, a new *Sabrina* to discover! With a feeling of adventure, she set off to town.

Children of all sizes and descriptions were walking or riding bikes in the same direction as she was walking. Sabrina waved at Terry as he came out of Nettie's Cookie Shop.

"Don't forget this afternoon!" she called. His smile was sickly as he hurried off.

Sabrina followed the parade of children over the bridge, the old boards creaking and groaning under their pounding feet, and down Tittletott Row. They turned off on a road to the right, where Sabrina surmised the school must be. There was a burned-down building on this corner, one that she had noticed before, but now she wondered if perhaps this wasn't Brad Tittletott's former office.

In a good mood, Sabrina tripped up Post Office Lane and stopped outside Sweet Island Music, where a table with books always stood. Wind chimes hung all around the store's porch and chimed pleasantly in the breeze.

Sabrina picked out an old Ngaio Marsh mystery and went inside the store to pay the suggested fifty cents. She recognized the pretty woman with long black hair behind the counter as one of the ladies with whom she shared the griddle cake stand.

"Hi!" Sabrina said. "I remember you."

Sondra Lane laughed and extended her hand. "And I remember you. Or more importantly, I've *heard* about you. I've never seen such a voracious grapevine until I came to this island! Let me see, you drive a red convertible and you're staying in the Old Wrightly Place. You're a Dunsweeney, but not related to Helen, and you feed the cats. How am I doing so far?"

"What, you don't know my dress size?"

"Give us time." She laughed. "My partner Katie and I own this store."

Music instruments of every description hung on the walls, as well as books, wind chimes and beautiful sun catchers. Near the back, a colorful selection of Halloween costumes hung on a rack. The sounds of a tortured trumpet bugled from the back room.

Sondra grimaced. "Katie's busy giving music lessons right now, or she'd come say hello. Are you on the island to stay or just to visit?"

"To visit." Sabrina realized that a little part of her wished she never had to leave.

"The natives been giving you the runaround? For an island that relies on tourism, some of our people can be rather standoffish."

"Really? I hadn't noticed."

"That bad?" Sondra laughed. "Sometimes it takes a while for them to warm up to visitors. Katie and I don't bite, though, don't worry. We've lived here for about five years, and we thank the Lord every day we made the decision to come here. I used to be an advertising agent, made tons of money, and lived in a beautiful house. I was absolutely miserable! Stressed out all the time, fighting traffic, the whole bit. Now I make about a quarter of the money, but I'm happy every day. That's what counts to us."

"It sounds wonderful." Sabrina fished in her purse for two quarters.

The two women said their good-byes and Sabrina went out into the lane. She wasn't surprised to hear the familial shrieks coming from the post office and she smiled as she climbed the steps of Tubbs General Store to sit beside Lima. Bicycle Bob was nodding off on the bottom step.

"Hullo, Miss Sabrina," Lima said. "Me and Bicycle were just talking about the state of the world today. What's your opinion?"

TEN

"I CAN'T SAY I've been paying attention to the state of the world, Lima," Sabrina said. "What do *you* think?" Which of course was what the old rascal wanted her to ask.

"Well, the way I see it, the rich get richer, the middle class gets more self-righteous, and the poor stay at home and watch that talk show host, what's his name, Jerry Springer. That's what I think." Lima huffed with amusement, slapping his knee.

"If it wasn't for the *Jerry Springer Show,* we wouldn't have anyone to whom we could feel superior." She paused, and then plunged ahead. "Speaking of class division, I was wondering why there's so much conflict between the Wavers and Towners? I mean, you've all been here the same amount of time, you've all grown up together, go to the same school and church, why hate each other?"

"We do have more than one church," Lima said in an injured voice.

"Do you?"

"The High Tide Church over in Waver Town is for the Baptists. The other one is over near the ocean, the Higher Tide Church, and it's for those fundamentalists folks, the ones who are so busy worrying about the rest of our souls that they don't notice they're beating their children and cheating on their spouses. Me, I'm not into any of that religion stuff. I'm half tempted to join Nettie's religion, whatever it is today."

"What about the feuds?" Sabrina was determined not to be sidetracked.

"Just always been like that, I guess. It was a lot worse when we didn't see them all the time, before the bridge across Down the Middle Creek. From early days, we've been different types of people. The Wavers were the fishermen, and the Towners, were, well, the Towners. Now that we see them all the time, I guess some of them aren't so bad. Some's worse than others, of course."

"So," Sabrina persisted, "what about the feuds? You said there were feuds between some of the Towners and Wavers."

"Well, let's see." Lima leaned back in his chair. "That's surely true. Back in the fifties, I remember Seimo McCall towed Ken Tubbs' boat out into the inlet and hit it with a shotgun, sent it right to the bottom. He said Ken was badmouthing him around town. Well, then Ken Tubbs refused to sell Seimo anything from the store until Seimo paid him back for his boat and Seimo's poor wife had to take the mail boat to the mainland to go shopping. It was uglier than a devil's blow, and everybody was on one side or the other."

"Goodness. And the Wrightlys and Tittletotts also have a feud going on?"

Lima nodded, and chewed on his toothpick for a bit. "Yup. That's been going on since the seventeen hundreds, of course."

"Since Lord Tittletott exposed Wrightly as a pirate," Sabrina supplied.

"Yup," Lima said, shooting her a dirty look. He didn't like his story being preempted. "But it just got dirtier and dirtier over the years. About a hundred years ago, a Wrightly daughter disappeared, just never came home one day, and the last person she was seen with was a Tittletott. The Wrightlys get together, there was a big clan of them in those days, and they march over to the Tittletott House and go all through the house looking for the girl, and of course they weren't gentle about it neither. Pretty much trashed the place. Well, the girl showed up a year later, turns out she ran off with a gypsy fellow. Those two families been at each other's throats for as long as anybody can remember. And then there's what happened to Rolo Wrightly and Bradford Tittletott, not fifteen years ago." Lima stopped and Bicycle Bob said "Yep" in his sleep.

"Who's Rolo Wrightly?" Sabrina had a tingling feeling that she was getting close to something.

"He's the oldest Wrightly son, Roland Thierry Wrightly. He's Thierry's older brother, but he left oh, nearly fifteen years ago, because he attacked a woman, and she lost her baby, and then he set her house on fire. His best friend, Bradford Tittletott, turned him in. It was a bad affair, and Rolo took off in his papa's boat and we've never seen him again. Good riddance, I say." Lima looked at Sabrina sideways. "Broke Ms. Lora's heart when he left. He was her favorite, you know. She had her stroke right after she heard he left."

"Yep," Bicycle said again, sitting up and automatically reaching for his bottle.

"Lima." Stacey Tubbs pushed open the screen door. "Could you go down to the house and tell Daddy that I'm going to need more beer than usual? The Regatta really wiped us out. He's making the order today, and he must already be doing it, because the phone's busy."

"All right." Lima stood up and made his way down the stairs, prodding Bicycle with his foot as he passed. "Bicycle!" he yelled. "I'll be back in a while."

"Nope," Bicycle said, and his head flopped forward on his chest.

"Lima," Sabrina called. "Where would I find a locksmith on the island? Lora's cottage needs some locks on the doors."

Lima paused, looked back at her and then snorted with laughter. "You're looking at him." He pointed at Bicycle Bob who was snoring peacefully again, his bottle clutched in both hands. "Bicycle Bob's the island's locksmith and jack of all trades. Buy him a bottle of whiskey and he'll do anything you want."

LATER THAT AFTERNOON she was digesting her excellent crabcake lunch, if she did say so herself, and putting away the fire extinguisher when there was a knock on the door. She opened the door to find Nettie Wrightly standing on her porch.

"The lunch rush at the cookie shop is over." Today Nettie's robes were white, plain cotton with no symbols. Though she still wore the flashing tiara on her head, it looked more subdued, as if maybe the batteries were running out.

"Come on in," Sabrina invited.

Calvin caught hold of Nettie's robes and swept along with her as she walked into the living room. Nettie looked up at the dark smudges on the ceiling, and shook her head. "I meant to get Bicycle in here to repaint the ceiling. But he went on a real bad binge, and then you were on the way and I didn't have time. I hope it's not bothering you. We're lucky the fire didn't burn the whole place down."

"Fire?"

"Yes. The night poor Lora fell and hit her head, she knocked over the candle burning on the coffee table. It set some magazines on fire, but it burnt itself out by the next morning when I came to bring Lora her new coffee cups."

"And you found her...deceased?"

Nettie nodded. "She was partly paralyzed on her right side, you see. It was hard for her to get around. She must have just...fallen, and it was bad luck she hit her head so hard it killed her."

"You hadn't thought about putting her in a nursing home? For her own safety?"

"Nursing home?" Nettie frowned, and adjusted her robe so Calvin could climb up to her knee. "We don't have any nursing homes on the island. I tried to get her to come and stay with us, but really, she was just down the road. Every time I brought it up she got upset. She was happy here, where she'd been living all her adult life." Nettie stroked Calvin and he whirred with pleasure.

Sabrina leaned forward and picked up the crayon pictures lying on the coffee table. Nettie accepted them and thumbed through them with a growing expression of horror on her face. "The poor, poor child," she whispered. "Such hate, such jealousy..." She pressed a hand to her forehead and closed her eyes. She stayed like that for a few moments and then she opened her eyes and flipped through the pictures again. "If Rolo or Thierry drew them, I don't remember seeing them before." She placed them back on the coffee table, her nose wrinkling with distaste.

"Lima said about twenty years ago the island had a bout of arsonist activity. Do you remember that?"

Nettie frowned. "Seems like someone was setting trashcans on fire, but no one thought too much about it. Childish pranks, and it stopped after a while." She started to say something and then stopped. She shook her head, as if refuting whatever was going on in her head.

"Do you have any idea why Lora decided to look through her old school folders? Was she looking for these pictures in particular, do you know?"

"I have no idea. Lora's always kept in contact with her old students. They came and visited with her, showed off their kids and she painted them coffee cups. Lora was a memorable woman." Nettie's voice was sad. "She could be ornery and impatient, especially when she got frustrated with her bad side, but she truly had a great heart. I say that, even though she was my mother-in-law. I loved that woman as if she was my own mama."

"Painting coffee cups?" Sabrina asked in puzzlement.

Nettie laughed, and pointed at the various coffee cups painted with simple, pretty designs sitting on tables and shelves all over the room. "That's how she kept herself occupied. She painted pictures on coffee cups with her left hand, and Sondra and Kate sold them down at Sweet Island Music."

Sabrina gazed at the pretty mugs, and felt an intense connection with Lora Wrightly. Would her own students come visit her when they were all grown up?

"She didn't explain why she wanted to look at those old school folders?"

Nettie shrugged. "She was impulsive. That's one of the reasons she got irritated with people, when she had to explain something that seemed obvious to her."

Nettie stared at the crayon pictures on the coffee table with troubled eyes. "I don't know why they bother me so much," she said, almost to herself. "Whoever drew them is twenty-five years older now, an adult. But something about them…"

Sabrina nodded, feeling the same. She wondered if someone had helped this child when he or she was younger, like she tried to help Tommy. No one had listened to her, and Tommy ended up trying to smother his little sister. Sabrina knew in her heart that Lora at least tried to help the child who drew those pictures. But why was she thinking about it twenty-five years later? Why was she looking at the pictures?

"Why were they under the hurricane hatch?"

Nettie stood and dragged the rug back from the hatch in the floor. She stooped and traced the uneven stain on the door. "I cut her some roses that day. She was always complaining that I didn't trim her 'ladies' right. I tried, but she would sit inside and yell at me out the window that I was taking too much off here, not enough there…" Nettie smiled in remembrance. "It got to be almost a joke with us, though I know it saddened her that no one was taking proper care of her roses. She was working on a coffee cup set that day, but she was fidgety and impatient. She had me take the file crate back upstairs and told me to make sure I cleaned the living room good because she was expecting company. This was before I opened the shop, so I got her situated and then went to work. I came back after the store closed and gave her her medicine and made sure she had her dinner. She was fussing that night, more so than usual I think, now that I look back at it. She complained that my clam chowder was too runny and she told me my new hairdo was crazy-looking." Nettie touched her tiara, a sad smile twitching her lips. "You get the picture. She was just fussy. I think she knew her death was near. I kissed her good-bye and left, and that was the last time I saw her alive. We think that sometime during the night she got up and overbalanced and fell. Why she lit a candle instead of just turning on the lights I have no idea, but Lora was never comfortable with anything high tech. When I found her the next morning she was lying on the floor. The magazines on the table and part of the coffee table were burnt, and there was soot all over the room, but everything else looked perfectly normal."

Nettie shook her head, and used the toe of her shoe to nudge at the rug. "The blood had seeped clear down to the floor, right through her favorite carpet. I had to throw it away and get another one."

Sabrina looked at the stain on the hurricane hatch door. "When you found her, she was lying on top of the hurricane hatch, but the rug was over it."

Nettie nodded.

"But why," Sabrina asked, "were the pictures under the hurricane hatch?"

Nettie shrugged, and stood up. "She had me open the hatch that afternoon. She said she heard noises and thought maybe a cat crawled under there to have kittens. I looked and didn't see anything, so I know the pictures weren't there the day she died. She must have put them there that last night, for some reason. I'm wondering… I'm wondering if maybe that's why she had me open the hatch. So she could hide the pictures there once I left. The hatch hadn't been opened for years, you see, and it took all my strength to break through the layers of paint and varnish to get it open. She couldn't have done it by herself."

Nettie and Sabrina were silent, each thinking about the crippled old woman and what she had done the last night of her life. What had been going through her head as she gazed at those horrible crayon pictures? Why had she put them under the hatch?

"I guess we'll never know," Nettie said sadly. "If only I had stayed with her that night. I knew she was feeling restless, maybe she wasn't feeling well. If I had been here, I could have gotten her whatever she needed, and she never would have fallen." Nettie sighed and then glanced at her watch. "I've got to get back to the store." She stood and Calvin squawked in protest.

After seeing Nettie to the door, Sabrina came back into the living room and flipped the rug back over the hatch. Then, after a moment, she threw a magazine over the pictures so she wouldn't have to look at them.

AN HOUR LATER, she stretched and looked around. She had been so involved taking notes on *Romeo and Juliet* that she hadn't noticed that her neck was aching and her hand was cramped. If she didn't watch out, she'd end up with carpal tunnel syndrome. She had brought a wrist brace—and a knee and neck brace, it was best to be prepared—in case she needed it.

She went outside onto the porch into the sheer, bright sunlight. She was a little lightheaded from standing up so fast and she clung to the porch rail for a moment.

Click-click.

The sound was coming from around the side of the house.

Click-click-click.

"Ouch!"

Sabrina hurried down the steps, around the side of the house, and stopped in stunned amazement when she saw a man holding a pair of clippers and sucking the edge of his finger.

"Hello," said Walk-the-Plank Wrightly, and smiled cheerfully.

ELEVEN

THE MAN WAS dressed all in black, with a big black hat and a sword hanging at his side. A dark furry beard covered the slight smile on his face.

"Hello," Sabrina managed. She was almost positive that this was the man she had seen in the woods the night of the Regatta.

"These poor ladies have been neglected shamefully over the years." The man reached out and tenderly touched a velvety red bloom.

"I—guess so." Sabrina forced herself to walk closer, her eyes picking out details. Though at first glance she assumed the man was wearing some type of eighteenth-century garb, on closer look she saw he was wearing black jeans and a long-sleeved black turtleneck with a black cowboy hat. Of course, the sword hanging at his side still did not fit anyone's idea of a modern wardrobe, but maybe he was making a fashion statement?

"Humans started cultivating roses a couple thousand years ago in China, but they've been around a lot longer than we have, you know. They've found fossilized rose flowers from thirty-five million years ago."

"I have to admit," Sabrina said, "I don't know that much about roses." She could see the light gray cat watching the man warily from under one of the rose bushes. Sabrina appreciated the way the cat felt. Who was he? Why was he pruning her roses?

"Most people don't," the man said. "But I happen to think roses are the best of the flowers. Back in 600 B.C., the poetess Sappho said—" He cleared his throat and intoned:

"If Zeus chose us a King of the flowers in his mirth,
He would call to the rose and would royally crown it,
For the rose, ho, the rose! is the grace of the earth,
Is the light of the plants that are growing upon it."

Sabrina smiled, charmed despite herself.

"That's Mrs. Browning's translation of the poem, of course," the man continued in his normal voice. "Roses have been domesticated, bred and tinkered with to produce a prettier rose, but this has hampered their ability to look after themselves. Just like with cats and dogs, now that we've domesticated the rose, we are responsible for taking care of them. To keep them healthy, you have to trim away the dead growth and the thin, tangled twigs to open up the center of the bush for circulation. I've had to do some radical pruning."

"I'm Sabrina Dunsweeney." She advanced and held out her hand. The man seemed harmless enough.

"I know," the man said, shaking her hand. He did not offer his own name.

"Well, I'm glad you have taken an interest in the roses. I'm afraid they were in rather bad shape."

"Very bad shape," the man agreed. "My grandma loved these ladies. She taught me all about taking care of them. But I guess she hadn't been able to take care of them these last years." His face was sad as he looked at the bushes.

"Your grandmother?"

He nodded. "She used to live here. I practically grew up in this house." He turned and clipped away some branches on the nearest bush. "Grandma Lora used to use horse droppings and fish bones to fertilize the roses. I remember telling her one day that we needed to get some of that stuff they sold in the store, and she just laughed at me. She said, 'Boy, I've been growing these roses without help of chemicals for longer than you've been alive. I don't need any of that stuff.' And of course, she was right."

Sabrina watched as he took a step back from the plant and considered it before taking the next cut. He set the resulting dismembered branch, covered with creamy rose buds, onto a growing pile beside him.

"I think I've seen your footprints on the beach," she said.

"I've always enjoyed taking a walk at sunrise. It's invigorating to watch the world wake up around you. I don't get much chance to walk on the beach where I live now."

Well, *that* explained why she had never been able to surprise him on his daily walks. At sunrise, she was still fast asleep in her warm bed.

He was pruning a large bush covered with silken white flowers streaked with vibrant crimson. He held the large pruning shears in both hands and was cutting with the precision of an artist creating a masterpiece. His face was rapt with childlike concentration.

He seemed unsurprised to see her, so she could only assume that she had not caught him unawares. He meant for her to find him.

Why?

"Do you live on the island?" She leaned her hip against the stair post.

"I used to."

An idea was taking shape in her mind, something he had said and snippets of conversation with Lima and Nettie congealing into certainty.

"Rolo?" She was rewarded by his abrupt stare, the bushes momentarily forgotten.

He turned back to the roses without answering, but she was sure she was right. This was Rolo, the long-lost Wrightly son who had gone away fifteen years ago. He had been running from a crime...theft? Rape? She couldn't remember, but she didn't feel very comfortable standing here alone talking to him.

She heard a tapping noise behind her, and looked up to see Calvin in the living room window, tapping at the window pane with his beak.

"I didn't figure you'd know who I was," Rolo said, and she turned back to find his brilliant blue eyes fixed on her. She should have recognized the thick black hair and bright blue eyes as distinctive Wrightly characteristics.

"I wasn't sure." She ignored Calvin, who was still tapping.

"I just wanted to talk to someone who—who didn't know who I was," he said, and Sabrina was touched by the sincerity in his words. "It's a small island."

"Yes, I understand," she said, and she did.

Rolo Wrightly had come back to Comico after leaving ignominiously fifteen years before. The population at large must not know of his return, otherwise tongues would be wagging. Those who had caught glimpses of him had assumed he was the pirate Walk-the-Plank Wrightly because of the strange way he was dressed—though close up, she saw that except for the sword buckled at his waist, his clothes were perfectly ordinary. Rolo must have been hiding since his return, and he simply yearned for human company, someone who would ask no awkward questions.

"I'm on a mission, myself," she said, surprising herself. Rolo looked at her in query.

"When I decided to come here, I decided to leave the old Sabrina in Cincinnati. She was shy, and dressed like a grandmotherly schoolteacher and would have been too scared to come all this way by herself. She'd never even thought of driving a red convertible. In fact, she let someone else do the thinking for her for so long she never even thought about what *she* really wanted to do."

Rolo studied her for a moment, then his face broke into a wide, approving smile. "So, what's the mission?"

"Why, to figure out who the real Sabrina is, of course. I'm not sure if I *want* to wear these new clothes, or drive a convertible, but I won't know until I try."

They grinned at each other, and Sabrina reflected that sometimes it was much easier to talk to a complete stranger than a loved one. She also wondered if talking about oneself in the third person was a sign of mental illness. She'd have to look it up.

"I hope you don't mind my pruning the roses. My daughter and I always prune ours together at home, and I miss her."

"No, not at all." Daughter? It seemed incongruous that this man, who was such an outcast on the island of his birth, could have a normal family life elsewhere. But obviously he did. "Your love of roses is a wonderful gift to pass on to your daughter."

She wasn't sure what to think. Why had he come back?

What had he been doing all these years? What exactly did he do fifteen years ago?

"I saw you talking to Bradford Tittletott." Rolo turned away from the roses and pinned her with his sharp blue gaze.

Sabrina thought quickly. Bradford was at her door yesterday evening returning her coat and assuring her that anything she may have overheard at the Tittletott House was untrue. Had Rolo been spying on her?

"He's no good," Rolo said, and all of a sudden there was nothing childlike about him. His face hardened, and the bushy black hair seemed to bristle around his face.

"Really?"

"You seem like a nice lady. I've seen you walking every morning and my ma likes you. I think you should know about Brad. He's like all the Tittletott clan, weak and bad."

"I thought you were friends with him."

"Yes, I was." Rolo's eyes gleamed with emotion. "We used to be really good friends. I loved him like a brother. Told him everything." His face softened a bit. "Brad wasn't that bad, then. He was just weak. He let people talk him into things. I thought he was my best friend, but believe me, I know better now. I don't know what games he's trying to play with you, but you'd be better off just staying away from him."

"I'll be careful," Sabrina said.

Rolo nodded. "It'll all be over tomorrow anyway. Then everyone will know about the Tittletotts and what they're really like. I just wanted to warn you. I didn't want you to get hurt in something that has nothing to do with you."

Sabrina studied him intently. She had caught a note

of something—was it indecision?—in the man's voice. He sounded hard, but his eyes were filled with sadness.

"You don't have to do anything you don't want to," Sabrina said quietly. She was speaking on instinct, moved by the anguish and indecision she sensed in the man.

Rolo stared at Sabrina in surprise. "I have every right to—he deserves—" He broke off. "It's just not right." There was no anger in his tone, just resignation.

Sabrina didn't know what to make of him. She didn't know what he planned to do tomorrow but she sensed that he was ambivalent about it.

Rolo hefted the shears and turned to one of the rose bushes, clipping another branch, and adding it to the pile.

"When I die," he said in a faraway voice, "and my body's lying under that cold, wet dirt, I hope someone plants roses on my grave. That way, part of me can grow into that rose and bask in the sunlight."

"What a nice thought," Sabrina said, disturbed by his tone.

"There we go, all done. I'll start on the Peace roses on the other side of the house tomorrow." He picked up the bunch of satiny roses lying on the ground and offered them to Sabrina. Surprised, she took them, barely feeling the prick of the tiny thorns.

"Did you know that they've figured out how to breed a blue rose? It's been the holy grail for rose breeders since 1840 and they finally figured it out."

"I'm sure the rose breeders must be thrilled that the mystery has been solved."

"I don't know. The quest is over, you see. Don't you find that sometimes anticipation is sweeter than the reality? The reality may not be what you really wanted."

Before she could speak, he turned and walked toward

the tool shed, saying over his shoulder, "It was nice to finally meet you, Miss Sabrina. You won't tell anybody you saw me, will you?"

"No, of course not," she said automatically. And then, unable to resist, she blurted, "Rolo?"

"Yes?" He turned.

"Why do you wear a sword?"

Rolo looked down at the sword as if he had forgotten it was there.

"It seemed fitting," he said at last, "considering what I've come to do. It's *his* sword, Walk-the-Plank Wrightly's, passed down through the generations. My father gave it to me when I turned eighteen."

Sabrina nodded, and watched as he went into the tool shed and came back out without the shears. He raised a hand toward her and walked down to the beach and out of her sight.

"My goodness," Sabrina said to herself, shifting the roses to the other arm. Calvin was watching her from the window, having given up trying to get her attention.

Sabrina let herself into the house and carried the roses into the kitchen.

"Rrrriiing." Calvin followed her into the kitchen. "Rrrriiing."

"Someone called? It's a pity you can't answer the phone for me. Oh well, I expect they'll call back. Calvin, you won't believe the bizarre conversation I've just had. I met a ghost, and I didn't ask him any of the questions that I meant to. I was supposed to ask him why he came back, and I forgot."

Calvin cocked his head.

"I didn't ask him where he's staying, or what he did

fifteen years ago to make him go away. About the only thing I asked him was why he was wearing a sword."

Calvin chattered a rebuke.

"I know, I know." Sabrina put the roses in the sink and began rummaging in the cabinets for a vase. "I wasn't thinking too clearly. And then I went and told him I wouldn't tell anybody I saw him. Now I can't tell all those people who think they've seen a ghost that they actually just caught a glimpse of Rolo Wrightly. Boy, would they be surprised! But I told him I wouldn't tell anybody, and in a strange way, I kind of liked him, Calvin. He was rough looking, with that big black beard and unkempt hair, but I think he's a nice person under the tough exterior. And I think he was genuinely worried about me, can you believe that? It's kind of sweet. Though I still don't have any idea why he would warn me off about Bradford. Is he afraid the man is going to seduce me?" Sabrina laughed and Calvin imitated the sound, bobbing his head up and down.

Calvin pulled on her pants leg and she lifted him onto her shoulder. No vase anywhere. She pulled out several large glasses and filled them with water, but she still couldn't fit all the roses. Sighing, she plugged the kitchen sink, ran some water, and placed the remaining roses in the sink.

"And what did he mean that it would all be over tomorrow?"

Calvin chattered at her.

"I wish I could remember what Lima said Rolo did fifteen years ago. It wasn't pleasant, whatever it was, I remember that."

Sabrina continued to talk to Calvin as she cooked a late lunch. She made homemade clam chowder and garlic bread and, after she had cleaned up (she made a mental note to buy the Wrightlys another sauce pan to replace the one she'd had to throw away), she went into the living room and settled down on the old pink recliner to read her book.

After a moment she realized she'd turned several pages without reading a word.

"Brad's rally is tomorrow," she said, staring down at Calvin who was perched on the armrest beside her. "You don't think Rolo would try to crash the rally, do you?"

TWELVE

PRECISELY AT THREE-THIRTY, seven miserable children were standing on Sabrina Dunsweeney's front porch. Sid and Terry stood in front, trying to ignore the pinches and nudges being rained on them from behind.

"This is all your fault!" hissed Maple Tubbs, a large girl who bore an amazing resemblance in both form and temperament to her Great-aunt Mary Garrison Tubbs.

"Is not!" Sid whispered back.

Terry resignedly knocked on the door. Once Miss Sabrina told his grandmother about the play rehearsal, it was all over. Grandma Nettie talked to Miss Piggy Perkins, their teacher, who "suggested" that the entire fifth grade class attend the rehearsal. Here they were, and Terry wished fervently that he had never set eyes on Miss Sabrina Dunsweeney.

"Why, hello, children!" The woman threw open the door and beamed at them. "Are we ready to start rehearsing?"

> "Two households, both awlike in dignity,
> In fair Verona, where we lay our scene,
> From ancient grudge break to new mutiny,
> Where civil blood makes civil hands unclean."

They were in the back yard, sitting at a picnic table under an oak tree, taking turns reading the script as Sabrina had been unable to find a copier to make copies. She had provided lemonade and cookies and waited while the boys rolled around on the sandy lawn before finally calling them to order. As the only girl, Maple was pressed into reading Juliet's parts, and it didn't take too long before she rebelled.

"I am *not* going to play any sniveling, stupid girl who doesn't know any better than to fall in love with a jerk like Romeo. She knew her parents hated him, didn't she?" Maple Tubbs crossed her arms and stared at Sabrina with malevolence.

"You don't think there's a chance that Romeo and Juliet's love will bring their families together?"

"Everybody knows the two of them drop dead as doornails at the end, so what's the point?"

"Well, of course, if you don't want the title role, one of the most important characters in the play, then I can understand," Sabrina said. "The nurse might be a good role for you—"

Maple was flipping through the play while the boys looked on. She had them cowed, Sabrina noticed. As the only girl in her fifth grade class, Maple could have felt left out and isolated. Instead, she was the queen bee and the boys waited on her hand and foot.

"I'll be the friar," Maple announced. "He manages to live through the play at least. I'll dress up in my grandma's burying dress and cut my hair short and wear one of those funny hats." She crossed her arms and stared at Sabrina.

"We'll see," Sabrina said noncommittally. "Let's continue reading. I'll read Juliet."

Sabrina listened as the six boys took turns reading and made mental notes. Sid Tittletott was a ham, waving his arms theatrically, and clutching his heart as he proclaimed undying love. He was so different from cool, impersonal Virginia and awkward, plain Gary, but perhaps he had resorted to flamboyance to get the attention of his undemonstrative parents.

Terry Wrightly was not nearly as theatrical as his best friend, but he had a fine speaking voice, and he was taking the reading seriously. He portrayed more emotion in his voice than Sid did with all his arm waving.

McCrorie McCall, the son of the local police sergeant, was heavy with freckles and laughed a lot. Karel Garrison, son of Missy the waitress from the Tittletott House, was very short, with glasses, and he constantly asked questions. Glenn Large, in his expensive clothes, was from the prestigious Lighthouse Estates and didn't let anybody forget it. Elbert Lowry was one of the numerous Lowry brood and spoke with a pronounced lisp.

Sabrina was pleasantly surprised at how well the children did with the reading. She knew from the beginning that Shakespeare was a bit heavy for fifth graders, and that they would have to leave out some of the hard bits. She'd expected to spend the entire first session explaining the "funny language." However, it appeared that their school teacher had already done that, and while they still thought that Shakespeare could have used "darn" just as well as "zounds," they were not overwhelmed.

They would do fine, Sabrina thought, but they would have to do some revising of the play. First thing would be to make it shorter, then she would tackle the problem of no Juliet. That was okay, though. *Romeo and Juliet* island style would be original and entertaining.

She hoped.

SHE SENT THE children home at five-thirty, carrying roses, extracting promises from them to be back the same time the next day to learn who would be playing what part.

"I might be busy tomorrow." Maple eyed Sabrina with dislike. She had declared war on Sabrina when the older woman insisted that she let some of the other children read Friar Lawrence's lines.

Sabrina smiled. "Of course, anybody who does not make it tomorrow will not find out what their part is and will miss out on the pizza."

"Pizza?" Maple glanced around at the boys who were whooping with excitement. "I suppose I might be able to make it."

"Don't forget that tomorrow is the spelling bee," Terry said. "It starts at six."

"Yeah, and Terry is going to be in it." McCrorie punched Terry's arm and chortled with laughter. "He thinks he's going to win, but everybody knows Kitty Tubbs is the world's best speller, so you might as well give up now."

"She's good," Terry admitted. "But I'm better."

"McCrorie, you just say that about Kitty because you got a crush on her!" Sid smirked at McCrorie. "But she won't even look at you, 'cause she's in the sixth grade and doesn't want a younger man."

"I do not!" McCrorie's ears were red.

"Do you want us to bring our scripts tomorrow?" Karel asked, small and serious.

"You have copies of the play?" Sabrina asked. At their nods—why on earth hadn't they brought them today?—she said yes, it would probably be a good idea to bring the scripts tomorrow.

"How much time will we be spending on this little endeavor?" Glen Large asked, rolling back his argyle shirt to glance at his ostentatious gold watch.

"An hour or so every day after school." Sabrina thought that with three weeks practice, which was the amount of time remaining to her on the island, they should be able to put together a pretty good short rendition of the play. She'd have to find out whether there was a stage of some kind on the island. Details, details!

Sabrina glanced around at the children's faces, and saw that for the most part, she had inspired their interest. They would be back.

"Bye, Miss Sabrina!" the children chorused as they trooped down the driveway.

"Good-bye, children," Sabrina said and smiled with contentment.

AFTER FIXING BROILED shrimp (the burners on the stove really did heat erratically), Sabrina hauled several logs in from outside and set about trying to light a fire in the downstairs fireplace. Calvin helped by darting into the fireplace and tearing twigs off the logs, and then parading around the room with his prizes. After an hour, Sabrina managed to light a small, very smoky fire that crackled and sputtered merrily.

With a sigh of contentment, she sat back in the comfortable armchair by the front window and opened her book.

"This is the life," she told Calvin, who sat on her knee, pecking at the edges of the book. "*Cough! Cough!* The peaceful, island life." Tears streamed from her eyes, and she pounded on her chest. "Sitting by the nice, warm fire, reading my book—*cough! cough!*—this is the way things ought to be."

She thought about what she would be doing if she was back in Cincinnati. Probably planning her next day's lesson plan, writing out progress reports, or sitting in Sally's kitchen enjoying a good gossip. She *did* miss Sally, and she missed her kids, but she thought if she never saw another schoolbook in her life she'd probably be happy. Teaching was just something she'd fallen into, because it was easier to go along with her mother than to go against her.

"What in the world is wrong with me, Calvin? *Cough!*"

"*Cough!*" Calvin imitated her.

"Everything's changed, I'm just not happy in my own life anymore. It's as if it doesn't quite fit, as if I went up to my closet and everything was too loose or too small. I don't want to be just Sabrina Victoria Dunsweeney, but I'm not sure I want to be anybody else either! *Cough! Choke!*"

She tried to concentrate on her book, which was rather good.

Finally, "Dammit, Calvin, why in the world won't the smoke go up the chimney like it's supposed to!" With that, she picked up the bird and fled the room, hacking and coughing as she slammed the door behind her and went up to her bedroom.

THE NEXT MORNING, the doubts and uncertainties of the night before seemed almost laughable.

"Listen to me, Calvin," she told him as she brushed her teeth and he swayed back and forth, his eyes slightly crossed as he tried to follow the movement of the tooth-brush. "I sound like an old woman crying because I never did anything with my life! I've had a fine life, and by goodness, it's not over yet! I can do whatever I want to do."

"Cheep," Calvin said distractedly. He was waiting for her to gargle. He loved it when she gargled.

"I mean really, I don't know what's wrong with me. I'm healthy, and that counts for a lot. I'm happy…" She paused and thought about that one for a bit. "Yes, I'm happy!" This was said in a drawn-out gurgle as she talked and gargled at the same time.

"Gurgle," Calvin repeated with delight.

She automatically started to pull her hair back into its accustomed bun, and then deliberately poofed the curls around her face. Then she went into the bedroom and picked out the most wildly extravagant outfit from her new wardrobe. She continued her self-motivational "I am wonderful, just hear me roar!" speech as she headed down to the kitchen. She briefly considered using her new pig teapot, and then she shuddered and threw a dishtowel over the pig's smirking face.

"I'm going to breakfast," she told Calvin, who had climbed up in his windowsill and was nodding off in the sunlight trickling through the leaves of the rose bushes and the thick trees.

Carrying a bundle of roses, she strode out the front door. It had rained the night before, and now everything sparkled and shimmered in the clean, morning sunlight.

She told herself she was hungry and needed sustenance, but she knew in her heart that she wanted to find out more information about Rolo Wrightly. Someone must know more about the fifteen-year-old scandal which had sent him away from the island. Of course, she would have to be careful not to give his presence away.

Though, now that she thought about it, several people in all likelihood knew he was in town. Nettie, for one. What had he said? *My ma likes you.* And she had the strong feeling that Gary and Elizabeth Tittletott knew as well.

"What is he doing back in town?" Gary had said. Was he talking about Rolo? And Elizabeth said that someone was threatening Bradford. Sabrina could imagine that Rolo might be angry at Brad for turning him in to the police fifteen years ago, but why didn't Tittletotts just call the police? Surely there was a warrant out for Rolo's arrest.

Sabrina was uncomfortably aware that she herself should probably call the police. But she *really* didn't know the details of Rolo's transgressions, did she?

She chuckled to herself, thinking that Rolo's reappearance must be the best well-known secret on the island.

The smile faded. Did Rolo draw those pictures? Considering Rolo's checkered past, the idea wasn't that farfetched. Somehow, though, she couldn't picture Rolo drawing those hate-filled lines, even as a child. There was a sereneness about him, an appealing naiveté. And if Rolo drew the pictures, wouldn't Lora have shown them to Nettie all those years ago?

But Sabrina couldn't shake the look on Rolo's face as he said, "It'll all be over tomorrow."

Sabrina shivered. *What* would be over tomorrow? Tomorrow was already today.

THIRTEEN

THE SUN WAS climbing the high, blue sky, and the temperature was slowly warming. Sabrina was amazed to think that Halloween was only a few days away. She thought about paper pumpkins, and tissue ghosts, and then turned her attention to the here and now.

Sabrina made her way through bustling, busy Waver Town, waving and smiling at people as she passed. They seemed startled by her friendliness, or maybe by the armful of dripping roses she carried. She passed Nettie's store, and would have stopped, but the little shop was busy with people buying coffee and morning rolls. She peeked in and waved, but Nettie didn't see her.

Over the bridge, she turned left onto Hurricane Harbor Road. She normally enjoyed a leisurely walk down scenic, tree-sheltered Tittletott Row, but this morning she was hungry and anxious to get to the Tittletott House.

She noticed the Blue Cam restaurant for the first time, a small blue building on the harbor front huddled in the shadow of the rowdy Ride the Big One Surf Shop and Pub. Sabrina peered in a window and saw May talking to a couple of dazed-looking tourists sitting at a plastic table. Sabrina winced and resolved that she would come back one day for lunch.

Virginia, sitting at the registration desk inside the Tittletott House, smiled at Sabrina as she came in.

"Hello, Virginia," Sabrina called. "How's business?"

"Slow." Virginia managed to give the appearance of grimacing without actually dimpling the pale, smooth cream of her skin. She was dressed in an immaculate green pantsuit, her fine blond hair woven into an intricate braid. "This time of year, we mainly just get busy on weekends."

"That's too bad," Sabrina sympathized and plunked the roses down on the registration desk. "I hope you have a vase. I don't have anywhere to put all these roses."

"Yes, thank you very much. We have vases. It's very kind of you. From the Old Wrightly House? There are some beautiful bushes there." She paused, and Sabrina saw the spasm of...what?—memory, regret?—cross the other woman's face.

"Are you all right?"

"Fine, fine," Virginia said. "I just thought of something.... Thank you so much for the roses."

"No problem. I'm going to get some breakfast. What's the special this morning?"

"I don't know. Gary's cooking, the cook called in sick." Virginia spoke absently and didn't seem to notice as Sabrina said good-bye and went into the dining room.

She seated herself at the same table she had occupied the day before. Missy hustled up to her in a T-shirt proclaiming "You are depriving some poor village of its idiot" and asked what she wanted to drink.

"Hot tea, please," Sabrina said. "And a menu."

"No menus this morning." Missy deftly scooped a plate off another table and looked over her shoulder at Sabrina. "Special number one, two and three is eggs benedict, country ham with homemade maple syrup, grits and fresh blueberry/raspberry muffins."

"That sounds wonderful. I'll have special number two,

then." Sabrina was already mentally justifying the extravagant breakfast. She was always meaning to try to cut back on her eating, but she could never say no to a good meal. And every meal was a good meal as far as Sabrina was concerned.

The dining room was mostly empty, except for a couple in the corner digging into their just-delivered plates. Missy bustled around the room, cleaning tables.

"Did you have a busy morning?" Sabrina asked.

Missy stood back and regarded the dirty tables. "Whenever the locals hear Gary's cooking, they come tramping in. His food's that good, not that anyone else in the house thinks so." Missy snorted. "The poor man doesn't get any respect."

"He seems like a nice man," Sabrina said diplomatically.

"*I* think so. But who am I to judge?" Missy snorted again. "I'm thinking about moving on to another line of work, anyway. I don't get paid enough to listen to them screeching and hollerin' at each other, and throwing things." She shook her head in disgust, but her eyes were troubled.

"Who?" Sabrina was fascinated. "Elizabeth?"

"Well, she's done her share. But no, I was talking about Mrs. Virginia and Mr. Gary. It was just terrible this morning!" She seemed about to say something else, and then didn't.

"Hmmm," Sabrina said.

Missy smiled with effort. "I wanted to thank you for giving the kids something to do after school. My son Karel was practicing Shakespeare all last night. Far cry from him playing those video games nonstop like he usually does."

Before Sabrina could reply, Elizabeth Tittletott swept into the room looking around as if she was wondering where her throne had got to. Today she was wearing a thick, violet, cape-like dress which could have come straight off a Graceland curtain rod. Her hair was shaped into a golden helmet around her head and Sabrina suspected it was a wig.

"Missy," she drawled. "This place is *such* a mess. Let's try to clear the tables a little quicker, shall we?"

Missy paused, a tray full of dishes on her shoulder. "Elizabeth, unless you want to spring for a busboy, this place isn't going to get any cleaner any quicker. By the way, have you read my T-shirt this morning?" Swinging her wide hips, she turned and disappeared into the kitchen.

"Well!" Elizabeth looked around the room for another victim. Her gaze passed over Sabrina, and then snapped back.

"Ah, Miss Dunsweeney," she crooned, and sailed toward Sabrina's table, a wide smile painted around large, false teeth. "How are we doing this morning?"

Sabrina regarded the older woman warily. "I'm doing fine, and you?"

"Just wooonderful," Elizabeth oozed. "I was just wondering how you were getting along in that old, icky Wrightly cottage. Kind of uncomfortable, isn't it? You should have stayed here."

"It's not uncomfortable," Sabrina said.

"Have you seen the pirate yet?"

"Walk-the-Plank Wrightly?"

"You've heard all about him, I'm sure. Nasty old pirate, tried to kill my late husband's ancestor. He's been seen out by your place."

"Really?" Sabrina looked down at the placemat, decorated with the many types of shells found in the ocean. She wasn't sure what to say. She had the feeling Elizabeth was fishing for information about Rolo, but how to find out without giving away that she had seen him? It was an ironical situation since she had come to town to see what information she could find out about Rolo.

"I'm afraid I don't believe in ghosts," Sabrina said.

"But they're *real*." Elizabeth paused, and with relief Sabrina saw Missy approaching with her plate of food. "I hope you're coming to the rally tonight, Bradford needs all the support he can get. I know it won't be like your big city shindigs—" she sneered slightly, and Sabrina was reminded of the Jester in *Batman* "—but it should be interesting for you."

"Yes, I was planning on attending. Thank you, Missy, it looks wonderful." Sabrina's stomach growled.

"Here's your food," Elizabeth cried. "I will leave you to it." Waving long, speckled fingers in Sabrina's face, she turned and steamed across the room.

"By the way, Mrs. Elizabeth, you haven't seen my cell phone, have you?" Missy called after the older woman.

"What? What? Your phone?" Elizabeth twisted her mouth sourly. "No, I haven't seen it. You really must be more careful with your belongings." She flounced out of the room.

Missy shook her head and turned back to cleaning a table.

"You've lost your phone?"

"My cell phone. Not many people on the island have one, but I run a cab company, Missy's Conveyance Company." Missy smiled self-deprecatingly. "Okay, okay, so it's a one-woman company, and my cab's my minivan, but the tourists call me sometimes, to pick them up at the airport, or to take them on sightseeing tours. Their calls come to my cell phone, which I put down on a table this morning, I think—I'm not sure where it got to."

"Well, I hope you find it."

As she ate (the food was wonderful; Sabrina herself could have only done a slightly better job on the eggs benedict, and the muffins were out of this world) Sabrina thought about Elizabeth's questions. Why did she have the distinct feeling Elizabeth was pumping her for information about Rolo? How could Elizabeth know that Rolo had been at the Old Wrightly House?

In retrospect, it wasn't a hard question to answer. Anybody who knew Rolo was on the island would know that the tall, black-bearded pirate was in reality the ghost's greatly removed grandchild, Rolo. After all, Rolo grew up on Jolly Roger Road. It was natural that he would gravitate back to that part of the island.

But why did Elizabeth care where Rolo was hiding? And why had Rolo contacted members of the Tittletott family? If she understood the overheard conversation correctly, Elizabeth said Rolo talked to *Bradford*. What did Rolo say to his childhood friend?

Sabrina scraped the last of the grits off her plate. As good as the food had been, and it had been heavenly, what she wouldn't give for some hot, fried goetta right now.

Gary, in a dirty apron, long sleeves rolled up, appeared at the door leading to the kitchen. He looked around at the empty tables, glanced at his watch and pulled off his apron. He was crossing toward the lobby when Sabrina called his name.

"Gary! Mr. Tittletott, I mean. How are you doing this morning?"

Gary looked over at her and as reluctantly as a child being forced to kiss his great aunt, the one who pinched your cheeks unmercifully and smelled like rotten peppermints, approached her table. "Uh—hello, Miss Dunsweeney," he said, shuffling his feet a bit.

"I just wanted to let you know that the food was wonderful. See? I ate every bite."

"Really?" Gary brightened. "My mother says—well, I'm glad you enjoyed the food. I enjoy cooking."

"Do you really? So do I. I make a wonderful Clam Tartlet, and my Tuna Extravaganzo is pretty darn good, if I do say so myself."

"An Extravaganzo, really? Not many, ahem, amateurs have the patience for an Extravaganzo. Tell me, do you add the white wine—"

"I always use a nice Pinot Grigio, it makes all the difference in the world."

"Really? Hmm. Anyway, do you add the wine before or after you add the gigantic mushrooms?"

"Definitely before. It gives the gigantics a chance to simmer in that wonderful sauce, and they just soak it up, don't you know?"

"That's what I do!" Gary cried. His thin, ascetic face was flushed, his pale blue eyes shining with excitement. It was a far cry from the pallid, shy man she first met.

"Have you taken classes? I've taken a few here and there, and I found that they helped immensely." It was a shame she could never take the advanced class, but each time she called to enroll the receptionist assured her that the class was full.

"No classes. Mother said—well, I'm happy here, running the house. When I was a kid, I thought I'd grow up to be a famous chef. I've been teaching Sid, and I think he's really showing an aptitude. Of course, he's so quick, he can pick up anything." Gary's face shone with pride for his son. "Anyway, I thought I might go to a culinary school, but then Brad decided to go into real estate, and I had to run this place. Wait a minute. You're from Cincinnati? Did you, by chance, ever go to the Maisonette?"

"Yes. Every month. It's wonderful, of course."

"Of course," Gary echoed reverently.

"Gary!" It was honey-covered steel.

Gary reflexively looked down at his grease-spotted pants and wiped at the flour on his hands.

Elizabeth was at the door, and she gestured at her son, her mouth pursed in disdain.

All the light went out of Gary's face, and with a quick look in Sabrina's direction, he shuffled toward his mother and they disappeared into the lobby.

Shaking her head, Sabrina paid Missy, left a good tip, and went into the lobby.

Virginia was still behind the desk.

"Did you enjoy your breakfast? Gary tends to go a little overboard." Virginia had regained her composure.

"It was outstanding, Gary really has a talent for cooking. I'm surprised he never pursued cooking professionally."

"It was all he talked about when we were kids. Brad was going to be rich, I was going to be a ballerina, Thierry was going to be a fireman in a big city, and Rolo was going to be president of the Sanitary Concessionary—" She stopped and looked away. "Well, you know how kids are."

Sabrina paused. "My group of friends ended up being shipped to different private schools, and we kind of lost touch. It must be nice to know people so well you remember them as children."

"Nice? I suppose so."

"Now, I know who Brad is of course, and Gary, and I'm pretty sure Thierry is Thierry Wrightly, and Rolo is...?" Sabrina was congratulating herself on her neat way of putting the question. She didn't actually lie and say she didn't know who the man was, but the question was definitely there.

"Just a guy we all grew up with. He went away a long time ago." Virginia was studying Sabrina as she said this.

"Really?" Sabrina tried her best to look innocent. "You must have been great friends."

"All of us were kind of wild when we were young. Thierry and Gary were two grades below us but we all hung out together. Until—" She broke off. "Well, everybody's got to grow up sometime. Brad and I ended up going to the same university, and of course, we all see each other almost every day, but it's never really been the same."

"Hmmm." Sabrina's brain was clicking along at a hundred miles an hour, but she couldn't think of anything else to say without revealing her interest in Rolo. "Anyway, I'm surprised Gary didn't go to culinary school."

"He wanted to," Virginia said indifferently. "But then he decided to run this place."

A deep, masculine voice interrupted whatever else Virginia was going to say. "Hi, Miss Sabrina."

She turned. "Hello, Brad."

If Sabrina didn't know better, she never would have thought he was island born and bred. He looked more like a corporate executive, handsome and assured in his blue power suit and red tie, with an elaborate gold and silver tie clip fastened to his snow-white shirt. He radiated confidence.

"Gary, I don't know why you can't just—" Elizabeth's high scolding voice drifted ahead of her as she followed Gary into the lobby. Gary wore a harassed look, the fox hounded by the dog.

"Mother, I—"

"Virginia, I have an appointment this afternoon at two, so tell anyone who calls I'll be back around three-thirty or so." Brad was rummaging in a copious shoulder bag, pushing aside a pair of white boots, an address book and various other miscellaneous objects in his search.

"Good luck with your, ahem, appointment," Elizabeth said, and allowed a slight smile to pass her lips.

Brad looked at his mother for a moment, and then his eyes shifted toward Sabrina. "Are you coming to the rally, Sabrina?"

"I wouldn't miss the spelling bee for the world."

"Well, good. I'll look forward to seeing you."

"Virginia and I were just talking about how you still know all the children with whom you grew up." The words surprised Brad, judging from the abrupt northern migration of his eyebrows.

Virginia's smile was fixed in place with super glue, not changing when Brad sent her a quick, questioning look.

Elizabeth drifted over to the reception desk, and sniffed the roses. "Oh, how bee-yoo-ti-full. Isn't it wonderful what our garden produces?"

"Sabrina brought them from the Old Wrightly House," Virginia said.

There was another strained silence.

"Well," Sabrina said, not understanding the undercurrents running like an electrified string from one family member to the next. "I'm off to the beach. It's such a beautiful day, I think I'll spend the whole day just lounging in the sand and reading my book."

"I've got to run too," Brad said. "I'll call in sometime to get my messages."

"I'm working the desk today," Gary said. "I'll try my best to keep up with your *important* messages."

Silence.

"I'm leaving in an hour or so to help get the school ready for the rally." Virginia's voice was strained.

"Well, have a nice day. Good-bye!" Sabrina headed out the front door, relieved to be away from the contentious family.

She wasn't getting very far with her Rolo questions, but she had a backup ace.

Lima. Lima knew everything about everybody, and Lima loved to talk.

FOURTEEN

"HI, MISS SABRINA!" Lima called from his rocking chair. Bicycle was humming the theme song to *WKRP in Cincinnati,* rocking back and forth on the steps.

"Hello, Lima. Hello, Bicycle Bob. You used to watch *WKRP in Cincinnati?*" She addressed the question to Bicycle, but he just continued to hum, watching her with bright, alcohol-fevered eyes.

Sabrina mounted the stairs to the porch.

"I hear you're doing a play with the kiddies." Lima's cheek was bulging, and he was working his mouth around a huge glob of chew.

"Yes. We're doing *Romeo and Juliet.*"

"Shakespeare, huh?" Lima shuffled his boots on the porch and recited in a falsetto voice. "'But soft! What light through that there window breaks?'"

"Why, Lima! You know Shakespeare?"

Lima spit over the edge of the porch. "It's the darndest thing what I remember nowadays. I can't barely remember if I put underwear on this morning, but ask me what Miss Georgia McCall pounded into my head when I was fourteen and I remember Shakespeare. Go figure."

Sabrina seated herself beside Lima. Bicycle was still humming, but the song had deteriorated into something a long way from the popular comedy's theme song.

"You just let me know if you need help with the play.

Everyone says I'm the finest drama-*tist* on the island. So how you doing this fine morning?"

"I'm doing fine, just ate breakfast at the Tittletott House."

"I heard Gary was cooking this morning. Got yourself some hut cwizine, I bet."

"He's a fine cook."

Lima snorted. "If you like that fancy schmancy stuff, I guess." He aimed spit at the edge of the porch and didn't quite make it.

"Lima!" Stacey's scolding voice came from inside the store. "Don't make me bring out the five gallon bucket again. I thought you quit that nasty old chew anyway."

"Ah, come on, Stacey. I just got a craving this morning."

"You know what Doc Hailey said."

"*I* do, but how the heck do *you* know what he tells me?"

Stacey's sweet, tinkling laughter floated from behind the screen door. "Just try to keep it off the porch, okay, Lima? I'm off this afternoon, and I don't want to come back tomorrow and find spit all over the floor."

"Yeah, yeah, yeah."

"Yep," Bicycle said, scratching at his callused, dirty bare foot.

"The play's going well, but no one wants to be Juliet," Sabrina continued.

Lima laughed. "That does kinda make it difficult, don't it?"

"Yep," Bicycle said with satisfaction.

"You make Juliet a John and you wouldn't have that problem, I bet." Lima leaned forward and took careful aim off the side of the porch. "Like I said, I have all kinds of ideas. We could turn it into a musical, and do sorta a *Romeo and Juliet* meets *Sound of Music.* How's that tickle your fancy bone?"

"Please?" Sabrina frowned. "Anyway, this whole thing should be interesting. I've got them coming over today before the rally."

Bicycle suddenly stopped humming and sat up very straight, wavering slightly in the breeze. The bottle had disappeared.

"Why hello, Sergeant," Lima said.

Sabrina looked up to see a man in cowboy boots and uniform walking by. He was not very tall, rather fat (he would make a very good Santa Claus with that belly), and a thick chocolate beard swirled over most of his face, topped with a pair of sharp brown eyes.

"Lima," the sergeant said in a pleasant voice.

Sabrina noticed that he had tattoos peeking out from beneath the short sleeves of his straining police uniform.

"This is Sabrina Dunsweeney, no relation," Lima said. "Sabrina, this is Sergeant Jimmy McCall."

"Yep." Bicycle was sitting very straight, his eyes focused on the sergeant's face.

"Nice to meet you, ma'am," Jimmy McCall said in a quiet voice. "Staying out in the Old Wrightly House, I understand."

"Yes." Sabrina decided she liked his voice. It was as if he were talking to a skittish colt, all the time.

"Robert, how're you doing?"

Bicycle started nodding, and then couldn't seem to stop. Finally he answered with a strangled "yep."

Sabrina remembered that Bicycle and Jimmy were brothers. They may have looked alike at one time, but the two-hundred-pound difference in their weight obliterated any family resemblance.

"Not going to ride that bicycle, right, Robert? You're going to walk home today?" Jimmy's voice held the wheedling note of someone who has said this same thing time and time again, with no result.

"Yep."

"Mama will be over to check on you tonight, bring you some more paint."

Jimmy McCall's eyes were sad as he looked away from his brother and up at Sabrina.

"Don't let Lima talk your ear off, ma'am." He raised his hand in a sort of semi-salute and continued down the road.

Lima was chuckling. Bicycle collapsed back on his step and produced his bottle from somewhere.

"Don't let *me* talk *your* ear off!" Lima chortled. "You're one of the most talkative females I ever met, always asking questions about this and that."

"Are you going to the rally?" Sabrina had to wait several moments until the old man's fit of hilarity had hiccupped its way to a stop.

"Rally?" Lima scowled and shuffled his feet. "I reckon so. I got things to do, you understand, but Brad is a relation of mine and I'll go support him."

"I understand Brad was kind of unruly when he was younger. I'm glad to see that he grew up nicely."

Lima guffawed. "That boy'll never grow up. He just learned how to hide it better. He wasn't any more rowdy than the rest of them, though. They were a crazy bunch."

"He and Virginia, Thierry, Gary and Rolo were good friends, I understand."

Bicycle was humming a song, and as part of Sabrina

tried to ignore him, the other part was trying to figure out what he was humming. It sounded familiar...

Lima fixed her with a bright, sea blue gaze. "Yup, they were all good friends. The rat pack, we called them. It's a shame it had to end the way it did."

"Were Virginia and Gary dating back then?"

"It's hard to keep up with those young'ns. From what I remember, Rolo and Virginia were kinda sweet on each other, though the three of them, Virginia, Rolo and Bradford, were inseparable when they were in school. They were the only three in their class, and it made them tight, you see. People were always wondering which of the two boys Virginia was going to marry. Think she had both of them in love with her. Turns out she didn't marry either of them. Life's funny like that, isn't it?"

Bicycle kept humming and Lima was tapping his toes. Something from *Wizard of Oz,* Sabrina decided. But what?

"Little Virginia—she's funny with men, she is. She has no problem falling in love, I'll say that."

Bicycle's humming was becoming louder.

"So what happened—"

In a surprisingly good baritone, Lima began singing the lyrics of the song Bicycle was humming, ending on his feet with his head thrown back and hand over his chest as he bellowed *"If I only had a dad-gummed heart!"*

Sabrina clapped as Lima sat back down and Bicycle began humming another song. She hoped it wasn't one that Lima knew, or she might never get any information out of the old man.

"Who knows what would have happened if Rolo hadn't've left?" Lima continued as if nothing had happened. "It shocked all of us, you understand. Our kids tend to spread some wild oats when they're young, but not many of them are just plain bad. And for Rolo Wrightly to do what he did—it was bad."

"He stole something? I've forgotten what he did."

"He broke into my great-nephew Mitch Lowry's house while Mitch was out on the water overnight, and stole some silver. Edie Lowry woke up, tried to stop him, and he pushed her down the stairs. Made her lose the baby, poor thing. Thank goodness she was able to have children after that. To make matters worse, he set the house on fire, with Edie lying there unconscious. She just barely managed to crawl outside before her house went up in flames. It was a bad business."

"You said Brad turned him in," Sabrina prompted.

"Edie Lowry didn't see who pushed her. The next day someone, probably Rolo, called and anonymously blamed the whole thing on Brad. But Sergeant Jimmy saw Brad that night, when Jimmy was on his way to the fire. Brad was way over in Waver Town. Normally, Jimmy would have stopped and asked him what he was doing out that time of night, but he'd already gotten the call about the fire. But when that anonymous call came in the next day, Jimmy remembered seeing Brad and knew it couldn't have been him that started that fire."

"Why not?"

"Why, because the fire bug specialist they called in from the mainland said that the fire was only set five minutes before Deena Tubbs saw it blazing and called the sergeant. It was just some newspapers that were doused with gas. It would have gone up immediately, you see? And Brad was way over in Waver Town. Even with a bike or a car, which he didn't have, he'd never been able to get way over there that quick if he'd set that fire. So Jimmy knew the caller was lying, though he did haul Brad to the station and ask him what in the world he was doing in Waver Town that time of night. That's when Brad said he was just out for a walk and then broke down and told Jimmy that Rolo confessed to setting Edie's house on fire. But before Jimmy could arrest him, Rolo took off to the mainland. Stole his pappy's boat and disappeared. Jimmy found the silver in Rolo's closet, so there was no question that he did it. I've told you the rat pack was into pranks back then, but Rolo went over the line. A prank's a prank, but he went much too far."

"Rolo confided in Brad," Sabrina thought aloud. "That's how Brad knew what Rolo had done." Fires, she was thinking. Was Rolo the child who had drawn those pictures?

"I guess." Lima squinted an eye at Sabrina. "Why all the interest in these old stories anyway?"

"It's interesting to me how children grow up," Sabrina said truthfully. "I seldom see what they grow up to be, and I'm curious. Did Brad Fowler, our class clown, grow up to be a comedian or an accountant? Did Cindy Hollers continue writing wonderful poetry, or did she outgrow it? Did Eddie Mills end up on the FBI's most wanted list? I'd like to know. But kids tend to forget their elementary school teachers, and it isn't very often that I find out what became of them."

"Yep," Bicycle said decisively and stood up. He staggered over to his bike and got on it backwards. He stood looking down at the back tire for several moments, befuddled.

"You mounted the horse backwards again, Bicycle. You gotta turn around."

"Nope." Bicycle carefully turned around so he was

facing the right direction. He pedaled off, just missing a young man coming out of the post office.

"You ran over my foot, Bicycle!" the young man yelled after the swerving figure.

"You're lucky he didn't run over your head, Pete," Lima said.

Pete shook his head and limped down the road, clutching his mail in one hand. He shook hands with Brad Tittletott who was coming up the road.

"You ready for your big speech tonight, Bradford?" Lima called. "Hope you don't choke."

"I hope not either, Uncle Lima," Brad said good-naturedly. "I've been practicing."

"Don't practice too much," Lima warned. "You won't sound natural, and no one likes to be read to."

"Yes, sir," Brad said. "I hope Stacey has some of her mama's homemade oyster stew left." He opened the screen door. "Good morning, Stacey."

"Brad—Mr. Tittletott," Stacey said, her voice startled.

Sabrina stood up. "I've got to be going. I've got to figure out what I'm going to do with *Romeo and Juliet,* with no Juliet."

Lima shook his head and laughed. As she walked away he aimed a stream of spit at the edge of the porch and missed again.

Sabrina patted her heavy beach bag. This morning she had packed *The Complete Pelican Shakespeare,* a beach blanket and a notepad. It was such a pretty day, warm and humid, the sun shining hazily, she knew she'd enjoy sitting on the beach. And she knew exactly where she wanted to go.

THREE HOURS LATER, Sabrina woke up and gazed at the hazy white sky above her. She couldn't make out any clouds, but an opalescent veil shrouded the entire sky. Sabrina looked at her watch and relaxed. She had only dozed for about a half an hour, thank goodness. She had plenty of time to pick up the pizza and get home before the kids arrived.

She sat up and looked out at the inexorable sweep of waves, foaming and hissing as they surged over the seashell-studded wet sand. A filigree of foam clung to the high water mark, a delicate necklace of salty enthusiasm. She was alone on the beach except for the boisterous seagulls, fighting over a dead fish, and the sand fiddler crabs scurrying before the waves. The heavy tang of brine and decaying sea life filled her nose and lungs and she closed her eyes, feeling the effervescent mist on her face.

She realized that she couldn't remember feeling this content in all her life. In a strange way she had Mr. Phil, the Phyllodes tumor, to thank for it. If it wasn't for the tumor, she would have gone on as before, ignoring the hole her mother's death had left in her life, ignoring the unhappiness that threatened to drag her down every day. Eventually she would have gone stark, raving insane, she was sure of it. But the tumor had forced her to take a break, giving her the opportunity to examine her life.

Sabrina thought about that for a while, enjoying the solitude, and then packed up her book and her notes and headed for the walkway leading over the dunes. The tall, white tower of the Comico Lighthouse rose above her, and Sabrina stopped to take in the neat white fence enclosing the patch of emerald grass and the immaculate Lightkeeper's House. A lady in a small shop at the foot of the white-washed tower waved to her and Sabrina waved back. It was all very picturesque, and Sabrina wished she had brought a camera.

She had stopped by the one pizza shop, imaginatively named Island Pizza, on her way to the beach and ordered two large pizzas to be picked up around three o'clock. The pizza shop was just down from the lighthouse in a brand-new strip mall holding the bank, the medical center, the liquor store and Maxorbitant's Gourmet Grocery. Sabrina had seen the mansions from the beach, and knew that this part of the island held the exclusive Lighthouse Estates, full of elaborate vacation homes big enough to house a small city.

Carrying her pizzas and her heavy bag, Sabrina walked toward home. As she came around the corner by the High Tide Baptist Church, a woman on a bike, with blond hair under a bright pink sun visor and reflective sunglasses, almost careened into her.

Sabrina had to step out of the road quickly to avoid being hit. The woman rode off, her back straight, and didn't even deign to acknowledge the near accident.

"Tourists," Sabrina said with a huff. "They should be restricted to one part of town, and not allowed out." After a moment, she laughed. "I think I'm starting to sound like a local."

She came to Nettie's Cookie Shop and saw Nettie unlocking the door, taking down a sign stuck to the door as she did so. Nettie, wearing what looked like a flowery bed sheet and the flashing tiara, turned and smiled.

"How are you doing, Nettie?" Sabrina called.

"Just fine. I think I got a smidgen of a message from the other world this morning when I was making the dough for my buttermilk biscuits. A voice inside my head said, 'Nettie, you done put in the butter already, girl,' and by the Stars of Juroon they were right! Here, I'll give you a bite of my new raspberry truffle." Over Nettie's shoul-

der, Sabrina saw Thierry glance out from the door leading to the back room and then duck back inside.

"Some other time," Sabrina said. "I've got to get these
pizzas to seven hungry children."

"Don't let me keep you from such a fine endeavor."

Sabrina said good-bye and continued on her way, wondering why Thierry had looked at her with such dislike.
What did she ever do to him? She also wondered if Nettie knew that she had spoken to Rolo. She wanted to ask
the old woman about her son, wanted to hear her version of what happened so many years ago, but something
held her back. Nettie carried a cloak of otherworldliness
around her, and as practical as she may seem at times,
she never seemed quite...here.

Pondering this, Sabrina mounted the steps to her house
and opened the door. The kids would be here soon, and
then it would be time to go to the rally.

A piece of paper, which had been lodged between the
door and the weather sealing, fell to the porch floor. At
the same time, Calvin came rushing out of the house,
chattering furiously, his eyes crazed.

"BARK! BARK! Trill, trill, trill," he shrieked. "Trill,
trill, trill!"

Sabrina picked him up and stroked his small, quivering body as he chirped incoherently. She *knew* she
shouldn't have left him out this morning. Usually when
she left the house she put him in his cage. Today, he had
looked so peaceful sitting on the windowsill that she
had let him be. Now, he was beeping, and booming and
chirping all at the same time, and Sabrina gazed down
at his little head in puzzlement. None of the noises he
was making made any sense to her. Her gaze fell on the

FIFTEEN

THE KIDS WERE back under the bleachers again, tying shoe laces together and sticking bubblegum on the bleacher seats.

Sergeant Jimmy McCall shifted his weight on the bleacher seat and then resignedly climbed to his feet. The spelling bee was nearing its close and Kitty Tubbs was spelling her way inexorably through "Neanderthal." She and Terry Wrightly were neck and neck, the only two kids left.

Jimmy moved around to the back of the bleachers. As he expected, it was Guy Garrison and Curly Lowry, poking each other and snickering while they looked up Stacey Tubbs' skirt.

"If I have to tell you one more time to keep out from under the bleachers, boys, you don't want to know what will happen."

He'd found that unspecified threats sometimes worked better than concrete ones, because the perpetrators tended to think of the worst that could happen to them. This was where Jimmy's misspent youth worked to his advantage. Everybody knew he had left the island and gone to California when he was eighteen, and spent ten years riding Hogs and living rough. People didn't forget things like that, and he was viewed with a sort of superstitious awe.

Of course, he had come back, like he always knew he would, and settled down to live the clean life.

"Yes, sir." Guy and Curly had the good sense not to play the smart-alecks. Though, at sixteen, they *were* smart-alecks and it was an effort for them to pretend otherwise. They made a fast exit and Jimmy sighed. Probably going outside to sneak a cigarette. Jimmy wondered if he had ever been that young and stupid, and knew that he had, and more.

"Why, Jimmy McCall, I certainly hope you're not under there looking up our skirts!" Jimmy looked up to see the painted and plucked face of Elizabeth Tittletott peering down at him, coquettishly holding her long skirts against her legs.

"No, ma'am." Jimmy ducked back from underneath the bleachers.

He looked around with satisfaction. Nobody crowding the fire exits, nobody trying to call out the answers to the two children still battling for the title of champion.

As usual, the spelling bee had turned into a Towner/Waver competition. The flannel-shirted Wavers, smelling of salt and mud, were loudly cheering on Terry Wrightly. The more restrained Towners, though many still in flannel shirts, were rooting for Kitty Tubbs. Jimmy just hoped it didn't dissolve into a free-for-all, Towners against Wavers. It had been known to happen, though not in recent times.

The gymnasium was almost full, and Jimmy had to admit that those rich folks over in Lighthouse Estates had really added a lot to the community. When Bill Large had realized that his boy would be attending a school with only five rooms, and no gym, he put together a coalition of the eleven year-round residents of Lighthouse Estates and raised money for the gymnasium. It was somehow annoying that the man who raised that monstrosity of a brick hotel on Hurricane Harbor had also significantly added to the well-being of the children on the island. Of course, Bill Large, who was unable to keep his mouth shut for very long, soon ruined any good feeling he had amassed when he commented that it was just like the lazy islanders to wait for an outsider to come along and do what needed to be done for their children.

Jimmy stifled a yawn as Terry Wrightly spelled "Trotskyism." Where did they get these words?

He looked up in the bleachers where Darlene and the kids were sitting. Joe had disappeared, and Jimmy hoped he hadn't joined his friends Guy and Curly out in the parking lot. If that was the case, he'd let Darlene handle it. She was a lot better at the discipline stuff than he was. She saw him looking at her and gave a small, private smile. She had promised him a backrub tonight.

His walkie-talkie crackled, and Jimmy listened as Billy eagerly reported that he was pulling over a brown Camaro, New Jersey license plates, for speeding out on Long Road. Jimmy sighed. Billy was a good boy, and he meant well. He really did.

He hoped the driver of the brown Camaro hadn't been drinking. Visitors to the island seemed to be under the impression that when they were on the island they were outside the reach of the law. They drove a hundred miles an hour down Long Road, drank ten shots of tequila at the Ride the Big One Pub and then drove through Selma Tubbs' flower bed, and smoked pot on the front porch of the Tittletott House.

The good news was that was about the extent of the crime on Comico, except for some small-time burglary of empty vacation houses. It was still enough to keep him and Billy busy. Hell, half the time poor Darlene had to dispatch for them. And if the driver of the brown Camaro was drunk, Billy would have to bring him to the station, and Jimmy would have to go down and administer the breathalyzer, since it was state law that the arresting officer couldn't administer the test. Then they would have to drag Bright Lowry away from the spelling bee, and have him set the bond for the guy.

"Caliginous. C-A-L—" Kitty was spelling.

The radio crackled again. Billy had issued a speeding ticket and a stern speech about the dangers of speeding. Jimmy relaxed. His dern back was hurting again, though he really didn't want to admit it. Every time he went to Doc Hailey, the man insisted that if he lost weight everything would be fine. It just got plain discouraging after a while. He was big-boned, and he hadn't been under two hundred pounds since he was in the tenth grade.

But Darlene always knew when his back ached, and made time to give him one of her special back rubs. She tried her best to feed him right. It wasn't her fault he'd rather have a cheese and ham omelet, with extra bacon, extra grits and hashbrowns for breakfast than the Grape-Nuts and lowfat milk that she tried to serve him.

Jimmy looked around the room again, and wondered how long this spelling bee was going to go on. Kitty and Terry had been spelling against each other for almost a half an hour. It was past time for Bradford Tittletott's speech to begin.

Jimmy looked for Bradford, and found him near the front of the bleachers, surrounded by Tittletotts. Jimmy looked away, frowned and glanced back at Bradford. The man looked ill. His face was as pasty as dough, and his eyes were flickering nervously toward the front door.

Ah, Jimmy thought, the great Bradford doesn't like

public speaking. But then, that wasn't right either. He'd heard Bradford speak in public before, and he had been his normal, self-assured self.

Sitting near the Tittletotts was the blond woman who was talking to Lima this morning. He searched his well-oiled memory: Sabrina Dunsweeney, that was her name. Fed the cats. Red convertible. He had been seeing a lot of her lately. She really had made inroads into the local population, which was not at all easy to do. She was organizing some sort of play for the kids, he'd heard. Lima was going around bragging that he was the "creative director" for the play, which wasn't surprising since Lima somehow or another had managed to worm his way into every dramatic production on the island for the last fifty years. Lima was a frustrated actor, was what he was. But it was good that the kids had something to do, besides smoking and looking up girls' skirts. Miss Dunsweeney was leaning forward, hands clenched as Terry Wrightly stumbled through "malevolence."

Miss Dunsweeney wasn't the only one holding her breath as Terry spelled. Nettie Wrightly, in her white robes and some godawful blinking hat (Jimmy couldn't shake the feeling that she looked like Luke Skywalker in those robes and half expected her to go around intoning, "The Force be with you." Maybe that would be next month) was watching with intense, dark eyes, her lips moving in what was probably some witchly incantation. Thierry, the boy's no-good father, was sitting beside her and he looked about half-lit. As Jimmy watched Nettie, he saw that *she* kept glancing to the front door, like she was expecting someone.

Terry got through his word, and the Wavers, who had segregated themselves on the opposite end of the bleachers, rose to their feet. Kitty Tubbs, her small face white and pinched, stood for her word.

Jimmy noticed that Bradford had started to shake. What was wrong with the man?

"Extirpate. E-X-T-I—" Kitty started.

At first, Jimmy couldn't see what everybody was staring at, though he heard the clanking as the front door slammed open. He wasn't very tall, and Albers Lowry was standing right in his view of the front door. He could see Kitty Tubbs though, and her mouth seemed to be frozen in a wide "O."

Then Dock moved out into the open floor in front of the bleachers, and Jimmy understood what everybody was staring at. And he knew that he had a serious problem on his hands.

"Billy, I think you better get over here," Jimmy said into his radio.

SABRINA WAS ENJOYING HERSELF, though she couldn't believe how long the two kids were holding out. Terry was pleased when she gave him the role of Romeo this afternoon, though he kicked his feet and tried to act nonchalant.

She was relishing her popcorn and listening to the various conversations going on around her. Most were about the choice of words, though several people were complaining about the rally preparations and the lack of organization.

"They paired me up with Virginia Tittletott to do the Fighting Flying Fish Float, and she spent the whole time drifting around and then just disappeared. I had to get Edie and Millie to help me with the streamers and balloons. Durn Tittletotts!"

When someone came banging through the metal doors of the gymnasium—the doors had been clanking and clanging every time somebody went through them, but this was especially loud—almost everybody had looked toward the doors. Kitty stopped spelling and looked confused, then terrified.

Sabrina blinked a couple of times to make sure she wasn't seeing things, and then she stared in horror at the old man who was slowly walking across the gymnasium floor, tears streaming down his face.

"Dock!" Nettie's shocked voice echoed through the gym, and it seemed to release the paralysis on the crowd's collective vocal cord. Low murmurs rose, like a strengthening breeze rushing through the dying leaves of the fall trees.

Dock stopped when he heard his wife's voice, but he just stood in the middle of the gymnasium floor, the tears coming faster, if noiselessly.

He was covered in blood, from head to toe.

SIXTEEN

EVERYBODY STARTED TALKING at once. Nettie tripped on her long robes as she scrambled down the bleachers, landing face down on one of the seats. Sabrina was the only one paying any attention, and she made her way over to the older woman who was struggling to right herself.

"Tippier than an egg on the day before the winter solstice," she said as Sabrina set her on her feet. "I call the Gods of Wind, Water and Earth—" She continued her muttering as Sabrina helped her down the stairs and over to Dock. No one had gotten near him, except for Sergeant Jimmy McCall, who was busy talking on his radio as he ran his hands over the old man.

"It's all right, Ms. Nettie," said the rotund police officer as Nettie put a shaking hand to her husband's grizzled, blood-streaked face. "Can't find a mark on him. I don't think the blood's his."

Dock reached out and grabbed Nettie's hand, tears flowing from his eyes, but no sound emerged when he worked his toothless mouth.

"Shush, it's all right, I'm here," Nettie crooned to the old man. "It's all right, honey, it's all right." She repeated the words over and over again, as if repetition would make them true.

"The ambulance will be here soon," Jimmy said. "I want to get him checked out, just in case."

"Where did all this blood come from, Dock? What's

going on? Oh, honey, don't cry, you're going to be just fine. Everything's going to be all right. I'm sorry I haven't watched TV with you for a while, I swear I will, if you'll just be all right." She stroked Dock's cheek over and over again, trying to wipe away his tears.

"Dock," Jimmy said in his gentle voice. "Look at me, Dock. Where did the blood come from? Are you bleeding?"

Members of the rescue squad, carrying a stretcher and medical bags, burst through the front doors of the gymnasium and hurried over to Dock. Within moments, they had him lying on the stretcher, his shirt open. Several people came out of the bleachers, presumably emergency squad volunteers, and assisted the paramedics. After verifying that there was nothing life-threatening about Dock's condition, they strapped him onto the stretcher and carried him out of the building. Nettie accompanied them, holding Dock's hand.

Sabrina followed Nettie and the stretcher. Outside, a fire truck, an ambulance and several blue H2O Rescue trucks were parked, their blue, red, white and yellow lights twisting in a dizzying kaleidoscope against the side of the building. A white police car with "Teach County Sheriffs" written in tan across the side careened around the corner into the parking lot and screeched to a stop in front of all the emergency vehicles. A young man in uniform tumbled out of the car.

"What's up, Sarge?" he asked as he swaggered over to Jimmy, hands on belt, chest out. He had a round cherubic face with apple cheeks, small blue eyes, and blond hair already thinning across a bright red scalp.

"Billy, could you please move your car out of the way of the ambulance?" Jimmy asked in a calm voice.

"Uh—ten-four, right away, sir." Billy hurried back to move his car.

"My God," Sabrina heard Jimmy sigh. His walkie-talkie was crackling with messages. From what Sabrina could hear, they were phone calls from concerned citizens, wanting to know what all the fuss was about at the school.

One of the calls was a bit more ominous. "Sheriff, is that you? It's Cue. I'm down at the New Dock, and I think you better get down here. You're not going to believe this, but I just found a body. A dead one, I'm pretty sure."

Jimmy was already moving fast. He slid into the passenger seat beside Billy, and the powerful police car accelerated out of the parking lot with a roar, narrowly missing a stop sign. The ambulance pulled out at a more sedate pace, with Dock and Nettie inside.

People were pouring from the gymnasium. Sabrina decided that Bradford probably wasn't going to speak tonight, so she hurried after the police car on foot.

It was almost dark, and the muzzy light rendered potholes and ruts in the road invisible. Sabrina walked quickly, wishing for just a couple of streetlights. By the time she got to Post Office Road, she heard the wail of sirens and saw the parade of emergency vehicles, minus the ambulance but plus several unmarked trucks with flashing lights in their windshields, careen past her and barrel down the road toward the docks. She got the feeling that these people were enjoying the lights and sirens entirely too much.

"What in the world is going on?" Sabrina said, stepping into the grass to avoid being run over by a monstrous four-wheel-drive truck.

She hurried down the road toward New Harbor and

found a crowd of people already gathered on the dock. Several short piers extended into the harbor, with boats tied up on either side. Billy was zealously guarding the entrance to one of those piers.

"I remember paddling your diapers, Billy-boy," one lady called out to him. "Don't think I can't still do it." Billy's ears turned bright red.

Jimmy and several people in the yellow of firemen and blue of rescue squad were standing around a work boat, lit by spotlights. Sabrina recognized it as Dock's old boat, usually tied up down the road from her house. What was it doing in the New Harbor, way over here in Towner territory?

Jimmy was talking into the walkie-talkie, but the distance was too great to hear what he was saying.

"Cue said it was a body," someone said in the dark. "Billy, is it a body? Do you know whose it is?"

Billy thrust out his chest and pretended he didn't hear.

"They said Dock just showed up at the rally, all covered with blood. You think he killed someone?"

"Been telling Nettie she needs to keep Dock locked up. He's been getting worse and worse."

"Crazy as he is, no telling what he'll do. I went over there the other day to talk to Thierry, an' the old man, he took one look at me and started yelling at the top o' his lungs. Tried to climb under the couch, he did."

"Can anybody see who it is? Who's dead?"

"I think I heard Jimmy say Dock didn't have a cut on him. Whoever it is must look wors'n he does."

Jimmy was walking around the boat, looking down inside it from different angles. It was impossible to see what he was looking at, but his face was grim.

"Know how to give DWIs, all right, but when it comes

down to something serious, they're lost," someone said maliciously.

"Am not!" Billy retorted. "We've taken courses for this type of thing. The sarge knows what he's doing."

"And what the sarge is doing," said Jimmy, coming up behind Billy, "is calling the Sheriff's department for backup, and the state police. The show's over, folks. Go on home. It's going to be a long wait before anything happens."

"Who is it, Jimmy?" several concerned voices asked.

The police officer hesitated, and Sabrina saw pain in his gentle, teak-colored eyes. "Can't say at this time, I'm afraid. Got to tell the next of kin first. You know how it works. Go on home, now."

Grudgingly, the crowd began to disperse, and Sabrina, with one last look at Dock's boat, walked back down Post Office Road. She was half-hoping Lima and Bicycle would be sitting on the general store's brightly lit front porch, but for once they weren't. Sabrina walked on, at a loss.

Finally, she decided to go see how Nettie and Dock were doing. She remembered seeing the medical center in the little strip mall where she had bought the pizza and hurried on in the sweating, heavy night. Thunder rumbled in the far distance, just a subliminal grumble she felt deep in her chest.

Another crowd was gathered outside the medical center, silent Wavers, waiting for news about Nettie and Dock.

"How is he?" Sabrina asked, and several people just stared at her.

"Dock? How is he?" she repeated.

"Not a mark on him," someone said, after a moment.

"He's in emotional distress, though." The words sounded strange coming from the stocky, taciturn fisherman, and Sabrina suspected that he was quoting verbatim what the nurse, or doctor, had said.

Several people, dressed in tennis whites or expensive-looking casual clothes, were going in and out of the pizza shop and the grocery store. They ignored the motley bunch of Wavers, and gave them a wide berth.

"Dern Estaters," one of the Wavers muttered.

Sabrina was surprised at the expensive cars in the parking lot. BMWs and gasaholic SUVs were a far cry from what she normally saw on the island. These must be the people from the Lighthouse Estates, the exclusive housing development of mansions. She had seen some of them at the gymnasium, but they obviously weren't too concerned about the fate of one of the nasty, dirty Wavers.

A few minutes later, a police car pulled into the parking lot. Jimmy maneuvered out of the front seat.

"There's Jimmy, he'll tell us what's what!"

"Hey, Jimmy, Dock didn't really kill someone, did he? Is he going to be okay?"

"You're one of us, Jimmy, give us the scoop!"

"I want to check on Dock, people, and talk to Nettie. As soon as I do, I'll come back and tell you what I can. Just give me a couple of minutes." Jimmy pushed his way through the doors of the little medical clinic.

The crowd waited, and Sabrina thought about going home. There was very little she could do. And Calvin had been very upset all afternoon, shivering, and making those strange noises, trilling and barking, at intervals. She hated to leave him at all, but when the sun started to sink, he had retreated to his cage and tucked his head beneath his wing.

She thought about Rolo's strange note. She couldn't help but be flattered that he wrote a note to thank her. Despite what she heard about him as a boy, she really felt that he had changed his ways. He'd been up to something, though. There was no mistaking that wayward gleam in his eye which she'd seen many times in the eyes of a young boy up to no good. But he changed his mind, and that was probably for the best.

Raindrops began to hit the ground, moving sluggishly through the thick air. Sabrina grimaced and stepped back farther under the cover of the porch. She would see what the police officer had to say, and then she would go home and see how Calvin was doing. Maybe she'd even cook an Extravaganzo—talking to Gary this morning had really got her taste buds humming for one.

"Nooooo!"

Nettie's cry rose from within the medical center, and the little group stirred in distress.

"Maybe we better go in there. It's not Doc Hailey in here, there's no telling what that so-called doctor is doing to Dock. Sounds like he's killing him."

Nettie's voice rose again in a wordless cry. In a surge of movement, the group pressed against the door and burst into the waiting room of the center.

"You just leave them alone!" one lady called out querulously. All they could see was the reception desk, and a woman in a cool white outfit staring at them in surprise.

"Oh my stars, no, no, no!" Nettie cried from within the bowels of the center.

The group surged forward again.

"Sergeant McCall!" the receptionist called nervously over her shoulder, eyeing the ragtag group.

"He was supposed to be there tonight. He said he was going to come and tell the truth about what happened all those years ago! He can't be dead!" Nettie cried.

Sabrina had an ugly feeling in the pit of her stomach. "No," she whispered to herself. *"No."*

Someone, overhearing her and misinterpreting her words, took up the chant and soon all the Wavers were saying, "no, no, no," in an elemental protest of the indifference of the receptionist, the presumed torture of Dock and the sterile unfriendliness of the place.

"People, people. Calm down." Jimmy stood at the door, looking tired. He somehow seemed smaller than he had a few minutes ago, his shoulders drooping over his big belly.

"What are they doing to him? What are they doing to Dock?"

Nettie's voice rose again in a wail.

"Dock's fine," Jimmy said wearily. "They're going to keep him overnight for observation. What Mrs. Nettie is upset about is something very different."

He paused, and Sabrina's stomach turned.

"She's upset because I just had to tell her that the dead man in Dock's boat was her son. It was Rolo."

SEVENTEEN

"SABRINA, CAN I come in?"

"Cheep," Calvin said, and Sabrina scooped the tiny bird off the floor. He immediately started into his repertoire of strange new noises. A weird loud cluck, then the trilling. It was unlike any sounds she had heard him make before.

"Nettie," Sabrina said warmly. "Please come in. How is Dock?" Nettie looked small and ordinary today, in normal clothes and no flashing tiara. Her face was drawn with grief, her eyes red and watery.

"They've taken him to a hospital on the mainland. For observation." Nettie's voice was flat and emotionless. "They think he killed Rolo."

Sabrina ushered the old woman into the living room as she thought about what to say. She had spent the whole night thinking about Rolo. She was grieving for the strange, enigmatic man who had managed to touch her heart in such a short time.

"Would you like something to drink?"

Nettie shook her head, her gaze far away.

"Nettie, I am so sorry about what has happened." Sabrina decided that brisk was in order. "I'm sure Dock will be cleared quickly. Nobody could seriously think he's capable of killing his own son?" Somehow the statement turned into a question.

"He's been acting so strange for the last couple of

years, people think he's capable of anything," Nettie said dully.

"But not killing his own son."

"They won't let me stay with Dock. They say it's best if I just stay here, and I do need to make the funeral arrangements. They took Rolo away to the mainland to cut him open, to determine the cause of death. I saw him last night. I made Jimmy take me to see him in the boat. It was sprinkling, and they had spotlights set up, and all these people were on the pier. And there he was, half covered with a ragged old tarp, lying there with those great big bloody holes in him. I overheard someone say he had been shot *and* stabbed. *Why?*" Nettie's face twisted in agony. "But his face looked so peaceful. And I'm sure I saw his ghost sitting on the end of the dock. It wasn't Rolo as I saw him last, it was a nine-year-old Rolo, sitting there with his fishing pole. And he smiled at me."

"He's at peace now," Sabrina murmured, letting the old woman ramble.

"I've never met them, his wife and daughter. Rolo sent me a few letters over the years; he moved around a lot, and he's never been good at writing letters. But I knew when he got married, and when his daughter was born. But he didn't want me to go out to Oregon, and of course he couldn't bring them here, so I never met them. I want to see them, but I don't know how…" Nettie waved a hand.

"We'll figure out some way for you to see them," Sabrina said gently.

"And of course, I wrote him letters back. He's my son, no matter what they say he did. Do you understand?" Nettie gave Sabrina a look of appeal.

Calvin had fallen asleep on Sabrina's lap, and she stroked his warm, little body.

"Yes," she said. "I think I do."

"It's my fault he came back. I was the one who wrote and told him Bradford was running for president. He hates Bradford for what he did, but I always told him that he couldn't trust those Tittletotts, and I was proved right. But he loved Bradford when he was a boy. Rolo was a wonderful person. He told me when he was twelve that he wanted to be just like his daddy when he grew up, wanted to be president of the Sanitary Concessionary, just like Dock. Rolo wanted to change things around here, like Dock wanted to. But the Tittletotts made sure Dock didn't stay president for too long. After Rolo got in trouble, they ousted Dock and put Ninja Tittletott in his place, and then it was back to the old status quo again.

"Rolo never wanted to leave the island. This was before he and Dock went through all that teen nonsense, of course, but even through that Dock and Rolo were close. I think that's why Rolo came back, because I wrote and told him Bradford was running for president. He wanted to be president, just like Dock. And then Bradford, this friend he now hated, was set to have the very thing Rolo had always wanted, you see?"

Sabrina nodded.

Nettie rose and began pacing across the floor, from the fireplace to the heavy sea chest and back again. She stepped nimbly over the hurricane hatch in the floor without even looking down.

"I know that Rolo talked to you. He told me he liked you, and he's right, I think you have a kind, old soul. I wanted to ask you, I wanted to know—did Rolo say anything to you that time he saw you? He told me he talked to you, but that was the last time I talked to him. I did *see* him yesterday, just a glimpse when I took him out some food, but he didn't see me and I didn't want to attract attention by calling out to him. If only I had!"

"What time did you see him?"

"It was close to two o'clock. But what did he say to you? Can you tell me that?"

Sabrina's heart hurt for the eccentric old lady, and she was glad she had something that might help. She retrieved Rolo's note from the kitchen and handed it to Nettie, who accepted it with trembling fingers.

"He must have left it sometime yesterday," Sabrina said. "I left the house around ten yesterday morning, and came back around three-thirty. The note was there when I got back."

Nettie read the note, and then her weary brown eyes moved up to the top of the paper bag and she read it over again. She shook her head, tears coursing down her wrinkled cheeks. "I don't understand. He changed his mind. And they still killed him."

"Who?"

"The Tittletotts." Tears splashed down onto the paper bag. "They killed my boy so he wouldn't expose their dirty laundry. He planned to go to the rally last night, when Bradford was going to give his speech. He said he was going to tell the truth about the Tittletotts, and it wasn't going to be pretty."

"Do you know what he was going to say?"

Nettie shook her head. "I didn't want to know. I—I knew it wasn't right. And Rolo knew it too. As much as I dislike the Tittletotts, I was not put on this world to be their judge. The Good Lord will take care of that. Rolo is a good boy, he knew what he was doing wasn't right." She waved the note. "This tells me that he went to heaven with a clear conscience. He changed his mind before he died."

Sabrina thought back over her conversation with Rolo. It was clear that he was ambivalent about what he planned to do. But what did he know about the Tittletotts? Was Nettie right? Did he die because of that knowledge?

"They killed him, and he had changed his mind!" Nettie cried.

"Shhh, calm down, shhh." Sabrina took the woman by her fragile, narrow shoulders and led her to a chair. "You've got to be strong, for your family, for Dock."

"Sabrina," Nettie said urgently, grasping Sabrina's hands in her cold ones and staring into her eyes. "I don't know what to do. I've told Jimmy, and the other police about the Tittletotts, but they just shake their head, they think I'm a foolish old woman. Jimmy knows better, but he thinks that all I care about is the feud. It's not true! When I was a child, you wouldn't believe some of the things the Tittletotts and the Wrightlys did to one another. Shot holes in each other's boats, fighting all the time. It was ugly. I don't want that again. But I know what Rolo told me! He *knew* something about the Tittletotts, and he was going to tell the whole island! They killed him to stop him from telling, I know it."

"What was he going to reveal?"

"I don't know! I wish I did!"

Sabrina made soothing noises, and Calvin imitated her, his bright eyes fixed on Nettie. Sabrina wasn't sure what to say. She couldn't help but think Nettie had spent her whole life thinking of the Tittletotts as her family's personal boogieman. When something horrible happened, like Rolo's murder, her mind automatically fixed on the Tittletotts as the culprits. But Sabrina couldn't dismiss what Rolo had said to her. It was clear that he had carried a lot of anger toward the Tittletotts.

"But what changed his mind?" She didn't even realize that she had spoken aloud until Nettie answered her.

"Because he was a good boy at heart." Nettie said the words wearily. "He always was, despite what they say he did."

"Did he ever talk to you about that? The burglary, and setting the house on fire?"

Nettie leaned back in her chair. She looked like an ancient crone, her face creased and ethereal. "He tried to, when the entire island was looking for him, after Bradford had told on him. But Dock was heartbroken, so hurt that his favorite son would do something so ugly. He told Rolo to leave, and never come back. So Rolo left. He took that silly sword that used to be Dock's, the one Dock gave him on his eighteenth birthday, and he left.

"I know Dock regretted telling him to leave, but he was too proud to take it back. Then Lora had her stroke, and there was nothing we could do about Rolo for a while. He wrote to me about a year after he left, and told me he wanted me to know he didn't do it, and of course he didn't. We never said much more about it. Didn't seem any point to it. He never asked about his father, either, and Dock never asked about him, though he knew that Rolo wrote to me."

"Maybe that's what Rolo was going to do: prove that he didn't commit the burglary and set the house on fire," Sabrina said hopefully. She didn't *want* Rolo to have committed those horrible acts. She had liked him, and it bothered her that he could have done something so cold-blooded as set a house on fire with an unconscious pregnant woman inside.

But Nettie was shaking her head. "I asked him about that. He said he didn't have any proof of his innocence except his word, and that should have been good enough except he was a Wrightly not a Tittletott."

"I guess Rolo blamed Bradford for turning him in," Sabrina mused. "That's what made him so angry at the Tittletotts. He loved Brad like a brother, and Brad betrayed him. I wonder if Brad was the one who actually stole the silver and set the fire?"

"Bradford couldn't've done it. Sergeant Jimmy McCall saw Bradford over here in Waver Town that night, right after the fire would have been set. Bradford didn't have time to do it, as much as I wish it was him that did it."

"That's right. Hmmm. And fifteen years later, Rolo comes back to ruin Brad's chances of winning the presidency." She thought about that. Rolo, who had loved his father so much that he had wanted "to be just like his daddy" when he grew up. Rolo, who never wanted to leave the island, but whose father had banished him. And Brad, running for president, living the life that Rolo had wanted for himself.

"But he had a daughter, a family," Sabrina protested. "Wasn't he happy with them?"

Nettie smiled. "He loved them, I know he did. He enjoyed his job, working with plants and trees, and even though he never could go to college, he read all the time and was very smart. But it was like a disease, this anger, gnawing away inside him all these years. He couldn't get rid of it, no matter how many times I told him he *had* to, to ever be truly happy." She shook her head.

There was a moment of silence, broken only by Calvin's self-absorbed chirping as he worked his way down Sabrina's leg and waddled over to Nettie. She picked him up and held him against her face.

"What was Rolo doing in Dock's boat? Was he trying to leave the island? That's how he left last time, he stole his daddy's boat."

Sabrina glanced out the side window that overlooked the dense copse of woods leading to the pier where Dock's boat was usually moored. "But why kill him if he was leaving?" Nothing made sense.

"I told the police about the note, and they just patted me on the arm and told me they would take care of everything. I thought that maybe…but no, it couldn't've been. No one believes anything I say, anyhow. They think I'm trying to protect Dock. I can feel their skepticism and their pity radiating off them in waves. Even Jimmy, who I've known since he was a little boy growing up a barefoot Waver, even he doesn't entirely believe what I tell him."

"What note, Nettie?" Nettie couldn't have told the police about the note Rolo left Sabrina. Nettie hadn't known about it until today.

"The note someone left under the door of the cookie shop the night before last. The note addressed to Rolo. They always knew I could get in touch with Rolo, so I really wasn't surprised to see the note. I took it out to the spot where I've been leaving food for him, out behind the shop at the edge of the marsh, hidden from the road by trees. That was yesterday morning. I checked that afternoon to see if he had got it, and the blueberry muffins I made just for him. They were both gone."

"Someone left a note for Rolo under the door of the cookie shop? What did it say?"

"I wish I knew! But I've never made a habit of reading Rolo's letters. And I don't know who left it." Calvin was perched on Nettie's shoulder, murmuring as she spoke. He squawked as she suddenly leaned forward, and she reached up to catch him before he slid onto the floor.

"Sabrina, I want you to help me. No one is listening to me. I'm afraid Dock is going to be charged with murder, just because Rolo was found in his boat."

Sabrina refrained from mentioning that Dock had also been covered with Rolo's blood, from head to foot.

"I know Dock isn't all there, but he would never kill his own son. He loved Rolo. Can you imagine what this must have done to the poor man? He was going fishing. The police found his fishing pole and cast net lying on our dock. He walked out there and saw Rolo in the boat, and I think he probably jumped down into the boat to see if he could help Rolo. That's why he was all bloody. And then he started the boat and went for help. He must have known, somewhere in that foggy brain of his, that I was at the school, because he drove that boat over to the New Harbor and came looking for me. And the police want to put him in jail for it. The man's worked himself to the bone all his life to support me and our family. Now that he's older, he deserves the chance to relax, go fishing and watch that awful television if he wants. Please don't let them put him in jail. Please help me, Sabrina."

Before she had time to think it through, just to ease the look of anguish on Nettie's face, Sabrina agreed to do whatever she could to help Dock. Nettie left not long after that, looking drained, but calmer than when she arrived.

"What in the world does she expect me to do, Calvin?" Sabrina carried the bird into the kitchen and opened the refrigerator. She knew it was too early for lunch, but she felt like doing something, anything, to take her mind off the subject of murder. "None of it makes sense. I've got so many questions, and no answers."

"Bark! Trill, trill, trill!" Calvin's eyes turned wild, and he started trilling and clucking again. Sabrina had noticed that he made the strange noises mostly when he came into the kitchen. She lifted him off her shoulder and put him on the floor, and he immediately made for the plant by his windowsill perch.

"I mean, what did Rolo know about the Tittletotts? Why did he change his mind about revealing it? How did he come to be killed in Dock's boat?"

Calvin climbed the plant and sat on the windowsill, his beak pressed to the window as he made his strange noises over and over. A loud, booming bark, but not like a dog, a sound that she was surprised could come out of his small body, then the three short trills. Always the loud cluck, and then the trilling, never the other way around.

Sabrina went to stand beside Calvin, reaching down to stroke his shaking body.

"It's all right, boy." She looked out the window, past the roses that framed the windows into the dark copse of woods. The woods that led right to the dock where Dock usually kept his boat.

Sabrina saw twisted rose branches lying on the ground, and she felt an ugly sense of foreboding.

What had Rolo said on Tuesday? *I'll start on the Peace roses on the other side of the house tomorrow.*

Sabrina looked down at Calvin, who was huddled against the window, chirping miserably.

"Did you see something, Calvin? Did you see Rolo yesterday while he was clipping roses?"

"Trill, trill, trill!"

Sabrina went outside and around the side of the house. She realized she had never explored this side of the house, where the roses grew thickly and the dark woods pressed up closer than they should.

The rose branches she had seen from inside the house were on top of a thick layer of leaves and pine needles. Brown stains, which hadn't quite washed away in the rain, were splashed across the trunks of the trees and stippled the leaves on the ground.

EIGHTEEN

SABRINA WATCHED OUT the window as uniformed personnel from Teach County Sheriff's Department and the State Police swarmed through her side yard, trampling the roses and snapping pictures of everything.

"Calvin, I wish they'd hurry up," she said, but he was asleep. He'd done his best to keep up with the ululating and whooping of the police cars' sirens, but the sounds were too varied, too loud. His eyes wild, his feathers standing on end, he'd tucked his head under his wing and succumbed to pure exhaustion.

Officer Gina Tozer, a young woman with a bad case of police-talk and a chip of unknown origin on her shoulder, asked Sabrina several peremptory questions but was more interested in explaining that the police would have found the murder scene quick enough *without* Sabrina's help, thank you very much.

"*Ms.* Dunsweeney, at what point did you ascertain that the victim allegedly became deceased in the side area of your yard?"

"I noticed rose branches on the lawn, and knew Rolo was planning to cut roses the day he died—that's why I went around that side of the house."

"It was reported that you have in your possession a piece of evidence that should have been immediately turned over to the TCPD."

"You mean, the note Rolo wrote me? Let me get it. I

would have given it to the police earlier, but it never occurred to me that it might be important. I'd like it back
when you're done, please."

"As the victim is a wanted criminal, why did you not
contact the TCPD 10-18, ASAP, on discovering a suspicious person in your yard?"

"It didn't occur to me to call the police when I met
Rolo. I've only been on the island for a little over a week.
I'm afraid it would be impossible for me to keep track of
all the island's alleged criminals."

Sabrina prided herself on not lying unless it was absolutely necessary.

"Ms. Dunsweeney, please give me your ETD and ETA
in regards to your residence yesterday."

Sabrina had to think about that one. "Oh! You mean
when did I leave and return? I was out of the house from
around ten in the morning to approximately three-thirty
yesterday. I don't think a murder could have occurred
outside my kitchen window while I was home."

Officer Tozer was hard put to conceal her skepticism.
"You've reported that your avian animal alerted you to
the location of the alleged murder scene. Could you give
me a 10-9 on that, please?"

"A what?"

"Repeat the story, please." Exaggerated patience.

"Yes, Calvin tipped me off. He was making strange
noises and has been acting odd since yesterday afternoon." Sabrina did her best to imitate the noises Calvin
had been making.

Officer Tozer raised an eyebrow at Sabrina's attempts
and scribbled busily in her book. Sabrina could only
imagine what she was writing:

The witness is allegedly displaying erratic behavior

*which leads this officer to conclude that the witness is
most probably a 32-45-86D, in need of the loony bin...*

"Unfortunately, my powers of imitation are not as well-
developed as Calvin's," Sabrina said frostily. She arched
a look down her nose and almost added, "young lady."

"Do not leave the vicinity as I may need to conduct
another interview at an as-yet-undisclosed time."

"Please?"

"Don't go anywhere. I'm not done with you," the po-
licewoman said over her shoulder before going outside.
Sabrina could almost imagine her practicing the line in
front of the mirror.

Sabrina was left to watch out the window, and think.

If Rolo was killed in her yard—and from the amount
of blood splattered on the trees, it seemed certain—then
the killer had dragged or carried Rolo's body through the
copse of trees to Dock's boat. Why? Why not leave Rolo
in Sabrina's side yard? Why not carry the body into the
woods and leave it there?

There was no plumbing a killer's mind, but perhaps he
or she was naive enough to think that the police would
never backtrack the killer through the woods to Sabrina's house. Perhaps it was just a way to throw the police
off for a while. Or maybe the murder was so spontaneous that the killer didn't get a chance to think his or her
actions through.

Rolo was shot. It wasn't normal for people to carry
around a gun, especially on Comico Island where crime
was almost nonexistent, and hunting had been outlawed
by the National Park Service when they took over most
of the island for a wildlife preserve.

Sabrina looked down at Calvin, who looked so small
and vulnerable as he swayed from side to side in his sleep.

She thought about his strange, loud BARK. Was he trying to imitate a shot? Did Calvin really see the murder take place?

"Poor little guy." Sabrina stroked his back with one finger. He fluffed his feathers a little and went back to swaying.

"A gun," Sabrina said. "That would seem to imply that someone planned to kill Rolo, now wouldn't it? That puts a whole new spin on things. But on the radio this morning, the announcer said Rolo was shot and 'stabbed with an unknown weapon.' Why bring a gun, and then kill someone with another weapon? Strange."

She checked to see that the coffee was finished brewing and set coffee cups, creamer and sugar on the table. After a moment's thought, she placed the remainder of Nettie's Millionaire Cookies on a plate beside the coffee cups.

"And if it was planned, how did the killer get here unobserved? It's a very small island. If *I* were going to kill someone on this island, I wouldn't come prancing down the road and not expect someone to see and notice me. It would be easy for someone to say later, 'Yes, I saw so and so walking down toward the Wrightlys'. I didn't think much about it then, but now...' That leaves two possibilities: Either the killer was someone who had every right to be on Jolly Roger Road, or it was someone in disguise.

"And how did the killer know Rolo would be at my house, assuming the killer had come to murder Rolo?" Sabrina stared at the ceiling, but no answer was forthcoming.

"And what about the note left anonymously under Nettie's door? How does that enter into this? Was it a request that Rolo meet his murderer here so he could be killed?

What else could it have been? But why in the world would the murderer pick my house to commit murder?"

Sabrina shook her head, frustrated. So many questions unanswered. The police were not very forthcoming about what was happening, and though she saw Jimmy McCall arrive in a car, she didn't feel comfortable asking him questions.

"I can't take this any longer," Sabrina said. "How can you sleep at a time like this, Calvin? I'm going into town."

She scooped up a protesting Calvin and put him in his cage. Then she headed for the front door.

"Ms. Dunsweeney, as I informed you earlier, I would appreciate it if you—" Officer Tozer was at the front door, her sturdy arms crossed.

"Officer Tozer, just the person I wanted to see. I've prepared cookies and coffee in the kitchen, so please tell your colleagues to feel free to help themselves."

"Thank you, ma'am!" a young man said from behind Officer Tozer, and he and several others made a beeline for the house.

Officer Tozer was not impressed. "I would like to advise you—"

"Oh, and I've been thinking. I know you're the police officer and I'm just a civilian, but I think I might have an idea about the murder weapon. Mr. Wrightly was pruning roses when he was killed, right? So where are the pruning shears?"

Officer Tozer was speechless as Sabrina made her escape down the steps.

THERE WERE MORE multi-hued uniforms at the Wrightly dock as she passed. Sabrina thought with relief that at least the discovery of the murder scene had cleared Dock.

He was a small, frail man and it would have been physically impossible for him to drag his son's body through the woods and deposit it in his boat.

That still bothered her. Why put the body in Dock's boat? Stirring that proverbial pot, Sabrina decided. Suspicion had fallen onto Dock, and perhaps that was what the murderer intended.

Or was there another reason? Perhaps the killer planned to come back that night and take Dock's boat out far enough to drop the body overboard. Then it would have been impossible to say where the murder took place. Or maybe no one would have known a murder took place at all. The few people who knew Rolo was on the island would just assume he had left again.

If the killer's plan was to make it look as if Rolo left the island on his own, then it did not work. First Dock had taken his boat out and found Rolo's body, and then Sabrina discovered the murder scene. How angry the killer must be that his or her carefully planned plans had gone awry!

It still seemed absurd to her that the killer would plan a murder in the middle of the day, at Sabrina's rental cottage, no less! Why not at night? Someone was in a hurry, Sabrina decided. If Nettie was right, the killer wanted to silence Rolo before he spoke out against the Tittletotts at Bradford's rally. Which, of course, pointed a suspicious finger right at the Tittletotts: Brad, Elizabeth, Gary and Virginia.

What did Rolo know about the Tittletotts that was so damaging?

SABRINA WAS NOT surprised to see several people gathered on the porch of Tubbs General Store. Lima was holding court, enthroned in his rocking chair and talking loud and fast.

"Everyone knows," he was saying as Sabrina sat beside Bicycle Bob on the steps, "that Dock has been dee-tee-ree-ating for the last five years or so. Mad as a Mitchell's Day crabber. Kind of like Jack Nicholson in that movie, 'One Fell Off the Cuckoo's Nest.' Hell, Dock's not been the same since Rolo left fifteen years ago. But I've known the man for years, and—"

"Humph," said a solid man wearing an apron and swinging jowls. He reminded Sabrina of some type of dog: Pit bull? Rottweiler? Doberman?

"Miss Sabrina!" Lima called, dashing Sabrina's hopes of gleaning information anonymously. "I hear they think Rolo was killed at the Old Wrightly place. Is that true?"

Everybody turned to stare at Sabrina.

"Looks that way," she admitted.

"So Dock killed him there," said the man in the apron with the air of someone who has been arguing unsuccessfully for some time. A bulldog, Sabrina decided, that's what he was. "Still doesn't mean Dock didn't kill him." He glared around the porch, daring anyone to contradict him.

"And carried him three hundred yards through heavy undergrowth and put him in his own boat?" Sabrina asked acerbically.

The man turned astonished eyes on Sabrina, but before he could say anything, Stacey Tubbs, looking young and appealing in pink shorts and a white "Ride the Big One" T-shirt, spoke. "Dock didn't kill anyone. He wouldn't do that."

"That old Waver—" began the Bulldog and Stacey interrupted him.

"Daddy, come on. Who cares about that Waver-Towner nonsense in this day and age?"

"Weeeell," Lima said. "I wouldn't go that far, but I don't think Dock did it neither. But what I want to know," he leaned forward dramatically, "is what was Rolo doing back on the island?"

"Nettie's going around saying that it's all the Tittle-totts' fault," said Sondra Lane from Sweet Island Music Store as she pushed back her long, black hair. "Sounds like more feud nonsense to me."

"God knows Rolo had reason to hate the Tittletotts," Lima said. "Especially Brad Tittletott."

"Brad didn't kill Rolo Wrightly," Stacey said sharply.

There was a moment of silence while Stacey looked at her sandal-clad feet.

"Had you seen Rolo, Sabrina?" Lima asked.

"Yeah, strange he ended up dead at your house," Mr. Tubbs said suspiciously, his jowls swinging like slabs of tender, pink ham.

"I understand he grew up around there." It was hard telling the truth all the time. She didn't feel right giving out information about Rolo that might be important to the investigation. Not that anybody else had any qualms, it seemed.

"What about the note?" Stacey asked. "Someone said something about a note found in one of Rolo's pockets."

"Note?" Heads turned at Sabrina's sharp tone. Yet another note?

"Yep," Bicycle said.

"I mean—what note?" Sabrina asked in a more moderate tone.

"Why, the note, all covered with blood, reading: 'Meet me at the pirate's tree—'"

"No, it was treasure," Sondra said. "I'm pretty sure it was 'treasure tree.'"

"That's right. 'Meet me at the treasure tree at two p.m.' That's right. I know, because Billy saw it, and he told his girlfriend, Mary, who's my niece, three times removed—well, anyway, nevermind all that," Lima said.

"Where in the world is the 'treasure tree'?" Stacey asked. "I've never even heard of it."

There were murmurs of agreement all around the porch. No one had heard of it.

"Wonder if it's got something to do with Walk-the-Plank Wrightly's buried treasure," Lima said. "People used to sell treasure maps to the tourists for fifty cents when I was a boy."

"And who drew up the maps?" Sondra asked the old man with a grin.

Lima didn't answer but his smug expression said it all. "Humph, well, anyway, everybody knew that Walk-the-Plank Wrightly's treasure was buried somewhere. They searched all over the island after he died, and no one could find his loot."

"Well, if Rolo had never come back, all this wouldn't be happening," said Mr. Tubbs.

"Who in the world killed Rolo? What if it was one of *us?*" Stacey said in a small voice.

There was a moment of silence, and Sabrina felt every inch the outsider.

"Weeeell, they've already checked out everybody who came over on the ferry yesterday," Lima said. "Only four cars, and they're just ordinary tourists. Looks like it must have been somebody on the island."

"Keystone cops at work," Mr. Tubbs said. "We'll be

lucky if they can find their way out of a paper bag, much less a murderer. I'm certainly not holding my breath."

Sabrina's stomach grumbled, and she rose and slipped away without anyone noticing. Sabrina wondered if Gary was cooking lunch, and if he was, what delectable treat he had prepared.

And she was just a little curious about what the Tittle-totts thought about this whole business.

NINETEEN

ELIZABETH TITTLETOTT COULDN'T remember the last time she felt so angry. She hoped her complexion wasn't suffering—one had to be careful as one advanced in age. She checked the mirror over her son's shoulder, but her skin was as tight as a drum, leaving no possibility for wrinkles. She couldn't resist smiling.

"If you are done admiring yourself, I have things I need to do," Bradford snapped, and Elizabeth turned an astounded look on her son. *Nobody* talked that way to Lady Elizabeth. She loved it when people called her that, though it infuriated her that some of her more irreverent neighbors shortened it to Lady E.

"Bradford Huntly Tittletott! Apologize at once! How could you speak in such a horrible way to your poor mother?" She decided that a small pout and welling tears might be in order. Men could never resist a crying woman, she learned that a long time ago.

"I'm sorry, Mother." Bradford sighed. He looked so handsome, enough to make a mother's heart swell with pride. Tall and blond with good posture (she had made sure of that—so many tall boys *slouched),* charming and confident. He was perfect.

"But how could you?" she whispered, reminded again of his betrayal. He wasn't quite perfect after all.

"What were you doing going through my trash?"

Elizabeth couldn't help checking the mirror again to

admire her oh-so-offended expression. Yes, very nice. "I wasn't going through your trash, Bradford. I was merely—assisting Julie with her duties. She's so slow, and the waste baskets simply had to be emptied." Elizabeth batted her eyes and dropped her voice an octave. "Sweetie, I just don't understand why you would want to throw everything away. We've—you've worked so hard to get where you are, and look at you, on the brink of becoming president! It's everything we ever dreamed of. And then I read the rough draft of that speech you were going to give last night, and I was shocked! Astounded—" Artfully widened eyes, Katherine Hepburn couldn't do a better job "—how could you say all that? You know it's not true!"

"And you know it is, Mother," Bradford said grimly. "You know better than anyone that it's all true."

Elizabeth was speechless for a moment. "Well!" she said, while she tried to think what to say. What a perfectly horrid thing for Bradford to say to her! She looked around the room, trying to think of something to put the boy in his place. They were alone in the back parlor, the doors firmly shut, the heady scent of burning leaves and fall roses drifting through the open windows.

"I don't know how you could say such an awful thing to your mother. After all I've done for you! I've always done what I thought was right for you, you know that. Everything I've done has been for you." Now she felt on safer ground.

"Sometimes I wish you lived for someone else besides me," Bradford said under his breath. Elizabeth believed that you should speak up if you had something to say and say it with conviction. She decided that she probably hadn't heard him right anyway.

"You have nothing to be ashamed of," she said in what she mistakenly thought of as her "soothing mother" voice. "Throw away that speech and forget all that nonsense. The election is in almost two weeks and I just know you're going to win by a landslide."

"I don't know that I want to win anymore."

Elizabeth saw movement out of the corner of her eye and turned quickly to look out the window. That awful blond tourist was standing right outside the window, sniffing a crimson rose, and her eyes met Elizabeth's.

"Some people!" Elizabeth said loudly, and went to slam the window shut in the impertinent woman's face.

"Who was it?" Bradford asked.

"That tourist staying in the Old Wrightly place. Nosy woman, and I hear she's never been married. Maybe if she had a family of her own she wouldn't be so interested in everyone else's." Elizabeth sniffed.

"Sabrina?" Bradford moved to the window and waved out the window. The woman had the audacity to wave back.

"Brazen," Elizabeth said with disdain.

SABRINA CONTINUED ALONG the stone path that meandered beside the Tittletott House through colorful flower beds. Virginia had told her that Gary was not quite ready to serve lunch yet, and had pointed her along the walkway that circled the house.

"I think we have the prettiest gardens on the island," Virginia said.

And Virginia was right, the gardens were beautiful. Chrysanthemums and marigolds and other fall flowers bloomed in profusion in sweeping flower beds nestled under ancient trees. A solitary stone bench stood beside a pond filled with lily pads and lazy koi already dressed for Halloween in varying combinations of orange, black and white.

Sabrina stopped enjoying the garden when she heard Elizabeth and Brad's voices coming from the open window. The Tittletotts really must learn to close their windows if they expected to have private conversations. She hadn't eavesdropped. No, she merely stopped to smell the roses.

What did Bradford plan to say in his speech that Elizabeth was so angry about? Was Brad planning to withdraw from the campaign? Why would he do that? It sounded as if he was going to confess to something. Did he steal the silver and set the fire after all? But how could he? He was on the other side of town when the fire was set.

Sabrina sighed. Since he was unable to give his speech, she might never know. Elizabeth Tittletott would probably be successful in browbeating her son into changing his mind.

Sabrina followed the path around the other side of the house, back to the front door. Hopefully, Gary would be ready to serve lunch.

Inside, Elizabeth was speaking to Virginia behind the desk.

"Hello, Sabrina," Virginia said. "I think Gary's ready now."

"Wonderful," Sabrina said. "You were right, the gardens are lovely. And how are you doing, Mrs. Tittletott?"

"Fine," the older woman snapped, the bright slash of her lips pressed together in annoyance.

I do believe I irritate the woman, Sabrina said to herself as she went into the dining room and sat at her favorite table. What a pity.

Missy brought her ice tea without asking. "Morning, Ms. Dunsweeney," she said. Today, her shirt read: "Friends help you move. Real friends help you move bodies."

"Let me see, we've got," she glanced at a note card, "fresh salmon spread on pita points with a celery relish and homemade potato chips, or fresh blackened mahi-mahi with a spicy salsa and potato and egg salad."

"They both sound wonderful. You'll have to explain to me what mahi-mahi is, however."

"Dolphin."

"Please?"

"That's what you want?"

"No."

"Then why did you say please?"

Sabrina's face was blank, and then she laughed as comprehension dawned. "Oh! I see. It's just something we say in Cincinnati. It can mean a number of things, but in this instance I guess it means 'what?' You're serving dolphin? I didn't know—"

"Not Flipper," Missy said, laughing indulgently. "Don't worry. It's the fish. That's why they call it mahi-mahi, 'cause people get all bent out of shape when we say dolphin."

Sabrina sighed with relief. "That makes me feel better. I think I'll have the salmon spread, though. That sounds refreshing."

Missy nodded and turned to go.

"What do you think about this murder, Missy? Pretty unusual for around here."

"It's horrible." Missy turned back and settled a well-cushioned hip against a nearby table. "And for it to be Rolo Wrightly! Enough to make someone cry. I used to baby-sit him and Thierry when I was in high school and I always thought he was such a good kid. Very solemn and sweet with a rare smile that would light up the room. Then he got older, and he was so good to his grandmother, always helping her with her roses. I couldn't believe it when they found all that stolen stuff from Edie Lowry's house in his room, and then he ran off. I guess you never really know people, though. We're all wondering what he was doing back, and who killed him. Live by the sword, die by the sword, I guess."

With that, Missy headed for the kitchen.

Sabrina glanced out the window and was surprised to see two policemen walking up the sidewalk to the front door of the Tittletott House.

"Uh oh. I wonder what this is all about?"

The police entered the lobby and Sabrina saw them talking to Virginia. They showed her a piece of paper, and she shook her head and picked up the phone. Hmmm.

After a few minutes, Virginia led the policemen through the office door.

Missy appeared with the food and Sabrina exclaimed with delight at the pleasing and original plate presentation. "How pretty! Is that a mango sauce used to decorate the edge of the plate? Yes, it sure is!"

"Anything else for you, Ms. Dunsweeney?"

"Do you know why the police are here?"

"Police?" Missy frowned. "Hadn't noticed them." Distracted, she went into the kitchen, and a few minutes later Gary, green apron still wrapped around his waist, emerged from the kitchen and went toward the lobby.

"They arrived about five minutes ago," Sabrina called helpfully. "Virginia took them into the back. By the way, this spread is simply out of this world. You did a wonderful job."

Looking paler than usual, Gary nodded and went in search of his wife and the policemen.

"Curiouser and curiouser," Sabrina said.

She lingered over her lunch, but the policemen did not emerge. After about fifteen minutes, Virginia returned to the desk. No one had come up to the reception desk while she was gone, though the phone rang non-stop.

Sabrina paid her bill and went into the lobby. Virginia was shuffling papers nervously, and despite her cool blue dress, she looked anything but cool.

"Are you all right, Virginia?"

The woman about jumped out of her skin at the sound of Sabrina's voice.

"What? Sabrina, you frightened me. I'm fine. The police have got me all worked up."

"I'm sorry, I didn't mean to frighten you. What do the police want?"

Virginia looked down for a moment. "I know I probably shouldn't be talking about it, but since you don't know anybody…they found one of Brad's business cards on Rolo's body. They just came in with a search warrant. They're searching the house right now! My God, I can't believe this. And they've been asking us where we all were yesterday afternoon. They're asking us for alibis! They didn't actually call it that, but they asked all of us where we were from ten in the morning to three-thirty in the afternoon yesterday, though they seem more interested in the afternoon. None of us has got an alibi to speak of, of course!" Virginia shook her head, and not a hair stirred in her elaborate braided coiffure.

"Of course not," Sabrina said. "Innocent people don't have alibis."

Nettie saw Rolo at just before two o'clock, she mused, and he was killed before Sabrina returned home at three-thirty. Only an hour and a half window in which a killer had to work.

"I was helping at the gymnasium most of the day," Virginia was saying, "getting ready for the rally. I got home around four. Brad was out at Lighthouse Beach. Usually you can't keep him away from his office with a stick, but ever since his office burnt down he's been out of sorts. He said he was nervous about the rally and was going over his speech. Gary was here working the desk all day. Elizabeth was helping Julie with her housework, and then she took a nap around two or so for a couple of hours. The water heater busted around one yesterday, and she and Gary spent an hour cleaning it up. Of course, she's complaining that I wasn't here to help clean up, but by the time I called from the school at three to tell Gary that Sid was going to play practice at your house after school, he said they had it all cleaned up..." Virginia's voice petered out. "I know I'm babbling, but it's all gotten to me. And now the police are questioning Brad, and he's still so sick from that twenty-four-hour flu he came down with. He's been throwing up all night. But his card was in Rolo's pocket, and Nettie Wrightly said Rolo saw Brad a couple of days before he died. Why didn't he tell anyone?"

He told Gary and Elizabeth, Sabrina thought to herself.

Virginia dropped her head into her well-manicured hands. Her shoulders shook, and Sabrina hastened around the desk to pat her on the back.

"There, there. The police are just doing their job. Everything will be all right, you'll see."

"Poor Rolo." Virginia's voice was muffled by her hands. "He was so beautiful when he was a boy. So cocky and masculine, but he loved those roses. Sometimes I thought I would marry him when we all grew up. And even after we grew up, I thought…and sometimes I thought I would marry Brad, he was so charming, and after Rolo left…" Virginia glanced up as if she hadn't meant to say what she just said. "Anyway, Rolo was always the good one. I can't believe he's gone. Always before, I knew he was out there, and that if I needed to talk to him, I could…now he's gone." She sobbed, her shoulders shaking silently.

Sabrina noticed that Virginia did not mention Gary as the subject of her adolescent dreams. Of course, most people never married their childhood sweethearts. Life had a tendency to smash the life and fun out of youthful fantasies.

Sabrina patted Virginia's back, murmuring calming, nonsensical words. Virginia pulled herself together quickly, as Sabrina expected. It must be very unusual for her to lose control.

"I'm sorry." She wiped away her tears with the tips of her pinkies and smiled.

"Sometimes you have to get it all out," Sabrina said, returning to the other side of the desk. "Do you feel better?"

"You have a gift for listening." Virginia smiled through her tears.

Sabrina smiled back. "I just thought of something. Did you hear that Rolo had a note on him, something about a meeting at a 'treasure tree'? It sounds like a name a child would make up for a favorite tree. Presumably Rolo knew what it meant. Have you ever heard of the 'treasure tree'?"

"Treasure tree? I don't think so." Virginia's face was calm and unruffled once more.

Sabrina and Virginia said their good-byes and Sabrina headed down the front steps.

Poor Virginia, feeling the loss of an old friend. Strange that she hadn't known what the "treasure tree" meant, when she and Rolo were so close as children.

In fact, Sabrina had the distinct feeling that Virginia had already heard about the note found in Rolo's pocket. Why would she lie?

And if Brad had been at Lighthouse Beach yesterday, then he must have been imitating the amazing invisible man, because she was there all day and never saw him. Why would he lie about being there, unless he had something to hide?

TWENTY

"RIIING, RIIING," CALVIN sang as Sabrina opened the front door. "Riiing, riiing." He rocked back and forth on his swinging perch.

"I hear it, I hear it." Sabrina ran for the phone.

"Sabrina! I almost hung up. You really should get an answering machine. They aren't that expensive—"

"Hello, Sally. How are you?" Sabrina relaxed when she recognized her best friend's voice. She glanced around the kitchen and saw the police officers had made themselves at home. Stained coffee cups were piled in the sink and the plate which had held Nettie's cookies was clean.

"I'm fine, dear. It's good to hear your voice. How are you doing?"

"Well…there's been a lot going on here."

"*What's* going on? You sound frazzled."

"Just a little murder to keep me occupied." Sabrina forced herself to keep her voice light so she wouldn't upset Sally.

"Dear Lord, murder? Who?"

Sabrina smiled at Sally's indignant tone. She knew her friend would be taking the issue up with God in her nightly prayers. "A man named Rolo Wrightly."

"One of the natives?"

"Yes."

Sabrina hadn't realized her voice was shaking until she heard the sympathy in Sally's voice. "It's okay, honey."

"Anyway," Sabrina said briskly, "the police are still here. I imagine they'll discover the identity of the murderer before too long."

"Well, you're certainly making up for lost time, aren't you?"

"What do you mean?"

"You've acquired a life! You didn't have one while your mother was alive. She wouldn't let you. I swear your father died just to get away from her."

"Sally!"

"It's true. She was a selfish, domineering alcoholic who never gave one thought to your happiness. Only her own. Whenever you would try to go your own way, she'd have one of those awful convulsions and have to go to the hospital. You never wanted to be a teacher. Your mother told you how much you wanted to be a teacher so many times that you finally believed it yourself. What do *you* want to do with the rest of your life?"

"I don't know. I've never thought about it."

"Well, think about it! How are you feeling? And don't try to throw me off track by telling me about your dishwater knee or your runner's ear. You've turned into a flaming hypochondriac ever since your surgery."

"I have not! I feel fine. Just peachy. Are you coming to visit?" Sabrina asked, in an effort to change the subject.

Sally was easily diverted. "I think I might. The weather's been abominable. And, humph, I'll be at loose ends shortly. Last night, I told Leanne Taylor to go jump in the river after she scheduled me to go visit child molesters in the state mental hospital. I mean, has she lost what little mind she ever possessed?"

"Did she really?" Sabrina asked, amused despite herself. Sally had a long and varied history with the local civic clubs. Most everybody she worked with loved her spirit and her dedication, but there were a few who didn't…and those people (with fragile egos, all, Sabrina thought protectively) hated Sally with a passion. It was just that Sally tended to *take over* in a not very subtle way.

"Yes, she did, the female Hun. Anyway, I've got some stuff to take care of—can I bring the kitties?— but if you're still going to be down there in a couple of weeks…"

"Sally, I'd love to see you. I've got the cottage for another three weeks and of course you can bring the kitties. We'll figure out some way to keep Calvin and the cats apart."

Calvin, hearing his name, squawked loudly.

"Is that Calvin? You give him a big, fat kiss for me."

"I will."

After Sabrina hung up, she stroked Calvin's back with her finger. Officer Tozer had been waiting for her when she arrived home. The police had found the murder weapon, and Officer Tozer wanted to know the last time she'd seen them.

The pruning shears were hanging in their usual place in the shed, but smudges of blood still clung between the blades and the handles were wiped clean of prints.

THE CHILDREN BEGAN arriving soon after, and Sabrina put aside her worry and spent a happy two hours directing a play that was taking on a life of its own. The children, naturally, were curious about the murder. They kept trying to sneak around the side of the house to watch the police. Sabrina noticed that Sid and Terry weren't talking to each other, and she asked them to stay afterward

for a few minutes after sending the other children home
for their dinners.

"Terry, I know this must be hard on you. I expect you
never met your uncle?"

"He left a couple of years before I was born," Terry
said, looking every inch a Wrightly with his bushy black
hair falling over his bright eyes. His gaze avoided Sid,
who was fidgeting beside him.

"The police have been coming around my house, asking all kinds of stupid questions. My family didn't do
anything!" Sid stared accusingly at Terry.

"Of course not," Sabrina said. "A lot of time, people
say things they don't really mean." She looked at them
both squarely. "I think it's very important for you two to
support each other through this. I know this is hard for
both of your families, but it needn't affect your friendship. Does that make sense?"

Both boys shuffled their feet and glanced at each other
sideways. In that look, Sabrina saw something in Sid that
she hadn't noticed before. It had been so fleeting, but—

"I'm sorry Grandma's been saying stuff about your
family," Terry said. "I know it's not true what she's saying, I don't care if it's true or not, anyhow. Still want to
meet me at the bridge tomorrow to walk to school?" His
sincerity was so palpable that Sabrina wanted to hug him.

"Yeah," Sid said, as if it didn't matter to him one way
or another. "I can do that. Long's you know my family
didn't do nothing to your uncle." He paused a moment.
"I'm sorry about him, okay?" He lunged forward and
tapped Terry on the chest yelling, "You're it!" and ran
toward the driveway.

Terry laughed and chased after his friend.

"Don't forget to learn your lines! And don't forget your

school homework!" Sabrina called after them, but they were too far up the driveway to hear her.

She smiled and went around the side of the house. The police were packing up.

"All finished?"

"Yes'm," one of the young men answered. "Thank you for the coffee and cookies. That's a pretty cool bird you got."

"I hope we haven't been too much of an imposition," Jimmy McCall said. "We're pretty much done, though someone might come by tomorrow." He looked tired, his full face sloppily shaved and haggard. His uniform had popped a button over his large stomach.

"No problem, Jimmy." Sabrina waved to the young policemen as they climbed into their cars and drove off in a cloud of dust.

Jimmy watched them go with troubled eyes and then turned back to Sabrina.

"I know Gina Tozer took your statement, but are you sure you didn't see anything unusual yesterday?"

Sabrina thought back. "No, everything seemed normal when I got home, except for Rolo's note, of course. But I had a lot to do, preparing for the kids and then getting ready to go to the rally. I didn't notice anything."

"And when you spoke to Rolo he didn't mention anything about a 'treasure tree'?"

Sabrina shook her head, "As I told Officer Tozer, Rolo and I mostly talked about the roses. He did refer to something taking place the next day, something about 'it will all be over tomorrow.'" She looked startled. "You don't think...?"

"No, it wasn't suicide," Jimmy said grimly.

"I really didn't know what he was talking about,

though he obviously was upset. I need to tell you something, Jimmy... I was at Lighthouse Beach all day yesterday and I never saw Brad. Maybe I somehow missed him, but—"

"No, you didn't. We already know he wasn't there, Miss Dunsweeney. I appreciate your candor. I'm a little concerned about you, actually. I'm going to make sure everybody knows that you didn't see anything. Since we know Rolo was killed between two and three-thirty, you might have just missed the killer. Do you understand what I'm saying?"

"And you think—that the killer might think I saw him? And come after me?" Sabrina felt cold.

"I'm not saying that," Jimmy said. "I'm just saying be careful. Use common sense. Lock your doors, don't walk around alone at night. I'm going to drive by tonight. I don't anticipate any problems, but I'd rather be safe than sorry."

"All right," Sabrina said. "I understand. Thank you for the warning."

Jimmy raised a weary hand in farewell and slid behind the wheel of his police car.

Sabrina watched as he drove away and turned to see Gray and Grayer sitting on the top step, watching her with tails twitching.

"I bet you're hungry," she said. "So am I, actually. That salmon spread seems like a long time ago." The cats pricked their ears and waved their tails as she climbed the steps. She retrieved their cat food and poured some in their bowl.

Then she closed the door behind her. Unfortunately, she couldn't lock it.

TWENTY-ONE

SABRINA WAS HUMMING as she left the house the next day.
Calvin, perched on her shoulder, was humming along
with her. She was glad that he seemed to have gotten over
his shock. He still seemed more needy than usual, so she
had decided to take him with her into town.

The night had passed without incident and, after a
few productive phone calls, she went to bed and slept
the sleep of the righteous. She felt well-rested and eager
this morning, and it was a far cry from the hopelessness
she'd been feeling every morning for the past few years.

The first person she wanted to talk to was Nettie, and
then she planned to go see if Lima had heard anything
new. She had a couple of ideas floating around...

She also needed to look for a Halloween costume.
She had several outfits at home in Cincinnati—she always dressed up for Halloween, and encouraged her kids
to dress up too, reasoning any outlet for creativity was
good—but she hadn't thought to bring them. She was a
little nostalgic about missing Halloween in Cincinnati,
but it sounded as if the island threw quite a party, and
she was looking forward to it.

When she walked through Waver Town, several people actually returned her enthusiastic waves and hearty
hellos, though they turned in surprise as Calvin added
his chirping greeting to Sabrina's.

The morning rush was just finishing up at Nettie's,

but she still had flaky, cinnamony apple Danishes left. Sabrina sat at one of the tiny tables with that and a cup of coffee. She usually didn't drink coffee, but Danishes and coffee seemed to go hand in hand.

Nettie was dressed in a brilliant green robe, the satiny fabric dwarfing her small frame.

"Green cheers me up," Nettie confided, as she took the seat opposite Sabrina. Her creped face sagged with weariness.

"It's a beautiful color." Sabrina fed Calvin a crumb.

"They're going to let Dock come home tomorrow. They say he's already forgotten finding Rolo's body."

"Perhaps that's a mercy."

"I guess so. I try to be positive, but sometimes it's so hard. If only Rolo would've stayed in Oregon, where he would have been safe, none of this would have ever happened. At least they don't think Dock killed Rolo anymore. Thanks to you. I appreciate your help, Sabrina, I really do. I think that maybe you're my guardian angel, come to me in my time of need."

Sabrina shook her head, but decided not to dispute the guardian angel notion. Nettie was going to believe what she wanted to believe, and if the belief made her feel better, then fine.

"I'm trying to find out what secret Rolo knew about the Tittletotts. I also think it's important to find out who left the note for Rolo under your door. Do you happen to know where the 'treasure tree' might be?"

Nettie frowned. "Jimmy asked me that yesterday. He said they found a note on Rolo—it has to be the same one I passed on to him, doesn't it?—but I don't know where the 'treasure tree' is. Probably has something to do with that old pirate, but... I don't know. Here's Thierry, maybe he knows."

Thierry came into the shop and went behind the counter to help himself to a muffin.

"What do you want, Ma?" he asked, his mouth full. He wore a baseball cap over his unruly black hair and a stained T-shirt. He looked like a spoiled, sulky child with stubbly cheeks.

"Do you know where the treasure tree is? Somebody sent Rolo a note asking him to meet there. Does that sound familiar?"

"What, does Nosy Neighbor want to know?" He waved his muffin at Sabrina.

"Thierry, she's trying to help us." There was an undercurrent of weariness in her voice, the tone of a woman who wished her child would fly out of the nest already.

Thierry grabbed another muffin and stuffed it into his mouth. "Got to get to work. Doing construction over in Lighthouse Estates today."

"Not working with Bradford Tittletott anymore?" Nettie asked, momentarily distracted. She couldn't help but sound pleased.

"Nah, he's gone off his rocker. 'Bout decided he doesn't want to be president anymore. Strangest thing I ever heard." A raspberry smear stretched across his cheek, and Nettie made unobtrusive wiping motions with her hand. He ignored her. "The Tittletotts are all uppity, every one of them."

"Have you ever heard of the treasure tree?" Nettie asked, returning to the previous subject.

Thierry chewed for a long moment and then shrugged. "Yeah, I have. Not in a long time, though." He opened the refrigerator and took out a gallon jug of milk.

"Don't you dare drink out of the—" Nettie began.

He took a long swig, straight from the container.

"Where is it, Thierry?" Sabrina asked after he had put the milk back.

"We used to hang out there when we were kids, drink some beer, smoke a coupla ciggies."

"Who did?"

Thierry gave her a disgusted look. "All of us. Me and Rolo, Virginia and Gary and Brad. Rolo was the one who found the tree. He got real weird when he turned eighteen and started wearing that stupid sword around. We used to go there at night and plan stunts, like going to the old pier and switching all the boats around so everybody had to run around looking for their boats in the morning, and painting Ernie Tubbs' house bright yellow one night. Had a lot of fun."

"All of you knew the tree by that name?" Sabrina asked.

"That's what we called it."

Sabrina took a sip of her coffee to hide her agitation. Why did Virginia lie to her about the tree? And it couldn't be coincidence that the five people who knew about the treasure tree were the five children of the "rat pack" who had interested Lora Wrightly the last days of her life.

"You really should tell the police about the tree," Sabrina said.

"Shoot, I'm not telling the police anything. They're smart ol' boys, they can figure out who chopped up my brother on their own."

"Thierry!"

"Well, if you won't tell the police where the tree is, can you tell me?" Sabrina asked.

"I can't tell you, hafta show you. It's deep in the

swamp." His eyes gleamed as he took in her white slacks and tennis shoes and her pale blue shirt.

"You take Miss Sabrina right now and show her that tree," Nettie said, standing up and glaring up at her son.

"Okay. I don't want to go to work anyhow."

Sabrina knew he was giving in too easily, but she was too excited about the prospect of finding the treasure tree to think about it much.

Until she was knee deep in dank, smelly marsh mud.

CALVIN HAD HIS little claws dug deep into the back of her neck, and Sabrina was too busy keeping tree branches from slapping into her face and keeping up with Thierry to try to loosen his grip. Thierry was almost out of sight and Sabrina sighed as she tried to slog through the mud faster.

They had entered the marsh behind Nettie's shop and followed a circuitous path through thick undergrowth, mud and trees. The rich, salty mud smell was almost overwhelming and tiny no-see-ums buzzed around her face. Sabrina was covered with the thick, black mud, and tired, but she refused to give up.

"Who do you think killed your brother?" she called to Thierry. He liked to talk, she had discovered. And when he talked, he slowed down. He was one of those people who was erroneously convinced he was Einstein reincarnated and everybody else had the IQ of a toilet plunger.

"I know who did it." Thierry slowed and looked over his shoulder at Sabrina. "Anybody with a lick of sense can see it."

"I guess I haven't been licked recently. Who then?" Sabrina wiped sweat out of her eyes, and in the process swiped a streak of mud across her cheek. She saw a mosquito the size of a humming bird feasting on her arm and swatted at it.

"Nah, I think I'll keep it to myself for now. Wouldn't want you to go and tell the police and take all the credit. I'll take care of it."

"Thierry, better let the police handle it."

Thierry shrugged and kept walking.

"Did you see Rolo over the past week? Did you know he was in town?"

Thierry slowed again. "I knew Ma was acting kinda strange, but no, I didn't know he was in town until…" He trailed off.

"Until Dock found his body?"

"Whatever." Thierry shrugged.

After that, Sabrina saved her breath for dragging her feet through the sucking mud, too tired to even care as a snake slithered across the trail in front of her. Calvin was in shock, chattering incoherently against her ear as he held on for dear life. After about forty-five minutes, Thierry disappeared into a stand of trees and Sabrina plunged in after him.

When she caught up with him, he was standing in a small clearing under a great, golden oak tree with limbs twisted in fantastical shapes.

"The wind does it," Thierry said. "Blows the tree limbs into such weird shapes."

Sabrina looked up at the tree. It was ancient and beautiful, and she could well believe that it might have stood in this spot for hundreds of years.

"Well, here it is, the famous treasure tree. Happy now?" Thierry leaned one shoulder up against the massive trunk and watched Sabrina as she walked around.

The grass grew tall in the clearing, turning amber in

the slight chill of the fall sun, and half obscuring the old leather bench seats where Sabrina could envision the teenage rat pack sitting around a fire, plotting their next exploit. Ancient beer cans and trash littered the clearing, and it looked as if an animal, a raccoon or perhaps a possum, had been digging for worms or some other tasty treat.

Near the tree the grass was flattened and fresh cigarette butts littered the ground. Someone had been here recently.

"Probably just kids," Thierry said, following her eyes. If there had been footprints, they'd been washed away by the rain the night before.

"Maybe." She looked Thierry right in the eye. "When was the last time you were here?"

"What, you think I was the one who met Rolo and killed him? I haven't even thought about this tree since Rolo left. Me and him had some good times growing up, goin' fishing and playing hide and seek in the marsh. That was before he started hanging around with Brad and Virginia more than me. And then he went and pulled a Houdini. After that, none of them had much to do with me. Virginia and Brad went off to college, and it was just me and Gary, and we never got along all that well anyway. He's a sissy boy."

Sabrina walked around the clearing, the tall nettles pulling at her mud-splattered pants. Calvin was making distressed little noises as he gazed around.

"Why did Rolo steal that stuff? Do you have any idea why he would do something like that?" Sabrina asked. "I can't help but think that what happened fifteen years ago has some bearing on what has happened to Rolo."

"You think Rolo didn't steal that stuff? He did, all

right, I can tell you. I saw him sneak out of the house
in the middle of the night, and I saw him come back
with an old burlap sack. The next day Jimmy McCall
found the silver in the sack, stuffed in the back of Rolo's
closet. Rolo ran like a rabbit." Thierry smiled nastily,
but Sabrina sensed an undercurrent of pain masked by
his bravado. "I figured Rolo and Brad and Virginia had
something planned, they were always trying to hide from
me and Gary, and do stuff on their own."

"Was Virginia dating either one of them?"

Thierry shrugged. "She was a regular tease. Even with
me and Gary, though not so much with us because we
were younger. I think she liked having all of us guys falling over her. But she and Rolo were close, real close."

Sabrina shook her head and looked around again at
the clearing. Did Rolo meet someone here? The trampled
grass and cigarette butts seemed to imply that *someone*
had been here within the last couple of days, and considering the note that Rolo had in his pocket when he died…
Rolo hadn't smoked during their conversation, but she
remembered smelling stale cigarette smoke when he had
handed her the roses. Did Rolo stand under this tree and
talk to someone, long enough for six or seven butts to
accumulate? Whom was he talking to? Most likely the
person who sent the note, Sabrina surmised, which could
have been any one of the rat pack. They all knew about
the treasure tree, if Thierry was telling the truth. Could
Virginia have forgotten?

What stumped her was why the killer, after luring
Rolo by note to this perfect killing spot, had followed
Rolo to Sabrina's rental house to kill him. Why not kill
him here, where it was unlikely that anyone would ever
find his body?

"I'm ready to go." Thierry shifted back and forth on his heels. He'd smoked a cigarette while they talked, and Sabrina saw that it was a different brand from the butts that littered the ground.

"That's fine." There was nothing more to learn here. Instead of answering questions, the trip to the treasure tree only added to the list.

Sabrina was so preoccupied with her thoughts that she didn't notice Thierry had led her down a different path. She was astonished when less than ten minutes later they emerged on the beach close to her house.

"It took us almost an hour to get to the tree," Sabrina said, turning to look at Thierry accusingly. "And less than ten minutes to get back?"

Thierry shrugged. "I wanted to see if you could keep up."

He sauntered away toward her house and the road, and Sabrina watched him, fuming. Calvin woke up and began squawking and Sabrina rubbed his head.

"What a jerk," she muttered, and the bird chirped his agreement.

TWENTY-TWO

"WHY IF IT isn't Miss Sabrina," Lima said as she climbed the steps and sat in the rocking chair beside him. She was glad to sit down. The hike through the swamp this morning had worn her out.

"Hello, Lima." Sabrina nodded at the several other people gathered on the porch. They stared at her, but soon ignored her presence and turned back to the subject of murder.

"It warse the pirate, I'm tellin' you," one emaciated gent proclaimed in an accent so thick Sabrina could barely follow him. "Sure as a devil's blow on Mitchell's Day, old Walk-the-Plank was walkin' the marsh like he does every night and came upon poor Rolo and tore him limb from limb. Didn't have no chance."

There were sounds of enthusiastic agreement, and Sabrina herself had to repress a chill as *something* (it was hard to distinguish amusement from terror in this instance) rolled up her spine. Someone had put a stop payment on the town's reality check, it was clear.

"Somehow I doubt he'd've taken apart a Wrightly," Lima drawled, his eyes glinting.

"Lima, you don't know everything under the god-derned sun, despite what you may think!" The old gent stood up and stomped down the steps.

"Well, Ralphie, if you weren't so stupid you needed to take your clothes off to count to twenty-one, maybe you'd see my point of view," Lima called after the retreating man. "I feel that it's my imperative to set people straight when they are so misguided that they're making fools of themselves. I happen to know for a fact that Rolo came into a whole bucket of money and he came back here to face the music, so to speak, and set his ma up for life. He's been wandering America all these years, with no family, and not a care in the world."

It was all Sabrina could do not to say something, but she really didn't feel it was her place. She did her duty this morning after Thierry left her on the beach. She went straight to the police station (well, she had stopped for a few minutes and changed her muddy clothes and tried to wash the worst of the black swamp mud off her face and hands) and told the eager young man in uniform, Billy, about the treasure tree. By the end of her tale, she was feeling foolish and half-convinced that Thierry had made the whole thing up and paraded her all over the swamp to some random tree. She wouldn't put it past Thierry.

"Can you take me there now?" Billy asked, already standing up and eagerly pulling at his gun belt.

"Oh no." Sabrina backed away from the desk. "I'm not going back in the swamp. Thierry is perfectly capable of taking you to the tree. Ask him." She made her escape before Billy could try to talk her into going back. She would be happy if she never went back to that creepy place, crawling with slithery snakes and buzzing bugs.

Lima and the others had continued with their discussion of Rolo's murder, and she tuned back in as Lima said, "Well, Mr. Bradford Tittletott, great nephew of mine or not, he's got a bit of explaining to do, let me tell you."

Conversation stopped, and everyone turned inquiring eyes on Lima, just as he intended.

"What do you mean, Lima?" The screen door slammed behind Stacey Tubbs as she came out of the store.

"Weeell," Lima said, settling back in his chair. "Of course you've heard the police done searched the Tittletott House." Lima paused and everybody leaned forward. "*Well,* I just heard that they found a gun in Brad's room! It came straight out of old CQ Tittletott's gun closet. Brad says he has no idea how it got into his closet. But he used to be a prize marksman, the only one in the family CQ managed to teach to shoot. Well, that's suspicious enough, but when the police asked everyone in that house where they were the day of the murder, Brad said he was out at Lighthouse Beach. The police talked to Jean Teasley, who runs the gift shop out by the lighthouse, and you know she sees everyone who goes past her shop out onto that beach, and she says the only people she saw were a couple tourists shell hunting early in the morning and Miss Sabrina here in the afternoon. She never saw Brad. The police go back to Brad and he clams up, won't say a word. So where was he while Rolo was being shot to death?" Lima leaned back in satisfaction.

Stacey disappeared back into the store with a bang of the screen door, and everyone sat for a few minutes, contemplating what Lima said.

"Have they arrested him yet?" Sabrina asked. It *did* look pretty bad for Brad.

"Nah, not yet. Apparently, Brad's got some kind of bad stomach flu. He can barely get out of bed, much less answer questions. I think it's only a matter of time, though."

"What I want to know is how anybody knew Rolo was on the island," said a woman in a pink dress decorated with tiny red rosebuds. "How did the killer know to send

Rolo a note through Nettie? I sure as heck didn't know he was on the island, and I'm related to the Wrightlys through my mother's sister."

Talk ebbed and flowed around Sabrina as she considered the woman's question. Why hadn't she thought about it like that? The killer knew Rolo was on the island. So who knew Rolo was on the island?

She could think of several people. Nettie, of course. Elizabeth and Gary knew, judging from the conversation she had overheard at the tea party. Brad knew, because Rolo contacted him. How about Thierry? Had he known Rolo was on the island?

At the moment, considering the gun, his motive and lack of alibi, Brad seemed a likely suspect for the role of killer. And from the talk around her, it sounded as if most of the town was beginning to agree with her. Several people had noticed the way he acted at the rally, trembling and white-faced—did he just come from killing Rolo? Of course, Sabrina knew something that the others didn't. Brad was nervous because he changed his speech and was going to reveal…what? What was he going to say in the speech that made Elizabeth Tittletott so angry?

Brad would know where the treasure tree was. He knew Rolo was in town. He lied about being at Lighthouse Beach. Brad wanted to stop Rolo from revealing a damaging secret about the Tittletotts. Everything pointed to Brad.

But something didn't feel right. If Brad was planning to kill Rolo, why did he change his speech with the intention of revealing something that made Elizabeth livid with rage? That didn't make sense.

"I wouldn't be surprised to find out Lady E was responsible for offing Rolo," somebody said. "She always hated him, hated that Brad was friends with a Wrightly."

Hmmm. Sabrina thought about that. Elizabeth and Gary knew Rolo was in town. Either one of them could have sent the note to Rolo, taken the gun from the cabinet and ambushed Rolo in the rose garden. And then what? Planted the gun in Brad's closet? Elizabeth would never do that. What about Gary? For that matter, what about Virginia? Sabrina didn't know if Virginia knew Rolo was in town or not—she said not—but why did she lie to Sabrina about the treasure tree?

Even more puzzling was the question of why Lora Wrightly was interested in the rat pack the week before her death. Did the crayon pictures have something to do with this whole business?

Sabrina stood up so fast the rocking chair thumped on the wooden porch. People turned to her in surprise.

"I uh—thanks for the seat, Lima!" Sabrina hurried down the steps, not even conscious of the avid hush she had created.

"Anytime, Miss Sabrina!" Lima called, never at a loss for words.

"Looks like she got a wahoo up her shorts," someone muttered at her retreating back.

"Methinks," Lima said, "that there goes a woman who knows more than she's saying."

"You never know," said Stormy Lowry, who was famous for her oyster pies and her discerning eye. "Maybe she's the one who killed Rolo."

"Yep," Bicycle said, and burped.

The rest of the townspeople stared thoughtfully after the blond stranger.

SABRINA WAS FEELING a sense of urgency. She wasn't sure why, but she felt she was *missing* something and she needed to find out what. Fast.

Or what? she asked herself. A man was already dead. What else could happen?

She wasn't sure, but she couldn't calm the anxious feeling in her stomach.

It had turned into a dim, overcast day, gray clouds marbling the sky, the light heavy and monotonous. The Tittletott House rose above her like some medieval gothic castle in the soggy light. Without pausing to think, Sabrina hurried up the stairs, her heart beating *hurry hurry hurry*.

Gary was on the phone behind the reception desk as she came through the door. As she waited for him to finish his conversation she wandered into the dining room. Missy had seen her coming and had her table ready, complete with a glass of ice tea.

Sabrina's stomach grumbled, and she saw when she glanced at her watch that it was close to two. Maybe she *would* eat.

"Thanks, Missy," Sabrina said, sinking into the padded wood chair Missy held out for her. Today, Missy's shirt said, "I don't suffer from insanity. I enjoy every minute of it."

"Gary's not cooking today," Missy said. "The special is a fried shrimp sandwich."

"Sounds good. Do you know if Brad's here? I wanted to talk to him about contributing some money to his campaign."

"I think the campaign's the last thing on his mind right now," Missy said. "He's still real sick."

When Missy came back with the sandwich, she reported that Brad was nowhere to be found. "You're not the only one looking for him," she told Sabrina. "Coupla those mainland cops here waiting for him too. Looks pretty serious. Mrs. E's in there talking to them now."

Sabrina nodded her thanks and took a big bite of the fragrant overstuffed sandwich. Mmmm. Not as good as Gary's cooking, but still good.

She thought about her next move, whom to talk to next. She wanted to speak with Brad, since he was the one Rolo had sought out. But Brad was unavailable, and once again Sabrina felt the sense of urgency. Whom else could she talk to? Elizabeth and Gary were aware of Rolo's meeting with Brad. Did they know what Rolo wanted?

"Missy, did you notice anything strange the day of Rolo's murder?" Sabrina asked when Missy came back with the check. "You were here most of the day, right?"

"I leave around two and come back at four for the dinner shift. I went over to Nettie's to get a cake for Karel's birthday, but she had a Be-Back-in-Five-Minutes sign up, so I had to go to the fancy Lighthouse Estates grocery store to get the cake. Elizabeth and Gary were just finishing cleaning up the mess from the busted water heater when I left. When I got back, Elizabeth was being a *bear*. She must have missed her daily nap, or she was just upset about the water heater, but she was in stellar form, let me tell you."

Sabrina finished up her sandwich, paid, and went back out into the lobby.

A soap opera was playing, judging from the big-hairdooed woman wearing an evening dress in the middle of the day, and the buff, tanned Adonis fawning over her.

"Airport Ecstasy!" Sabrina said in sonorous tones, as if she had just walked into a church and seen all twelve disciples doing a conga line though the aisles.

"You watch *Airport Ecstasy?"* Gary tore his eyes away from the show and looked at Sabrina in astonishment.

"I always try to schedule my planning hour between two and three so I can watch it. I've been watching it for thirteen years, ever since it started," Sabrina said. "I actually remember when Vansola was a man—and a Mexican! Now look at her!" Sabrina glanced around. "I don't usually tell people that I'm a soap fiend. People look at you funny, if they don't watch themselves."

"I know," Gary said with fervor. "I usually watch the desk in the afternoons—hold on—" he picked up the ringing phone and answered a few questions about the Tittletott House "—but even though the phone is always ringing off the hook this time of the day, I usually can take in the whole show."

"I haven't been able to watch the last couple of days— did Durham reveal to Pookie that he slept with Gordan? Or did he ask her to marry him? Or did he ask Gordan to marry him? Do tell, I'm dying to know."

The phone rang, and Gary raised one finger and answered it. The reservation seemed to take an inordinate amount of time, and Sabrina was beginning to fidget by the time Gary had asked for the person's credit card number, its expiration date, the person's driver's license number, its expiration date, the person's mother's maiden name, *her* expiration date...

"Durham?" Sabrina prompted, when even after Gary hung up the phone it appeared he had forgotten about her.

"What?" Gary looked up from writing. "I'm not

sure—the phone's been ringing nonstop the last couple of days."

"I was wondering," Sabrina said, leaning a casual arm on the counter. "Why did Rolo come and see Brad? Do you know?"

Gary's eyes widened as he looked at her in astonishment. Sabrina worried that she might have come on too strong.

"What? I don't know—"

"I heard you and your mother talking."

"She'll kill me if I talk to you."

"Do you always do what your mother tells you?" Sabrina asked, feeling a little mean, because she had the feeling that for the most part he did. And who was she to talk?

"Uh—no. No," Gary said with more feeling.

"So you can tell me anything you want."

"I guess I can." Gary looked emboldened and confident for a moment, and then his face fell into the familiar, pinched, sallow lines. "Except I really don't know. I know he was threatening Brad, but no one ever told me what he was threatening to do."

"But you must have an idea."

"Well, I guess I thought it had something to do with all that business when we were kids, when Rolo stole the silver and set Edie's house on fire. What else could it be about? I'm sure Rolo was still pissed that Brad told on him."

"But was he threatening to reveal something?" Sabrina pressed.

Gary's eyebrows rose. "Reveal something? Like what? I figured he told Brad he would get him for what he did when they were kids. That's what I meant by threatening."

"No," Sabrina said. "He came back to expose something about the Tittletotts. What could it have been?" She knew she was right. Why else would Rolo have said: *everyone will know about the Tittletotts and what they're really like.*

Gary shrugged. "I'm afraid I'm not the depository of our family's dirty secrets. As a matter of fact, I'm honored if they bother to tell me what day the family reunion falls on."

"Do you remember anything about that time when Rolo stole the silver? Why would he do something like that?"

"Rolo and Brad were nuts back then. Always doing something crazy. Right before Rolo left, they had something going on, I know they did, but as usual they left me out." Gary still sounded bitter over a fifteen-year-old slight.

"What did Rolo and Brad have going on?" Sabrina felt she was close, but to what?

"I have no idea. But they were always poring over some map, and they kept digging holes under the treasure tree."

TWENTY-THREE

SABRINA WENT OUTSIDE, her mind whirling. Gary wasn't able to add anything else to his statement, and after the phone rang two more times, Sabrina gave up.

Digging under the treasure tree? For what?

Of course, the obvious answer would be: for treasure, stupid. But what treasure? Again, the answer seemed obvious. For Walk-the-Plank Wrightly's treasure.

As obvious as all these answers seemed to Sabrina, she was still in the dark as to what it all meant. Did it have anything to do with Rolo's murder?

Sabrina tripped over Virginia and then fell on top of her.

"Oomph." Virginia gasped as Sabrina struggled to lift herself off the smaller woman and succeeded only in elbowing her in the ear.

"I've been meaning to diet." Sabrina finally managed to untangle her arms from Virginia's and got to her feet. "I'm sorry. I usually *am* capable of walking along without falling over stationary objects. What are you doing?"

"I was planting bulbs." Virginia rubbed at her hip as she looked up at Sabrina. She sat on the ground in her pressed jeans and white T-shirt, with an impeccable pink bandanna protecting her golden hair.

"Here," Sabrina said, offering her hand, and pulled Virginia to her feet. "Are you okay?"

"Yes." Virginia rubbed at the back of her jeans again,

and let Sabrina lead her to a wooden bench in the side yard shaded by a large weeping willow.

"Did I hurt your, um, hip?"

"No, no. Please don't worry about me. It was just an accident." She looked away, her face drawn in unaccustomed lines of strain.

They sat in silence for a few moments, and then Sabrina said, "You don't look happy, Virginia, if you don't mind my saying so. Is anything wrong?"

Virginia looked at Sabrina for a long moment. "No. Yes. I mean, I'm fine," she said, and then caught her breath in a sob.

"Obviously not." Sabrina drew the woman into a hug and patted her back. "There, there. It can't be all that bad."

"I'm just so unhappy!" Virginia wailed, and pressed her head into Sabrina's shoulder.

"What do you have to be unhappy about?" Sabrina asked gently. "You've got a wonderful son, a caring husband, and you live in what's got to be the one of the most beautiful places in America." As if to prove her point, a pony ambled down the street and tore a chunk of grass out of the Tittletott lawn.

"Go away, Paint!" Virginia sat up and wiped at her eyes. "It's really silly. And you probably wouldn't understand since you've never been married."

Sabrina held her face straight. "You might be surprised to know," she said, "that I'm not completely ignorant about the relationship between a man and a woman."

"Sabrina, I didn't mean to say, to imply—oh damn. I'm sorry." Virginia looked contrite, and Sabrina smiled her forgiveness.

"You and Gary are having trouble?"

"Not really. Not any more than normal. But..."
Virginia looked out over the harbor, her face remote.
"There's something wrong with me. I can't love my husband like I should. I try, but I just can't. I guess that's part of my problem. I love the idea of being in love!"
Virginia's troubled gaze came to rest on Sabrina's face. "But it never lasts, do you understand? I fall in love with men all the time, I just can't help it. I've been like that since I was a girl."

"Why did you marry Gary?" Sabrina asked. "You had to know that you would keep falling in love with other men, even if you married him."

Virginia flushed and looked down at her wedding ring. She twisted it, and then pushed a nonexistent strand of hair under her bandanna.

"You had to, didn't you?" Sabrina asked gently. "You were pregnant with Sid."

Virginia hesitated and then nodded. "Yes. I had to." She looked at Sabrina appealingly, and Sabrina sensed that there was something more.

"Is Sid Gary's child?"

Virginia started, and looked at Sabrina with wide eyes. "How did—can you really tell—oh, it's worse than I thought. Everyone must know." She hid her face in her hands.

"Who's the father?" Sabrina asked in a mild voice. She thought she knew.

"It was just a momentary thing. We were in college, and both just homesick for something familiar. We got together for dinner one night, and well, that was that. Nothing more ever came of it. That one night didn't mean anything to him and I know now we should have just stayed friends. I was hurt that he avoided me after that, and I was more lonely than I ever was before. It was right before summer break, and when I came home Gary still looked at me as if I walked on water... Then I found out I was pregnant with Sid and it seemed like an easy decision."

"Brad's the father?" It was a calculated guess, but Sabrina wasn't surprised when Virginia hesitated and then nodded. "Does Gary know?"

The other woman shrugged. "Why would I tell him? He always had a crush on me, even when we were kids. When I came back from school that year, I didn't know I was pregnant until I got back to the island. Gary was so...kind, and quiet. He was exactly what I needed right then. We were married within the month, and he was so grateful, so happy, he never even asked why I was in a hurry. He's always treated Sid as his own. He loves that boy, more than anything." Virginia shrugged. "And since we haven't been able to have any more, Sid is extra precious to him. I've always wanted a little girl, but well, it just wasn't meant to be."

"And Brad? Does he know?"

"I never told him. There didn't seem to be any point. I knew by then I wasn't in love with him and that he wasn't ready to settle down with anyone."

Sabrina sat back and studied Virginia. "So why are you so unhappy now?"

"I don't know. I made my bed, and I have to lie in it. But Gary's just not what I always wanted in a husband."

What, he's caring, sensitive and honest? Sabrina wasn't sure why she was feeling so protective of Gary, but she kept the thoughts to herself.

"He's almost *feminine*," Virginia said, her face twisted in distaste. "He loves cooking, he watches soap operas for God's sake, and I think he may wear my clothes when I'm not around. I called two days ago when I was at the school setting up for the rally to tell him Sid was going to your house after school, and do you know what he was doing? Darning holes in his socks and watching that stupid soap opera. What kind of man is that?"

"Did you ever consider that he may be as unhappy as you are? Have you talked to him?"

"What's the use?"

"What about Brad? You don't think he's ever suspected about Sid?"

"Brad very rarely thinks about anybody but Brad," she said, her voice hard. "He treats me like a favorite younger sister, as if nothing ever happened between the two of us, and he loves Sid like an uncle should love his nephew. Nothing more, nothing less."

"Do you want more?" Could Virginia's disdain toward Brad hide deeper, stronger feelings for her handsome brother-in-law? After all, Brad was the father of her son.

"No, no." Virginia shook her head impatiently. "I was cured of Brad Tittletott twelve years ago. He doesn't bother me. I guess... Rolo coming back and dying, it's just brought back all the old memories. I miss how we were back then, Rolo, Brad and I. We were still kids, and everything was so innocent, and I was happy. I look back on those days as the happiest of my life."

"Those days you spent in the marsh under the treasure tree?" Sabrina kept her voice calm.

Virginia was nodding before she thought. "Oh!" She looked at Sabrina guiltily.

"You *do* know where the treasure tree is."

"I didn't mean to lie, Sabrina, but everything is so crazy. I didn't want to admit I knew what it meant, because I was afraid the police would think I had something to do with writing the note." Virginia fidgeted with the knot on her bandanna, and then pulled it off her head, shaking her fair hair with a fierce shake.

"Did you?" Sabrina looked at Virginia with steady eyes.

"No! But I knew—I knew who it had to be. I didn't want to talk about it until I had a chance to think about it."

"Who wrote that note? Do you know who killed Rolo?" Sabrina tried to keep her excitement at half-throttle.

"Not exactly. But it would have to be one of us, wouldn't it? One of us who knew what the treasure tree was. I didn't want to think about it being one of the rat pack."

Sabrina sat back, deflated. She'd hoped that Virginia somehow knew who the killer was, but Virginia had come to the same conclusions that Sabrina herself had. Rolo's killer was most probably one of a small group of people who knew about the treasure tree: Bradford, Virginia, Gary or Thierry.

"What's the story behind the treasure tree, anyway?" Sabrina asked, changing tacks. "Why did you call it that?"

"Rolo found it. It was in the diary his dad gave him when he turned eighteen. At first, Rolo only showed Brad where it was and the two of them would disappear for hours at a time. But then he took us all to the tree and we hung out there for months, built fires, roasted oysters. None of our families knew about it, so we could effectively disappear. It was very peaceful." Virginia's gaze was soft and faraway.

"Dock gave Rolo a diary when he turned eighteen?"

"It was an old-timey diary and a sword. Rolo started

wearing that sword around everywhere he went. We used to make fun of him, but Rolo was always so serious, we finally just left him alone. He was saying the strangest stuff, saying that he had proof that the Tittletotts didn't rightfully own the island, that his family did. Which was funny, since no one *really* owns the island, now. The Tittletotts own a lot of property which has been passed down to them through the years. I guess if someone proved that all that land didn't belong to the Tittletotts, they—we— would be pretty poor."

Virginia looked thoughtful for a moment, and then continued. "Rolo was dead serious about the whole thing. He wouldn't tell the rest of us what he meant, but I'm pretty sure he told Brad. He and Brad were always digging under the treasure tree looking for old Walk-the-Plank Wrightly's treasure. Rolo was convinced it was under the tree."

"Whose diary was it?"

Virginia shrugged. "I have no idea. Rolo was pretty secretive about it all. I guess I always thought Rolo was making it up, except of course, he wouldn't. He wasn't like that. But I just remember feeling left out, because Rolo and Brad were palling around and leaving me out. I had to hang around with Thierry and Gary." She wrinkled her nose and laughed. "I was such a snotty kid."

Sabrina heard crunching gravel and looked up to see Brad Tittletott coming up the front walk, carrying an armful of his election posters crumpled and torn in his arms. His face looked strained and white, and a little green around the mouth.

"Brad, the police came around again," Virginia called. Was that malice sharpening the woman's voice?

Brad stopped, his posture weary and defeated. "I'm

sure they'll be arresting me soon. Why is all this happening?" He looked a shadow of his former self, his coat wrinkled and stained, his hair hanging over his eyes.

Buzz, buzz, buzz. Brad fumbled in his coat, brought out a cell phone, and continued walking toward the house. Sabrina stared after him, her brow wrinkled.

"Yes, I heard," Sabrina heard him say into the phone. "No! I don't want you doing that, do you hear me?"

Sabrina's eyes narrowed as he disappeared into the house.

TWENTY-FOUR

SABRINA WALKED ON down the road, her mind racing.

Dock gave a sword and a diary to Rolo when he turned eighteen. What was in the diary that convinced Rolo that Walk-the-Plank Wrightly's treasure was buried under the treasure tree? Did it matter? And what evidence did Rolo have that proved that the Tittletotts didn't own the island?

"No," Sabrina said. "That's not quite what she said, is it? She said that the Tittletotts didn't *rightfully* own the island. Not quite the same thing, is it?"

Sabrina stopped in the middle of the street. Could that be a motive for murder? Would someone kill to keep Rolo from revealing that the ancient deed that Elizabeth Tittletott hung so proudly over her mantel proclaiming her family's ownership of the island was a fake? What proof could he possibly have? And would his proof affect the Tittletotts' current landholdings?

But all this happened fifteen years ago. If Rolo didn't spill the beans then, why now?

Did he bring this proof, whatever it was, back with him and plan to reveal it at the rally? Is that why he was killed?

"But that's crazy," Sabrina said.

"Look who's talking," a woman said loudly.

Sabrina realized that she was standing in the middle of the street opposite Tubbs General Store, her mouth gaping open and her eyes slightly crossed as she thought.

She looked around and focused on Lima who was leering at her from the porch of Tubbs'. Mary Garrison Tubbs stood beside him.

"Hello." She climbed the steps to the porch and sat down in one of the rocking chairs. Lima watched her, his eyes sparkling with delight.

"Miss Sabrina, you look as if you're thinkin' awfully hard."

"It looks like hard work." Mary swung the plastic bags she carried.

"It's all so sad," Sabrina said impulsively. "Why did someone have to kill Rolo?"

"Ah," Lima said, nodding. "Yes, it's sad. Sadder yet is that one of us on the island saw fit to do him in. I shore hope Brad knows what he's doin'."

"It does look bad for him, doesn't it?"

"Of course he didn't do it," Mary said. "No one else on this island did it either. It was some tourist come down here from the mainland, all hopped on some drug or another. You know how these tourists are." She stared at Sabrina.

"I heard several people saw a blond woman who looked suspiciously like Mrs. Virginia Tittletott going through Waver Town around the time of the murder. I thought she was supposed to be helping with the rally," Lima said. "I wonder what she was doin' there?"

"Just walking through, I suspect, like anybody's got a right to do," Mary said. "Anyway, everyone saw her at the rally. She was there the whole time, I know it."

"Just because she's your kin…" Lima said. "Anyway, I also heard the police found Rolo's camp, and the boat he used to get to the island. It was in the marsh, right close to the old Wrightly House." Lima looked at Sabrina.

"I also heard that the gun they found, the one in Brad's room, was almost certainly the gun used to shoot Rolo, but that it was jammed, and that was probably why the murderer had to finish Rolo off with the pruning shears."

Mary sucked in a breath, her face twisted in consternation.

"And I hear tell everybody in the Tittletott House is under suspicion, because they found old CQ's gun in Brad's room," Lima continued, ignoring Mary. "Anyone could have put it there, you see. I hear they got alibis from everybody at the house, and handwriting samples to match to that note they found in Rolo's pocket, I suppose. Ms. Elizabeth was in the house all day, though I 'spect she could have slipped out if she wanted to, but someone would have seen her, wouldn't they? She's not exactly subtle, if you know what I mean. Ms. Virginia was supposedly down at the school gym, though she looks to have a double going through Waver Town about the same time. Gary was manning the desk, probably watching that godawful soap opera of his, but was he there the whole time? Brad definitely lied about where he was. Why on earth did he tell the police he was at Lighthouse Beach when he most assur-red-ly wasn't?"

"The police don't have no right to be poking into a body's private life," Mary said. "I'm glad they don't think *I'm* guilty of murder, they'd be asking what type of shampoo I use, and what I write in my diary. I'm sure Brad has a pretty good reason for not telling the police where he was that day. And, you know perfectly well Elizabeth always takes a nap in the middle of the day. Virginia was at the school, everyone saw her. I know Gary was at the Tittletott House that afternoon, because he called me and asked if I knew where Henley's daddy was, because they needed a plumber for their water heater. I called him right back at the house and told him Big Henley would be there later that afternoon. So there, it couldn't have been any of them, it must have been some tourist, just like I said!"

Lima shrugged. "If you say so, Mary, you've always been the smartest, brightest woman I ever knew. Prettiest, too." He winked at Sabrina as Mary looked mollified. "I'm just saying it doesn't look real good, aren't I?"

Sabrina got up to leave.

"I think I'll just go check on Roxanna, make sure she's not sending the letter to my sister to the pope by accident," Mary was saying as Sabrina stepped over Bicycle on her way down the steps. He was humming a song, something she recognized.

It wasn't until she was down the street that she realized what it was:

It was a Police classic called *Murder by Numbers*.

NETTIE WAS PULLING taffy when Sabrina entered the cookie shop.

"Did you hear about Rolo?" Nettie's eyes were red and she looked old and papery like a sixty-year-old newspaper. "They've released his body. We're burying him tomorrow, on Halloween."

"Where will you bury him?"

"They won't let us bury people in our yards anymore, like we used to. The only cemetery on the island is Dunetop, but at least Rolo will be home on Comico." Nettie looked down at the blue-green goop she was stretching between her tiny hands.

"Have you made the arrangements for the funeral? Do you need any help?"

"Oh no." Nettie punched at the taffy and sighed.

"Howard Dunsweeney, who runs the bait shop, he owns Dunetop and he's going to get Bicycle Bob to dig the grave, and he's shipping over a nice oak casket from the mainland. Pastor Josh, my nephew once removed who owns the little car lot over by the gas station, will give the service, and then everyone will come back to the house. The ladies have already started bringing food over." Nettie glanced at the telephone. "I've been trying to get in touch with Rolo's wife, but I haven't been able to reach her."

"Sounds like you have everything well in hand," Sabrina said, resolving to cook something delicious to bring. Maybe a nice tiramisu or chocolate-raspberry ganache. "I have a question for you, Nettie. About Rolo."

Nettie put the taffy aside, and went to the sink to wash her hands. "Thank you for being a friend to Rolo in his last days. It means a lot to me. What do you want to know?"

"Do you know why Dock gave Rolo the sword and a diary on his eighteenth birthday?"

Nettie stared at Sabrina in amazement. "How did you know about the diary? I didn't think anyone but the Wrightlys knew about that. Dock swore me to secrecy when we were first married, but I don't see where it matters now. Dock's dad had just given him the sword and diary, you see, and Dock told me it was a family tradition that had been going on for almost three hundred years in his family. The pirate's wife started it after Walk-the-Plank died. When their son turned eighteen, she gave him his father's diary and sword. Ever since then, when the oldest Wrightly son turns eighteen, he receives old Walk-the-Plank Wrightly's legacy. It's like a right of passage in the Wrightly family."

Sabrina nodded slowly. Walk-the-Plank Wrightly's diary. What she wouldn't give to read that diary, to see the eighteenth century through the eyes of someone living it. It was a shame the family kept the diary a secret. It belonged in a museum.

"What does it say?" Sabrina asked. "Why is it such a secret? And what proof does it hold about the Tittletotts?"

"The Tittletotts?" Nettie frowned. "I don't know. I never read the diary. I do remember Dock told me once, when I was really put out with Elizabeth Tittletott, that the Tittletotts were no better than the Wrightlys and he had proof. He said, some day, when the time was right, everybody would know the truth. But he wouldn't say anything else about it. And then, when he gave Rolo the diary, Rolo started walking around with that sword as if he were ten foot high. It made me proud, to see him with so much confidence."

"Hmmm." What could it possibly say that could affect so many generations of Wrightlys?

"And then he brought it with him when he returned to the island. The diary and the sword. I saw them when I put some of my cookies in his bag one day. When I asked him about it, he started talking about righting old wrongs, and that it was time to tell the truth about this island's history. I was so happy to see Rolo after all these years, but he wasn't easy to talk to. I didn't understand what was going on with him. I wanted to talk about his wife and daughter, and all he wanted to talk about was what the Tittletotts had been doing for the last fifteen years. When he found out Thierry was going around with Brad, he got so angry he almost couldn't talk. I told him that Brad was only using Thierry to get the Waver vote, but he wasn't listening."

"But they didn't find the diary when he died. Or the sword," Sabrina said. "They didn't find anything on him but that note. Why wouldn't the killer take the note? It was incriminating. But maybe he or she was in too much of a hurry. Yet he or she still had time to take the sword and the diary?"

Did Rolo *have* the sword and the diary when he was killed? Wouldn't Rolo have been able to defend himself if he had been wearing the sword when he was attacked? And it seemed unlikely that the killer took the sword after the murder. It would have been almost impossible for the killer to conceal the sword as he or she made an inconspicuous exit from Sabrina's yard. The diary, yes, the sword, no. It was possible that the killer hid the items, but the police searched the woods thoroughly. Maybe in the sound? But the water was shallow for yards and yards... Maybe Rolo hid the sword and diary before he was killed. Or maybe the killer hid them. Suddenly she had a pretty good idea *where* the sword and diary might be. It was the perfect place to hide treasure, after all.

"Nettie," Sabrina said as she stood. "I've got to go. I think I know where to find the sword and diary."

THERE WAS NO wind in the marsh. At least, not down among the roots and mud. Above her head the top of the marsh grass fluttered in the sunny breeze, but among the rustling, scratchy stalks the air was green and stale.

"I know I'm going the right way," Sabrina said, trying to convince herself. She trudged on through the stinking mud, slapping at bugs and watching as new battalions of the little beasties hummed their way toward her. Brown goop covered her legs well past her knees, and sweat glued her shirt to her back. It was the smell that was overwhelming, however, not the heat, the mosquitoes or even the creepy crawlies she kept seeing out of the corner of her eye. The smell of rotting vegetation, stagnant water and rich soil was almost overwhelming.

"Almost there, almost there." She didn't know that at all, but the words made her feel better, so she kept saying them. She heard a splashing, sliding noise off to her right. Alligator? She shivered and hurried on.

Just about when she had decided she was completely lost, and doomed to wander the marsh of Comico Island for the rest of her short, miserable life, she stumbled upon the small clearing holding the treasure tree.

"Thank goodness," Sabrina gasped as she stumbled over to one of the rotting old bus seats and collapsed in a cloud of dust and gnats. She breathed heavily for several minutes, gazing around at the quiet clearing as her breathing slowly returned to normal.

"I made it!" For a woman who was convinced that her car moved itself every time she went into the grocery store, leaving her to wheel the grocery cart in futile pursuit, she was delighted with her accomplishment.

After she caught her breath, she stood up and walked to the far side of the clearing. She'd noticed the ground was freshly disturbed the first time she was here. At the time, she thought an animal had been digging in the clearing, but now she thought she knew what lay under the raw dirt.

She had been in such a hurry that she didn't think to bring a shovel or a spade, so she started digging with her bare hands. She didn't have long to dig. No more than a foot under the ground she struck the long hard shaft of the sword. Digging carefully, she uncovered the plastic bag lying under the sword.

Inside was a small, leather-bound book.

Sabrina took the book and sat back down on the bus seat, not even noticing the dust billowing around her.

Two pieces of paper were slipped within the pages of the book. Carefully, she extracted one and unfolded it, wincing as the ancient paper tore a little along where it had been folded.

It looked familiar. It didn't take her long to recall where she had seen something like it. Over the mantel at the Tittletott House. This was also a deed to the island, dated 1716, which was four years earlier than the Tittletotts' deed.

And it was made out to Roland Thierry Wrightly.

Sabrina had heard the story from Lima. She knew that Roland Thierry Wrightly the First legally owned the island before it was given to Lord Tittletott when Wrightly was exposed as a pirate.

It was the letter folded up beside the deed that surprised her.

It was a letter to a real estate lawyer, from Rolo, asking the lawyer to review the enclosed information and give his opinion on whether the Wrightlys could lawfully reclaim their rightful property, namely, much of the land on Comico Island.

TWENTY-FIVE

IT TOOK HER the rest of the night to decipher the story from the diary. The curlicue letters and the awkward language made the diary hard reading, but even when her eyes started drooping she wasn't able to put the book down. Roland Thierry Wrightly the First started writing in the diary when he was sixteen, and while he wasn't a consistent diarist, he was conscientious about writing whenever anything important happened in his life.

Sabrina read about the death of Roland's father, and how the young man threw himself into learning his father's commerce business. Roland increased his father's small concern into a booming business with over ten ships. As he grew older, Roland began questioning the wisdom of importing everything from England, and switched his focus, at great cost, to selling within the colonies themselves, carrying tobacco and rice to New England and trading for meat and wheat. He met his wife, Sarah Campbell, a Scottish immigrant who came to America with her parents when she was a child.

Sabrina shook her head in bemusement, putting the diary down and fixing herself a cup of hot tea. For a notorious pirate with a reputation for viciousness, Roland Wrightly's words were imbued with thoughtfulness. Though he didn't dwell on his own kindness, he obliquely mentioned several occasions when he helped his less wealthy neighbors through a particularly hard winter, or after a summer storm. He loved his wife to distraction. He did not sound like a vicious, bloodthirsty pirate.

It wasn't until near the end of the diary that the treacherous story began to unfold. Roland was awarded the deed to Comico Island as a token of the governor's esteem. Roland was proud, and he took his new responsibilities very seriously.

A few years after that, reports of vicious pirate attacks began to appear more often in Roland's diary. Roland was very concerned, as twice his ships were hit by Walk-the-Plank Jack, and he was heartbroken when all the men on the ships were killed. Finally, the governor appointed Lord Russell Tittletott, a retired admiral in the English navy, to hunt down the pirates.

Roland was impressed with Lord Tittletott's progress as the retired admiral hunted down and brought to justice several less notorious pirates. They were friends, though Roland knew Tittletott resented the fact the governor had not deeded Comico Island to him instead of to Roland. As the months passed, and Walk-the-Plank Jack was still at large, Roland began having doubts about the man he had considered a friend. Small things: a fleeting glimpse Roland caught of the pirate ship which looked suspiciously like Lord Tittletott's ship. And then, there was the cuckoo clock. It had hung on the wall of the captain's cabin inside one of Roland's ships. The ship was attacked, the cargo and several miscellaneous items including the cuckoo clock stolen, and all the crew killed. Roland Wrightly saw the cuckoo clock on the wall in Lord Tittletott's house.

After confronting Tittletott about the clock and being genially rebuffed, Roland began to suspect he was being framed. Booty from a ransacked ship was found on his property on Comico Island. Authorities in different ports were tipped that some of his cargo may be illegal, which caused him inconvenience and time.

That was when Roland Wrightly gathered together a small fortune in gold and silver and buried it, drawing a small map in his diary to show where it was buried. He saw the end coming and wanted his wife and unborn child to be provided for.

A week later, Wrightly sailed out of Hurricane Harbor on his way to the West Indies on a routine trip.

There was no other entry from Roland Wrightly.

There was a short letter on the very last page, written by Sarah Campbell Wrightly to her son. By that time, Lord Tittletott had sailed triumphantly into Comico Harbor with Roland Wrightly's ship, complete with stolen cargo and pirate flag as proof that Wrightly had been the infamous Walk-the-Plank Jack. The governor rewarded Lord Tittletott the title to Comico Island.

But a crew member, Cedric, who was on Roland Wrightly's ship when it was attacked, managed to escape the drowning fate of his shipmates. And he recognized Lord Tittletott as the vile pirate who cut down Roland Wrightly and then forced the rest of the crew to walk the plank, one by one. Cedric clung to a piece of wood for three days before washing up on shore, after which he made his way back to Comico Island to tell Sarah what really happened to her husband.

In the letter, Sarah wrote that she was saving the diary and her husband's sword—apparently it was an heirloom and not Roland's everyday sword—as a legacy for his son, so he would know the truth about his father. She urged him to continue searching for his father's treasure, as she wasn't able to locate it. The map that Roland Thierry Wrightly the First had drawn was torn. The directions to the treasure tree were clearly discernible, but the other side of the map was indecipherable. Sarah wrote that the Tittletotts had grown too powerful for the Wrightlys to hope to challenge. She hoped succeeding generations would know the truth about their famous, maligned relative, and that sometime, when the time was right, a Wrightly could right the wrong.

Sabrina put down the diary and yawned. Calvin had fallen asleep a long time ago, and his little body twitched as he dreamed.

Was this diary a motive for murder? Would someone kill Rolo to keep him from revealing the truth behind the ancient story? If this diary could be used to prove that Lord Tittletott won the title to the island illegally, then it was just possible that all of the Tittletott island holdings could be questioned. That was a powerful motive for murder. What response had the real estate lawyer given to Rolo? And why were the diary and sword buried under the treasure tree?

Carrying the book with her, Sabrina climbed the steps to her room and lay down without even taking off her clothes. Tomorrow would be a long day. It was Halloween.

And Rolo's funeral.

HE HAD TO come out sometime. He couldn't stay in there forever.

Thierry shifted position and patted his pocket, feeling the reassuring lump of the pistol. The morning sun licked at the dew around his pants cuffs.

"Hiya, Thierry, whatcha doing?" Wayland McCall hefted the crab trap he carried and nodded at Thierry.

"Hanging out," Thierry said, and turned his head back toward the Tittletott House. He was conscious of Wayland's gaze on him but Thierry ignored it. He never much liked Wayland anyway, ever since they were kids and Wayland turned them all in to his daddy for holding midnight races on the island ponies. As a matter of fact, he'd love to give Wayland a fist in the gut right now, that's just the way he was feeling.

"Pshaw," Thierry said, which was one of his dad's favorite expressions before he went crazier than a Mitchell's Day surfer. He shifted position against one of the posts holding up the pier.

The front door of the Tittletott House opened and Virginia came out onto the front porch with a water pitcher. She took so long watering the potted palms and picking off dead fronds that Thierry almost went up there and took the pitcher out of her hands and did it himself. The whole time he was worried she would see him over here and wonder what he was doing.

He never liked Virginia the way the rest of them did. She was good-looking if you liked a trim body and pretty face. No, Thierry wasn't immune to a pretty face. But she was cold inside. Pure ice. Thierry liked a girl with a little more fire, like curvy Molly Lowry. Now *she* was something, though she wasn't talking to him since she found out he wasn't going to be the big shot president's assistant like he told her he was going to be. She didn't seem interested in just a plain old carpenter.

Virginia went back inside and Thierry shifted so he faced the house full on again.

"Thierry, you better get on home and get dressed for your brother's funeral, you hear? You can't go dressed like that, and it's in two hours."

Thierry scowled at Aunt Mary Garrison Tubbs. She was always looking down on him, like he smelled or something. She had always raved about his brother Rolo, and look at what he had gone and done. After Rolo left the island, Aunt Mary never said another word about Rolo, but it didn't make her like Thierry any more.

"I'll go when I'm good and ready," he grumbled.

"What did you say? Speak up, boy, you're always mumbling." She stopped in the middle of the street, oblivious of the car behind her. She tapped her foot, and glared at Thierry.

"I got something to do first," Thierry said, a little louder.

"Well, see you get home soon. Your mama needs your help." Aunt Mary stared at him a moment longer, trying to catch his eye, but Thierry acted like he was looking at an old work boat coming across the harbor. Was it Nick Teasley? Why, yes it was.

Aunt Mary snorted and marched on down the street. The car behind her roared past her, the driver making obscene gestures. Tourist.

Thierry resumed his watch of the Tittletott House, massaging the butt of the pistol in his coat. He had to come out sometime.

Thierry remembered not too long ago when he would have walked right inside like he belonged there. His mama always sniffed at him, like he was getting uppity because he was hanging out with Towners. But his mama had plenty of Towner friends, it was just the Tittletotts she hated. Well, hated was kinda strong. He couldn't imagine his mother hating anybody. But Nettie and Elizabeth Garrison Tittletott had a long history. Nettie was the pretty one, from what Thierry heard, and Elizabeth the snobby one, with all the money behind her. Elizabeth was sweet on Dock when they were in school.

Thierry could almost recite the story by heart, Nettie had recounted it so many times. Dock had those dark Wrightly looks, and he was a smooth-talking, handsome young man. And he only had eyes for Nettie. They married the day after they both graduated from high school. Elizabeth Garrison eventually married CQ Tittletott, who was fifteen years older.

And that should have been that. But over the years, the two women kept up a rivalry that started in kindergarten. Thierry wondered if when he was old and wrinkled he would still hate Wayland McCall because Wayland finked on him when they were twelve years old.

Brad came out the front door of the Tittletott House. Thierry started and then turned away and pretended he was inspecting one of the boats tied up on the pier. Brad didn't even look in his direction as he hurried down the street.

Thierry abandoned his pretense and ran after him. Brad was walking so fast Thierry almost lost him when he turned down Post Office Road.

"Don't think you can lose me," Thierry muttered, though he was pretty sure Brad hadn't even noticed him. Wasn't that just like a Tittletott? A couple of days ago, Brad acted like Thierry was his best friend. I'll make you a director of refuse, Brad said. Just help me with the campaign, and I won't forget about you when I'm in office.

And Thierry helped him. He'd admit it now, he was flattered when Brad started talking to him that night down at the Pub. Brad had just announced that he was running, and everybody was buying him drinks. They started talking, and the rest was history.

Brad never noticed him much when they were kids. Brad and Rolo were best friends, and they didn't have much time for the "junior rats," as Brad called Thierry and Gary.

Then Rolo went away and things changed. Lately, people looked at Thierry with respect because he was always with Brad, and wasn't that a hoot!

But all that was over now. Thierry grasped the butt of the pistol and increased his speed. He wasn't going to let him out of his sight.

Brad turned and ducked into the back of Tubbs' store. Thierry stopped, confused. What in the heck was he doing going in the back of Tubbs'?

Thierry found a nearby tree and leaned up against it. He could wait.

Brad had to come out sometime. He couldn't stay in there forever.

And then Thierry would have him.

TWENTY-SIX

IF IT WASN'T for the cast iron skillet, Sabrina wouldn't have been late for Rolo Wrightly's funeral.

Sabrina overslept that morning, and then she couldn't decide what to wear. And then she felt a stabbing pain in her eye, and it had taken her almost fifteen minutes to look up her symptoms in her medical book. She ruled out entropion and a stye, and it was only a matter of time to see if acute glaucoma developed.

And then, she couldn't find the cast iron skillet.

"STOP that!" Sabrina snapped at her tiny yellow companion.

"CHEEP cheep!" Calvin replied in perfect imitation of her tone. Calvin had taken to following Sabrina from room to room, wagging his head and imitating her agitated mumblings.

"Do you see the skillet?" Sabrina asked in exasperation, standing in her stockinged feet in her best dark blue dress as she stared around the kitchen.

Calvin glanced around the kitchen and then back up at her face.

"I don't either." Sabrina sighed, and glanced at her watch again. Almost twelve.

If she knew why she was looking for the skillet she might have searched for the darned thing with a bit more patience. But Nettie didn't explain when she called this morning and asked Sabrina to bring the skillet, the one she knew was in the house somewhere.

Calvin grew tired of her antics and pulled himself up onto his favorite windowsill where he nodded off. Sabrina started pulling out drawers and opening cabinets which she knew she'd already looked through.

Finally, she found the skillet in the living room, being used to catch water for a rampant fern.

Sabrina grabbed her hat and dashed for the door.

It was already twelve noon, and the streets were deserted. "Closed" signs were posted in all the shop windows, and the old boat dock was full of battered work boats which usually would have been out on the water this time of day. The island of Comico had turned out to mourn the passing of one of its sons, no matter how wayward that son had been.

She heard the music as she neared the High Tide Baptist Church. For all the world, it sounded like a jazzy blues band playing "Love Me Tender."

It *was* a jazzy blues band playing Elvis' "Love Me Tender." Led by Sondra Lane from Sweet Island Music on a keyboard, the four-person band sat behind a wall at the front of the church and sweet-talked the strains of music from their various instruments. Judging from the misty smiles and nods of approval, the funeral-goers deemed this an entirely appropriate choice of music.

The church was packed with islanders wearing their best flannels and house dresses. Sabrina stood at the back of the church until Bicycle Bob, sitting on the edge of a pew, began subtly edging closer to the plump matron beside him, who edged against her husband to retreat from Bicycle. Soon the entire row of people was squishing, and

Bicycle patted the seat beside him. Sabrina gratefully sat down, balancing the rusty skillet on her lap.

"Thank you, Bob," she whispered and he nodded.

The interior of the church was paneled with wood and painted a light pink. Narrow windows emitted cheerful shafts of light which played over the varnished pine pews. There were no flowers in the church, but instead vases of gold, green and auburn marsh grass adorned the coffin.

At the front of the church, Sabrina saw Nettie, Dock, Thierry and an unfamiliar young woman with a little girl. Sabrina smiled.

"Pssss, Miss Sabrina," someone hissed, and Sabrina saw Lima Lowry waving from three rows away to gain her attention.

Sabrina smiled and averted her eyes, hoping he would take the hint and stop waving his arms like a pinwheel.

"Miss Sabrina!" His tone was definitely increasing.

Sabrina tried a small wave and looked away.

Lima wasn't having any of it.

"Pssss, Miss Sabrina!"

By this time the entire church was watching Lima.

"What?" Sabrina mouthed silently.

"Did you hear that someone shot at Brad Tittletott this morning?" Lima said in a whisper as subtle as a shotgun blast, especially when Sondra Lane brought her band's rendition of "Heartbreak Hotel" to a snazzy finale, and Lima's words echoed in the sudden silence.

"Thank you, Lima," Sabrina said firmly. Lima nodded in satisfaction and turned back toward the front, oblivious of the stir he had caused.

Sabrina saw Brad sitting by himself two rows in front of her. He stared stonily ahead and ignored the curious looks directed his way.

Sabrina gave him a thoughtful look and looked back toward the front where a man dressed in a flannel shirt and suspender pants had wandered to the front of the church. A black robe hung down his back like Batman's cape. He seemed to be looking for something behind the pulpit.

Someone shot at Brad this morning? Who? And why, with all the suspicion flying around him, was Brad at Rolo's funeral?

Because Brad and Rolo were best friends when they were children, she realized, despite all that had happened since then. That kind of pure friendship is unsullied by complicated adult emotions.

The man in the cape was down on his hands and knees behind the pulpit. He said "aha!" and pounced on a polished stick and held it up triumphantly. He turned to stare at the congregation, swaying slightly, the stick raised like a director's baton.

The congregation stared back.

"Marriage," he said, waving the stick experimentally. "We are all gathered here to celebrate—" His confused glance fell on the coffin.

"It's a funeral, Pastor Josh!" someone yelled.

"I see. Yes, that would explain the—" Pastor Josh put down the stick, fumbled for his glasses and began sorting through the paper on the pulpit. "Oh yes," he said with some relief, "here we go. We are all gathered here in memory of our beloved brother, um..." He paused, flipping through some papers. "Our beloved brother, um..." The flipping became frantic.

"Roland Thierry Wrightly the Eleventh," Nettie said from the front row. "Get it together, Pastor Josh, or I'll preach the sermon myself."

"Oh yes. Certainly. We are all gathered here in memory of our beloved brother, Rolo, my dear cousin Rolo."
A big fat tear rolled down Pastor Josh's cheek.

"My dear cousin Rolo has gone on to heaven now," he said in a stronger voice, falling into the familiar sermon-giving rhythm, "and while we all will certainly miss him, we must remember that heaven is like a used car lot, can I hear an amen. Just think about how you feel as you walk around that lot with a wad of money in your pocket and you know that you can buy any car there, and that emotion is pure happiness. That is how Rolo will feel for all eternity, and we can rejoice for him.

"This reminds me of something that happened to me the other day. A young man came onto my lot—I won't use any names—and this young man was looking at a low-mileage, clean Ford F-150, and he liked that truck, yes he did, can I hear an amen, and he wanted to buy that truck, but he said to me, he said, 'Pastor, I surely like that truck, but I don't think I should have to pay that price you have stuck to the windshield,' and I said, 'Wayland McCall—'"

A couple rows in front of Sabrina, a young man jerked upright and looked around as his neighbors turned to snicker at him. Pastor Josh had picked up the stick again and he was using it to point at the blushing young man.

"I said, 'Wayland McCall, let me ask you a question. Do you go into a restaurant and order a hamburger and fries and then when the bill comes, say, 'I don't think I should have to pay that?' Do you go to the general store and pick out twenty dollars' worth of groceries and then tell Greg Tubbs, 'I don't think I should have to pay for these?' There is something wrong with people today, can I hear an amen, there is something wrong when they think that the world owes them a big-screen TV, a nice car and a Foreman grill. Nobody ever got something for nothing, that's what I say, and that's what the good book says, I think in John or Luke. Responsibility!" Pastor Josh roared, slamming the stick down on the pulpit, and half the congregation jumped. "That's what we need, a sense of responsibility! If you want to buy a house, save for it. If you want good roads, pay your taxes! And do it with a smile, and a 'Thank you, Lord, for giving me my health and the road signs that warn me that some poor, unsuspecting critter may be crossing the road!'"

Sabrina looked around and saw people nodding, with thoughtful expressions on their faces.

"So here we are to say good-bye to our brother Rolo, a good man, and lest you feel sad, lest you have tears in your eyes, just remember, that in our own time, we will see him again, and we too will be spending eternity in our own personal car lot with plenty of money—money we earned, mind you—in our pocket."

Pastor Josh seemed drained, and he swayed for a moment, toying with the stick on the pulpit. "So then, ashes to ashes, dust to um…" He stopped and fumbled through his papers. "Dust to, um…"

"Dust," people were saying under their breath, so many of them that a sibilant hiss rose through the air.

"Um, let's see…ashes to ashes, dust to…hmm…"

"Dust!" Lima roared. "Dust to dust!"

"Yes, of course. Dust to dust. God is good, God is great, thank the Lord it's time to eat."

With that, Josh used his arms to spread his cape like great wings over his head and trotted down the middle of the aisle. Six men went to the front of the church and surrounded the coffin, bearing it carefully out of the church.

Shaking her head, Nettie, dressed in a plain dark dress, and holding a candle topped with a flickering flame, came down the aisle, followed by Dock, Thierry and the strange woman and child, all holding white candles.

Sabrina looked around in consternation as the people around her began pulling candles out of their pockets and a pack of matches was passed down the aisle. Even Bicycle Bob had a candle, though his was a red candle, burned down to almost a nub.

Sabrina forgot about the candles when she saw Elizabeth Tittletott, Gary and Virginia pass down the aisle and out of the church. She'd assumed Brad came alone. As the last of the islanders streamed out of the church, holding their lit candles, Sabrina fell in behind.

The crowd of people walked down Lighthouse Road and took a right down Long Road, the paved road that headed toward the deserted end of the island. Sabrina had driven down to the far end of the road when she first arrived on the island and was rewarded with views of marshland, rolling dunes and ponies.

Once on Long Road, the crowd took another right and Sabrina saw a metal archway bearing the name "Dunetop Cemetery." The hill of sandy dirt was dotted with tombstones.

Sabrina followed the crowd up the hill and down the backside, where a mound of fresh dirt and a hole in the ground marked Rolo's final resting place. The six burly men lowered Rolo's coffin to the ground beside the grave site and Nettie opened the lid. Sabrina joined the gathering around the edge of the grave behind Nettie and her family. Pastor Josh had disappeared, though Sabrina could hear something that sounded suspiciously like snoring drifting from a nearby bush.

"Thank you all for coming out today. Rolo would have been happy to know that we didn't forget him." Nettie paused, and wiped at her eyes. "Despite what everybody may think, Rolo was a good boy. He didn't deserve what happened to him." Nettie gestured toward the young woman and she stepped forward, holding the hand of the little girl. "This is Rolo's wife, Sherry, and his daughter, Little Nettie, who wouldn't be here if Miss Sabrina, our new neighbor, hadn't made a couple of phone calls and arranged the whole thing!" Nettie had to stop again. "They came all this way from Oregon to see where Rolo was born, and where he died. I'm trying to talk Sherry into staying here."

Sherry, who had shoulder-length auburn hair, a thin face and eyes blotched from crying, smiled at her mother-in-law.

"Now, I'd like to call up Bruce Teasley who was one of Rolo's good friends when they were kids."

Bruce Teasley, carrying a cast iron skillet, stepped to the front and talked about Rolo and some of the stunts they pulled when they were boys. As he finished, he placed the skillet in the coffin.

One by one, several people spoke about Rolo and placed a skillet in the coffin.

"It's amazing how people who hadn't thought about Rolo Wrightly for fifteen years have so many nice things to say about him," Lima said.

"Don't be cynical," Sabrina said out of the corner of her mouth. "All right, I give up. What's with the iron skillets?"

"Weeell now." Lima shifted his weight from one bright white boot to the other. Sabrina thought he had probably spray-painted the boots for the occasion. "It's a tradition that goes back to my grandpappy's day. We don't have much high land on the island, and when it came to a-burying, most folks just put their loved ones in their back yards. Kept it all in the family, so to speak. The only problem was, when a hurricane or nor'easter came along, the winds pushed the water right up into everybody's back yards. It was common after a storm to have coffins bobbing around in the harbor like buoys. So people started thinking about weighting down the coffins a little, so they wouldn't float off. And about the heaviest things they could think of, and something almost everybody had, were cast iron skillets. Now, whenever anybody gets buried, we make sure there's at least five or six skillets in the coffin, just in case a storm comes and tries to float that coffin away. And then there's Shelby's Fishing Pole—"

"Sabrina, would you mind saying a few words?" Nettie asked.

Sabrina was speechless as Nettie looked at her inquiringly.

She stepped to the front of the crowd, carrying her skillet, and looked down at the peaceful, bearded face in the coffin. Rolo was dressed in a dark suit, and his hair had been trimmed. Any signs of his murder must have been covered by the suit, because he looked serene and whole, as if he would open his bright blue eyes and ask Sabrina if she was taking care of his grandmama's roses.

"I didn't know Rolo very long, or very well," Sabrina began, turning to face the crowd, and using her carrying voice, the one she used when she spoke in the echoing auditorium, and wanted to make sure the squirming boys in the very back could hear. "But in the short time I knew him before his death, I think Rolo and I made a connection. He told me about his family and talked about his love for his grandmother's roses. We talked, really talked, and if I was able to help him during a difficult time, then I'm glad."

Sabrina noticed that Sergeant Jimmy McCall was waving a hand at her, and she paused a moment, staring at him in puzzlement. "Rolo Wrightly was a good man," she continued. "I feel honored that I knew him, even for so short a time." She turned to the coffin and placed the skillet beside Rolo in the coffin. She felt the tears burning in her eyes, and she wanted to go before she started crying in earnest.

"Thank you all for coming out." Nettie stood beside the coffin, holding a fishing pole. "All that's left is Shelby's Fishing Pole—"

"Wait," a voice said from the crowd, and Brad Tittletott stepped forward. "I'd like to say a few words."

Nettie looked at him for a long moment, and then nodded and stepped back to let him speak.

"Rolo was," Brad began, and swallowed hard. "Rolo was the best friend I ever had when I was a kid. He showed me what friendship is supposed to be. I wanted to say—"

"You have no right," Thierry cried, pushing to the front of the crowd. "You have no right to act as if you cared about my brother *when you killed him*!" He pulled out a pistol from his pocket and aimed it at Brad. "I won't miss this time. Blood for blood, Brad! You're going to die for killing a Wrightly!"

TWENTY-SEVEN

"THIERRY ROLAND WRIGHTLY, you put that down!" Nettie said sharply, her voice thin with fear. "Right now, do you hear me?"

"He killed Rolo, Mama." Thierry's hands were shaking as he held the gun. "Can you believe it? A Tittletott killing a Wrightly, imagine that." He gave a harsh laugh. "I should have known better than to have ever trusted a Tittletott." His voice rose as he gestured with the gun.

"Thierry," Sergeant Jimmy McCall said calmly. "Give me the gun, and we'll talk about this. If Brad killed Rolo we'll take him to jail, I promise you. He won't get away with this. You know me, Thierry. I wouldn't lie to you." The fat police officer in his tight uniform and sweat stains spreading across his back should have looked ludicrous, but Jimmy McCall was anything but ludicrous. His voice was calm and soft, as if coaxing a wild dog from a burning building.

"Ha!" Thierry jeered. "You expect me to believe that a Tittletott can't get away with murder on this island? They've been doing it for centuries."

Sabrina raised her head in surprise. Had Thierry read the diary?

All this time Brad had been standing quietly, his head bowed as if accepting whatever fate was meted out to him. He looked up then, and Sabrina realized that Brad, at least, knew about the diary. She could see the recognition in his eyes.

"I didn't kill Rolo," Brad said, but his voice was defeated, and he didn't sound convincing.

"Yes, you did," Thierry cried. "I saw you put the note under the door that night! I was coming back from the Pub, real late, and I saw you in front of Nettie's Cookie Shop, looking around as if you didn't want anyone to see you. Then you put the note under the door. I saw you! Rolo met you at the treasure tree and you killed him! I know you killed him!"

"No, no." Brad was shaking his head. "I didn't kill him, I swear I didn't."

"Then where were you the day of the murder?" Thierry asked in a hard voice.

"Yeah," someone shouted from the crowd. "Where were you, Brad Tittletott? You weren't at the Lighthouse Beach, we all know that. So where were you?"

Brad was shaking his head, back and forth like a metronome.

"What's more," a rotund lady said as she stepped out of the crowd, "I saw 'im that day, plain as day. I didn't want to say nothing, because I wasn't sure, but I know I saw him coming down the street, down in Waver Town, hat pulled low, and he had mud on his boots. He thought nobody knew who he was, but I sawed him."

Brad stopped shaking his head, and stared straight ahead, his eyes unseeing.

"Well, Brad," Jimmy asked. "Did you arrange to meet Rolo at the treasure tree? We have a sample of your handwriting, remember. If you wrote the note, we'll find out soon enough." Jimmy was now standing next to Thierry, facing Brad. Jimmy had assessed the situation, it was plain, and saw that Thierry was so wrapped up in the public spectacle that he had let the gun drop to his side. Jimmy was in easy reach of the gun if Thierry raised it again.

Brad shut his eyes.

"He was with me! He didn't kill Rolo! He was with me!" Stacey Tubbs, looking very young in a white dress, her hair tied in a ponytail at the back of her neck, stepped forward out of the crowd to stand at Brad's side.

"Stacey!" Greg Tubbs, heavy chins swinging, stared in disbelief at his daughter.

"He was." Stacey slipped her arm through Brad's.

"No, Stacey," Brad said, almost inaudibly.

"We've been together for over a month now. And the day Rolo was murdered we were at my house. Mummy and Daddy were at the store. We were there all day. In bed." She looked around at the faces of her family and friends, as if determined to share every nitty-gritty detail now that the truth was out in the open.

"No, Stacey," Brad said in a louder voice. "I don't want you lying for me." He took the girl by the shoulders and moved her away, out of the possible track of a bullet. "I wasn't with Stacey all afternoon, though we were together earlier in the afternoon. I love her," he said simply, and Stacey glowed with happiness. "But I left to go meet Rolo at two. I did send him the note asking him to meet me at the tree. Thierry was right about that. But I didn't go to kill him. I went to tell him that—" He broke off, looking around at the curious, concerned faces of those around him. "I went to tell him that I would tell everyone the truth the night of the rally. That I would tell what really happened the night the silver was stolen."

There was an excited murmur of voices, and a shifting of the crowd as people pushed closer to Brad so they could hear.

"When Rolo first got back to the island, we met and he swore that he would tell everybody about the Tittletotts, and what I did that night. He was so angry. I think he must have kept the anger bottled up for all these years. There was something about me running for president that really set him off. I'm not sure why, but that made him angrier than anything else." Brad grew more confident, and his voice strengthened.

"I asked him not to, told him I would give him money to go away, that I was sorry, but that I couldn't give up my whole life for him." Brad laughed, a harsh cynical sound. "I won't repeat what he said. I left then, and he swore the truth would come out. I asked who would believe him?

"But over the next couple of days, I couldn't get him out of my mind. I knew he was still around, and I found myself wanting to talk to him, like we used to when we were kids. We used to tell each other everything. He was the best friend I ever had. I wanted to tell him about Stacey, and my campaign, all the things I had done over the past fifteen years. I think that's when I realized how wrong I had been, and how much I wanted to make it all up to Rolo. So I left him the note at Nettie's shop, and asked him to meet me at the treasure tree. The next day, I went to see Stacey and then I went to the marsh and saw Rolo. I told him it was all over, that I would tell everything at the rally that night. He didn't believe me at first, but I convinced him. He planned to go to the rally anyway, and we agreed that he would meet me there, and I would tell what happened.

"We—we made up, in a way. I think in time we could have been friends again. When I left the clearing at the treasure tree he was still there, sitting on one of the old bus seats, and smiling. I swear he was still alive when I left. And that night at the rally, I was going to tell the truth, I was, but Dock came in covered with blood. Then when I found out Rolo was killed, I couldn't say anything, because I knew everybody would think I killed him to stop him from telling what happened." Brad stopped, his chest heaving with his emotion. There was silence except for Brad's gasping breaths, almost as if he was breathing for the entire group.

Jimmy McCall broke the spell. "What really happened that night?" he asked quietly. "Fifteen years ago, you and your mother said Rolo told you he stole the silver, and when we went to his house it was in his closet. What really happened?"

"I stole it," Brad said, and the sun went behind a cloud, and shadows rippled across the blowing grass. "Rolo and I were always playing jokes on each other. Not just on each other, on the whole island too, I know. But we played them on each other as well. Rolo—Rolo had gotten it in his head that Walk-the-Plank Wrightly's treasure was buried somewhere in the marsh around the treasure tree. He had a map that he said proved the treasure was buried there, somewhere."

Brad paused, and his eyes sought out Dock. Dock, who had given the diary to Rolo and pledged him to secrecy. And Rolo, young and trusting, had told his best friend Brad, who just happened to be a Tittletott. Dock returned Brad's stare stonily.

"We dug for it. We dug holes until our fingers bled from the blisters, but we couldn't find it. So one day, I was over at Edie Lowry's house. I was delivering a note from my mother, and Edie was polishing her silver. And it occurred to me, what if I planted treasure for Rolo to find? Wouldn't that be a hoot? That night, when I stole the silver, I didn't know Edie was in the house, I thought she had gone to my mother's Oyster Cram party. And of course everyone knew Edie's husband was out to sea. I swear I didn't know she was there until I looked up and she was standing in the doorway. It was dark, and I didn't think she could see me, so I jumped up. She backed away from me until she was standing at the top of the stairs leading outside. I pushed by her, not hard, just trying to get by her. I guess she fell. I was running so fast I didn't realize that she had fallen until the next day. I buried the silver, and Rolo and I went later that night to dig for the treasure, and he found the silver. He was excited, he really thought it was Walk-the-Plank's silver! I was going to tell him eventually, and put back Edie's silver, but I wanted the joke to last a little longer. Rolo took the silver and I went home. The next morning I heard about Edie's fall and that her house had caught on fire. And then someone called and blamed the whole thing on me! I swear I didn't set Edie's house on fire. It must have been an accident. I didn't do it. All I could think was that Rolo had found out I tricked him, and had made that phone call. I felt so horrible about it, but I was so young… I didn't know what to do." Brad looked up and locked eyes with Elizabeth Tittletott. Her eyes were narrow, and two spots of color flared high on her cheekbones. Brad turned away. "I was scared. I was stupid. I told the sergeant that Rolo did it. I'll live with that mistake the rest of my life."

Stacey had slipped to Brad's side again, and he didn't protest as she took his arm. He stared at the ground now, his posture defeated. Around him voices broke out in excited conversation.

"I'll just need to get an official statement, Brad." Sergeant Jimmy McCall reached over and took Thierry's gun. Thierry didn't protest as he stared at Brad in bewilderment.

Sabrina took the opportunity to make her way through the crowd to Brad.

"One question," she said in a quiet voice, and Brad looked at her in surprise.

"Did Rolo threaten anything else? Weren't you just as worried about the Tittletott deed as you were about your reputation?"

Brad looked over at Stacey who was arguing with her father. "I'm not going to even ask how you know about that," he said in a low voice. "Yes, Rolo had proof that the Wrightlys were the rightful owners of all the Tittletott land. He told me about the pirate's diary years ago, when we were kids. Back then I told him that when I got control of the Tittletott property I would give back half to the Wrightlys." He smiled and shook his head. "Kids are so idealistic, aren't they?"

"Why did Rolo decide to come forward now, though? The Wrightlys have had this information for three hundred years."

"A lot of people live on Tittletott land—including most of the extended Wrightly clan. The piece of land with your cottage and the New Wrightly House is on Wrightly land, but Nettie rents the cookie shop from us and a lot of Wavers have been renting from the Tittletotts for generations. The Wrightlys have been scared, plain and simple. If they challenged us and lost, they were afraid they would lose everything." His face grew sadder. "Rolo hated me so much and was so angry that I was going to be president, he just didn't care anymore.

"That day at the rally, I was going to admit the truth about the silver. Rolo promised if I did that he would keep quiet about the diary until my mother passed away. I asked him that favor, and God knows he didn't owe me anything, but he agreed. Since I'm the sole heir of the Tittletott property, I was going to start making over deeds into the Wrightlys' name. It was the only thing I could do."

"You never saw the diary? You don't know what happened to it?"

Brad shook his head, and then Jimmy took him by the arm and led both Brad and Thierry down the hill.

"Ahem," Nettie coughed. "This is still a funeral. I'm glad Bradford Tittletott saw his way clear to telling the truth about Rolo. Now all of you know that he really was a good boy." Nettie turned to face the coffin. She placed the old wooden fishing pole she carried inside the coffin with Rolo, and leaned down to kiss his face. Then she lowered the coffin lid as Bicycle Bob moved forward with a shovel.

"One more thing." Nettie gestured to Terry and little Nettie who picked up two potted rose bushes lying in the shade of a nearby bush and brought them to their grandmother. "Rolo loved his grandmama Lora's roses. These are from Lora's house and they'll be planted on his grave."

Sabrina closed her eyes, feeling the sting of tears behind her eyelids. She was glad she remembered to tell Nettie what Rolo had said.

When I die, and my body's lying under that cold, wet dirt, I hope someone plants roses on my grave. That way, part of me can grow into that rose and bask in the sunlight.

TWENTY-EIGHT

SABRINA HAD NEVER been to a wake quite like the one
held after Rolo's funeral. She was puzzled by the jackets
most of the islanders wore to the funeral, considering the
mild temperature, and even more puzzled by the identical
bulges in each of the pockets. As they filed into Nettie's
big green house, she was astonished to see person after
person pull a bottle of liquor out of his or her coat and
place it on a table set up by the front door, which was already groaning with its heavy load of bottles.

Lima saw Sabrina studying the growing pile of liquor
in perplexity.

"Don't have nothing like this in Sin-city-nati, huh?"
Lima swaggered over to Sabrina, munching on an hors
d'oeuvre.

"Not quite," Sabrina said, accepting her defeat grace-
fully. She just wished she could take the old man to Cincinnati and see how *he* felt in the big city. She was still
absorbing Brad's amazing story, and from what she could
hear, so was everybody else.

"Weell," Lima said in satisfaction. "There was a day
when there was no money on the island to speak of. We
didn't need it, you understand? We had our gardens, the
cows and goats in the marsh, and the bounty of the bitch
in blue. The ocean," Lima explained quickly, seeing Sabrina's disapproving look. "We had everything we needed
right here. Except liquor. That we had to ship in. Of

course, you had your random stills and toxic moonshine, but it wasn't quite the same thing. Liquor became more precious than gold. Whenever anybody died, the people would all get together and chip in for a bottle of liquor, and gave it to the bereaved. It was better than money, you see. Now, we all give a bottle of liquor to show our respect. Every day before a funeral the liquor store's wiped out completely."

All these old traditions were making her head spin. "What," she asked, "does Nettie do with all this liquor?"

"We'll open it before too long, don't you worry," Lima said, winking.

"I see." Sabrina gazed around the room. None of the Tittletotts were in sight. Apparently the truce between families only lasted through the funeral. Either that, or the scene at the funeral had changed their plans. It was too bad, because Sabrina wanted to talk to them.

Lima and Sabrina went through the crowded front room to the kitchen, where a fire was blazing and the counter was laden with food in mismatched plates. She could see her own coconut and saffron rice pudding at the dessert end of the table. While she watched, Bicycle Bob loaded a scoop of the pudding on his plate and took a big bite. He burst into a coughing fit, his eyes watering.

"Cut out your heart," Horatio crooned, swaying back and forth on his perch and unfurling his top feathers. "Raawk! Here kitty!" Horatio glared at a child who strayed too close to the cage.

Sabrina tsked in the bird's direction and loaded a plastic plate with food.

"Um, Lima? What's this?" Sabrina held up a dark gray ball studded with what looked like nuts.

"Oyster ball."

Sabrina took a tentative bite and then a larger bite. She went through her plate, asking Lima to identify the more bizarre items, and ate with gusto. Dock was wandering around the kitchen, drinking from other people's cups and digging into the food on the serving plates with his fingers. He seemed oblivious to the people around him and was making sounds in his throat that sounded like: "Bugabugabuga."

"Have you got your costume for tonight?" Lima asked. "I'm going to be Elvis, in honor of Rolo. He loved Elvis when he was a kid. I got a purple leisure suit and I've been practicing my sneer. What do you think?" He twisted his face into a grotesque grimace.

"Er—yes, Lima, very nice. You don't think it would be disrespectful to celebrate Halloween when someone's just been buried?"

"Oh Lordy. Nothing could stop Halloween. We don't get much of a chance to let loose around here, so when we do, we go all out."

Sabrina hid a smile. From what she could see, the islanders got plenty of chances to let loose, and they took advantage of every occasion.

"On Comico, Halloween's more for the adults than the kids. The kids go around to the houses and trick or treat from five to six-thirty or so, but then they go home and their parents go out. We all get to pretend we're someone else for the night. You don't get too many opportunities like that."

Sabrina nodded thoughtfully and chewed on a scallop pancake.

"I've got a question," she said after a moment, aware that both she and Lima had stayed far away from Brad's confession. It was still too fresh. "Who is Shelby? And why did Nettie put his fishing pole in Rolo's casket?"

"Weeell, back in my great-great-grandpappy's day, there was a huge storm that hit the island, nicknamed the Black Friday Storm because the sun never came up that Friday, or at least not that anybody could see. Shelby Wrightly was out on his boat, and while he was trying to get back to harbor, a big wave came up and swamped his boat. Shelby was washed away by the waves, and he knew as sure as grits ain't groceries that he was going to drown. He drank so much of that ocean that afterward he never drank a glass of water again. Right about that time come a casket just a-bobbing along—this was before they started putting skillets in the caskets, you understand, so it was floating along just as pretty as you please. So, Shelby, he grabbed onto that casket and held on to the handles for dear life. Well, the storm rolled on for that day and then the next, but eventually it died down and Shelby looked around and found himself far out to sea, just a-bobbing on top of that casket. Well, days passed, and Shelby grew awful hungry and thirsty, and the day came that out of pure desperation he opened up that casket while it was floating on the sea. And lo and behold he found a fishing pole next to the dried-up old corpse. Someone had buried the man's favorite fishing pole with him, and it saved Shelby's life. He used that pole to catch fish, and rain came and he drank. After a month, he finally washed up on shore. And the only reason he stayed alive was because of that fishing pole. After that, everybody thought it was such a fine idea that they started burying a man's favorite fishing pole with him when he died. And who knows, if ever those skillets don't work, some poor adrift soul might need to use that pole to catch his dinner."

Lima took a bite of Sabrina's rice pudding. His eyes got wide, and his face turned red as he swallowed.

"What in the hell is that?"

"It's coconut and saffron rice pudding. Do you like it? I made it. Here, there's plenty left." Sabrina ladled another heaping spoonful onto his plate and went over to help with the cleanup in the kitchen.

IT WAS ALMOST three o'clock when Sabrina hurried toward town.

The afternoon was glorious, the cool breeze adding a salty tang to the golden air, like a perfect margarita. Sabrina strode through Waver Town, over the bridge and along the harbor where the pubs were doing brisk business as people geared up for Halloween. Sabrina was still not done with her costume, and she needed one last touch to make it perfect.

"Miss Sabrina!" a voice called, and Sabrina turned to see Sergeant Jimmy McCall bearing down on her, as unstoppable as a dump truck.

"Hello, Sergeant." Sabrina stopped on her way up the Tittletott sidewalk. "How is Thierry?"

"Upset. We released him into his mother's custody a little while ago. We'll have to charge him with something, but nobody wants to see him go away for this. He genuinely thought Brad was responsible for killing his brother."

"And did he?"

Jimmy shrugged his massive shoulders. "What Brad did fifteen years ago is despicable. And whether or not he actually set Edie's house on fire, we'll never know, though *someone* did it on purpose, I know that much. But it doesn't mean he's Rolo's killer, though it certainly gives him a motive. As it is, we've got no proof. They're still questioning him at the station, but he'll be out soon."

Sabrina nodded.

"Hmph. Well, what I wanted to tell you was this: be careful. I'm not sure if you meant to or not, but your eulogy made it sound as if Rolo told you something, maybe the something that Rolo was killed for. Do you follow my drift?"

Sabrina thought back on her words, and remembered Jimmy McCall's frantic hand waving. She hadn't meant to imply anything, of course, but she saw what the sergeant meant.

"My goodness. I did at that, didn't I?"

"What are you doing here?" Jimmy glanced up at the Tittletott House.

"I came to give my condolences to the family."

Jimmy narrowed his eyes. "Lady, you haven't been here two weeks, and already you've got your fingers in every pie on the island. I can't imagine what would happen if you lived here full time!"

Sabrina waved good-bye to the sergeant and went up the sidewalk, letting herself in the front door.

Virginia looked up as she entered. She was still wearing the slate gray dress she wore to the funeral, and her eyes were red and puffy.

"Hello, Sabrina." Virginia leafed through some papers on the desk and dabbed at her eyes.

"I'm so sorry for your family, Virginia. This must be hard for you."

"I'm just glad the truth's out about Brad."

"You knew?"

Virginia nodded, and picked up a pen and wrote something.

"How long have you known?"

Virginia looked up, and Sabrina saw that her beautiful eyes brimmed with tears. "Brad told me years ago, that night we were together. I didn't know what to do, who to tell." Virginia shook her head. "What could I do?"

Sabrina said nothing. "Is Elizabeth here? I'd like to talk to her."

Virginia nodded. "She's supervising the girl cleaning a room for a check in. Come on, I'll show you."

Sabrina followed Virginia up the wide stairs. The dim hallway stretched the length of the house and doors marched down the white walls. Floor boards creaked under their feet, and sounds from a TV floated from behind one of the closed doors.

"Gary, would you mind watching the desk? I need to get dressed." Virginia paused before an open door. Sabrina glanced over Virginia's shoulder at the large, luxurious bedroom, complete with fireplace and sitting area. Gary was feeding another log into the fireplace.

"I'll be right down." Gary's voice was devoid of emotion. He had changed from his funeral clothes into threadbare khaki slacks and a rumpled shirt.

"Don't be too long," Virginia said irritably.

Sabrina saw a costume, white toga, black wig, golden mask and serpent bracelet, laid out on the bed and whistled in admiration. "Is that what you're wearing tonight, Virginia?"

Virginia preened. "I can't wait to put it on."

"It's revealing who a person decides to impersonate, isn't it?" Gary sat back on his heels.

Virginia ignored her husband. "I've always been fascinated by Cleopatra. What a woman!"

Sabrina smiled at Gary. "Are you going as Marc Antony?"

He made a sound halfway between a horrified snort and a laugh and indicated the monk's long robe and cowl on the bed next to the Cleopatra costume.

"I asked him to, but he wouldn't. Gary, the desk?" Virginia continued down the hall.

Near the end of the hall, Virginia poked her head into another open door. "Mother Elizabeth, Sabrina is here to see you."

Virginia left and Sabrina faced Elizabeth, who was laboring to make the bed by herself.

"Well, don't just stand there. Help me!" Elizabeth snapped. Sabrina went to the other side of the bed and helped tuck the top sheet under the mattress.

"Can't keep good help around here," Elizabeth said, smoothing her hand over the sheet. She had changed from the turquoise dress she wore to the funeral, but the gauzy mauve concoction she wore didn't look any more appropriate for making a bed. "The girl walked out just because I told her she was more than a few peas short of a casserole and that she couldn't empty a trash can without instructions on the side. It's true! She just didn't think. But she got all huffy-puffy and walked out, so now I have to do it all myself."

They pulled the comforter up, and Elizabeth arranged the pillow shams until she was satisfied. "So what did you want?" She stood up and smoothed her frizzy hair away from her face.

"I wanted to ask you about these." Sabrina pawed into

her copious handbag and pulled out the crayon pictures she'd found under the hurricane hatch.

Elizabeth's eyes flickered as she glanced over the horrific pictures, but no expression dared to pass over her face. She handed the pictures back to Sabrina.

"Well?"

"Well, what?" Elizabeth snapped. "Why are you showing me those?" She turned her back on Sabrina to arrange the knickknacks on the dresser top.

"I thought you might have seen them before."

Elizabeth shook her head. "I don't know where you got those horrible pictures, but I've never seen them before."

"Not even twenty-five years ago?"

"I said I never saw them!"

Without comment, Sabrina put the pictures back in her bag. She knew in her heart that old Lora would have shared those pictures with the child's parents, seeking to help. Both Nettie and Elizabeth claimed they had never seen the pictures. Did that mean their respective children didn't draw the pictures? And did the pictures really have something to do with Rolo's murder, as she strongly suspected?

"Let's talk about Brad, then."

"What about him?" Elizabeth crossed her arms. "It was a boyish prank. You can't hold a man responsible for something he did when he was a boy."

Sabrina nodded, as if in agreement. A boyish prank, stealing silver and setting an unconscious woman on fire? "I'm really surprised Brad would set Rolo up, considering how close they were."

Elizabeth's lips thinned as she turned and started rearranging the knickknacks on the dresser, slamming them down with unnecessary force.

"What I really wanted to talk to you about is in the spirit of Brad's defense. Brad admits he sent Rolo the note, and admits he met Rolo at the tree. I'm wondering if anybody else knew Brad was going to meet Rolo."

Elizabeth stared at her with opaque eyes, her face blank as she tried to figure out Sabrina's reasoning. "He told us that he was going to meet Rolo that day, but not what time, or where. He said he was going to clear all this up, that everything would be better. I thought—I thought…" Elizabeth twisted a large diamond ring on her pinkie.

"You thought he was going to bribe Rolo into shutting up about what happened. You may have even thought he was going to kill Rolo. You didn't think that he was going to agree to tell the truth. You never would have let him do that."

Elizabeth huffed with indignation. "How dare you say that to me!"

Sabrina smiled sadly. "A woman who would tell her eighteen-year-old son to turn his best friend over to the police for something his friend didn't do is capable of anything, as far as I'm concerned. Brad told you about the Wrightly diary, and what was in it. When Brad confessed to you that he stole the silver you saw a way to get rid of the Wrightly threat. With Rolo gone, no one else but you and Brad knew what was in the diary. And that's the way you wanted it."

"I don't know who you think you are, but I suggest you get out of this house—immediately!" Elizabeth's eyes were cold and nasty, and she didn't bother to deny the accusations.

"Have a nice night," Sabrina said. "I wouldn't want to live with your conscience."

As she went toward the stairs, she passed a cracked door and something golden and shiny caught her eye. Pausing, she pushed open the door. The well-appointed room was clearly Elizabeth's, with expensive silken clothes tossed on the bed and chair. Sabrina looked at the array of wigs, long and short, from platinum blond to honey auburn, arranged in a cherry armoire.

Thoughtfully, she closed the door and continued on her way.

TWENTY-NINE

SABRINA STOPPED TO pick up the final touches to her costume and headed home. Only a few lights burned at the New Wrightly House when she passed, and all the bicycles and golf carts had disappeared from the front yard. It was growing chill as the sun sank into the water, sparking a bonfire of glowing crimson and orange and pink.

Due to the funeral and the upcoming festivities, Sabrina had given the kids the day off from play practice. She went into the house and let Calvin out of his cage. He waddled to her, complaining.

"I know, I've been leaving you alone far too much. But I've got a lot on my mind, Calvin." Sabrina scooped the bird off the floor and carried him with her into the kitchen. "I'm not any closer to figuring out why someone killed Rolo. In fact, now I've got too many reasons. It seems like everyone on the island had some secret that they might have killed Rolo to keep him from repeating. That's the problem, don't you see? No one knew *which* secret Rolo intended on revealing. Anybody with a secret to hide could have thought that Rolo planned to reveal *their* particular secret. Rolo really should have been more specific."

Sabrina fixed herself a cup of hot herbal tea—she'd done extensive research to discover just the right combination of soothing herbs—while a muttering Calvin climbed into the window.

"I wish you could talk, Calvin. You saw the killer. Who was it? How did the person get through Waver Town without anybody seeing him or her? Through the marsh? Brad did that, and someone saw him. You can't sneeze around here without someone saying 'Here's a tissue.' Is Brad the killer? It would make so much sense. He was the last one to see Rolo alive. He arranged the meeting. Rolo was killed with a gun taken from the Tittletott House. But somehow… I believe him when he said he had decided to tell the truth. I think."

Sabrina sat at the table and stared out the window as the sun was extinguished in a puff of lavender and pink clouds. The kids should be coming around trick or treating soon, and she had a basket of Reese's Cups and Milky Ways all ready to go. She wasn't one of those people who forced apples and oranges on kids for Halloween. Why, it would be like eating a cucumber instead of pumpkin pie at Thanksgiving. Just not the same.

"What am I missing, Calvin? Let's take this logically, from the top. Elizabeth Tittletott. She's got so much invested in Brad. Would she kill to keep him from being ruined? Even more likely is that she would kill Rolo to keep him from telling the truth about her ancestor. Her position on the island is everything to her. She knew that Brad was going to meet Rolo, but she says she didn't know where or when. She could have lied. Her alibi is shaky—she says she was at the house sleeping. But wouldn't someone have noticed if she was all the way over in Waver Town? And would she have the strength to kill Rolo with the garden shears? And then drag his body through the trees to Dock's boat?

"Brad. He's the most obvious. He's got the motive, the opportunity…but you know, if everybody in that house knew he was going to meet Rolo, wouldn't it have been easy to set him up? Plant the gun in Brad's room, which would point suspicion at Brad. That would explain why the killer left Brad's note, the one asking Rolo to meet Brad at the treasure tree. But then again, why kill Rolo at my house? Why not in the swamp? What about the gun? Maybe the killer jammed the gun because he or she didn't know how to use it. That would rule out Brad, who, according to Lima, was a prize marksman. Then again, maybe it was Brad, and in the heat of the moment he got excited and the gun jammed. That's possible, I guess.

"Gary. There's no love lost between Gary and Brad, so I can't imagine Gary killing Rolo to keep him from revealing Brad's secret. In a way, I think he was happy when his brother's pedestal crumbled. By the same token, I don't think he takes his family seriously enough to kill Rolo to keep him from revealing the truth about the Tittletott ancestors. But is he so far under his mother's thumb that he could have killed Rolo at her direction? And then there's Sid. But Rolo didn't know anything about Sid being Brad's child. Nobody but Virginia knew about that, and I can't see where she would have had reason or opportunity to tell him. Rolo had been gone three years before Sid was conceived. And Gary was working the desk when Rolo was murdered, both Virginia and Mary Tubbs said they called him.

"Finally, there's Virginia. She has lied to me, at least twice that I know of. And I don't understand her, or her penchant for falling in love with someone every other week. Does that make her a killer? Why would she kill Rolo? Could she have killed Rolo to keep him from ruining the family's name? It's a little far-fetched, but possible, I suppose. She said she was at the school helping set up for the rally, and presumably the police checked out her alibi. But I seem to remember someone saying that Virginia disappeared while she was supposed to be working on a float. How long was she gone? People thought they saw her in Waver Town.

"And what about Thierry? Could he have something to do with Rolo's death? Maybe he faked that incident at the funeral to further frame Brad. But why would Thierry kill Rolo? Out of jealousy? Did he kill him for Brad?"

Sabrina drummed her fingers on the table, running the options over and over through her head. Something was bothering her, something May had said…but what was it?

"I wish Lora Wrightly was alive so I could ask her what she knew about all this."

Loud knocking on the door interrupted her thoughts and woke Calvin.

"CHEEP, CHEEP!" he complained.

Sabrina got up and glanced around the kitchen for a weapon. She took up a knife and padded to the front door.

The loud knocking again.

Sabrina wished devoutly that she had had Bicycle Bob put the lock on the door.

"Who—" She cleared her throat. "Who is it?"

"Trick or treat!" several young voices called.

"It's just the trick-or-treaters, Calvin. And you were afraid!"

AFTER AN HOUR, the trick-or-treaters, dressed as witches, Cinderella and Spiderman, trickled to a stop. Sabrina went upstairs, took a bath and began putting on her own costume. She'd agreed to meet Lima at the Walk-the-Plank Pub at eight, and she had one small errand to do before that.

Sabrina finished her makeup, and after smoothing her hair into a rumpled coif she surveyed herself in the mirror. The rose, she had forgotten the rose. Calvin sat next to a vase that held three perfect red roses.

He cheeped in admiration as she pinned a rose to her dress. There. That was perfect.

In the mirror was an old-fashioned-looking woman in a button-up dress with full skirts, blond hair, a red rose pinned to her bodice and a lantern in her hand. It was Sarah Wrightly, as she walked the shores looking for her lost husband.

Sabrina knew that it could not be an original costume on this island, but it was original for her. And when she had seen the dress among the Halloween costumes at Sweet Island Music, she knew it would be perfect.

"Calvin," she said, pirouetting in front of the mirror. "Let's go catch a killer. I've got an idea."

"SABRINA! LOOK AT YOU!" Nettie said in delight as she opened the door.

"Cheep!"

"And Calvin. So good to see you both." Nettie looked tiny and fragile, but she was smiling. Sabrina could see Rolo's wife and daughter sitting in the living room with Dock. "I can't thank you enough for arranging for Sherry and little Nettie to come. We just got back from taking Nettie trick-or-treating. It's made this whole thing so much easier knowing that Rolo has left something behind in this world. He's not happy. He's trying to tell me who killed him...but I can't quite get it. I see a lady on a bike..." Nettie squeezed her eyes shut and Sabrina patted her arm.

"I've got something for you." She passed the long, awkward bundle she was carrying over into Nettie's arms.

Nettie unwrapped the towel from around Rolo's sword. "Oh, Sabrina! You found it!"

"I thought that since Rolo didn't have a son, maybe you could give it to Terry when he turns eighteen. There's something else in there as well." Sabrina explained about the diary and the letter to the lawyer, and Rolo's promise to Brad to keep the truth about Lord Tittletott and Walk-the-Plank Wrightly a secret until Elizabeth passed away. "It's up to you, of course, and Brad said he would start passing over some of the Tittletott land to the Wrightlys."

"My stars and moons," Nettie murmured.

"I was hoping that there might be some way to find the treasure that Roland Wrightly buried so many years ago, but if eleven generations of Wrightlys haven't found it by now, I think it may be a lost cause."

"When the time is right, someone will find it," Nettie said positively. "And with all this—" she waved at the diary and the letter "—I don't think we really need it, do you?"

"I think you're right. I do have a question for you, Nettie, about something else. Right after Rolo was killed, we were talking about the letter that Brad put under the door of the cookie shop for Rolo, though of course we didn't know then who had done it. You said, 'They always knew I could get in touch with Rolo.' Who did? Did someone give you a letter to send to Rolo?"

Nettie looked troubled. "Virginia has been sending him letters for years. She was actually the first person I thought of when I saw the letter under the door addressed to Rolo. I told Jimmy about it, just in case, though it turns out Brad did it after all. I remember the first time Virginia came to me, and said, 'Mrs. Nettie, I'd like to send a letter to Rolo. Would you be able to pass this along for me?' I said yes, of course. Those two always were special to one another. I was worried about Virginia. She had just come back from college, and she looked so pale and…" Nettie shook her head. "She looked like she had a lot on her mind."

Sabrina nodded her head grimly. "This was about three years after Rolo left? Shortly before Virginia married Gary?"

Nettie wrinkled her forehead. "Why yes. You're right. Over the years she has sent several more letters. Every couple of years or so. I thought it was sweet that she never forgot Rolo."

Sabrina thanked Nettie and hurried down the dark street. So Virginia *had* kept in contact with Rolo. And when May had talked about seeing Walk-the-Plank Wrightly and Sarah Wrightly walking in the swamp, she had probably seen Rolo and Virginia.

As she came around the corner and Old Harbor came into view, she caught her breath in delight. Glowing colorful buoys bobbed in the water, shedding ghostly light over the waves. People in costumes filled the streets, streaming in and out of houses lit only with candles. The town looked as if it had been transformed into a fantasy land of dark shadows and flickering light, inhabited by monsters and princesses and past presidents.

Sabrina whistled idly, and Calvin cheerfully took up the tune. So Rolo could very well have known about Sid's parentage…

Almost there. Just one more person to talk to.

Candles in paper bags lined the street facing New Harbor and barricades were set up at the entrance to

Hurricane Harbor Circle, blocking all motorized traffic from the road. Here on the Towner side of the bridge the costumes were more elaborate. A knight in armor rode by atop an island pony, followed by a queen in flowing regalia.

Sabrina mounted the steps to the Tittletott House and let herself into the lobby. A table was laid out beside the reception desk, covered with food and lit by candles. No one was in the room.

Missy hurried in, wearing an alien costume with long arms, a glowing finger and bobbling head. She wore a T-shirt over the costume that read: "Do not meddle in the affairs of aliens, for you are crunchy and taste good with ketchup."

"E.T.!" Sabrina said in delight.

"Sarah Wrightly," Missy said with appreciation.

"Is anybody around? I'd like to speak to Virginia."

Missy shook her alien head. "The family's not taking callers. Brad came back to the house about an hour ago, and there was a big blow up. After that they went to their rooms and haven't come out."

"Hmmm." Sabrina thought fast. "Missy, I know you are a discreet person, and would not normally tell tales outside of school. But this is very important. You mentioned that Gary and Virginia had a fight the morning of Rolo's murder. I know you wouldn't eavesdrop, but did you hear any of the conversation? It's very important."

Missy took off her mask and looked at Sabrina. "I've thought about it a lot, actually, debating whether I should tell anyone. It'll be a relief to share it with someone. They fight all the time, you know. I don't pay much attention to it. Most of the time they just snip at each other in a very civil manner. It's uncomfortable to listen to them.

Virginia will say how *sweet* it is that Gary likes to cook, and why, wouldn't it be nice if he took up cross-stitching. And Gary sneers about how Virginia is easy. They're nice people apart, but together they're horrible.

"Virginia threw a vase that morning, which caught my attention. It was before breakfast, and Gary was helping me set up the tables. Virginia came in, and Gary said, 'Out and about again? You better be careful or people are going to start to talk about you.'

"Well, I left the room and started prepping the creamers in the back. But then I heard this crash and as I went to the door, I heard Virginia say: 'Gary, sweetie, I can see whoever I want. He was my high school sweetheart, after all. You think you and your mother are the only ones who can keep a secret? Don't you raise your hand to me! You think you're macho? You're not even man enough to give me a baby. Did you really not know? Haven't you guessed who Sid's daddy is? About the only good thing your no-good brother ever accomplished in this world.' Or something to that effect. I was flabbergasted, you understand, because I never suspected that Gary wasn't Sid's father. About that time I went through the swinging door, and the looks on their faces! Gary looked…horrified, and Virginia looked so smug I wanted to slap the look right off her face. It was ugly. I turned around and went right back out. I thought about telling the police all this, but I couldn't see where it would help anything, and I didn't want to hurt Sid."

Trill, trill, trill.

Missy lifted her cell phone off her belt. "Some darn tourist wanting a ride this night of all nights—"

"TRILL, TRILL, TRILL." Calvin's eyes were wild, his small body quivering. "BARK! TRILL, TRILL, TRILL."

"Goodness," Sabrina said.

Out of the corner of her eye she saw a flash of movement through the cracked dining room door. Sabrina went over and swung it open, just in time to see a woman in a long white dress, black hair and gold mask, holding a big beach bag, disappear into the kitchen.

"I'd like to talk to you," she called to Cleopatra. "Virginia?"

Cleopatra ran.

THIRTY

"VIRGINIA?" SABRINA SAID, as she followed the woman through the spacious kitchen. "I just want to ask you a question!"

"CHEEP!" Calvin called.

Virginia apparently didn't feel like answering any questions. She reached the side door leading outside and spent a few precious moments fumbling with the lock. Sabrina almost reached her when she threw the door open and vanished into the darkness.

"Sabrina? What's going on?" Missy called.

Sabrina ducked out the door into the velvety darkness of the side yard garden. The smell of burning logs and crackling leaves filled her nose as she pushed through bushes and branches and ended up in the front yard of the house next door to the Tittletott House. A white form was fleeing across the yard and Sabrina suddenly realized that a killer was escaping.

"Halt! Police!" she cried. Behind her she heard crashing and cursing as Missy struggled to follow her through the brush.

"Sabrina?"

She turned to see Lima decked out in an awful purple leisure suit, dark sideburns and wig, and a pair of cheesy sunglasses. "What on earth are you doing?"

"I'm catching a killer!" Sabrina took off in pursuit of Cleopatra and Lima lumbered after her.

"Stop!" Sabrina yelled.

"Cheep!" Calvin clung to Sabrina's shoulder, his tiny wings beating in excitement.

As she ran, thoughts zoomed through her mind, misplaced pieces of the puzzle falling into place. The missing phone, the mud boots, the woman on the bike. It all was beginning to make sense. It was a spur-of-the-moment plan, with several unforeseen obstacles, but it had been pulled off in the end. Sabrina even had the motive.

Heads turned as Cleopatra crashed into a street-side trashcan and it clattered into the road, spilling trash everywhere. Mouths gaped as Sabrina, Lima and Missy came barreling down the street behind Cleopatra, doing a pretty good imitation of an Army training exercise sans tires as they tried to avoid the rolling cans and rotten vegetables.

Sondra Lane's band, dressed as Mozart, Beethoven and other musical figures, had set up on the corner of Post Office Road and they were playing rousing tunes as couples in matching costumes danced in the middle of the street. Cleopatra tried to dash through the middle of the crowd, but right at that moment the dancers handed their partners off and Henry the Eighth grabbed Cleopatra's free hand and spun her around into Cupid's arms, who surreptitiously pinched her behind as he twirled her around. Cleopatra dropped the beach bag, and the powerful smell of gasoline filled the air. Out of the corner of her eye, Sabrina saw two gallon milk jugs leaking gasoline slide out of the beach bag.

A punch to the stomach dropped Cupid to the ground, and Cleopatra took off down the street again. Henry the Eighth tried to grab Sabrina as she raced by, but stepped back when he saw Lima bearing down on him.

"Well I never!" Aunt Mary Garrison Tubbs, who was dressed as a pudgy Cat Woman, was livid. "Lima Odel Lowry, what on earth do you think you're doing?" She fell in behind them, followed by Henry the Eighth.

They were nearing the ferry docks, which were closed. On the other side of the docks was the small public beach where families waiting for the ferry often picnicked. Tonight, a huge bonfire had been built, and crowds of people bobbed for apples, tried to dunk the pirate dressed up as Walk-the-Plank Wrightly, and rolled watermelons at the bowling pins.

"Where we going?" bellowed Henry the Eighth.

"Lima!" screeched Aunt Mary.

"Sabrina?" called Lima.

"Clear the way!" Missy shouted.

"Stop that Cleopatra!" Sabrina yelled at the top of her lungs.

"Cheep!" Calvin shrieked in delight.

Cleopatra looked back over her shoulder at her noisy entourage and then dove into the crowd. Sabrina was right behind her.

"Hey, lady, wait your turn!" said an irate man as she trod on his toe and elbowed him in the stomach.

"Sorry," Sabrina panted.

Cleopatra dodged around the barrel full of water where Mother Teresa was doing her best to fish an apple out of the water with her teeth, and pushed past a lady dressed as a VW, who bumped into Mother Teresa, who ended up headfirst in the barrel.

Cleopatra came to a screeching halt as she came face to face with Sergeant Jimmy McCall, who was standing massively in front of the bonfire. He turned in surprise as Sabrina yelled, "Stop her, Sergeant!"

"Now, what exactly is going on here?" Jimmy said as Sabrina, Missy, Lima, Aunt Mary and Henry the Eighth pushed through the crowd into the firelight. Cleopatra was looking around desperately, from Sergeant Jimmy and the bonfire, to the waters of the sound on her left, to the six-foot bulkhead on her right. Backed up to the bulkhead was the dunking stand, and the pirate on the dunking bench was startled as Cleopatra made up her mind and dove for the dunking booth.

She climbed the side, clutching at Walk-the-Plank Wrightly as she struggled to stand on his bench and step over to the edge of the bulkhead. The pirate pushed at her as Cleopatra wrapped her arms around his head and tried to keep her balance.

"I'll get her!" Mother Teresa sputtered in rage, and she took up an apple and aimed it right at the bull's-eye.

Walk-the-Plank Wrightly and Cleopatra dropped into the water with a resounding splash.

"Sergeant, I suggest you do your duty," Sabrina said, as the two in the tank struggled to reach the surface.

"What exactly is going on?" asked Sergeant Jimmy McCall. "Who were you chasing?"

"Lima," Aunt Mary spat.

"Sabrina," Lima said.

"Cleopatra," said Missy.

"The murderer," Sabrina said as a head, without the black wig and mask, appeared at the edge of the tank. She shook her head sadly. "Gary Tittletott, it didn't have to come to this." Calvin chirped nervously, and hid behind her neck.

Gary, coughing, looked like a wet, half-drowned rat, not the murderer that he really was. He glared at Sabrina. "Why couldn't you mind your own business, you damned tourist?"

A sudden thought occurred to Sabrina. "Where is Virginia?" she asked urgently. "What have you done with her?" She came up close to Gary's face, lit eerily by the crimson flames from the firelight. "Have you hurt her?"

Gary coughed again. "She's just sleeping," he said, but Jimmy was already on the radio, calling to Billy to get over to the Tittletott House right away and check on Ms. Virginia Tittletott.

"Did you kill Rolo?" Aunt Mary demanded. "Gary Russell Tittletott, what have you done?"

"Get me out of here!" Walk-the-Plank Wrightly wailed, flailing around in the water of the dunking pen. "I didn't know he was a murderer!"

Jimmy grabbed the pirate by the back of his shirt and hauled him out of the water.

"I don't get it," said Henry the Eighth, who was actually Greg Tubbs. "Gary killed Rolo?"

Sabrina nodded. "I didn't realize until Missy told me about the fight she heard between Virginia and Gary the morning of Rolo's murder. You see, Gary knew that Rolo was in town, and was threatening to reveal a Tittletott secret. He thought Rolo was going to tell everybody what Brad did fifteen years ago, about stealing the silver, and Gary wasn't all that upset by the prospect. Brad always got all the attention, and Gary was tired of living in his shadow. But Wednesday morning after his fight with Virginia, Gary realized *he* had something to lose if Rolo started revealing all the Tittletott secrets. You see, it was possible Rolo knew about—"

"Sid," Gary moaned. "He was going to tell everybody about Sid. That bastard Brad."

"And Gary couldn't bear if everybody knew that Brad was actually Sid's father," Sabrina said softly. "That was just too much to bear. He started planning the murder right then. He knew Brad was going to meet Rolo that afternoon, because Brad had told them he was, but Gary didn't know what time or where. He took Missy's cell phone because already he was thinking about his alibi. In the lobby that morning, as Brad was leaving, Brad mentioned that he had an appointment at two. Of course, Gary and Elizabeth knew what appointment he was talking about. And just like I did, Gary saw the mud boots Brad carried in his bag. Unlike me, he realized where Brad was going. To the treasure tree. It was the only thing that made sense. Now he knew that Brad was meeting Rolo at the treasure tree at two and the rest should have been easy. He would kill him after his meeting at the treasure tree, there in the swamp where no one would find his body.

"But the water heater broke, and by the time Gary and Elizabeth had cleaned the water up, it was almost two. He had to hurry now, he could only hope that Brad's meeting with Rolo lasted longer than just a few minutes. He dressed in some of Virginia's clothes and donned a blond wig—it was one of Elizabeth's, I believe—and put on one of those neon visors and sunglasses. He meant to look like a tourist, knowing nobody would pay him any attention, but he was wearing Virginia's clothes and from a distance a few people thought it was her over in Waver Town. He took the gun out of the gun closet and while Elizabeth took her daily nap, he rode one of the Tittletott rental bikes over to the Old Wrightly House. Behind the house was the shortest path to the treasure tree. He knew I wasn't going to be home, because I told everybody that morning I was going to spend the day at the beach. He parked his bike there, and was planning on heading to the tree, but that's when he must have heard Rolo snipping roses on the other side of the house. I brought roses to the Tittletott house that morning, you see, and everyone knew how Rolo felt about the roses. What happened then, Gary?"

Gary spit out water, and looked around at the circle of townspeople.

"I shot him," he said. "I came around the side of the house, and I shot him. I wanted to do it at the treasure tree, but it was too late by then. I had to shut him up, don't you see? I had to keep him from telling everybody about Sid. But the gun wouldn't fire again, and Rolo was lying there, kicking his feet and cursing. I picked up the pruning shears, and I—and I—"

"You finished him off," Sabrina said. "And then you knew you had to provide yourself with an alibi. You called Mary Tubbs and asked her to get hold of Henley to see if he could come fix the water heater and call you right back to let you know. You called the Tittletott House and forwarded the calls to Missy's phone. When Mary— one of the biggest gossips on the island—"

"Excuse me—" Mary began, and was shushed impatiently.

"When Mary called back, you answered the phone, and she thought she had called you at the Tittletott House. You chatted with her, as Rolo died in the grass at your feet. After you hung up with Mary, Virginia called you from the school, which just improved your alibi." Sabrina paused and the silence was complete except for the gentle washing of waves on the beach and the crackle of flames.

Calvin chattered excitedly.

Sabrina smiled, and stroked Calvin's small, quivering body. "If it wasn't for Calvin, I'm not sure I would have figured it out. He saw the murder, you see. The night of the murder, he was making strange noises that I didn't understand. One was the sound of the gun, but the other... the other was the sound of Missy's phone ringing, when Mary called Gary back.

"It wasn't much of an alibi, but Gary never expected to be a suspect. It was an extra precaution, wasn't it, Gary, because you didn't plan on anybody finding Rolo. You're a careful man, and you wanted to cover all your bases. You may or may not have known that the police could find out the calls were forwarded from the hotel, but really, what reason did they have to subpoena phone records? The case against Brad looked pretty open and shut.

"When you hung up with Mary, you cleaned the pruning shears, put them back in the shed, and you dragged Rolo's body to Dock's boat. That was dangerous, because someone could have seen you from the water, but you were careful, and made sure no one was around. You put the body in the boat and covered it with a tarp, and rode your bike back to the house in your blond wig and tourist costume. In fact, you almost ran me over, and I didn't recognize you. You planned on coming back that night and taking Rolo's body out into the sound and dumping it. But Dock decided to go out in his boat that afternoon, and that was when it started to go bad. But you still had your alibi, and you planted the gun in Brad's room for extra protection."

"I don't know why they didn't arrest him," Gary said. "It was all his fault. I would have never done any of this if it wasn't for him. If only—" Gary's mouth shut with a snap, and Sabrina saw the small secret smile on his face.

"Jimmy." Sabrina turned quickly to the police officer. "I suggest your officer at the Tittletott House warn Brad that Gary might have set him a trap—maybe a broken balcony rail, or his brake lines cut, or something like that. After all, the first attempt failed, didn't it, Gary?"

The secret smile vanished.

"First attempt?" Jimmy inquired.

"Gary tried to poison Brad right after the murder, I think," Sabrina said. "That's why Brad was so sick. I suspect Brad's life expectancy would have been limited if Gary hadn't been caught. And where was he going tonight, disguised as Virginia, with two gallon jugs of gasoline? I have a feeling that he was going to tie up another loose end. Me."

"But why, Gary?" several people called out. "Why would you do such a thing?" Jimmy stepped forward and hauled Gary out of the dunking booth.

Gary stared at his neighbors, looking pitiful as he stood dripping in the sand. "He was always better than me," he finally said. "I never could do anything right."

Sabrina fished the crayon pictures out of her purse and held them up in the firelight. "Did you draw these, Gary? Back when you were a little boy, and you first started feeling like your best was never good enough, and that nobody was paying you any attention? Soon after that you started setting fires around town, trying to get attention. Isn't that right, Gary?"

Gary shrugged, but his mouth twisted in distaste at the sight of the pictures. "He was always *better*," he said. "Everything just fell in place for him, while I struggled and slaved and nothing ever worked out right."

"As you grew older, you learned to quietly undermine Brad whenever you could. I've heard about how Brad, the golden boy, is jinxed. You—you set Edie's house on fire, didn't you? After Brad stole the silver."

"I figured they'd have to notice if he did something bad enough," Gary said. "I followed him that night because I knew he and Rolo were up to something. I saw him come running out of Edie's house and I found the gasoline in the shed. Brad wasn't such a golden boy after all, was he?"

"So you set the house on fire. But then, even after your anonymous phone call, Brad got away with it," Sabrina said. "And so it went for years, I'd imagine. Subtle things, not too obvious, that always went wrong when things were going right for Brad. Like laxatives in the tea at the tea party. And Brad's campaign office burning down." Sabrina stopped, aware of the islanders' collective gaze on her. It felt like an almost unbearable weight. Suddenly she felt so tired, and all the pieces fit.

"But that's when you made your mistake," she said. "You hadn't used fire for all these years since you set fire to Edie's house, which was blamed on Rolo. Old Lora Wrightly had accepted that her grandson Rolo was responsible for the fire at Edie's house, as hard as it was for her to believe. She actually had a stroke because of it. But when you burned down Brad's office, things began to connect for Lora. She remembered those pictures you drew as a child. She remembered the awful jealousy you had for Brad. She tried to help you when you were a child, I suspect, but Elizabeth wouldn't listen to her. Lora had Nettie bring down the old file folders and she found the pictures you had drawn as a child, pictures of hate, and jealousy…and fire. Did she call you, Gary? I'd imagine she'd want to confront you in person."

Gary stared at the fire, and then he continued the story

almost mechanically. "She called me, and asked me to come over. I was surprised, naturally. I hadn't spoke to Lora since I graduated from high school, though I knew Brad and Virginia went to see her sometimes. I went over to her house that afternoon and she told me she thought I was the one that set fire to Brad's office. She showed me the pictures I drew when I was a kid. She told me that I should go confess to Jimmy the next day, or she would have to tell Jimmy what she guessed. I knew those pictures I drew twenty-five years ago weren't really proof, but I couldn't take the chance that Jimmy would start looking into things." Gary trailed off, staring into the fire. "I couldn't find the pictures. I searched everywhere. What did she do with them?" His voice was inflectionless.

"She put them under the hurricane hatch for safety. You pushed her so that her head hit the coffee table hard enough to kill her. You didn't find the pictures or the hurricane hatch because Lora was lying on top of it. When you couldn't find the pictures you overturned Lora's candle, thinking that the house would burn down, burning up the pictures as well, but the candle burnt itself out."

Gary stared around at his neighbors, his friends. "I just couldn't let her ruin my life like that. They'd have made me go away, put me in an institution. I didn't *want* to hurt anyone, but everyone was conspiring against me! Rolo was threatening to reveal—Brad has everything! I couldn't just stand there and let Rolo tell the world that my son is actually Brad's!"

Jimmy moved forward and began reading Gary his rights. The townspeople all began talking at once, crowding around Sabrina in their excitement.

"How in the world did you figger it was him?"

"A killer on our little island!"

"I never would have thought—Gary, of all people!"

"It wasn't such a big surprise," Lima said, adjusting his robes and swelling his chest. "I knowed it all along. Well, Miss Sabrina, you sure are something, sure as a doomed kayaker on Mitchell's Day."

"Lima, I've been meaning to ask you…what in the world is Mitchell's Day?"

Laughter sounded from all around.

"You stick around for a while and you just might find out," he said.

"Well, it looks like I might get the chance." Sabrina looked around at the islanders' faces—some friendly, some still skeptical, but all familiar and welcome.

"I have an announcement to make," she said. "I've decided that we really need several more months to finish practicing our new play, *The Island Adventures of Romeo and John*, even with Lima's help."

There was silence.

"Does that mean you're giving up the play?" Aunt Mary Garrison Tubbs asked.

"Actually," Sabrina took a deep breath, "I've come to see that I've never cared enough to do what *I* really wanted, just for myself, until I came to this island. I've never felt so alive as I have these past couple of days. I don't want to lose that, so I've decided to stay. Permanently."

Amid the cheers and congratulations, Lima turned to Sabrina.

"Are you going to teach school here?"

"No, I don't think so. In honor of the new me, I think I'm going to do something completely different. I'm just not sure what yet. I could sell conch shells like Missy

Garrison did, or rent kayaks, or, since I'm no slouch in
the kitchen, maybe I could even open a restaurant!"
    Now why did Lima look so horrified?

THIRTY-ONE

"Go on, go. You can't hang around here in the rose garden forever."

A fish splashed in the sound, and the roses rustled dreamily in the chill night breeze.

"I know you don't want to go, but believe me, Comico Island will do just fine without you two wandering around scaring people." The woman's voice was sad. "Go on now."

Two shadows moved though the rose garden and just for a moment she could see them. The first was tall and strong, with bushy black hair and bright blue eyes. The roses seemed to reach out to him as he walked by. The other shadow, slim and straight again, laughed as she did a little dancing step.

"I'll see you both soon enough," Nettie Wrightly said. "Go on. Get."

A cloud skidded across the moon's face, and the two shadows were gone.

* * * * *

AUTHOR NOTE

Comico Island is strictly a figment of the author's over-active—some say deviant—imagination. It is loosely based on islands where the author has lived and visited, and in the interest of creating a plausible history for the island, the author utilized several books, including the interesting *Ocracoke, Its History and People* by David Shears. However, Comico Island and the people who inhabit it are not real.

Truly.

But wouldn't it be grand if it did exist?

REQUEST YOUR FREE BOOKS!
2 FREE NOVELS PLUS 2 FREE GIFTS!

⊕ HARLEQUIN

ROMANTIC suspense

Sparked by danger, fueled by passion

YES! Please send me 2 FREE Harlequin® Romantic Suspense novels and my 2 FREE gifts (gifts are worth about $10). After receiving them, if I don't wish to receive any more books, I can return the shipping statement marked "cancel." If I don't cancel, I will receive 4 brand-new novels every month and be billed just $4.74 per book in the U.S. or $5.49 per book in Canada. That's a savings of at least 12% off the cover price! It's quite a bargain! Shipping and handling is just 50¢ per book in the U.S. and 75¢ per book in Canada.* I understand that accepting the 2 free books and gifts places me under no obligation to buy anything. I can always return a shipment and cancel at any time. Even if I never buy another book, the two free books and gifts are mine to keep forever.

240/340 HDN GH3P

Name	(PLEASE PRINT)	
Address		Apt. #
City	State/Prov.	Zip/Postal Code

Signature (if under 18, a parent or guardian must sign)

Mail to the **Reader Service:**
IN U.S.A.: P.O. Box 1867, Buffalo, NY 14240-1867
IN CANADA: P.O. Box 609, Fort Erie, Ontario L2A 5X3

Want to try two free books from another line?
Call 1-800-873-8635 or visit www.ReaderService.com.

* Terms and prices subject to change without notice. Prices do not include applicable taxes. Sales tax applicable in N.Y. Canadian residents will be charged applicable taxes. Offer not valid in Quebec. This offer is limited to one order per household. Not valid for current subscribers to Harlequin Romantic Suspense books. All orders subject to credit approval. Credit or debit balances in a customer's account(s) may be offset by any other outstanding balance owed by or to the customer. Please allow 4 to 6 weeks for delivery. Offer available while quantities last.

Your Privacy—The Reader Service is committed to protecting your privacy. Our Privacy Policy is available online at www.ReaderService.com or upon request from the Reader Service.

We make a portion of our mailing list available to reputable third parties that offer products we believe may interest you. If you prefer that we not exchange your name with third parties, or if you wish to clarify or modify your communication preferences, please visit us at www.ReaderService.com/consumerschoice or write to us at Reader Service Preference Service, P.O. Box 9062, Buffalo, NY 14240-9062. Include your complete name and address.

HRS15

REQUEST YOUR FREE BOOKS!

2 FREE NOVELS
FROM THE SUSPENSE COLLECTION
PLUS 2 FREE GIFTS!

YES! Please send me 2 FREE novels from the Suspense Collection and my 2 FREE gifts (gifts are worth about $10). After receiving them, if I don't wish to receive any more books, I can return the shipping statement marked "cancel." If I don't cancel, I will receive 4 brand-new novels every month and be billed just $6.49 per book in the U.S. or $6.99 per book in Canada. That's a savings of at least 19% off the cover price. It's quite a bargain! Shipping and handling is just 50¢ per book in the U.S. and 75¢ per book in Canada.* I understand that accepting the 2 free books and gifts places me under no obligation to buy anything. I can always return a shipment and cancel at any time. Even if I never buy another book, the two free books and gifts are mine to keep forever.

191/391 MDN GH4Z

Name	(PLEASE PRINT)	
Address		Apt. #
City	State/Prov.	Zip/Postal Code

Signature (if under 18, a parent or guardian must sign)

Mail to the **Reader Service:**
IN U.S.A.: P.O. Box 1867, Buffalo, NY 14240-1867
IN CANADA: P.O. Box 609, Fort Erie, Ontario L2A 5X3

Want to try two free books from another line?
Call 1-800-873-8635 or visit www.ReaderService.com.

* Terms and prices subject to change without notice. Prices do not include applicable taxes. Sales tax applicable in N.Y. Canadian residents will be charged applicable taxes. Offer not valid in Quebec. This offer is limited to one order per household. Not valid for current subscribers to the Suspense Collection or the Romance/Suspense Collection. All orders subject to credit approval. Credit or debit balances in a customer's account(s) may be offset by any other outstanding balance owed by or to the customer. Please allow 4 to 6 weeks for delivery. Offer available while quantities last.

Your Privacy—The Reader Service is committed to protecting your privacy. Our Privacy Policy is available online at www.ReaderService.com or upon request from the Reader Service.

We make a portion of our mailing list available to reputable third parties that offer products we believe may interest you. If you prefer that we not exchange your name with third parties, or if you wish to clarify or modify your communication preferences, please visit us at www.ReaderService.com/consumerschoice or write to us at Reader Service Preference Service, P.O. Box 9062, Buffalo, NY 14240-9062. Include your complete name and address.

SUS15

READERSERVICE.COM

Manage your account online!

- Review your order history
- Manage your payments
- Update your address

> ### *We've designed the Reader Service website just for you.*

Enjoy all the features!

- Discover new series available to you, and read excerpts from any series.
- Respond to mailings and special monthly offers.
- Connect with favorite authors at the blog.
- Browse the Bonus Bucks catalog and online-only exculsives.
- Share your feedback.

Visit us at:

ReaderService.com

RS15